Finding God

Following Jesus

As I open this book, I open
to God's presence in my life.
When I allow God's grace to help me,
I see with truth, hear with forgiveness,
and act with kindness.
Thank you, God, for your presence in my life.

Barbara F. Campbell, M.Div., D.Min.
James P. Campbell, M.A., D.Min.

LOYOLAPRESS.
A JESUIT MINISTRY
Chicago

Imprimatur	In Conformity
In accordance with c. 827, permission to publish is granted on August 1, 2012 by Rev. Msgr. John F. Canary, Vicar General of the Archdiocese of Chicago. Permission to publish is an official declaration of ecclesiastical authority that the material is free from doctrinal and moral error. No legal responsibility is assumed by the grant of this permission.	The Subcommittee on the Catechism, United States Conference of Catholic Bishops, has found this catechetical text, copyright 2014, to be in conformity with the *Catechism of the Catholic Church*.

Finding God: Following Jesus is an expression of the work of Loyola Press, a ministry of the Society of Jesus, the Jesuits.

Senior Consultants
Joe Paprocki, D.Min.
Tom McGrath, M.A.
Robert Fabing, S.J., D.Min.
Richard Hauser, S.J., Ph.D., S.T.L.
Jane Regan, Ph.D.

Advisors
George A. Aschenbrenner, S.J., S.T.L
Most Reverend Gordon D. Bennett, S.J., D.D.
Paul Brian Campbell, S.J., Ph.D.
Paul H. Colloton, O.P., D.Min.
Gerald Darring, M.A.
Eugene LaVerdiere, S.S.S., Ph.D., S.T.L.

Catechetical Staff
Jeanette L. Graham, M.A.
Jean Hopman, O.S.U., M.A.

Grateful acknowledgment is given to authors, publishers, photographers, museums, and agents for permission to reprint the following copyrighted material. Every effort has been made to determine copyright owners. In the case of any omissions, the publisher will be pleased to make suitable acknowledgments in future editions. Acknowledgments continue on page 331.

Cover design: Loyola Press
Cover Illustration: Rafael López
Interior design: Loyola Press

ISBN-13: 978-0-8294-3671-6
ISBN-10: 0-8294-3671-5

LOYOLA PRESS.
A JESUIT MINISTRY

www.loyolapress.com
www.ignatianspirituality.com
www.other6.com

22 23 24 Web 10 9 8

Contents

GRADE 7

One True Faith

Saint Augustine grew up in northern Africa around A.D. 350. His mother was a Christian, and his father was a pagan. Augustine was intelligent, but like all of us, this did not stop him from making bad choices. It is said that he and his friends once stole pears from a farm, not because they were hungry, but for no good reason. At the time, Augustine didn't seem to care that he and his friends were stealing. He didn't think about how his choices affected other people, who may have sold the pears for a living or who needed them for food. Some of his actions were thoughtless and hurtful to others. But his ideas would change over time.

How the Saint Relates { Saint Augustine represents a person who needed to take some time to discover the one true faith—Christianity. In the same way as Saint Augustine, we are on a faith journey that leads us closer to God.

Past Meets Present

PAST: Sometimes insights into our faith come when we least expect them. According to legend, as Augustine reflected on the Trinity while walking along the seashore, he saw a child drawing water out of the sea with a seashell and pouring the water into a sand pit. When he asked the child what he was doing, the child answered that he was emptying the sea into the pit. Augustine commented that such a task was impossible. The child responded, "So too is it impossible for the human mind to understand the mystery of the most Holy Trinity." Augustine turned away to ponder this. When he looked back, the child was gone. This mysterious event revealed to Augustine that the human mind can no more fully understand the mystery of the Trinity than a seashell can empty out the sea.

PRESENT: Cardinal Joseph Ratzinger chose a seashell as part of his coat of arms when he was appointed archbishop in 1977. The seashell was a reminder of the story of Saint Augustine. Elected pope in 2005, Cardinal Ratzinger, now Pope Emeritus Benedict XVI, had seashells embroidered on the vestments he wore at his installation Mass. This sign and other **sacramentals,** such as rosaries, medals, and statues, are given by the Church to help us celebrate our faith with greater awareness and devotion.

Gift of Faith

As a young man, Augustine began to question his thoughtless actions. He sought to learn from a religious group that seemed to have the answers about the meaning of life. Eventually he became disappointed in what they taught. Augustine tried reading the Old Testament but thought it was too simplistic to tell a real story about God and how he relates to us. Following the custom of his time, Augustine put off being baptized until he figured out what he believed. Throughout it all his mother, Saint Monica, prayed for him and encouraged him in his search for the true **faith.**

Augustine kept searching, and gradually he developed some important friendships, especially with Saint Ambrose, bishop of Milan, Italy. These new relationships, as well as a series of life-changing personal experiences, helped Augustine learn about Jesus and his Revelation of God the Father. Augustine's faith in Jesus and in the Church blossomed, and he chose to be baptized. He became a famous theologian and spiritual writer. The people of Hippo in northern Africa made Augustine their bishop.

Augustine's journey opened his eyes to faith. Faith means saying yes to God when he reveals himself and gives himself to us. Faith is a gift from God that helps us believe in him. Faith exists in relationships. In our relationship with God, faith enables us to respond with love to God and to others. For faith to be complete, we need to believe, accept, and respond.

Augustine's life shows us that God doesn't force us to believe. Faith is a free human choice. Faith grows in people through different experiences and at different times in their lives. To grow in faith, we need to be open to what God has in store for us. Faith grows when we watch, listen, and search for God. Our faith grows stronger when we love and serve others. When we are honest, open, and willing, our faith can grow.

Three Persons in One God

Think of a time when you've listened to an idea or a story and thought to yourself, "I don't get it. How can this be?" Do you accept the idea or reject it and move on? Or do you search and dig deeper to find answers?

PRAYER

Loving God, help me in my search to find direction so that I may grow closer to you.

The Blessed Trinity

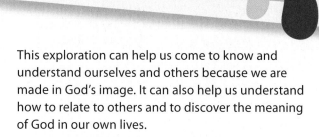

WHAT traits or habits did you inherit from your parents? A quick wit? A flair for music? We gain insight into ourselves by learning more about our parents, who gave us life. Because God made us in his own likeness, we can gain a better understanding of who we are by learning more about God.

For Catholics the most powerful insight that we have about our God is the **mystery** of the Trinity. A mystery of faith is a religious truth that we cannot fully understand. A closer look at this mystery can unlock profound insights into our identity as children of God.

The **Trinity** is the mystery of the existence of one God in Three Persons—the Father, the Son, and the Holy Spirit. Each of these Three Persons is God, whole and entire. Each is distinct only in relationship with each of the others.

The Trinity is the most important mystery of our Christian faith and life, a mystery for us to enter into and ponder. We can state this mystery in just a few words—Three Persons in one God. But even after a lifetime of studying this mystery, we will never be able to completely understand it. God is not a mystery to be solved. He is a mystery that we explore and a relationship into which we enter.

This exploration can help us come to know and understand ourselves and others because we are made in God's image. It can also help us understand how to relate to others and to discover the meaning of God in our own lives.

One God

God made it clear in the Old Testament that there is only one God, not many gods ruling over a fractured world, as some people believed. The one God who created and sustains the world is the same God who chose Abraham and his descendants to be his special people. He is the same God who liberated the Hebrews from the slavery of Egypt. He is the God who spoke through the prophets. And he is the God who sent his Son to be born of the Virgin Mary. These are not all different gods. There is only one God.

Three Persons

The New Testament reveals Three Persons in one God. The First Person of the Trinity is God the Father. God the Son, Jesus, is the Second Person of the Trinity. He is begotten of the Father, which means that he was not created, but rather, existed before he was born of Mary. In fact, the Father and the Son have always existed. The Third Person, God the Holy Spirit, proceeds from the Father and the Son. The Holy Spirit was not created either because, like the Father and the Son, the Holy Spirit exists from before time.

Our Catholic Character

Our belief in the mystery of the Trinity—Three Persons in one God— does not imply that we believe in more than one God. Christianity, Judaism, and Islam are all major monotheistic religions, which means they are based on a belief in one God. Other religions, such as Hinduism, Buddhism, Jainism, and Shinto, have varying degrees of polytheism, the worship of many gods. Despite this fundamental difference, the Catholic Church respects other faith traditions.

In teaching us about the Trinity, God has told us that each Person of the Trinity is distinct from the others, equally God. In other words the Father is not the Son, the Son is not the Holy Spirit, and the Holy Spirit is not the Father. And yet, because their love for one another is so strong, they are inseparable in who they are and in what they do—there is only one God. Since we are made in the image and likeness of God, we are called to live in unity with others, just as the Father, Son, and Holy Spirit live in unity. We best live up to our name as children of God when we are united with others in loving relationships.

The Church and the Trinity

The Church realizes that the Three Persons of the Trinity have a single purpose for the human family. Each Person reveals this purpose. The actions of the Father, the Son, and the Holy Spirit are all for our benefit.

→ The Father is our loving Creator. He continues to act in the world and in each of us in the ongoing act of creation.

→ The Son, the Second Person of the Trinity, shared in our humanity without loss of his divinity so that we could know and love God as our Father. Through the life, Death, and Resurrection of Jesus, we are brought into God's own life. We are baptized into Christ so that we can join him in the praise of the Father.

→ The Holy Spirit fills us with grace so that the life and love of the Father and the Son breathe within us. The gift of the Spirit opens us up to faith in Jesus, who unites us with the Father.

Study Corner

DEFINE

mystery, Trinity

REMEMBER

The Trinity is the most important mystery of our Christian faith and life.

Through the Church our faith is received, supported, and nourished.

Explore

When it comes to the mystery of the Trinity, God invites us to come closer and to experience fully his love through the gift of faith. This faith is connected to the faith community. It is in and through the Church that our faith is received, supported, and nourished. The Church helps our faith grow when we pray, participate in Mass, and receive the sacraments.

In faith we turn to the one God who gave us all that we have. God—Father, Son, and Holy Spirit—is our destiny, our final goal, the one for whom we will always reach, and the most important relationship in our lives.

SACRED ART

From the earliest times, the idea of the Trinity was difficult to understand. In trying to portray the Trinity, iconographers turned to the story of the hospitality of Abraham when three wanderers visited him. Iconographer Andrei Rublev represents the Trinity through three haloed figures that visited Abraham. This image shows the unique nature of the Trinity and the Eucharist as a symbol of unity and divine love. Rublev designs a wordless way to appreciate the mystery of the Trinity by setting the three figures within a single circle, making their faces identical, and including a blue garment, signifying divinity.

Holy Trinity (Troitsa), Andrei Rublev, 1425–1427, Russia.

God Is Our Creator

REMEMBER what it feels like to be awed by a blazing sunset or a black sky full of stars? What do you do in reaction? Point? Comment? Simply stop and stare? The next time you notice beauty in nature, pause for a moment and think about this idea: The created world around us is God's first gift of love to us.

God is our **Creator.** The world was not created as an afterthought or by a God who set it in motion and then sat back to watch. The world was created by a God who passionately desires to share his truth, goodness, and beauty. All that we see and experience in the created world is an expression of God's great love for us. We recognize him in the beauty, wonder, and harmony that surrounds us in the natural world and acknowledge him as the cause and end of everything.

The story of creation tells us that God made us in his likeness and gave us dominion over the earth and all the creatures on it. (Genesis 1:26–30) How comforting it is to know that when God looked at everything he had made, he found that it was very good. (Genesis 1:31) Believing that God created us body and soul in his image and finds us good makes it easier for us to accept the idea that God loves us and that we, in turn, should love ourselves and one another. God blesses us with life and love.

To help us know this love and friendship, God sent us his Son, Jesus, to make us sharers in his divinity. Likewise, the Father and the Son sent the Holy Spirit to guide us and make it possible for us to live in love and happiness in this world and the next. In this way God invites us to live in close relationship with him, but it is up to us to respond to his invitation of friendship. God has given us **free will**—our ability to choose to do good and stay in relationship with him or our choice to sin, which distances us from him. We thank God for calling us into existence when we live Christian lives, and we recognize him in the loving actions of others.

Acting in Faith

Recognizing that God has blessed us with many gifts, we respond to God's love by loving him and by loving others. We can do this in many ways. For example, we can worship God through the celebration of the sacraments. We can use our words wisely to promote peace rather than harm others. We can show respect for ourselves and others in our actions. We can take care of God's creation. We can encounter God through volunteer work. We can pray—all the while knowing that God lovingly receives our prayers. Whenever we give back to God and others, we show a recognition of his infinite love for us.

Catholic Social Teaching: A Response to God's Love

Because human beings are the height of God's creation, we have a responsibility to work toward making a more just world. As members of the Catholic Church, we are called to witness for Jesus Christ. For example, during the Industrial Revolution in the 1800s, machines changed the workplace. Because products and goods could be mass produced, the kinds of jobs changed. Society changed, and so did ideas about labor and government authority. In response to these developments, the Church increasingly began addressing economic and social matters that relate to the basic rights of people and communities. We are still called to address social issues today in our ever-changing world.

Those baptized, or the People of God, under the leadership of bishops and priests, are one body with many parts. The Church applies this image of organization to society and calls it the principle of **subsidiarity.**

Catholic social teaching is a rich treasure of wisdom about how to build a just society and how to live holy lives amid the challenges of the modern world. A core principle is that society is responsible for building up the **common good.** The bishops of the United States have defined seven areas of social concern:

- **Call to Family, Community, and Participation**
- **Care for God's Creation**
- **The Dignity of Work and the Rights of Workers**
- **Life and Dignity of the Human Person**
- **Option for the Poor and Vulnerable**
- **Rights and Responsibilities**
- **Solidarity**

The Church's Catholic social teaching helps us find direction on how to care for all of God's creation and how to thank God actively for his gifts.

Catholic Social Teaching

Think more about a theme of Catholic social teaching. Choose one of the Catholic social teaching themes listed. Read more about it on pages 299–300. Write about one injustice that you see in the world that relates to the theme you chose. Then discuss how you can respond.

Theme:

_____

One injustice and what I can do to respond:

_____

_____

_____

_____

_____

_____

_____

_____

Explore

Study Corner

DEFINE
Creator, free will, subsidiarity, Catholic social teaching, common good

REMEMBER
Everything in the created world is an expression of God's love for us. We respond to God's love through prayer, word, and action.

Catholic social teaching helps us build a just society.

Signs of Love

As Catholics we begin our day and our prayers with the Sign of the Cross. It's a simple reminder that our whole life is lived under the sign that saved us, the Cross of Jesus, by the power of the Trinity—one God, who is Father, Son, and Holy Spirit.

It is an important sign that places before us and on us the shape of the cross that saves us. It is the sign traced on our foreheads when we become a Christian in Baptism, and it is made over us in death as we complete our Christian life.

When we bless ourselves with the Sign of the Cross, we remember the God who created us, the one who saves us, and the Spirit whose wisdom guides us. This sacramental helps us grow in our spiritual life because it reminds us of our core beliefs.

The Sign of the Cross is also a visible sign of a **disciple,** a person who accepts Jesus' message and tries to live as he did, including sharing his mission. Jesus' words in Luke 9:23 remind us to take up his cross daily and follow him. Though short and simple, the Sign of the Cross lets the whole world see that we belong to God—Father, Son, and Holy Spirit.

Reflect on the Sign of the Cross

Leader: Let's pause for a moment to become aware of God's presence with us as we prepare ourselves for prayer. Trace a small cross on your forehead. Reflect on the ways you use your mind to know and understand God better.

All: Faithful God, you created us with a mind that we might seek and know you. Help us recognize you in all the people and events of our lives.

Leader: Next, trace a small cross on your chest. Pause for a moment to thank God for all the ways he has shown you how much he loves you. Let's pray together.

All: God of love, thank you for the gift of your Son, Jesus, who died on the cross for love of us. Help us know how to love others the way you love us.

Leader: Now slowly trace a small cross on each shoulder. Reflect on anything in your life that feels heavy to you, or reflect on a burden that you could use help carrying. Now let's pray together.

All: Merciful God, your Son bore the weight of our human suffering on his shoulders. Help us take up our cross each day and follow you. Inspire us through your Holy Spirit to be generous in offering help to others who carry heavy burdens.

WHERE Do I Fit In?

We've all heard the message "God loves you." But do you really believe it? This concept is often easier to believe when our lives are going well. But how do we have faith in God's love when things fall apart? How can we use knowledge of God's love to help us cope and get past our problems?

by Tom McGrath

How Do We Know God Loves Us?

I'm glad to be a Catholic because as a Catholic I believe that God loves me. I don't just believe it; I know it. I know God loves me because I've experienced that love in many different ways.

I haven't always felt God's love. In fact, there have been times when I felt God was distant and remote, and quite frankly, uninterested in me or my life. But it wasn't God who moved away from me during those times; it was quite the opposite. I had simply quit responding to him. At other times I have experienced the closeness and love of God so fully that it left no doubt that not only did God exist, he also knew all there was to know about me—and loves me anyway. My experience and my religion teach me that God is always on my side and at my side.

How do I experience God's love in my life? I could list hundreds of ways, and I bet you could, too, if you put your mind to it. I don't usually experience God's love as a bolt of lightning or a thundering voice but rather as a gentle nudge or the still, small voice inside me that is an echo of God calling me into life. Open your mind and heart, and be ready to be surprised.

We experience God's love in many ways. The activity shows three places where you can look for signs of God's love. Read each section and respond on a separate sheet of paper.

Reflect

In Nature

Nature gives us witness to God's existence upholding the world and our presence in it. Think of a time when you felt the loving presence of God in nature. Write about it, or find another creative way to express it—drawing, painting, poetry, or music.

In Your Family

Describe a time when you experienced the love of God through the care and concern of a family member. In the week to come, make a point of thanking that person.

In the Kindness of Others

Summarize a time when you experienced God's care through the actions of others, maybe someone you didn't even know.

TOM McGRATH is the author of *Raising Faith-Filled Kids.*

What's What?

For each main idea, write a supporting detail.

1 Saint Augustine's faith journey led him to live a holy life and become a great Catholic theologian and writer. (PAGES 1–2)

Example: Saint Augustine made mistakes, but he kept searching and eventually had experiences that helped him have faith in God.

2 The Trinity is the most important mystery of our Christian faith and life. (PAGES 4–5)

god is not a mystery to be solved, he is a mystery we explore and enter

3 Through the Church, our faith is received, supported, and nourished. (PAGE 5)

The church helps our faith grow when we pray, participate in mass, and recieve the sacraments

4 God sent us his Son so that we would know his love. (PAGE 6)

To help us know this love and friendship, god sent us Jesus to make us sharers of divinity

5 We can respond to God's love through prayer, word, and action. (PAGE 6)

Whenever we give back

6 Catholic social teaching gives us direction on how to show love for others and to care for all of God's creation. (PAGE 7)

A core principal is that society is responsible for building up the common good.

7 We pray the Sign of the Cross to remind us that our lives are lived under the sign that saved us—the Cross of Jesus. (PAGE 8)

When we do the sign of the cross, we remember God, Jesus and the holy spirit

Say What?

Know the definitions of these terms.

Catholic social teaching	free will
common good	mystery
Creator	sacramentals
disciple	subsidiarity
faith	Trinity

Now What?

Through faith in the Holy Trinity, we can learn to live a life of holiness. What can you do this week to live as a holy person?

I can be kind to others, follows the commandment and beatitude and pray

Jesus Is the Answer to a Promise

Making promises is easy—keeping them is the difficult part. Think about a time when you made a promise. Did you keep your promise or did you break it? What makes some promises difficult to keep? Can you recall a promise made to you? How might faith play a role in believing a promise?

PRAYER

Loving God, you always keep your promises. Help me be faithful to you always.

John the Baptist

THE Old Testament tells us that the Jewish people had already been waiting several centuries for the promised Messiah, the Son of David. *Messiah* is a title that means "anointed one."

Someone called to speak for God is a **prophet.** Scripture captures times when God spoke to his people through prophets so that they would remember and follow his laws, keep in mind his promises, and be prepared to accept the salvation that he was going to bring for all people.

John the Baptist is the prophet who announced the coming of the Messiah, so he is often considered the last of the prophets, the bridge between the Old Testament and the New Testament. God chose John to be the **precursor,** or immediate forerunner, sent to prepare the Messiah's way.

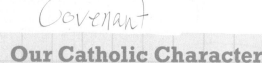

Our Catholic Character

Even though Jesus chose to be baptized by John in the Jordan River, he was free from sin. As Jesus rose from the waters of the Jordan, the Holy Spirit came to rest upon him.

As Catholics, we celebrate Baptism, which frees us from **Original Sin,** the consequence of Adam and Eve's disobedience when human beings lost God's blessing and became subject to sin and death. In Baptism, we receive new life in Jesus Christ through the Holy Spirit. Baptism makes us sons and daughters of God, fills us with grace, and makes us members of the Church. The **priest** or deacon pours water, a reminder of both death and life, over us at Baptism and says, "I baptize you in the name of the Father, and of the Son, and of the Holy Spirit."

Miraculous Beginnings

The Gospel of Luke tells us that John the Baptist's parents, Zechariah and Elizabeth, were a righteous, elderly couple who had no children. Zechariah, a Jewish priest, was performing duties in the Temple when the angel Gabriel appeared to him. The angel told Zechariah that his prayers had been heard and that Elizabeth would bear a son to be named John. (Luke 1:5–13) When Mary visited and greeted her pregnant cousin Elizabeth, the infant John leaped in her womb. (Luke 1:39–41)

A Voice in the Desert

John grew up and became the "voice . . . in the desert" announced by the prophet Isaiah. (Mark 1:3) John kept things simple—his clothes, his diet of locusts and wild honey, and his message to repent. He was not worldly, rich, or politically powerful. John admonished the people, saying "[E]very tree that does not produce good fruit will be cut down and thrown into the fire." (Luke 3:9) He instructed them on how to repent. (Luke 3:10–14) Luke's Gospel shows the great importance of John the Baptist's supporting role in proclaiming God's Word and preparing the way for Jesus. Everyone, even those who are not thought of as great or powerful, can take part in proclaiming the Word.

SACRED ART

It is said that John the Baptist's voice resembled that of a roaring lion like those found in the Judean wilderness. A winged lion is used to represent the Gospel of Mark. Mark's Gospel account begins with John the Baptist "crying out" in the wilderness that "[o]ne mightier" than he is coming. (Mark 1:3,7)

Stained glass at St. Thérèse Church in Appleton, Wisconsin.

The Promise of the Messiah

Because John the Baptist was a charismatic and popular preacher, he attracted many followers. Some of his followers believed that he might be the one promised by the prophets. But John was not confused about his role in God's plan. He pointed the way to Jesus and announced "One mightier than I is coming after me. I am not worthy to stoop and loosen the thongs of his sandals." (Mark 1:7)

A Sign of Repentance

As a way to show that they had heard and accepted John's message of repentance, many followers allowed him to baptize them in the Jordan River. When John baptized, the act of washing was a symbol of forgiveness and a willingness to start a new life. John continued to instruct that his baptizing was not the fulfillment that is found in the Messiah. "I have baptized you with water; he will baptize you with the holy Spirit." (Mark 1:8)

John Baptizes Jesus

John's testimony to Jesus raised interest. "Behold, the Lamb of God, who takes away the sin of the world." (John 1:29) At hearing these words, two disciples, one being Andrew, the brother of Simon Peter, began to follow Jesus. These early disciples told others about Jesus, and as Jesus' reputation grew, so did the number of his disciples.

Jesus began his public life on the banks of the Jordan River when John baptized him. Jesus had no need to repent for sins. He was without sin and totally faithful to the will of his Father. By submitting to the baptism given by John the Baptist, Jesus set the example of how we should empty ourselves in obedience to

God's will as a way to reconcile with the Father. Mark wrote "On coming up out of the water [Jesus] saw the heavens being torn open and the Spirit, like a dove, descending upon him. And a voice came from the heavens, 'You are my beloved Son; with you I am well pleased.'" (Mark 1:10–11) God fulfilled his promise of the Messiah in Jesus.

Explore

Jesus' Testimony to John

Read Jesus' testimony concerning John the Baptist in Matthew 11:7–19 and Luke 7:24–35. Summarize the key ideas here or on another sheet of paper.

_____

_____

_____

_____

Study Corner

DEFINE

prophet, precursor, Original Sin, priest

REMEMBER

John the Baptist announced the Messiah. Jesus begins his public life following his baptism by John.

The Inspired Word of God

IN a variety of ways, both the Old Testament and the New Testament tell a single story of God's love for us.

The Old Testament records how God made a promise to Abraham, our father in faith, and his descendants. This **covenant** was a solemn agreement between God and his people. The New Testament tells us how this plan came to completion in Jesus Christ. Everything we need to know about what it means to live in relationship with God our Father is revealed in Jesus. Throughout many generations, God was faithful to the covenant. God kept his promise, a promise fulfilled in Jesus.

We read about God's covenants throughout the ages in the Bible. The Bible is the collection of books containing the truths of God's Revelation to us. The Bible, written by human beings, is the inspired Word of God. Because of this, God is really the author of the Bible. The two main parts of the Bible are the Old Testament and the New Testament. After several centuries the Church established the official list of the 73 books that make up the Old and New Testaments of the Bible. This official list is called the **canon,** which comes from a Greek word meaning "measuring stick" or "rule," because the writings contained within the Bible are our rule of faith.

The Old Testament

The Old Testament contains 46 books that tell stories about the Jewish people and their faith in God before Jesus was born. The first five books are referred to as the Torah, meaning "instruction" or "law." The central story in the Torah is the Exodus, the liberation of the Hebrew slaves as Moses led them out of Egypt. During the journey God gave the Ten Commandments to Moses and the people. Many prophets, such as John the Baptist, were called by God to speak for him and to urge the Jewish people to be faithful to the covenant. A total of 18 books in the Old Testament present the messages and actions of the prophets.

This part of the Bible was originally written for the Jews. The books of the Old Testament were their Scriptures. Jesus and his disciples grew up studying Scripture and praying the psalms. The early Christians began to refer to these writings as the old covenant, or Old Testament, as they began to understand that God was forming a new relationship with them through Jesus—the new covenant.

The Bible is God's personal message to us. It is important for us to know the Old Testament in order to understand fully the New Testament. Both the Old and New Testaments tell about God's great plan for the human family.

The New Testament

The New Testament consists of 27 books. For Christians the most important books of the New Testament are the four **Gospels:** Matthew, Mark, Luke, and John. Even though each Gospel gives a unique portrait of Jesus, together they teach the essential truth that Jesus is the **Son of God** become man, sent by the Father for the sake of our salvation. The end of the Gospel of John states that if all the stories about Jesus were told, there would not be enough books to record them. What we do have is a special treasure, helping us know Jesus.

The books of the New Testament tell the story of Jesus' life, Death, **Resurrection** from the dead, and **Ascension** into heaven, and the experience of the early Christians. For about 25 years after these events, just about everything we know about Jesus was passed on through word of mouth. The Apostles and the other disciples preached the Gospel, and followers of Jesus gathered in their homes to worship God. Then, around the year A.D. 51, the Apostle Paul began writing letters to communities of Christians in different parts of the Roman Empire. The four Gospels followed. In its final form, the New Testament is made up of the Gospels according to Matthew, Mark, Luke, and John; the **Acts of the Apostles;** the letters of Saint Paul to the Romans; 1 and 2 Corinthians; Galatians; Ephesians; Philippians; Colossians; 1 and 2 Thessalonians; 1 and 2 Timothy; Titus; Philemon; the Letter to the Hebrews; the Letters of James; 1 and 2 Peter; 1, 2, and 3 John; Jude; and Revelation. The Church accepts and venerates as inspired both the Old and New Testaments.

Scripture tells us much that we need to know about our faith. The beliefs and practices of the Church that Christ entrusted to the Apostles continue to be passed down from generation to generation under the guidance of the Holy Spirit. This **Tradition,** together with Scripture, makes up the single deposit of faith which remains present and active in the Church.

Past Meets Present

PAST: For centuries, monks and nuns living and working in monasteries copied the Bible by hand. The process was painstaking, sometimes taking almost a year to complete a single copy. A calligrapher would try very hard not to make mistakes and would have a companion check all the work. The Catholic Church developed a tradition of adding elaborate illuminations to the sacred text. These beautiful illustrations brought to life the story or theme of the sacred text. The invention of the printing press around the middle of the fifteenth century helped make Bibles accessible to more people.

PRESENT: The Bible is the all-time best-selling book in the world. Today you can read a Bible in book form, online, on a smartphone, or on another electronic device. You can listen to it as you exercise or while riding the bus to school. No matter what form the Bible takes, it is the Word of God, so it should be received with respect.

Study Corner

DEFINE

covenant, canon, Gospels, Son of God, Resurrection, Ascension, Acts of the Apostles, Tradition

REMEMBER

The Bible is the inspired Word of God. Together the Old Testament and the New Testament reveal God's message. Faithful accounts of Jesus' life are presented in the Gospels of Matthew, Mark, Luke, and John.

Praying the Gospel

Reflecting on **Scripture is a form of prayer. Each time we open the Bible, we have an opportunity to meet God in a new way.**

When we read or listen attentively to the Gospel, we become open to receiving the Word of God and allowing it to form us. Just as the Apostles preached the Good News of God's mercy and love, we learn religious truths by experiencing the stories of Jesus' life, Death, Resurrection, and Ascension through the Gospels.

And the Word Was God

Leader: The Word of God is like a light that shines in the darkness. It shows us the way to God by teaching us to live as followers of his Son, Jesus. Aware of God's presence with us as we gather in Jesus' name, let's pause to prepare ourselves to offer our prayers to God in thanksgiving for this gift of light.

Reader 1: God of all creation, through you all things came to be. Through our study of Scripture, help us grow closer to Jesus, your Word. Let us pray to the Lord.

All: Lord, hear our prayer.

Reader 2: God of love, in Scripture you reveal how close you are to us. Through our study of Scripture, open our hearts to accept your friendship with us. Let us pray to the Lord.

All: Lord, hear our prayer.

Reader 3: God of all truth, in Scripture you teach us all we need to know for our salvation. Through our study of Scripture, guide us along your path of truth. Let us pray to the Lord.

All: Lord, hear our prayer.

Leader: And now let us pray in the words that Jesus taught us. **TOGETHER** pray the Lord's Prayer.

Leader: Your Word, O God, became flesh and made his dwelling among us. We thank you for the gift of your Word. Help us recognize your presence in the Scripture we study. We ask this through Christ, our Lord. Amen.

WHERE Do I Fit In?

I think many people believe that trusting God involves no effort—that no matter what, God will work out your problems for you. Truly trusting in God requires effort. You have to do the work and have faith that what happens is part of his plan.

by Daniel Kennedy

Trust in God

I have never had an easy time trusting God, but one night a few years ago I learned how. It was mid-January, and I was driving my two best friends home from basketball practice. The temperature was slightly above freezing, and it was raining. The temperature of the ground was colder than the air, which is a dangerous condition, as was explained to me later. When rain hits the ground under these conditions, it freezes, causing what is known as black ice.

I was driving about 70 miles per hour on the freeway when I noticed something unusual. I saw one taillight on a car in the lane up ahead, like a left-turn signal. This struck me as odd because we were in the left-most lane, and there wasn't anywhere to turn further left. I suddenly realized that this car was completely stopped. I hit my brakes hard, but nothing happened. The freeway was covered with black ice. We started to skid. I realized that we were going to hit the car.

Instantly, my head was full of so many thoughts that I couldn't keep track of them: my parents, my friends, my car, my future, my past. My life really was flashing before my eyes. Just before impact, my mind emptied out. I gave up. There was nothing more I could do. "God, save us," I prayed.

DANIEL KENNEDY is a college sophomore from Ann Arbor, Michigan, who hopes to combine his interests in history and travel with study abroad in Rome.

Impact. My car spun off the road. Five more cars piled up after mine. All but one of the cars was totaled, but no one was critically hurt.

Before my crash, I didn't really know how to trust God. Now I've learned how to pray "God, save me" practically every day. After I have done all I can to help myself, I've learned that I must trust that God will take care of the rest.

Learning to Trust

Think about a time in your life when you resisted trusting either God or others. Describe this experience. Then write a trusting response. Continue on a separate sheet of paper, if needed.

No Trust

_____

_____

_____

Trust

_____

_____

_____

What's What?

Respond

Complete each sentence with details from the text.

1 John the Baptist is called the bridge between the Old Testament and the New Testament because _____ . (PAGE 12)

_____

_____

_____

2 John fulfilled the prophecy of Isaiah when he became _____ . (PAGE 12)

_____

_____

_____

3 Jesus began his public life when _____ . (PAGE 13)

_____

_____

_____

4 We know that God is faithful to his promise of the Messiah because _____ . (PAGES 14–15)

_____

_____

_____

5 The two main parts of the Bible are _____ . (PAGE 14)

_____

_____

_____

6 These two main parts work together because _____ . (PAGE 14)

_____

_____

_____

7 The books of the New Testament tell about _____ . (PAGE 15)

_____

_____

_____

Say What?

Know the definitions of these terms.

Acts of the Apostles	precursor
Ascension	priest
canon	prophet
covenant	Resurrection
Gospels	Son of God
Original Sin	Tradition

Now What?

Because God keeps his promises, we are free to share in his plan of salvation for us. What is something you can do this week to strengthen your relationship with God?

_____

_____

_____

_____

_____

_____

_____

_____

_____

Think about a close relationship you have with someone. Is it hard to know someone on a deep level? When you want to know someone better, do you have to reveal more of yourself to that person? Does that person have to reveal more to you?

Jesus Reveals God to Us

PRAYER

Loving God, you have revealed and given yourself to us. Help me continue seeking you.

The Genealogy of Jesus

The Nativity, Bartolome Esteban Murillo (1618–1682)

PEOPLE are often curious to know where they came from and how they are related to others. For many it seems that the more they learn about their families, the more they learn about themselves. As Catholics what might we learn from Jesus' heritage?

As a Jew, Jesus shared in a Jewish religious heritage. The Gospel of Matthew begins with the promise that God made to **Abraham,** our father in faith, centuries before Jesus was born. "I will bless you and make your descendants as countless as the stars of the sky and the sands of the seashore; . . ." (Genesis 22:17) God promised Abraham that he would always be his God and that his descendants would be his people. Through this covenant with Abraham, the Chosen People were set apart by God to have a special relationship with him.

The Gospel of Matthew begins with a **genealogy,** which is a listing of ancestors. The genealogy of Jesus, described in Matthew 1:1–17, traces the covenant from the time of Abraham through 42 generations, including Abraham's son, Isaac; Isaac's son, Jacob; and Jacob's 12 sons. The 12 sons would become the 12 tribes of Israel. God revealed his Law through Moses. Kings ruled at this time, the greatest being King David. David's son, King Solomon, built a Temple in Jerusalem. The genealogy ends with Joseph, the husband of Mary and foster father of Jesus. God worked through Jesus' ancestors to prepare them for the salvation that Jesus would bring to humanity.

Our Catholic Character

People are social beings. We are born into a family, our first example of how to live in a larger society. Participation in family life and life in society is important to our formation as people. Pope John Paul II expressed in the encyclical *On Social Concern* in 1987 that it is vital that people work together to ensure that families and individuals have the ability to participate in the life of society. He wrote: "Today perhaps more than in the past, people are realizing that they are linked together by a common destiny, which is to be constructed together, if catastrophe for all is to be avoided. . . . The idea is slowly emerging," he stressed, "that the good to which we are all called and the happiness to which we aspire cannot be obtained without an effort and commitment on the part of all, nobody excluded."

We All Belong

The genealogy of Jesus includes Gentiles and Jews, people who are upright, and people who are immoral. The genealogy of Jesus reveals not only examples of faith and fidelity but also examples of imperfect people who made poor choices. Some are the most well-known members of the Jewish family, and some are obscure. God keeps his promise—a promise now fulfilled in Jesus—for better or for worse, even when some of the ancestors of Jesus were undeserving. In a similar way, each of us is part of a story that began long before we were born and will continue long after we die.

Explore

Your Family

Ask family members about yourself and your family history. Record the responses on another sheet of paper.

1. Where and when were you born?
2. What do you remember about growing up?
3. Where did you go to school?
4. What did you want to be when you grew up?
5. How did your parents meet?
6. What do you know about your grandparents? Your great-grandparents?
7. Were any of your ancestors born in a different country? If so, who and where?
8. What are some of your family traditions?
9. Was anyone well-known in your family?
10. What is your favorite family memory?

Study Corner

DEFINE

Abraham
genealogy

REMEMBER

God is revealed to us through the history of the Chosen People.

We all belong to Jesus' family tree.

God Makes Himself Known

SACRED ART

Michelangelo's marble statue of Moses was the last of his projects for the tomb commissioned by Pope Julius in 1506. The unusual small horns on Moses's head are symbols of wisdom and enlightenment. In Exodus 32:1–30 we read about Moses's 40 days on Mount Sinai with God and how the Israelites turned to the worship of a false god, a golden calf. Moses becomes so infuriated with the people that he breaks the tablets containing the Ten Commandments. The artist captures an angry Moses as seen in the tense face, posture, and flexed arm of the sculpture.

Sculpture of Moses from the tomb of Pope Julius II, Michelangelo Buonarroti, ca. 1513–16

GOD is a loving God. He seeks a loving relationship with all people.

Revelation is God's communication of himself to us. Revelation occurs through the words and deeds that God has used throughout history to show us the mystery of his plan for our salvation.

The process of Revelation took centuries to unfold. In the creation story, we learn that God entered a personal relationship with humanity through Adam and Eve. God set all happiness before them and asked only one thing—that they not eat the fruit of the tree of good and evil. Adam and Eve found the temptation hard to resist. When they lost their battle to temptation and ate the fruit, they broke their agreement with God. This resulted in all their descendants being born with Original Sin. Because God is merciful, he restored the human family so that we could live fully with him as he had intended. God had his plan of salvation. He promised to send a descendant from Eve who would conquer the Devil.

The Covenant with Noah

As we read Genesis, we realize that God continued to reveal himself and lead all people back to him. When the sinfulness of humanity separated the unity of the human race, God made a covenant with Noah and all living beings. God promised that never again would the waters of a flood destroy the creatures on earth. God gave a sign of the covenant. "When the bow appears in the clouds, I will see it and remember the everlasting covenant between God and every living creature—every mortal being that is on earth." (Genesis 9:16)

The Covenant with the Chosen People

Eventually, God chose Abraham to become the father of a great nation. (Genesis 17:5) Over the course of many generations, the **Israelites,** the descendants of Abraham, Isaac, and Jacob, would suffer many trials and hardships.

The Book of Exodus tells us how God called Moses to lead the people, who were enslaved in Egypt, to freedom and the Promised Land, the land first promised by God to Abraham. At Mount Sinai, God gave Moses the Ten Commandments, the rules that sum up God's Law and show us what is required to love God and our neighbor. The Old Testament tells how God revealed his plan through Abraham and his descendants. The New Testament tells how this plan came to completion in Jesus Christ.

Jesus, the Divine Revelation

As Catholics, we believe that Jesus fulfills the Revelation of God found in the Old Testament. When God helped Moses lead the Israelites across the Red Sea, it was a preview of the salvation and freedom Jesus would bring. Jesus is the fulfillment of the promises made to Moses. Matthew describes how Jesus retraced the steps of Moses' journey. He tells how Joseph and Mary took Jesus to Egypt to save him from King Herod. Like his Hebrew ancestors, Jesus was called out of Egypt, and he retraced their journey to the Holy Land. (Matthew 2:15)

In both the Book of Exodus and in the Gospel of Matthew, God is at work saving his people. Chapters 19 and 20 of Exodus describe how Moses went up on Mount Sinai to receive the Law from God. Chapters 5–7 of Matthew recount how Jesus went up a mountain to deliver the new Law. Moses spoke with God's authority, but Jesus spoke with his own authority as the Son of God. As the Son of God, Jesus understands and proclaims the true meaning of the Law. Matthew knew that God used the Passover to help create a people of his own. Now Jesus would create a new People of God.

When the people agreed to the covenant at Mount Sinai, it was sealed with an animal sacrifice and a meal. Moses united the people to God and his covenant by sprinkling them with the blood of the sacrifice. At the Last Supper, Jesus explained to the Apostles that he was going to be the new covenant. "This cup is the new covenant in my blood, which will be shed

for you." (Luke 22:20) God completed everything he wanted to say about himself by sending his own Son and establishing in him a new covenant. Jesus' Crucifixion revealed the meaning of who he is. Looking at the bruised and battered Jesus on the cross, the Roman centurion recognizes Jesus. "Truly this man was the Son of God!" (Mark 15:39)

Jesus Helps Us Know God

Jesus helps us understand the kind of father we have in God. He tells us to go to God the Father for everything we need. Even if we run away from him, our Father will throw his arms around us and welcome us back just as a father would greet his children. Jesus calls us to friendship. "I no longer call you slaves, because a slave does not know what his master is doing. I have called you friends, because I have told you everything I have heard from my Father." (John 15:15)

In Jesus we see a God who is for all people. Jesus recognized human imperfections and sinfulness. He showed a special concern for sinners, not just the righteous, and could see beyond human failures. Jesus' forgiveness for those who repented and had a conversion of heart demonstrates the mystery of God's deep and infinite love for us.

Explore

Study Corner

DEFINE

Revelation, Israelites

REMEMBER

Jesus fulfills the Revelation of God found in the Old Testament.

God has revealed himself fully by sending his own Son to establish a new covenant.

The Family and Prayer

Litany of Thanksgiving for Who I Am Today

Leader: We begin our prayer, in the name of the Father, and of the Son, and of the Holy Spirit. Amen. Let us pray our intentions.

For our parents and families and the faith we've received . . .

Response: We give you thanks, O Lord.

Leader: For our relatives, those we know and those we've never met . . . ℞.

Leader: For our deceased relatives who live now in the presence of God . . . ℞.

Leader: For our faith that has been lived and passed down to us through so many generations . . . ℞.

Leader: For our relatives who struggled through tough times . . . ℞.

Leader: For our ancestors who showed their trust in God when faced with difficulty . . . ℞.

Leader: For those whose forgiveness of one another taught us to do the same . . . ℞.

All: God of love, our families are your gift to us. Thank you for their witness of faith and fidelity to you and one another. May their lives inspire us to look for your presence in times of joy and times of challenge and to find you in all things. We ask this in the name of Jesus, the Lord. Amen.

For many people, family is the first place we learn about prayer. We pray as a family before meals and in church.

But learning to pray is much more than simply reciting words. We take our prayers to heart, meaning that we intentionally think about them as we pray them.

Jesus promised that wherever two or three were gathered in his name, he would be in their midst. Because of this, everyday family events become opportunities for prayers of thanksgiving, for petition, and for entrusting ourselves into the hands of God, our Father. In this way the family becomes more and more a school of prayer.

WHERE Do I Fit In?

by Suzanne Ecklund

Where does God make himself known? God is everywhere. He is in the song of a spring chickadee and in the arms of a winter tree. He is in our times of joy and in our times of suffering and hardship.

God Makes Himself Known

When I was a little girl growing up on a farm in Pennsylvania, I used to put God to the test. I would lie on my bed, look up at the ceiling and pray, "God, if you are there, please place a bird in the tree outside my bedroom window." I would then peel myself off my bed and peer out the window. And there in the thin, gray arms of the tree, I would either find a bird, or I would not. Thinking back on this time, I realize that I was using my prayer as a kind of test. The kind of test that began, "God, if you are there . . ." And I never stopped looking.

I'm much older now, and although birds continue to serve as winged reminders of God's presence for me, I realize that God extends far beyond the branches of that little Pennsylvanian tree. And God doesn't even have to wait for tests from little farm girls to make his presence known. On the farm, work was defined by what nature brought—and the seasons gave this work its shape. There was a season for planting, a season for growth, a season for harvest, and a season for rest. And God's pulse was at the center of each turning.

To be human is to follow a similar path. Spiritual seasons bring joy and sadness—and everything in between! But just as God is at the center of nature's changing essence, he is also at the center of our turnings of the soul. Sometimes it's hard to imagine that God is with us during times of loss and hardship. It's easier to imagine God's presence in our lives when things are going well. But summer and winter are born out of the same mystery; autumn and spring dance in the same wind. God is present throughout our rich, colorful journey, no matter what it brings.

Reflect

God Is Present

Take a picture, draw a sketch, or find pictures in magazines that show places, people, or events where God makes himself known. Explain your ideas below or on another sheet of paper.

_____

_____

_____

_____

SUZANNE ECKLUND is working toward a master of divinity at Emory University's Candler School of Theology in Atlanta, Georgia.

What's What?

Circle the letter of the choice that best completes each sentence.

1 God promised _____ that his descendants would be "as countless as the stars of the sky." (PAGE 20)

   a. Jesus

   b. Abraham

   c. Moses

   d. Adam and Eve

2 We can read about Jesus' genealogy in _____ . (PAGE 20)

   a. the Book of Genesis

   b. the Book of Exodus

   c. the Gospel of Matthew

   d. the Gospel of Mark

3 After Adam and Eve's fall from grace, _____ . (PAGE 22)

   a. God breaks his promise

   b. the Devil is defeated

   c. the human family is restored

   d. God promises a plan of salvation

4 God called _____ to lead the Israelites to freedom. (PAGE 23)

   a. Moses

   b. Abraham

   c. Noah

   d. Isaac

5 The Revelation of God found in Old Testament events is fulfilled with _____ . (PAGE 23)

   a. the Ten Commandments

   b. King David

   c. Jesus

   d. Moses

6 At the Last Supper, Jesus explained that he was going to be the _____ . (PAGE 23)

   a. new king

   b. new covenant

   c. last Apostle

   d. greatest prophet

Say What?

Know the definitions of these terms.

Abraham	Israelites
genealogy	Revelation

Now What?

God has revealed himself fully to us by sending his own Son. What is something you can do this week to help you find God or realize his presence in your daily life?

_____

_____

_____

_____

_____

_____

_____

_____

_____

Respond

Jesus Calls Us to Say Yes

Recall a time in your life when you did something good all on your own, without being asked. What made you want to do it? Was it something you planned to do, or did a little prompting in your heart make you think it was the right thing to do?

PRAYER

Lord, grant that in all things, great and small, today and all the days of my life, I may do whatever you require of me. Amen.
Saint Teresa of Ávila

The Annunciation: Will You Say Yes?

The Annunciation, Francesco Furini.

IN the Gospel of Luke (1:26–38), the young Mary is given a glimpse into the future, one in which she gives birth to the Savior. This announcement is delivered by the angel Gabriel, who is acting as a messenger of God.

Gabriel's announcement, called the **Annunciation,** reveals to Mary that her Son will be named Jesus. The word *Jesus* means "God saves."

Gabriel tells Mary that she will conceive a child through the Holy Spirit. This fulfills a prophecy in the Book of Isaiah (Isaiah 7:14), which says that the Messiah will be born of a virgin and be a descendant of King David's.

Mary asks Gabriel how this is possible. Although she and Joseph were betrothed, she was living with her family and apart from Joseph. Gabriel assures Mary that "nothing will be impossible for God." (Luke 1:37) With God—through God and with God's help—nothing is impossible. Nothing is closed to possibility.

Mary's Act of Faith

Mary accepts the announcement that Gabriel describes. She chooses it. She embraces it. The future will hold bright moments (Jesus' healing ministry) and sorrowful moments (Jesus' Crucifixion), but such is Mary's faith. She says yes to God. "Behold, I am the handmaid of the Lord. May it be done to me according to your word." (Luke 1:38) In saying yes to God, Mary shows complete faith and trust in him. In saying yes to becoming the mother of Jesus, she becomes Jesus' first disciple.

Gabriel tells Mary that her cousin Elizabeth has also conceived a child. This child, Jesus' cousin, is John the Baptist. Because Elizabeth is pregnant in her old age, she reminds us of Sarah, the wife of Abraham, who conceived her only son, Isaac, in her old age. (Genesis 17:19)

Our Catholic Character

During the time that Jesus lived, women were not treated with equality. Jesus set a new example. Unlike many people of that time, Jesus treated women with openness, respect, acceptance, and tenderness.

Likewise, our Catholic character is to treat all people with justice and equality. In his 1995 apostolic letter *Letter to Women,* Pope John Paul II acknowledged that the Church, along with the rest of society, had not always followed Jesus' lead in his treatment of women. He thanked all women for their contributions in every area—social, economic, cultural, artistic, and political. The pope continued to say that it is a matter of justice, but also of necessity, that social systems be redesigned in a way that favors the processes of humanization that mark the "civilization of love."

Celebrating Mary

Throughout Scripture many people say yes to God, but Mary's yes gives profound insight into how we as Catholics see and celebrate Mary. The Catholic teaching of the **Immaculate Conception** proclaims Mary free from sin at the moment her parents conceived her and teaches that she remained free from personal sin all her life. In this light, Mary's yes to God truly does fulfill who she is, from the moment she is given life.

Gabriel's announcement and Mary's acceptance change the course of her life. Her yes to Gabriel is sometimes called her *fiat,* a Latin word that means "let it be done." Mary's willingness to respond to God's call is why we as Catholics hold her in high regard and with such devotion. Her yes to becoming the mother of Jesus makes her a model of discipleship. When we respond to God with our own fiat, we embrace a direction that centers around Jesus.

The Gospel account of the Annunciation ends with the words "Then the angel departed from her." (Luke 1:38) We might imagine Mary as being quite alone to contemplate this startling announcement, this Annunciation. But in making her choice, Mary is not alone. She has Jesus, and he will be with her during her journey of faith.

Explain the Annunciation

Write a scene for a movie or play that uses the words from Luke's account of the Annunciation. Continue on another sheet of paper if needed.

_____

_____

_____

_____

_____

_____

Explore

Study Corner

DEFINE
Annunciation
Immaculate Conception

REMEMBER
The angel Gabriel told Mary that she would become the mother of Jesus, the Son of God, by the power of the Holy Spirit. Mary was the first person to say yes to Jesus.

SACRED ART

At age 15 French painter Maurice Denis was sure about what he wanted to do. He felt a calling and said yes to it. He wrote in his journal, "I have to be a Christian painter and celebrate all the miracles of Christianity; I feel that it has to be so." In this painting, the figures are in a modern setting rather than a historically accurate one. The artist wanted to use color and symbols to communicate emotion or intimacy. The Virgin Mary was one of his favorite subjects.

The Annunciation, Maurice Denis, 1913.

Grace

MARY believed; she had faith. Complete faith requires a response, a yes, when God reveals himself and gives himself to us.

When we pray the Hail Mary, the first thing we say about the Mother of God is that she is "full of grace." By **grace** we don't mean that Mary has poise or is graceful in movement. We mean that she lives wholly and fully in the grace of God.

We recognize the Lord God as a source of human help in the many professions of faith found in the Book of Psalms. For example, Psalm 28:7 recognizes God's grace as a source of protection and help:

> The LORD is my strength and my shield,
>   in whom my heart trusts.
> I am helped, so my heart rejoices;
>   with my song I praise him.

Psalm 121:1–2 acknowledges the Lord as guardian:

> I raise my eyes toward the mountains.
>   From whence shall come my help?
> My help comes from the LORD,
>   the maker of heaven and earth.

Actual Grace

When we need help, strength, and support to accomplish a task or endure a difficult time, God is there to bestow on us his grace—that is, a share in his divine power and life. Grace that helps us make choices to live as God wants us to live is called **actual grace.** We don't need to be going through hardship to ask for and receive God's grace. We may, for example, begin our day by asking God for his grace to help us do his work throughout the day. We may ask for God's grace to help us concentrate in class or to lend depth of feeling to our praying.

Grace is a deep and intimate connection between God and us. Grace is the gift of God's own self to humans. It makes us capable of living in God's love and acting in that love in our daily lives.

"Grace is the gift of God's own self to humans."

Sanctifying, or Habitual, Grace

The word *sanctify*, meaning "to make sacred," has a similar root word in Latin as the word *saint* and refers to holiness as a state of being in the human soul. **Sanctifying grace** is imparted to us first through the Sacrament of Baptism and produces in us a permanent condition in which we are pleasing to God as God's children. Through the state of sanctifying grace, we participate in God's divine spirituality. The Catholic Church teaches that without this grace, we cannot achieve this participation in God's spirituality.

Our sanctified soul predisposes us to live in goodness in God's eyes and to follow God's Law. This predisposition becomes a condition of our character, or in Latin, *habitus*. Sanctifying grace, then, as it refers to our God-given inclination and capacity for good, is sometimes called **habitual grace.**

God's gift of grace to us, his children, is unique and special. It cannot be bought, bargained for, traded for, or even earned by a particular number of good deeds. God alone bestows the gift of grace freely and unconditionally, because God gives this gift out of abundant love for us.

Grace is without limit and without quantity. Imagine a candle receiving a flame from another lit candle. The first flame is not diminished, and yet now there is twice the light and twice the warmth.

Although grace is not ours to give, we may certainly wish God's grace on other people. Saint Paul wishes God's grace and peace to the Philippians, the Ephesians, and the Galatians: "grace to you and peace from God our Father and the Lord Jesus Christ." (Ephesians 1:2)

Study Corner

DEFINE

grace, actual grace, sanctifying grace, habitual grace

REMEMBER

God's grace is a gift, freely given and not earned. With God's grace we live in his love and make decisions about our actions that will lead us to do what is good.

Past Meets Present

PAST: Saint Ignatius of Loyola was born in Spain in 1491. A nobleman who became a soldier, his life changed when he was injured in battle and began to read the Bible and about the lives of saints. He became a priest and founded a religious order called the Society of Jesus (the Jesuits). One of his greatest contributions to Catholicism is a book he wrote called the *Spiritual Exercises*, which includes a special prayer. Through the prayer a person dedicates all of himself or herself to God. The prayer asks to use all of one's talents to do what God wills. It asks that God give his love and grace because that is all a person wants in life. God's love and grace are enough.

PRESENT: Matt Maher is one of the most critically acclaimed Catholic musicians today. He has received several awards, and young people especially find that his vibrant music speaks to the heart. One of his most popular songs, "Your Grace Is Enough," is included on *Empty and Beautiful*. Saint Ignatius knew that God's grace is enough, and Matt Maher's song with the same phrase gives us the chance to pray it and sing it at the same time.

Explore

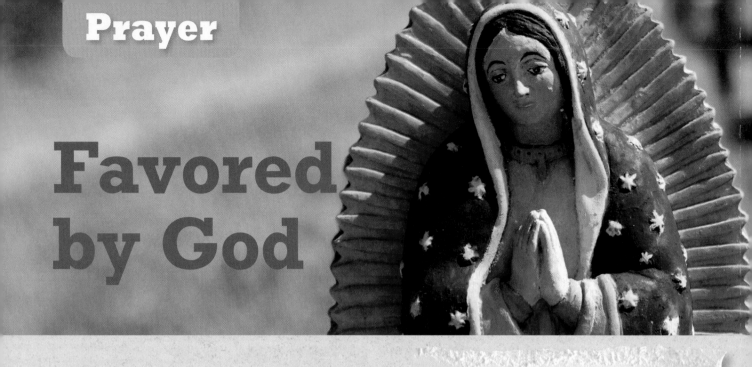

Favored by God

Most hymns and prayers to Mary contain two elements. The first element is praising God for the great things he did for her and through her for all human beings. The second element is entrusting our needs to her.

Because Mary knows our needs, we rely on her **intercession.** These elements are found in the Hail Mary. The angel Gabriel greets her with the words "Hail, favored one! The Lord is with you," and we pray "Hail Mary, full of grace, the Lord is with you." (Luke 1:28) Mary is wholly given to God, who has come to dwell in her. God promises she will not be alone.

When Mary visits Elizabeth, she greets Mary with the words "Most blessed are you among women." (Luke 1:42) Because of her faith, Mary becomes the mother of all believers. All the nations of the earth receive the blessing of God through Mary. Then we pray "Holy Mary, Mother of God." We entrust all our cares and petitions to her. Like Mary, whose response to God was "May it be done to me according to your word," we abandon ourselves to the will of God. (Luke 1:38) We ask her to "Pray for us sinners, now and at the hour of our death." We acknowledge our weakness and ask for her support. We look for her to welcome us into God's presence.

What do you think of when you think of Mary's Annunciation? This meditation may help you better understand the place of honor she holds for followers of her Son, Jesus.

Annunciation Meditation

Imagine yourself in Mary's place. What would you think if an angel appeared to you? Would you be surprised? Would you be nervous or even laugh? Would you be so filled with awe at seeing an angel standing before you that you'd be afraid? What would you want to ask the angel?

Now imagine that the angel Gabriel speaks to you. Hear the angel say "Hail, favored one! The Lord is with you." Reflect on this message. How does it feel to be favored by God?

Imagine pondering the message the angel tells you. Think of the many feelings and questions you would have. Now hear yourself saying yes. Feel a sense of calm wash over you.

As you pray the Hail Mary, meditate about each line's meaning to your life.

Pray the Hail Mary.

Take note. What is God asking you to do at this time in your life? Be still and see if anything surfaces in your heart. Hear yourself respond with the same words that Mary spoke: "May it be done to me according to your word." Now become aware of your acceptance of God's call. Remember that Mary is our mother and that she is always ready to help us grow as disciples of her Son.

WHERE Do I Fit In?

Life is a roller-coaster ride of changes and challenges. When you find yourself in a difficult situation and you are not quite sure what to do, how do you respond? Do you worry? Get angry? Avoid the problem altogether? God invites you to respond to challenges with faith, courage, strength, and generosity.

by Claire Gillen

Waiting

I was just a day away from finishing my first semester in college. Soon I would be traveling home to spend Christmas with my family. So why was I miserable? Maybe it was because I still had to take an exam in my least favorite subject, and I panicked every time I thought about it. To be honest, I thought about this class as little as possible. I knew that I hadn't studied with the same diligence that I had applied to the classes that I liked.

Weary, I reported to my part-time job in the library. I usually found the task of shelving books tedious, but on this day I discovered that the time passed more quickly, and I was enjoying the work. I began to think about reasons *why*. Shelving books was a job I had to do, but this time I threw myself into it and focused carefully—something I *didn't* do all the time. It occurred to me that my failure to throw myself wholeheartedly into the work right in front of me was part of a broader pattern. For example, in eighth grade, if I encountered a challenging class, I would reassure myself that high school was the real time to buckle down. In high school, I daydreamed about buckling down in college. I wasn't dealing with the present so much as I was imagining an easier future.

If I kept waiting for tomorrows instead of meeting my todays with faith, I would never become the kind of person God wanted me to be. If I didn't respond

positively to the challenges right in front of me, I was not living fully as God intended. It was a moment of grace. God used my simple work at the library to remind me that some of life's larger battles can be conquered by facing the work right in front of me. During this moment of grace, I realized the exhilarating truth—the present moment is the only moment that I have to say yes to God and to ask for his help so that I may follow him better.

YES to God

Saying yes to God is an act of faith. Copy and complete this idea web on another sheet of paper. Make the surrounding ovals large enough to write your ideas. Then write ways to say yes in each one.

school
friends
myself
YES
church
family
community

CLAIRE GILLEN is a history major at the University of Notre Dame.

What's What?

Use details from the text to answer each question.

1 Who delivered a message to Mary, telling her that she would have a Son named Jesus? (PAGE 28)

_____

2 Mary is our model in faith. As the first of Jesus' disciples, what was she the first to do? (PAGE 28)

_____
_____
_____

3 What does the word _Jesus_ mean? (PAGE 28)

_____
_____

4 What does the Immaculate Conception mean? (PAGE 29)

_____
_____
_____
_____

5 How does actual grace help us? (PAGE 30)

_____
_____
_____
_____

6 How is sanctifying, or habitual grace, first given to us? (PAGE 31)

_____
_____
_____
_____

Say What?

Know the definitions of these terms.

actual grace

Annunciation

grace

habitual grace

Immaculate Conception

intercession

sanctifying grace

Now What?

Compose a brief prayer. In your prayer dedicate yourself to God, telling God that you say yes to what he wants you to do. Think of one or two talents or gifts God has given you that you can use in God's service. Then pray the completed pray in the silence of your heart.

_____
_____
_____
_____
_____
_____
_____
_____
_____
_____

Respond

Celebrating Ordinary Time

JUST as we use a calendar to mark important days in our lives, the Church's liturgical calendar helps us remember and celebrate important events from Jesus' life. From the time before his birth to his Death, Resurrection, and Ascension, the liturgical calendar helps us celebrate the life of Jesus.

Ordinary Time occurs twice a year and lasts a total of 33 or 34 weeks. The first period begins after the Christmas season and ends on Ash Wednesday, and the second period begins after the Easter season and ends in late fall. All Saints Day and All Souls Day are celebrated during Ordinary Time.

The "ordinary" in Ordinary Time means "counted time." We number the days and weeks to remind us that all time belongs to God. A good way for us to celebrate Ordinary Time is by growing as a disciple of Christ and deepening our commitment to him. In the Gospel of Matthew, Jesus tells his followers "Whoever wishes to come after me must deny himself, take up his cross, and follow me." (Matthew 16:24)

But what does this mean? A disciple is a person who accepts Jesus' message and tries to live as he did, sharing his mission, his suffering, and his joys. Because you are one-of-a-kind, with your own talents, gifts, personal circumstances, and challenges, the way you grow in discipleship will also be unique. Denying yourself might mean putting someone else first. Taking up the cross might mean working in the parish food pantry, even though some of your friends might pressure you to do something else.

As disciples we are called to live out our faith. Every word, thought, and action show others and Jesus our commitment to living the life we're called to live as one of his followers.

Take a moment and think about your first thoughts and words today. Jesus lived his life as an example of how we should live. How did your first thoughts and words mirror the way Jesus calls you to live? How can you remind yourself to live the way Jesus asks?

PRAYER

Jesus, guide my words and actions so that I may live my life according to your will.

Helping Faith Grow

DO you play an instrument or participate in a sport? Think back to when you first began. You probably didn't feel very confident about your abilities at first. You may not have been able to play an entire song or dribble a basketball the first time you tried. You probably set small goals for yourself, working to gain little skills that would add up to success over time.

Similar to sports or music, we need to practice our faith too, so it grows, so we're confident in it, and so it "feels natural." Faith is a beautiful gift from God that helps us believe in him. It is our responsibility to nurture it and help it grow.

Doers of the Word

We can practice our faith in thought, word, and action. We can turn to our Church and to Scripture for guidance as we practice our faith. In a letter to early Christians, James says, "Know this, my dear brothers: everyone should be quick to hear, slow to speak, slow to wrath, for the wrath of a man does not accomplish the righteousness of God. Therefore, put away all filth and evil excess and humbly welcome the word that has been planted in you and is able to save your souls. Be doers of the word and not hearers only, deluding yourselves." (James 1:19–22)

The original doers of Jesus' Word were the Apostles. After Jesus died and rose from the dead, he appeared to the Apostles and sent them out into the world to make disciples of all nations—the **Great Commission.** "Go, therefore, and make disciples of all nations, baptizing them in the name of the Father, and of the Son, and of the holy Spirit. . . ." (Matthew 28:19) They did as Jesus asked, spreading his message, even when it meant putting their lives in danger. Not everyone was ready to hear what they had to say. Some became frightened and turned away. Others became angry. Many people did not understand what it meant to become a follower. As the disciples shared Jesus' message of love and compassion, people began to open their minds and hearts. They accepted Jesus and became living examples of how Jesus asks us to live our lives.

Our Catholic Character

The *Catechism of the Catholic Church* (767) tells us "As the 'convocation' of all men for salvation, the Church in her very nature is missionary, sent by Christ to all nations to make disciples of them." All over the world, the Church reaches out through various ministries and in everyday parish life to bring Christ's help, healing, and love, and to inspire individuals to take up Christ's mission.

Everyday Disciple

The Gospels tell us about many people who followed Jesus. We too are called to be disciples of Jesus. Like the disciples in the Gospels, we realize that following Jesus is not always easy. We may experience worries and fears and question ourselves, others, and God. How can we be doers of the Word and practice our faith? How do we experience Jesus in our daily lives? In Jesus' time the disciples traveled, spoke, and set examples. They actively and passionately practiced their faith.

You are called to do the same. To be a disciple means to be bold and to have trust that God is with you. With the help of the Holy Spirit, you find the courage to do good deeds, such as sharing a kind word with someone you might not normally speak with, lending a hand without expecting a thank-you, or beginning each day in prayer asking Jesus to guide you. Each time your thoughts, words, and actions reflect Jesus' teaching, you are a disciple because you are actively engaging your faith and experiencing Jesus in your life. Just as a musician or athlete practices to play better, the more you practice your faith, the stronger it becomes.

The decisions you make every day and the actions that become habits shape your faith over time. Think how you interact with people you meet. Opportunities to practice your faith are everywhere. Your chances to be an everyday disciple may not be obvious, but they are there if you are alert and watch for them.

Study Corner

DEFINE

convocation
Great Commission

September 2013

SUNDAY	MONDAY	TUESDAY	WEDNESDAY	THURSDAY	FRIDAY	SATURDAY
1	2	3	4	5	6	7
8	9	10	11	12	13	14
15	16	17	18	19	20	21
22	23	24	25	26	27	28
29	30					

REMEMBER

Ordinary Time means "counted time." It's a time for us to grow in discipleship.

As disciples we are called to live out our faith.

Practice Your Faith

Write what you would do to practice your faith in each scene that follows.

School

The math teacher just announced he is giving a surprise quiz. The boy next to you is on the yearbook staff. You know that he has been struggling in math, and his parents told him that if he does not improve, he has to quit the staff. During the test he tries to copy from your paper. What do you do?

_____

_____

_____

_____

Grocery Store

A mother is pushing a cart full of groceries with a baby in the infant seat and two toddlers walking alongside her. As she opens the refrigerated dairy door and pulls out a gallon of milk, she knocks another carton down. It explodes on the ground. What do you do?

_____

_____

_____

_____

Library

A group of students is finishing a project. They discuss taking a break outside. One girl sits quietly and continues her work. The others gather their belongings and leave without saying good-bye. The girl is alone and upset at being excluded. What do you do?

_____

_____

_____

_____

Explore

Responding to the Gospels

THE word *Gospel* means "good news." During Ordinary Time we hear stories from the Gospels that speak to us about what it means to be one of Jesus' disciples.

Throughout the centuries, followers of Jesus have found many ways of living as his disciples. Some have done so in extraordinary and dramatic ways. For most Catholics, however, discipleship is lived out quietly through everyday experiences and encounters with others. One way we can live as disciples of Jesus is through charitable actions by which we help our neighbors in need.

Works of Mercy

Many people have been inspired to practice works of mercy as a way of showing discipleship to Jesus. There are two types: **corporal works of mercy** and **spiritual works of mercy.**

Saints Respond

Choosing to live the works of mercy is challenging. During Ordinary Time, we celebrate the lives of many saints who were examples of how we can respond to Jesus' call to follow him.

Works of Mercy

Corporal works of mercy are kind acts that help others with their material and physical needs.

- Feed the hungry
- Give drink to the thirsty
- Clothe the naked
- Shelter the homeless
- Visit the sick
- Visit the imprisoned
- Bury the dead

Spiritual works of mercy are compassionate acts that help others with their emotional and spiritual needs.

- Counsel the doubtful
- Instruct the ignorant
- Admonish sinners
- Comfort the afflicted
- Forgive offenses
- Bear wrongs patiently
- Pray for the living and the dead

Ste Thérèse de Lisieux

Study Corner

DEFINE
corporal works of mercy
spiritual works of mercy

REMEMBER
The Gospels inspire us to perform works of mercy. Saints show us how to devote our lives to Jesus' teaching.

Saint Thérèse of Lisieux

Thérèse was born in 1873, the youngest of nine children, to devout Catholic parents. At a young age, Thérèse's mother died, and she was raised by her father and older sisters. Years later, her oldest sister left home to enter a Carmelite convent, and Thérèse became very sick. Through prayers and intercession to Mary, Thérèse was healed. After a pilgrimage to Rome, Thérèse knew she wanted to devote her life to God.

When Thérèse was 15, she entered the Carmelite Order. Always honest about her feelings, Thérèse realized there were things in life she would never like, such as certain chores. But her devotion to God inspired her to show love and compassion in quiet, little ways. She would smile at people she did not like or aid another sister who was not kind to her. She learned that any small task done in God's name brought her joy.

Throughout her life Thérèse prayed spontaneously. Whether she was sad and sick or happy and well, she carried on conversations with God. The head of her convent asked Thérèse to write about her faith and how she lived her life. Her autobiography is called *The Story of a Soul,* and it is read today by people all over the world. Here is some of what Thérèse tells us in her work: "Then, beside myself with joy, I cried out: 'O Jesus, my Love, at last I have found my vocation. My vocation is love! Yes, I have found my place in the bosom of the Church, and this place, O my God, Thou hast Thyself given to me: in the heart of the Church, my Mother, I will be LOVE!'. . ."

In 1925 Pope Pius XI declared Thérèse a saint. Pope John Paul II declared her a Doctor of the Church in 1997.

Saint Vincent de Paul

Vincent de Paul was born in Gascony, France, in the late 1500s. He was ordained in 1600. Vincent led an exemplary life. He began his ministry by visiting prisoners in jail. Barely surviving in damp, dark cells and given very little food, these prisoners were in terrible health and had little or no faith in God. Deeply moved by their condition, Vincent tended to their needs and showed them tremendous compassion. Many prisoners, overwhelmed by his kindness, became followers of Jesus. Years later Vincent helped found a hospital for people suffering such hardship.

Later, Vincent founded the Congregation of the Priests of Mission. This is not a special order but an institute with special vows. These priests, who add the letters C.M. to their names, help the poor in Jesus' name. Vincent also founded the Sisters or Daughters of Charity, a congregation devoted to performing corporal and spiritual works of mercy. They care for those who are poor, sick, and orphaned. To this day the Sisters or Daughters of Charity perform their ministry in schools, hospitals, and orphanages.

Vincent was canonized a saint on June 16, 1737. Today the Society of St. Vincent de Paul still helps those in need. Volunteers provide services through thrift stores, food pantries, home and hospital visits, and lend support wherever needed. A very strong and vital youth movement exists within the Society. Young adults across the country are working together to serve others.

Explore

The Paupers' Meal on a Winter Day in Paris, Norbert Goeneutte, 1881

SACRED ART

Images of hunger bypass language and time barriers. This painting portrays the emotion and need of those who experience hunger. Painted in the late 1800s by Norbert Goeneutte, a French artist, we still understand the concept 100 years later. The expressions in the painting range from quietly resigned to fearful and wounded, and even contentment. Feeding the hungry, one of the corporal works of mercy, is a universal theme.

For Those Who Are Sick

Regarding those who are sick, Jesus gives the Apostles this commission in Matthew 10:8: "Cure the sick. . . . Without cost you have received; without cost you are to give."

The Church carries out this commission in the Sacrament of the Anointing of the Sick. This sacrament, a way through which God's life enters our lives, also calls all of us to care for those who are sick and to be present with them in their illness through prayer and physical care.

Sunday is a special day for reflection, silence, and meditation that can help us grow in our Christian life. When we go to Mass on Sunday, we pray the Prayer of the Faithful. This prayer is a special time to pray for family members, relatives, and friends who are ill or who are in need in some other way.

Have you ever thought of illness as an opportunity for grace? Most people don't. But Jesus sees things differently. He sent his Apostles to anoint and cure those who were sick. Today the Church continues to anoint those who are seriously ill. We, as his disciples, are called to care for those who are sick. By doing so, we help them experience God's healing grace. Through our prayers we can support and serve those who are sick and suffering.

Prayers of Intention

Leader: Think about relatives, friends, or neighbors who are ill. Also recall media reports that you've seen or heard from around the world that tell about those who are ill. In your imagination, picture God's healing love surrounding each person.

Become aware of the power of prayer and the promise of Jesus to be in the midst of those who gather in his name.

Let's join together in prayer for those who are sick. Feel free to speak aloud the first name of someone you want to pray for, and, if you wish, describe the situation he or she faces.

Pray aloud intentions and respond after each.

Response: Jesus, heal us.

Conclude praying aloud intentions.

Leader: Let us pray aloud together.

All: God of Mercy, your Son, Jesus, walked our earth and shared our humanity. In his name we ask you to hear our prayers and to comfort all those who are ill in body, mind, or spirit. Amen.

WHERE Do I Fit In?

From the tiniest mustard seed, a magnificent tree springs, giving shade to all. Every ordinary day is an opportunity for extraordinary discipleship. Your choices in daily life, whether big or small, are powerful, and you are completely free to make them.

by Bert Ghezzi

Little Things Mean a Lot

Ron, my neighbor, has a serious lung disease. His doctor cannot do anything more to make Ron get better, so he put him on oxygen and painkillers to keep him comfortable. Ron is strong-willed, fights for life, and tries to take care of himself. Early one morning not long ago, I walked outside and found him dragging a heavy oxygen tank and struggling to get into his car. "What are you doing, Ron?" I asked. "Taking short breaths," he said. "I'm going to try to go to the store to buy a light bulb." I persuaded him to get back into the house. And I went and bought him a light bulb.

That simple act triggered my decision to help Ron. I began dropping by regularly and offering to do things for him. He didn't like asking for help, but I persisted, and he finally let me serve him. So I began to shop for his favorite foods—spinach, black olives, and custard pie, which you might not like very much, but Ron craves. Every morning I pick up his newspaper from the driveway and put it on his doorstep. I take out his garbage for him. I'm not very handy, but I figured out how to reset the switches on his garage door opener and garbage disposal. Several evenings a week I visit him, and we share our day. And I always make the Sign of the Cross on Ron's forehead and ask the Lord to strengthen him, clear his lungs, and give him a good night's sleep.

Ron and I have become good friends. I know that if he were well, he would be offering to help me. My friendship with Ron has taught me an important lesson about living the Christian life. That is, I show my love for God by serving others. As Mother Teresa said, "The needs are great, and none of us, including me, ever do great things. But we can all do small things, with great love, and together we can do something wonderful."

BERT GHEZZI is a father, grandfather, and author of 20 books, including *Voices of the Saints*.

A Full Heart

Our actions show our love. Small choices, such as choosing to smile at someone who doesn't like you, express your faith. In the heart below, list small ways you can serve others as a way to show your love for God.

What's What?

Use each phrase in a brief paragraph that tells what the idea means to you and how you can think, speak, and act as a young Catholic.

1 take up your cross (PAGE 35)

_____

_____

_____

_____

_____

2 everyday disciple (PAGES 36–37)

_____

_____

_____

_____

3 responding to the Gospel (PAGES 38–39)

_____

_____

_____

_____

_____

4 caring for those who are sick (PAGE 40)

_____

_____

_____

_____

_____

Say What?

Know the definitions of these terms.

convocation

corporal works of mercy

Great Commission

Ordinary Time

spiritual works of mercy

Now What?

Saint Thérèse of Lisieux and Saint Vincent de Paul answered Jesus' call to be disciples. They dedicated their lives to performing works of mercy. Jesus is calling you today. How will you answer him? How will you find courage and strength to share the gifts God gave you with others? Write your ideas below.

_____

_____

_____

_____

_____

_____

_____

_____

Faith in ACTION

Faith is alive when we put it into action every day of our lives. Faith is expressed in our attitudes and values and in the way we relate to people and the world around us. Taking action to make a more just world is an essential part of living the Gospel. Jesus preached not only with words but also with actions. We are called to do the same.

In this unit we explored important beliefs of our Catholic faith—the Trinity, God's Revelation, and our response to God. We were also introduced to the Church's rich tradition of Catholic social teaching. The Church calls us to put the needs of people who are poor and vulnerable first. Here are some ideas for how you can do this.

Become Gleaners

Purpose

Learn about the practice of gleaning as a way for people who are poor and hungry to get food; become a gleaner by collecting food and distributing it to those in need.

Background

The Gleaners is a famous painting by the French artist Jean-François Millet. Painted in 1857, it portrays peasants scavenging a harvested wheat field. Life was rough for people at the time, and they often resorted to gleaning, which is the collecting of crops left over in farmers' fields after harvesting. Today mechanical harvesting often leaves behind crops that would normally go to waste. With the farmers' permission, humanitarian groups practice gleaning in these fields so that they can distribute the food to those who are poor and hungry.

Steps

1. Read Leviticus 23:22. What do you learn about God from this passage? What is God's message to you in this passage?

2. Initiate monthly food drives and drop-off locations to collect nonperishable food to share with people who are in need.

3. Ask volunteers to coordinate the pickup of donated food each month, sort it into bags or boxes, and store it.

4. Form a partnership with local churches, food pantries, shelters, and soup kitchens that could use the food. Ask adults in your school or parish to help you deliver the food.

"It is an eternal obligation toward the human being not to let him suffer from hunger when one has a chance of coming to his assistance."

—Simone Weil, French philosopher

Detail from *The Gleaners*, Jean-François Millet

Living Faith

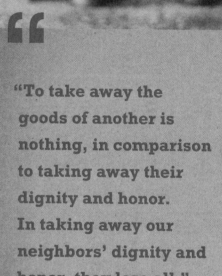

Purpose

Identify areas in your community where people who are homeless live; work with your community to provide basic necessities to people in need.

Background

Many communities provide shelter and services for people who are homeless. Although these services are helpful, the need for basic necessities and continued assistance is an ongoing problem. Some people in need of assistance are reluctant to seek help in shelters, soup kitchens, or other places where services are provided. They may be afraid. Others worry about losing their dignity. Some suffer from physical or mental illnesses that make them unable to seek help, and others have simply lost hope. Whether or not they seek help from service providers, people who are homeless need help and protection.

Steps

1. Mobilize a group to collect basic necessities for people who are homeless, such as combs, soap, toothbrushes, and toothpaste. Determine the best way to collect the items. Your group may sponsor a drive, collect financial donations and then purchase items, or get businesses to donate items.

2. Contact local organizations that provide services to those who are homeless. Schedule a date and time for dropping off donations.

3. Organize a group to assemble and package the collected items. Ask adult volunteers to help distribute the packages to the organizations of your choice.

4. Consider sharing your project with others in the school or parish by videotaping the assembly and distribution of packages. Show the videotape at an open house, parent meeting, or other assembly to increase awareness and encourage greater participation in helping those who are homeless.

> "To take away the goods of another is nothing, in comparison to taking away their dignity and honor. In taking away our neighbors' dignity and honor, they lose all."
>
> —Saint Vincent de Paul

Act

The Early Life of Jesus

Saint Marie Guyart (1599–1672), wife, mother, missionary, and mystic, was born in Tours, France. In the 1600s, it was traditional for parents to arrange marriages. Marie wanted to become a nun, but her parents arranged for her to marry a silk manufacturer named Claude Martin. After two years of marriage and the birth of a child, Claude died. At age 19, Marie was a widow. Her desire to enter the religious life had never left. At the age of 30, she joined the Ursuline nuns in Tours and began her work for God as Sister Marie of the Incarnation. Eventually this work took her far from her homeland.

How the Saint Relates

{ Sister Marie of the Incarnation imitated the life of Jesus, who lived humbly among the people. She sought to serve him by immersing herself in the culture of the native people she served, learning their language and customs as a way to teach and spread Jesus' message.

Saint Marie of the Incarnation

Why would Marie Guyart choose to name herself after the **Incarnation?** God's supreme act of love for humanity is the Incarnation. The Incarnation means that Jesus Christ, the Son of God, is God made flesh. Jesus is fully God and fully man in one Person. In Jesus, God became one of us and gave his life for us to save us from sin. The humanity of Jesus is made known in his human joys, sorrows, and emotions. Because Jesus has a divine nature, we know God's faithful love. And since Jesus also has a human nature, in him we see the best example of humanity we could ever know. Perhaps Jesus was the inspiration for Marie's work. Jesus showed her how to live a life full of love for God and others.

In the city of Tours, Sister Marie cared for **novices,** young women who entered the convent but had not yet taken vows. She enjoyed instructing and felt a great enthusiasm for proclaiming Jesus. Marie answered a calling to leave her homeland and spread the Gospel to North America as a **missionary.** A missionary is a person sent by Church authority to spread the Gospel through evangelization and catechesis. Sometimes a missionary goes to a country where few people have heard about Jesus. Other times a missionary is sent abroad to serve the spiritual needs of the faithful who live in isolated or underserved regions.

Marie eventually made the four-month journey to Canada, arriving in a French colony in Quebec in 1639. Immediately upon her arrival, she learned the Algonquin and Iroquois languages to be able to explain the Good News of Jesus. Because there were no materials about the Catholic faith in those languages, she took up the task herself, writing dictionaries for the people with whom she worked. For the next 30 years, she dedicated herself to the Algonquin and Iroquois peoples while learning about their culture. Marie served God well as a missionary because she became one of the people.

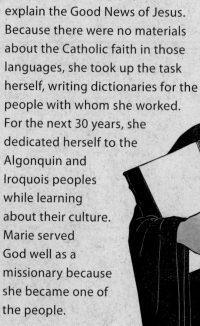

Past Meets Present

PAST: Saint Paul, like Sister Marie, traveled to other countries. He preached the Gospel while enduring hardships and imprisonments. He established churches and wrote letters that became part of the Bible. Saint Paul wrote, "To the weak I became weak, to win over the weak. I have become all things to all, to save at least some. All this I do for the sake of the gospel, so that I too may have a share in it." (1 Corinthians 9:22–23)

PRESENT: Five Catholic missionaries, each notable to his or her state's history, are honored today in the National Statuary Hall Collection in the U.S. Capitol. One statue honors Saint Damien of Molokai, who traveled with a shipload of parishioners suffering from leprosy and devoted the rest of his life to the settlement on Molokai, Hawaii. Father Damien cared for their physical and spiritual needs until he himself died of the disease in 1889.

Jesus Became One of Us

Think about a time when you confided in someone. Perhaps the person gave you good advice or encouragement, or showed compassion. Maybe the person simply listened. How did it feel to be understood? Why do you think that person understood you so well?

PRAYER

Jesus, you gave yourself to us in love. Help me come to know you so that I may better know the Father who sent you.

The Word Became Flesh

Martha and Mary mosaic, Franciscan Church, Israel.

AS Catholics, who do we believe God is? How can we understand him? How can we understand the relationship between God the Father and God the Son? Each time we pray the Creed, we proclaim our beliefs.

In the Gospel of John, we learn that the Son of God, the Word, existed from the beginning of time with the Father. Divine in nature, the Son of God brings the light of life to the human race.

> In the beginning was the Word,
>   and the Word was with God,
>   and the Word was God.
> He was in the beginning with God.
> All things came to be through him,
>   and without him nothing came to be.
> What came to be through him was life,
>   and this life was the light of the human race;
> the light shines in the darkness,
>   and the darkness has not overcome it.
>
> *John 1:1–5*

The Word of God taking on human form in the Person of Jesus is called the Incarnation (literally "in flesh"), a core belief of our Christian faith. In the Incarnation we see God's great love for us. By God's great sacrifice, we are saved and reconciled to God. We know that God is our loving and caring father.

> And the Word became flesh
>   and made his dwelling among us,
>   and we saw his glory,
>   the glory as of the Father's only Son,
>   full of grace and truth.
>
> *John 1:14*

Our Catholic Character

As Christianity steadily grew and spread around A.D. 100, the distance and differences in beliefs, customs, cultures, philosophies, and other factors threatened the unity of various Christian communities. Those who believed in a united and worldwide, or **catholic,** expression of faith wanted to distinguish their beliefs and traditions from other communities of believers. As Jesus' identity as both God and man was disputed over the years, the decisions of two ecumenical councils, Nicaea and Chalcedon, formulated the basic Catholic doctrine that identifies Jesus Christ as having two natures, divine and human, that exist together. This understanding of Jesus Christ's identity is a core belief of our faith that lasts to this day.

SACRED ART

Catholic devotion to the Sacred Heart reminds us that Jesus was a man. Saint Margaret Mary Alacoque, a 17th-century nun, spread the devotion after having visions of Christ, who told her about his loving heart. Images of a burning heart, either pierced or surrounded by thorns, symbolize Christ's burning love for humanity, even though pierced by our sins. By imitating the heart of Jesus in its limitless love, we best reflect the image of God.

Fully God, Fully Man

Jesus was not part man and part God. As the Son of God, Jesus is at the same time both fully God and fully man. He is not one or the other; his divine nature and his human nature are distinct but inseparable. Without ceasing to be God, Jesus assumed human form and became our brother.

Jesus lived among us, as a man at a specific time and place in history (A.D. 1, Palestine). He was human in every way except sin. Born to a Jewish woman, the Virgin Mary, he grew up in the town of Nazareth and learned the trade of carpentry. He had intellect, will, and a body that was susceptible to suffering and death. Jesus knew what it was like to be loved and befriended, as well as abandoned and misunderstood. Throughout his life Jesus expressed human qualities.

In the raising of Lazarus, we read about the human and the divine natures of Jesus. When Jesus arrived in Judea, his friend Lazarus, the brother of Martha and Mary, had been dead for four days. Jesus was overcome with grief at Lazarus's tomb. (John 11:34–35) Later in this account, Jesus performed a **miracle** of truly divine nature—he raised Lazarus from the dead. (John 11:41–44)

In the early days, the Church defended the true divine and true human natures of Jesus Christ against any **heresy,** or false teaching. In 325 the first ecumenical council in Nicaea composed a Creed to clarify that the Son of God is of the same substance as the Father. We affirm this belief when we pray that Jesus is "true God from true God, begotten, not made, **consubstantial** with the Father." We believe that today Jesus sits at the right hand of God and intercedes for us.

As we think about Jesus in heaven, we must remember that Jesus was truly man, with eyes and hands and a voice and a heart. In his ever-present spirit, Jesus asks us to be his hands and his voice in the world today.

Explore

God and Man

Read and categorize these Scripture passages as the Revelation of either Jesus' divine or human nature. Put an *X* in the correct column.

	Divine	Human
Luke 8:1–3		X
Mark 2:1–12	X	
Luke 5:5–11	X	
John 2:13–16		X
Matthew 14:22–33	X	
Matthew 26:36–46		X

Study Corner

DEFINE

catholic
miracle
heresy
consubstantial

REMEMBER

Jesus is the Son of God. Without losing his divine nature, he assumed human nature. Jesus Christ is true God and true man in the unity of his Divine Person.

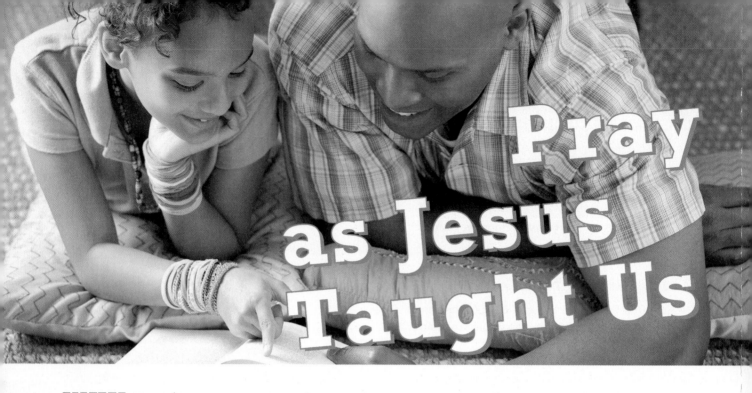

Pray as Jesus Taught Us

WHY is the Incarnation meaningful in our daily lives? God's deep love for us and his desire to share divine life is revealed. In Jesus, God became man, and because of Jesus, our salvation was won.

Jesus' last days gave witness to his true humanity. He experienced joy at a triumphant entry into Jerusalem, anger at money changers in the Temple, and betrayal at the hands of one of his own Apostles. His Passion and Death are stark reminders of his human suffering. "For God so loved the world that he gave his only Son, so that everyone who believes in him might not perish but might have eternal life." (John 3:16) In such great sacrifice, we come to know the pure love of a caring God.

Jesus became one of us and is our model of humanity. He experienced life with others. He was present at weddings, at dinners, in the gatherings of friends and of strangers, in a room in a house where a small girl lay dead from illness, and among people so ill, poor, and disabled that others wanted to stay far away.

Jesus, the Son of God, was fully God but humbled himself to share in our humanity. Jesus did not come to be served but to serve.

Who, though he was in the form of God,
　[Jesus] did not regard equality with God
　　something to be grasped.
　Rather, he emptied himself,
　taking the form of a slave,
　coming in human likeness; . . .

Philippians 2:6–7

Jesus is a model of holiness, and we look at his life on earth as the greatest example of how to live. Following Jesus' example is a way to come to know God and a way to become closer to him. After all, Jesus gave his disciples the **Great Commandment,** "This is my commandment: love one another as I love you." (John 15:12)

Jesus Prays to Abba

Jesus modeled a deeply personal and intimate relationship with people and with God the Father. When Jesus addressed God in prayer, he used the Aramaic word *Abba,* meaning "father" but more like "Papa" or "Daddy." (Mark 14:36) This informal way of addressing the Almighty was unprecedented in Hebrew culture.

Jesus became one of us and is our model of humanity.

When Jesus tells us to call on God in heaven as our Father, he shows us the kind of relationship we are called to seek with God. We approach God as our own parent—a parent who is near, who requires no formal language, and to whom we can turn for daily matters, both large and small. We approach God in this way when we have gratitude in our hearts for the abundant love he has shown us. We can trust in God's wisdom, express sorrow for our sins, make amends, and surrender to his plan for us. God, as parent, is always inviting us.

Relationship with God

Belief in the Incarnation changes the way we see everything. A window to God opens, inviting us to find him in all things. We know that God is with us, and we seek him in everything that surrounds us. We know that God is not far away. Our God is close to us, he is concerned for us, and he recognizes our human triumphs, sorrows, friendships, and pain.

Jesus opened up a new way of relating to God, our Father. In the Gospel of Luke, one of Jesus' disciples said, "Lord, teach us to pray." He said to them, "When you pray, say:

> Father, hallowed be your name,
> your kingdom come.
> Give us each day our daily bread
> and forgive us our sins . . ."
> *Luke 11:2–4*

Study Corner

DEFINE

Great Commandment
dignity of the human person

REMEMBER

Because of the Incarnation, we know Jesus is our model of humanity.

Jesus showed us how to pray to God the Father.

In addition to relating to God through prayer, Saint Ignatius of Loyola believed that we invite God to speak to us through life's experience and the use of our senses. Jesus taught us that God is the best of fathers. He understands our human imperfections and frailties and welcomes us back over and over when we stray. Jesus' personhood, prayer, and example tell us that our relationship to God is and can be deeper and far more personal. Jesus' wisdom, guidance, and holy counsel apply to our identity today, what we face, and what we need.

Jesus reminded us that we could find God everywhere. He tells his disciples, "In my Father's house there are many dwelling places." (John 14:2) Jesus says he prepares a place for us there. He invites us to be in his presence.

Explore

SACRED ART

The artwork of painter Michael O'Brien expresses the holiness of existence and the **dignity of the human person.** Because of the Incarnation, the guiding principle of Catholic social teaching is the dignity of the human person. In their pastoral letter *Economic Justice for All*, the U.S. bishops insisted that every economic decision and institution must be judged in light of whether they protect or destroy the dignity of the human person. "We believe the person is sacred—the clearest reflection of God among us. Human dignity comes from God, not from nationality, race, sex, economic status, or any human accomplishment. We judge any economic system by what it does for and to people and by how it permits all to participate in it. The economy should serve people, not the other way around."

Jesus and the Children, Michael O'Brien, 1998.

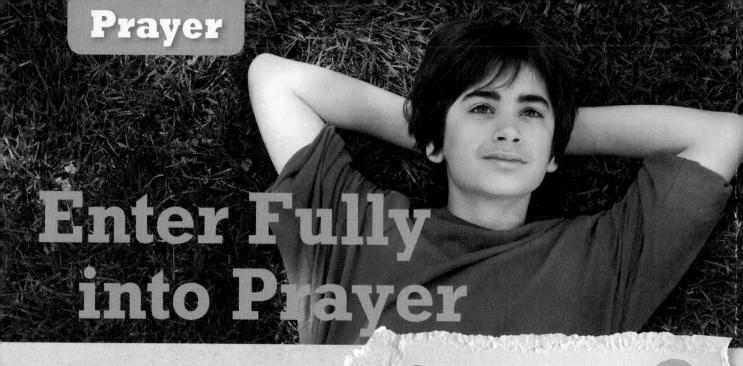

Enter Fully into Prayer

Jesus taught us to enter fully into prayer by engaging our whole being, including all our sorrows, joys, fears, and loves.

Jesus expressed joy to his Father for revealing the kingdom not only to the educated and the leaders of the time but to everyone. (Matthew 11:25) In the garden of Gethsemane before his Crucifixion, Jesus prayed with great anguish. (Matthew 26:38–39) No matter which form of prayer you enter into, you can feel comfortable bringing all that you are to the experience.

Lectio divina, Latin for "sacred reading," is an ancient form of Christian prayer in which you use your imagination while reading Scripture. It is a way of spending time with the Word of God and having a prayerful conversation with him. To get ready for *lectio divina*, quiet your thoughts. The first step is to read a Scripture passage slowly. The second step is meditation—letting the words sink in and echo within you while you reflect on what God might be saying to you. The third step is prayer. God speaks to you, and you respond with your own words. The final step is contemplation, sitting quietly with God, beyond words and feelings.

Lectio Divina
Jesus and the Scribe

Read: Mark 12:28–34 (The Great Commandment)

Meditate: In your imagination, place yourself with Jesus and the scribe. What do you see? Who is gathered? Listen to the conversation. Picture the clothing, mannerisms, reactions, and facial expressions. How do you think the scribe feels at the beginning of the conversation? At the end?

Read a second time: Mark 12:28–34 (The Great Commandment)

Meditate: Now imagine yourself as the scribe. Ask Jesus the same question: "Which is the first of all the commandments?" Listen as Jesus answers. Think about what Jesus' words mean in your life right now. If you wish, draw your ideas or take notes.

Pray: Share your reflections with God. Ask him if there is anything else he wants you to notice. Thank God for his presence and this time of prayer.

Contemplate: Spend a few moments in prayerful silence with God.

All: Jesus, through your life you showed your deep love of God and your limitless love of all people. Help us love God with our whole heart, our whole mind, and our whole strength. Help us love others with a heart like yours. Amen.

WHERE Do I Fit In?

Because Jesus became one of us, we know we are never alone. Not only is God present with us every step of the way, but as members of a faith community, we also help and support one another.

by Annie Azrak

I Am Not Alone

Last summer my parents packed their bags and left for a two-week vacation. This was the first time that I was left alone to watch over my sister, who is an adult with special needs. On the very night my parents left for their vacation, a tremendous rainstorm engulfed our area. I found myself driving through deep, fast-moving water. I had to stop the car. When I called my sister at her apartment, she spoke through panicked sobs. "My apartment is flooding, and I don't know what to do!" she cried. "I am so scared!"

I was overcome with worry and questions. I thought, "How do I get to my sister?" I was stranded in my car, miles from her, and I knew that she needed my help and assurance. I felt completely helpless and alone. I closed my eyes and asked, "God, what do you want me to do?" Just then my phone rang. The caller was my good friend, and she volunteered to take my sister to her home until I could arrive. I felt relieved.

I remembered a joke about a man caught in a flood. As the water lapped at his knees, a boat came by. "Get in!" the crew shouted. "No, thanks," said the man. "God will save me." As the water reached his waist, a helicopter hovered overhead and threw him a rope. "Don't bother," the man shouted. "God will save me any minute now." Finally, the water swallowed him, and he drowned. At the gates of heaven, he asked Saint Peter, "Why didn't God save me?" Saint Peter replied, "He sent you a boat and a helicopter! Were you expecting a chariot of fire?" Help had been there the whole time—the man just didn't take it.

ANNIE AZRAK is a premedical student who hopes to treat those who do not have access to medical care.

I used to think that it was up to either me or God to fix problems. But when I reflect on that rainstorm, I see that God does not want me to face every challenge alone. Neither does he want me to wait around, expecting a miracle. God answered my prayer when the phone rang. My experience taught me that God wants us to turn to him for help, but he wants us to turn to one another too.

Living for Others

The writer understood her experience when she remembered a joke about a man in a flood. Tell a short anecdote or make up a joke of your own that illustrates how God provides people to turn to for help. Write your notes on the lines below. Then write your anecdote or joke on another sheet of paper.

_____

_____

_____

_____

_____

_____

_____

_____

What's What?

Fill in the letter blanks to complete each sentence. Use the circled letters to discover the secret phrase.

1. Jesus is like us in all things but ◯_ _.
(PAGE 49)

2. Jesus had two _◯_ _ _ _ _,
human and divine. (PAGE 46)

3. Blessed Marie of the Incarnation spread the Gospel to native peoples in
◯_ _ _ _ _. (PAGE 46)

4. _ _ _ _◯_ _ _ _ _ refers to the belief that God was made flesh in Jesus.
(PAGES 46, 48–49)

5. The pastoral letter ◯_ _ _ _ _ _ _
Justice for All teaches about the dignity of people. (PAGE 51)

6. The Son of God, the _ _ _◯, existed from the beginning of time with the Father.
(PAGE 48)

7. Jesus is fully ◯_ _ _ _ and fully divine. (PAGE 49)

8. All of us can be the hands and
_ _ _ ◯ of Jesus on earth. (PAGE 49)

9. Jesus was made flesh and gave his life for us to _◯_ _ us from sin. (PAGE 46)

10. A _ _ _ _ _ _ _◯_ leaves a homeland to spread the Gospel. (PAGE 46)

11. A prayer in which you use your imagination while reading Scripture is called
_ _◯_ _ _ _ _ _ _ _.
(PAGE 52)

Secret Phrase:

_ _ _ _ _ _ _ _ _ _ _

Say What?

Know the definitions of these terms.

catholic

consubstantial

dignity of the human person

Great Commandment

heresy

Incarnation

lectio divina

miracle

missionary

novices

Now What?

What can you do this week to embrace both your human strengths and weaknesses while you grow closer to Jesus?

_____

_____

_____

_____

_____

_____

_____

_____

_____

_____

Jesus Is God with Us

Is there a particular reason or story behind the name given to you at your birth? Why do you think names are important?

PRAYER

Bless the LORD, my soul;
all my being, bless his holy name!

Psalm 103:1

Explore Names for Jesus

Annunciation mosaic, St. Thomas the Apostle Church, Phoenix, Arizona.

WHEN the angel Gabriel announces to Mary that she has been chosen to be the Mother of God, Mary accepts with joy. Joseph also receives a message from an angel. The visit to Joseph proclaims Jesus as divine.

Matthew's Infancy Narrative

An **Infancy Narrative,** an account of the infancy and childhood of Jesus, appears in the first two chapters of Matthew's and Luke's Gospels. In the Gospel of Matthew, we learn that Joseph was troubled by the news of Mary's pregnancy. Joseph and Mary were not married and hadn't had sexual relations. Who was the father? Joseph, a kind and just man, was unwilling to expose Mary to public disgrace. Instead, he planned to leave her quietly. (Matthew 1:18–19)

Before Joseph could do this, an angel of the Lord appeared to him in a dream. "Joseph, son of David, do not be afraid to take Mary your wife into your home. For it is through the holy Spirit that this child has been conceived in her." (Matthew 1:20) This is when Jesus was proclaimed divine.

Son of David

In Matthew's narrative, the angel addresses Joseph with the title "son of David." The angel is saying that Mary's child is the fulfillment of the covenant of old. As the foster father of Jesus, Joseph passes on this title to Jesus, showing that Jesus fulfills the covenants with Abraham and David. The prophecy that the Messiah will rise from the House of David is fulfilled.

Name Him Jesus

The angel tells Joseph, as he told Mary, that the child will be named Jesus. "She will bear a son and you are to name him Jesus, because he will save his people from their sins." (Matthew 1:21) This is the first time that the words *sin* and *save* appear in the New Testament in a meaningful way.

The name *Jesus* is an English (or anglicized) version of the Greek for the Hebrew name *Yeshua*. Yeshua was not an uncommon name in Jesus' time and place. In Aramaic the name *Yeshua* means "God saves." Joseph would have understood the meaning of the name. He did not understand how Jesus would save his people, but he believed the angel's words. In response to the visit from the angel, Joseph accepted Mary into his household and cared for the child Jesus as his own son.

God Is with Us

Matthew's narrative gives new meaning to events in the Old Testament by shedding light on the birth of Jesus. Matthew connects Jesus' birth to the fulfillment of the prophet Isaiah, who foretold a child born to a virgin and named **Emmanuel.** (Matthew 1:23) *Emmanuel*, Matthew writes, means "God is with us." Joseph and Mary, as faithful Jews, would have known the meaning of the word. They would have understood that Jesus would be God's presence among us. The name Emmanuel expresses the terms of the covenant. God promises to be with us, and we promise to have faith in Jesus and to follow him.

The name Emmanuel is a key statement of faith—God is with us. Matthew emphasizes this idea at the start of his Gospel and again in the middle when Jesus tells his followers, "For where two or three are gathered together in my name, there am I in the midst of them." (Matthew 18:20) And he mentions it at the end of his Gospel when Jesus says, "I am with you always, until the end of the age." (Matthew 28:20) When Matthew wrote about Jesus being Emmanuel, God with us, he was telling about the presence of Jesus to all of humankind.

Matthew's Infancy Narrative includes additional events in the story of Jesus' birth. It tells of the star leading the Magi to Jesus' stable, King Herod's plot, the massacre of the infants, and the flight into Egypt. Matthew's Infancy Narrative reveals Jesus as the fulfillment of prophecies and hopes throughout the ages. Matthew's audience would recognize that Jesus retraced the steps of Moses's journey when Mary and Joseph took the infant Jesus to Egypt to escape the murderous rage of King Herod. Jesus himself is the new covenant.

Jesus the Christ

Another name for Jesus is **Christ.** The word *Christ* is the Greek version of the Hebrew word for *Messiah.* In Jesus' time, and for a long time afterward, people did not have surnames. People with the same first name distinguished themselves by adding where they came from, who their father was, or what they

did for a living. The Jews of Jesus' time would have addressed him as either Yeshua Ben Yosef or Yeshua Bar Yosef (both meaning "Jesus, son of Joseph") or Yeshua Ha-Nozri ("Jesus of Nazareth").

In Latin the letter *J* is rendered as *I,* so when Pontius Pilate ordered that the inscription "Jesus of Nazareth, King of the Jews" be placed on Jesus' cross, it was abbreviated *INRI:* Iesus Nazarenus Rex Iudaeorum. Even on the cross, the name Jesus, "God saves," is written for all to see.

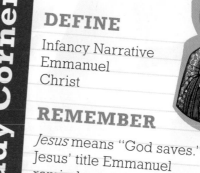

Study Corner

DEFINE

Infancy Narrative
Emmanuel
Christ

REMEMBER

Jesus means "God saves." Jesus' title Emmanuel reminds us that Jesus himself represents the new covenant.

Explore

SACRED ART

George Adamson was a 20th-century author, illustrator, and cartoonist. In this artwork, how does the artist draw attention to the figure of Jesus? Who are the other people? The Son of God chose to live in the common world of our human experiences. Therefore, when we are looking for the presence of God, we don't have to look "out there." God became man so that we would be able to discover the presence of God in one like us in all things but sin. Jesus Christ continues to dwell in and among us each day, in our ordinary lives. Jesus is Emmanuel.

Nativity Scene, George Adamson, 1973.

How Does God Speak to Us?

IF you know someone by name, you probably find it easier to talk to him or her than if the person is a stranger. We know God by name. The prophet Isaiah teaches us that God certainly knows our names.

> But now, thus says the LORD,
>   who created you, Jacob, and formed you, Israel:
> Do not fear, for I have redeemed you;
>   I have called you by name: you are mine.
>
> *Isaiah 43:1*

Our Catholic Character

The Mass is the "source and summit" of our spiritual life—the perfect environment to communicate with God. Our Lord is present through the priest, the Scriptures, the Holy Eucharist, and in the people gathered. You are with God, and he is with you as you listen, pray, and sing.

Your name is personal; it belongs to you. Your name is a reminder that no one else is exactly like you. God calls you by name. You belong to God, and he wants you to grow closer to him. Just as finding ways to communicate keeps people closely connected, in a similar way, God seeks a loving communication with each of us. Jesus showed us a warm, caring relationship with the Father when he prayed to Abba.

How can you know when God is speaking to you? God is always present, talking to you often and at length. God's voice may be hard to recognize if you aren't listening or haven't figured out that God speaks to you in more than words. Sometimes you need to listen for God speaking through your thoughts, ideas, feelings, memories, and desires. It is important to listen with your heart.

Through Mystery and in Word

The Bible shows different ways that God speaks to people. It offers clues that tell how we might hear God's voice.

When Moses first encounters God, God's voice seems to come from a burning bush. Then on Mount Sinai, God gives Moses the Ten Commandments. These stories show that God speaks in miracles—in the wonderful, the unlikely, the mysterious. God also speaks to us through his Law and through Scripture, the Word of God.

Through People

God has always used people to speak to us. Remember that God spoke through the prophets, and Jesus chose the Apostles to make disciples of all nations. God may speak to you through people who love you and who want to help you in your spiritual growth. Think about a person who has your best interests at heart, a person who tries to keep you safe, healthy, and moving in the right direction. How might God be speaking to you through this person?

In Dreams and Other Ways

In the Bible, God speaks through the power of dreams. God spoke to Abraham in dreams, as he spoke to Jacob and his son Joseph. He spoke to Joseph when he was betrothed to Mary, and even, in the time of Moses, he spoke to Pharaoh in Egypt. There is no one way by which God speaks to people. The prophet Elijah sensed God's presence in a quiet whisper, and God spoke to Job in a mighty whirlwind.

Ask God to help you listen for God's voice, from wherever it might come. Every dream or prompting may not be a message from God, but he may be heightening your awareness about something in your life that needs your attention.

Through Your Own Deepest Longings

It's natural to reflect on your own hopes and desires. However, God's plan for you may not match yours. You will sense that God's voice is present when your desires are at one with God's values and how God wants you to live.

In Memories, Thoughts, and Feelings

When you enjoy pleasant memories of family, friendship, holiness, or service to others, you may feel a sense of peace or a call to action. In ways such as these, you might hear God's voice because you feel God's presence. God is with you every moment of your life. He is with you in times of great happiness, and he is with you in moments of utter despair. God never abandons you. If you keep your heart open, you will hear his voice.

Through Scripture

Every time we read the Gospels, we discover that the words of Jesus are as relevant today as when he first spoke them. Jesus' central message is forgiveness. Jesus gave his disciples his example of forgiveness and healing over and over again. You follow Jesus every time you forgive a friend, ease a burden, or act as a peacemaker.

Past Meets Present

PAST: The worship of the real presence of Jesus can be traced back many centuries. As an established practice by the 14th century, the Blessed Sacrament was displayed in some churches in Danzig, Germany, in a transparent **monstrance,** a vessel usually made of precious metal, so people could pray before it and adore the presence of Christ in the Holy Eucharist. The act of giving reverence to God, called **adoration,** includes one's body, mind, and soul. In Eucharistic adoration, people invite God to speak to them. During Eucharistic adoration, people come to church throughout the day and sometimes the night to pray and worship Jesus Christ present in the host.

PRESENT: A new generation of Catholics is discovering the beauty of this ancient Catholic practice. For example, Eucharistic adoration is a part of World Youth Day when young Catholics around the world gather to celebrate the Catholic faith and deepen their spiritual formation.

Study Corner

DEFINE

monstrance, adoration

REMEMBER

God speaks to us in many ways, such as through his Law, Scripture, people, dreams, and our own deepest longings.

Prayer

Called by Name

When God created human beings, he created within us a desire for himself. Just like a stomach hungers to be satisfied with food, our whole being hungers to be satisfied with God.

God's deepest desire is for you to turn to him. Everyone is created with this hunger for God. Even when you stray from God, he doesn't abandon you. Instead, God tirelessly calls you by name, urging you to a change of heart and a conversion back toward him.

God created you to be unique. No two people are exactly the same. You do not have to become like someone else to serve God. You will serve God with the special talents, personality, and characteristics that make you unique.

God calls you into relationship with him, and he calls you by name, meaning he calls you to take what is best and what is good about yourself and be his voice and his hands in this world in some way that perhaps only you can best accomplish.

Guided Reflection: Am I Who I Say?

Imagine yourself in a quiet place with Jesus. Jesus asks you to describe yourself. Think about it for a moment. What is your personality? What makes you special? What is important to you?

Now Jesus asks you a question. If you could call yourself by any name in your everyday life, what would it be? What name really describes who you are in your heart? Is it a conventional name like John or Emily? Is it a symbolic name like Sun? Is it a descriptive name like Dances with Joy? Share the name with Jesus and tell why you chose it.

Hear Jesus ask you one more question. If someone observed you for 24 hours, would that person be able to tell what you value the most? How does the way you live your life reveal your values—the choices you make, the friends you have, the things you do? Do your choices reflect what you say you value? Share your thoughts with Jesus and listen to whatever he wants to share with you.

All: Jesus, we want to be your disciples. Grant us the strength and courage to let our lives be signs of your kingdom by the choices we make. We ask this in your name. Amen.

WHERE Do I Fit In?

by Jim Cruise

We are all created by God with a distinct and wonderful purpose, ultimately to live with him forever. But because of the effects of Original Sin, we can be easily distracted from this goal and follow the temptations that lead us away from God and others. Through the Church and the sacraments, God continually offers us the grace to reorient our lives to him and to a loving relationship with others in our lives. This is the true path he calls us to.

Answered Prayers

When I was in seventh grade, I wanted to make the basketball team in the worst way. All of my friends were trying out, and I wanted to be with them. For months I begged my dad for a basketball hoop. He finally gave in, and I practiced hard on the lopsided cement driveway. Almost every day I was dribbling, shooting, and passing the ball with friends.

Team tryouts lasted for three days. I missed the first two days because I was sick in bed with a fever. I had only one more chance to make the team, but I wasn't the only one. A kid named Benny also missed the first two days.

I did my best in the tryout, but Benny was a much better player than I was. Afterward, I walked home because I wanted time to pray. I begged God to let me make the team. I said Our Fathers and Hail Marys all the way home. When I reached home, I went to my bedroom and started reading the Bible. I had never read the Bible on my own before. I was hoping for a miracle.

The next day we gathered in the gym to hear Coach Wagner announce who had made the team. My friends whooped and cheered as each of their names was called. Benny's name was called. Mine wasn't. I didn't make the team. I was devastated. I didn't understand. I had prayed so hard.

Coach Wagner took me aside afterward and encouraged me. He urged me to consider another

sport and suggested the swim team. I took his advice and discovered I really liked swimming. I also made a good friend named Bill who became my best friend. Many years later I was the best man at his wedding.

In retrospect, not making the basketball team wasn't the catastrophe I thought it was. My prayers *were* answered—just not in the way I wanted them to be. Instead, God led me to a lifelong friend and the discovery of a new talent.

Becoming You

Describe how God answered a prayer in either an expected or unexpected way. Copy the boxes below on a separate sheet of paper. Then add your ideas to each one.

> **My Prayer**
>
> ↓
>
> **What Happened**
>
> ↓
>
> **How God Answered My Prayer**

JIM CRUISE, the "Spoon Man," is a Catholic evangelist who performs his musical interactive comedy routine all over the country.

What's What?

Write the letter of the phrase that best matches each term.

1. _____ Jesus [Yeshua]

2. ___ ___ Emmanuel

3. _____ Christ

4. ___ ___ *INRI*

5. _____ Joseph

6. _____ adoration

7. _____ Infancy Narrative

8. _____ Elijah

9. _____ Scripture

10. _____ Mass

a. adoring the presence of Christ in the Eucharist (PAGE 59)

b. told by an angel that Mary's child was conceived through the Holy Spirit (PAGE 56)

c. a celebration that is the source and summit of our spiritual life (PAGE 58)

d. a name that means "God saves" (PAGE 56)

e. reveals Jesus as the new covenant (PAGE 57)

f. the Word of God (PAGE 58)

g. a name that means "God is with us" (PAGE 57)

h. the Greek word for *Messiah* (PAGE 57)

i. a prophet that heard God in a whisper (PAGE 59)

j. translates to "Jesus of Nazareth, King of the Jews" (PAGE 57)

Say What?

Know the definition of these terms.

adoration

Christ

Emmanuel

Infancy Narrative

monstrance

Now What?

Identify times at home or at school when you feel that you most need to hear God speaking to you. Describe one of these times and tell what you will do to be sure that you're aware of God's message to you.

_____

_____

_____

_____

_____

_____

Respond

Jesus Is for All People

What do you think goes through the minds of people who have lost their homes because of natural disasters, political unrest, or financial instability? What might they fear? For what might they hope?

PRAYER

Lord, I am grateful for shelter. Please come to the aid of all those who are living as refugees, separated from their homes.

The Birth of Jesus

Modern icon of the Nativity, Israel, 1980.

ON the surface, countries run by dictators might appear unified and peaceful. The truth is that what seems like unity and peace on the surface is actually brought about by force, brutality, or fear tactics. This kind of "peace," defined as a fearful, silent population, is only temporary.

In Jesus' time the Roman emperor Caesar Augustus was a dictator in this regard, vanquishing his enemies and expanding the Roman Empire. The citizens he ruled called him not only a man of peace but also, in Latin, *divi filius*—the son of god.

Luke's Infancy Narrative

The Gospel of Luke introduces the story of the birth of Jesus, citing Caesar Augustus by name. (Luke 2:1) Jesus too is a bringer of peace but not a peace as Caesar made it—by violence and fear. Luke's narrative helps us understand that Jesus' peace is the salvation of God for the entire world, a kingdom not limited to the Roman Empire. Jesus alone is the true Son of God.

Son of David

In Luke's time it was common for people to think that great and powerful people were born into privilege. But Jesus was born to Mary in Bethlehem, a small city near Jerusalem. This city, according to Scripture, is where David was born and crowned king. Joseph, as a descendant of David's, traveled to the city with Mary to register for the **census,** the count of citizens. (Luke 2:4–5) So the place of Jesus' birth contributes to his identity as the Messiah and as the Son of David.

Firstborn Son

Luke records that Mary gave birth to her "firstborn son." (Luke 2:7) Jesus is the firstborn of many brothers and sisters in a spiritual family. He is the first of the always-growing community of people who work together to serve God's kingdom on earth. Mary is the spiritual mother of all Jesus came to save.

Swaddling Clothes

Luke's Gospel helps us understand that while Jesus is a king, he is a humble king who serves all. Mary wrapped Jesus in **swaddling** clothes, symbolizing the poverty and humility of Jesus' birth in a stable among animals. The act of swaddling, or wrapping the infant with strips of cloth, also reminds us that King Solomon was wrapped in swaddling clothes as a baby. (Wisdom 7:4–6)

Birth Announcement

Imagine that an advertiser hires you to write a billboard message for teens about the meaning of Jesus' birth. Write your tagline, an effective slogan that identifies your purpose.

_____

_____

_____

Manger

Mary placed the infant Jesus in a manger. Mangers were troughs used by shepherds and farmers to feed the animals. Luke tells us that because there was no room for Joseph and Mary at the inn, Jesus, the "Son of the Most High," (Luke 1:33) started life in a stable with simple accommodations. Placing the swaddled Jesus in the manger can remind us that Jesus himself will be food for the world.

Shepherds

Jesus' birth announcement was significant because it was made to shepherds, the humblest members of society. Shepherds were usually poor and dismissed by society as uneducated and unable to keep Jewish Law. Because shepherds lived outdoors in pastures with their sheep, many people considered them undesirable company.

Jesus is "the good shepherd" who "lays down his life for the sheep." (John 10:11) Because the proclamation of Jesus' arrival came first to shepherds, Luke showed that Jesus came to save everyone, not just a privileged few.

Savior

Jesus came from humble beginnings and demonstrated humility throughout his life. He brought a message of love to everyone, from simple fishermen to tax collectors. He is our example for living in a way that brings God's love to the world.

Jesus is our Savior, not a worldly leader. He comes to restore us to wholeness, to rescue us from sin, and to make it possible for us to be reconciled with others and with God.

In Luke's Infancy Narrative, Jesus is proclaimed the Son of God who came to save the world. Those who first recognized him were those who recognized their own need and dependence on God. Like Mary, they reflected in their hearts on the true meaning of salvation. Today we are still called to reflect on how Jesus comes into the world, where he is recognized, and where society neglects its obligation to help those in need. Every time we open ourselves to the concerns of others, we discover the birth of Jesus in our own hearts.

Past Meets Present

PAST: Saint Francis of Assisi (1181–1226) wanted people to share his devotion to the Christ Child. In 1223 he made a living image of the scene of Jesus' birth. Francis built a small stable out of wood and gathered farm animals. At midnight Mass he placed a baby in a manger and gathered people around a scene of the Holy Family. Francis spoke of Christmas as a time of gentleness and generosity, and he reminded people of Jesus' humble beginning.

PRESENT: A **novena,** a Catholic prayer tradition, is prayed for nine days in a row. The Mexican celebration of *Las Posadas* is a Christmas novena that reenacts Mary's and Joseph's search for shelter. The celebration lasts for nine days from December 16–24. Some Spanish-speaking Catholics celebrate *Las Posadas* in various ways, depending on their culture. Often people dressed as members of the Nativity go house-to-house, singing a song that asks if there is room at the inn. The hosts of the home sing a reply. Christmas carols are sung, and food is sometimes served.

Explore

Study Corner

DEFINE

census
swaddling
novena

REMEMBER

Jesus came from humble beginnings. Jesus is the Savior who came to save everyone, not just a privileged few.

Hardship in Jesus' Life

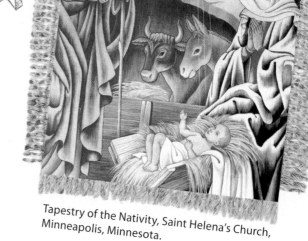

SOME people around the world have no homeland and bear the burden of terrible hardships. They may live as exiles or **refugees** because of natural disasters, such as famine, or because of man-made disasters, such as civil war. Newly arrived immigrants may feel hardship and alienation in an unfamiliar culture.

Early hardships of Jesus' family serve as a reminder that God exalts unexpected people.

> "Rather, God chose the foolish of the world to shame the wise, and God chose the weak of the world to shame the strong, and God chose the lowly and despised of the world, those who count for nothing, to reduce to nothing those who are something, so that no human being might boast before God."
>
> *1 Corinthians 1:27–29*

Tapestry of the Nativity, Saint Helena's Church, Minneapolis, Minnesota.

Our Catholic Character

Catholic social teaching tells us that as we grow in faith in God, we grow in **solidarity** with people all over the world. Faith, instead of isolating or dividing us, makes us more aware of the interdependence among individuals and nations. We are affected personally by the human suffering following natural or man-made disasters in distant countries. Pope John Paul II, in his encyclical letter *On Social Concern*, says, "Solidarity helps us to see the 'other'—whether a person, people or nation . . . as our 'neighbor,' a 'helper,' to be made a sharer on a par with ourselves, in the banquet of life to which all are equally invited by God."

The Magi

Even though the heavens opened up and angels sang of Jesus' birth, (Luke 2:13–14) Jesus was born into very dangerous circumstances. Matthew's Infancy Narrative tells how King Herod, greatly troubled by the prophecy of the Messiah's birth, wants the **Magi** to locate Jesus, supposedly so he may do Jesus homage. The word *Magi* refers to the men who came from the East by following a star, the first Gentiles to believe that Jesus was the Messiah. After finding Jesus, the Magi, who were warned in a dream not to return to Herod, depart for their own country.

Out of Egypt

An angel of God appeared to Joseph in a dream, telling him to flee with Mary and Jesus to Egypt. Joseph listened, and they stayed in Egypt until the death of Herod.

In a similar way, people all over the world pick up their families and flee persecution, fearing for their lives. Jesus, in Egypt, is a refugee. Throughout his ministry, he continues to advocate for those who are poor, outcast, and unwanted.

SACRED ART

This African artwork, a painting from the Jesus Mafa Collection, is a visual response to an event in the life of Jesus Christ. Originating with a group in Northern Cameroon in Africa, this painting portrays the Holy Family's flight into Egypt. To make the painting, group members dramatically interpret a reading from the Bible, photograph the dramatization, and paint from the photos.

The Flight into Egypt, Mafa Collection.

Massacre of the Infants

Matthew described how Herod gave orders for the death of every male child under the age of two in the vicinity of Bethlehem to ensure that the Messiah would not reach adulthood. Herod, a ruthless dictator, tried to hold on to power through violence. The bloodshed of the massacre of the infants surrounds the beginning of Jesus' life, and bloodshed surrounds it again with his Death on the cross. Herod attempted to rob Jesus of life, and on Calvary, Jesus' Death and Resurrection secured eternal life for humanity.

Prophecy

Jesus' early hardships fulfilled many prophecies about the Messiah. A **prophecy** is a divine communication that comes through a human being. When Herod asked the Magi where the Messiah was to be born, they recited the words of the prophet:

> "And you, Bethlehem, land of Judah,
> are by no means least among the rulers
> of Judah;
> since from you shall come a ruler,
> who is to shepherd my people Israel."
>
> *Matthew 2:6*

Another prophecy said that the Messiah, similar to Moses, would come out of Egypt:

> "Out of Egypt I called my son."
>
> *Matthew 2:15*

When Herod ordered the massacre of the infants, Jeremiah's prophecy was fulfilled:

> "A voice was heard in Ramah,
> sobbing and loud lamentation;
> Rachel weeping for her children,
> and she would not be consoled,
> since they were no more."
>
> *Matthew 2:18*

After the angel told Joseph to return to the land of Israel, his concern over Herod's son Archelaus, who was ruling over Judea, prompted Joseph to take the family to Nazareth, fulfilling the words of the prophet:

> "He shall be called a Nazorean."
>
> *Matthew 2:23*

Jesus' Life, Our Lives

We see God's prophecy fulfilled in moments of hardship as well as moments of blessedness. We know that Jesus' love for us leads to his Crucifixion and that through his saving act, Jesus comes into glory, and we are saved from sin. Jesus' Incarnation is to share in human suffering so that we may know Jesus is with us and that through Jesus we can bring God's love to others.

Our compassion and solidarity with refugees, immigrants, and persecuted people around the world are our recognition and response to hardships endured by Jesus' family and his saving actions on the Cross.

Study Corner

DEFINE

refugees
solidarity
Magi
prophecy

REMEMBER

Mary and Joseph fled into Egypt to save Jesus' life. King Herod inflicted violence to maintain his power, but Jesus willingly submitted to violence; through his Death and Resurrection, he triumphs over sin and death.

God Delivers the Just

Psalms, prayers in the form of poems that were written to be sung in public worship, express some aspect of the depth of human prayer.

Jesus knew the psalms and even prayed part of Psalm 22 on the cross. The psalms express a variety of human emotions, desires, and needs. They reflect real-life situations and problems. Although the style of language may be unfamiliar, their poetry draws us in and helps us express our human emotions in prayer.

Psalm 34 is a prayer of thanksgiving that speaks of God's justice. This prayer makes reference to fearing God. In this case, synonyms for the Hebrew word *fear* are *awe* or *respect*. This fear acknowledges the greatness of God, not the condition of being afraid of him. Even though hardships are part of human life, God is greater than these hardships. Injustice, poverty, disappointment, misfortune, hunger, and cruelty are part of our world. Prayer touches on all these things while reaffirming our hope in the Lord at the same time.

God Delivers the Just

Leader: Let us pray together the Response and become aware of God's justice.

Response: Magnify the LORD with me;
and let us exalt his name together.

Side 1: I sought the LORD, and he answered me,
delivered me from all my fears. R⁄.

Side 2: Look to him and be radiant,
and your faces may not blush for shame. R⁄.

Side 1: This poor one cried out and the LORD heard,
and from all his distress he saved him. R⁄.

Side 2: The angel of the LORD encamps
around those who fear him, and he saves them. R⁄.

Psalm 34:4–8

WHERE Do I Fit In?

It can be hard to make a place for yourself in the world. You may not always be welcomed, and sometimes you might be altogether rejected. A sense of belonging can make all the difference. God always makes a welcoming place for you.

by Cara Mia Cicciarelli

I Belong Wherever I Am

Every summer our family spent a vacation at Pennellwood, a 100-year-old family camp in the woods of southwestern Michigan. The camp was a hot, sticky, mosquito-filled place—and wonderful. Pennellwood consisted of 20 screened-in cabins, a lodge for meals, a few activity centers, and a "lake" that was really a dammed-up river. Pennellwood was closed off from the outside world, a little nook of unchanging charm from decade to decade. We would trade in our cell phones and video games for fishing poles and outdoor games of Capture the Flag. We forgot about TV shows that went unwatched and text messages that went unanswered. Young people wandered freely without causing parents any concern because once the dinner bell rang, we would surely appear, ready to heap our plates with comfort food. At the end of each season, we gathered to sing and tell stories around a bonfire. The sense of community was very strong, and I never felt more comforted than I was at those campfires.

After Pennellwood's final season of operation, our close summer community disbanded. That first summer without the campground, the weeks dragged on and on for me. I felt hollow without the familiarity of lazy days full of camp activities and the cool lake waters. I felt as if a part of me was auctioned off along with our beloved cabin.

I began looking for other places where I could feel the acceptance, love, comfort, and freedom that I had found at Pennellwood and now missed. I discovered that if I looked for God's presence in my ordinary life at school, while doing chores, or while spending time with friends, I could reclaim those feelings.

When I paused to notice the beauty of nature, the goodness in myself or others, or the bonds of my community, I knew that Pennellwood lived on in my heart. God lets me know that I belong wherever I am, and that he is present with me—anywhere.

Always Welcome

On a separate sheet of paper, write an e-mail message to a friend that either describes a time when you felt God's welcoming presence or a time when you needed to respond in a certain way to rediscover God's presence and love.

To: Becca

Cc: Mary

Subject: My Trip to Pennellwood

CARA MIA CICCIARELLI is a high school student who enjoys the fine arts, including vocal and dance studies.

Reflect

What's What?

Circle the letter of the choice that best completes each sentence.

1 _____ was the Roman emperor at the time of the birth of Jesus. (PAGE 64)

  a. Julius Caesar   **c.** Caesar Augustus

  b. Nero   **d.** Pontius Pilate

2 Jesus, Son of God, starts out life among _____ . (PAGES 64–65)

  a. those who are poor

  b. those who are lowly

  c. animals

  d. all of the above

3 After his birth, Jesus was laid in a manger, which is _____ . (PAGE 64)

  a. a feeding trough for animals

  b. a typical crib

  c. a loft in a barn

  d. a vehicle for travel

4 Jesus was wrapped in swaddling clothes just like _____ . (PAGE 64)

  a. King Herod   **c.** King Tut

  b. King Julius   **d.** King Solomon

5 Jesus, the Savior, comes for _____ . (PAGE 65)

  a. religious people

  b. smart people

  c. all people

  d. good people

6 In 1223 _____ built a scene of the birth of Jesus with a stable and animals. (PAGE 65)

  a. Saint Patrick   **c.** Saint Matthew

  b. Saint Francis of Assisi   **d.** Saint Stephen

7 The massacre of the infants refers to an order by _____ to kill every male under the age of two years. (PAGE 66)

  a. Herod   **c.** Pontius Pilate

  b. Caesar Augustus   **d.** Romans

8 An angel of the Lord appeared to Joseph in a dream and told him to take Mary and Jesus and flee to _____ until the danger had passed. (PAGE 66)

  a. Bethlehem   **c.** Egypt

  b. Nazareth   **d.** Galilee

9 After Herod's death, the Holy Family leaves Egypt and settles in _____ . (PAGE 67)

  a. Bethlehem   **c.** Jordan

  b. Nazareth   **d.** Galilee

Say What?

Know the definitions of these terms.

census	refugees
Magi	solidarity
novena	swaddling
prophecy	

Now What?

Jesus' message is for everyone. Describe ways you can help someone who is excluded, experiencing rejection, or in need of help.

_____

_____

_____

_____

Respond

Jesus Grew in Wisdom, Age, and Grace

Imagine how you'd like your life to be in 10 years. What does your family, home, schooling, or career look like? To realize these dreams, what steps do you likely have to take?

PRAYER

Lord, show me the gifts you have generously given me. Help me give my gifts and talents back to you, to serve you in some way.

Jesus in the Temple

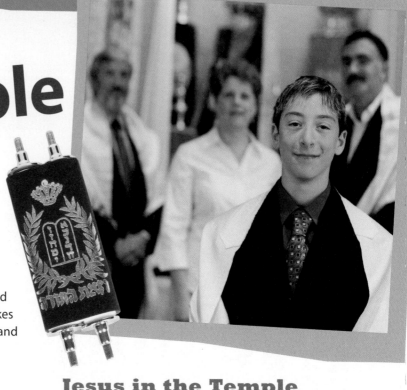

IN Jesus' time there were no Bar or Bat Mitzvahs, the Jewish ritual in which young people read the Torah in the **synagogue** and become "children of commandment."

Today a Jewish male has a Bar Mitzvah when he turns 13 years old. Luke's story, commonly referred to as the Finding in the Temple (Luke 2:41–52), takes place during Passover when Jesus is 12 years old and represents an important time in his life.

Lost

Passover, the Jewish festival celebrated every spring, recalls how the Lord delivered the Hebrews from slavery in Egypt. In Jesus' time the Temple in Jerusalem would have been crowded at Passover with men and women, families, pilgrims, and holy people preparing for the great celebration. It is not that surprising that Jesus got separated from Mary and Joseph or even that his absence wasn't noticed until Mary and Joseph were on their way back home. They may have assumed that Jesus was somewhere else in the huge caravan.

Jesus in the Temple

Mary and Joseph returned to Jerusalem to look for Jesus. After searching for three days, they discovered him in the Temple among rabbis. Jesus was not lecturing or preaching to the Jewish elders. Rather, he was "listening to them and asking them questions." (Luke 2:46) His ability to understand and speak about the Jewish faith at such a young age impressed the teachers who had studied the faith and the Law their entire lives. Luke 2:47 says that "all who heard him were astounded at his understanding and his answers."

Carving depicting Jesus found in the Temple.

Our Catholic Character

In Luke 2:51–52 we learn that while Jesus was living with his parents in Nazareth, he advanced in wisdom, age, and favor before God and others. He did so by practicing the virtues that lead a person to live in relationship with God and others. These four virtues—prudence, justice, fortitude, and temperance—are called the **Cardinal Virtues.** Jesus learned to be prudent, choosing the right course of action. He learned to be just, giving God and his neighbors what was due them. He learned to be strong, determined to do what was right in the face of obstacles. He learned to practice temperance, being moderate both in seeking pleasure and in using his possessions.

Why Have You Done This to Us?

Mary and Joseph were astonished to see Jesus in the midst of the teachers. But why? Were they astonished that he wasn't afraid? That he wasn't looking for them? That he was so comfortable with adults—important adults? That he knew so much about Scripture despite being so young?

Mary and Joseph must have experienced a variety of thoughts and feelings, including immense relief that Jesus was safe. Mary might have wondered how her son could disregard the worry she would feel as a parent. Mary has a question of her own: "Son, why have you done this to us?" (Luke 2:48)

My Father's Business

By way of reply, Jesus asks a question of his mother: "Why were you looking for me? Did you not know that I must be in my Father's house?" (Luke 2:49) For Jesus, the calling to be near the Father is obvious. Perhaps Jesus is surprised that he has even caused them worry. He might be wondering why his parents would look for him anywhere else. The story is not one of Jesus' disobedience to his parents but of an awakening that the Father is calling him to a special mission. Jesus has a sense about his future. He is beginning to know and understand his special relationship with God, his Father.

But Luke writes that Mary and Joseph do not understand the meaning of Jesus' words. Even so, seeing Jesus in the Temple among the teachers must have planted the seed of understanding about the work the Father was calling Jesus to do.

This is an extraordinary time for both Jesus and his parents. Jesus is obedient to them and returns to Nazareth. He knows the commandments, and the Fourth Commandment instructs him to respect and obey his parents. The commandment applies to parents, as well, calling them to help their children live full, healthy lives and to prepare them for the work that God wants them to do. Scripture tells us that "his mother kept all these things in her heart." (Luke 2:51) Mary would think about Jesus' words later on, knowing that her Son loved her but was answering his Father's call.

Mutual Respect

For families to live in harmony, it's important for parents and children to respect one another and understand their respective roles. Think about a time when you and a family member showed each other mutual respect. Record your ideas on the lines.

_____

_____

_____

_____

_____

_____

_____

_____

_____

_____

_____

Explore

Study Corner

DEFINE

synagogue
Cardinal Virtues

REMEMBER

Mary and Joseph found Jesus in the Temple with Jewish teachers, who were astounded at his understanding and answers.

Jesus begins to understand that God, his Father, is calling him to a special mission.

Past Meets Present

PAST: Saint John Bosco (1815–1888) took care of poor and forgotten youth in need. He was ordained a priest in 1841 and sent to Turin, Italy. John inspired young people who lived on the streets by the way he taught and by his life of prayer. Soon he was running a boarding house with the help of his mother, Margaret. Many more young people came to him for faith instruction and boarding, and he founded the first Salesian Home to care for their needs.

PRESENT: Today the Salesians number in the tens of thousands and are found in over 100 nations. Offering more than just food and shelter, the ministry rebuilds lives and helps young people learn a trade that will lead to employment. Other work includes assistance for women, food programs, youth clubs, health services, and emergency relief. Salesians also staff many mission foundations in developing countries. Today the Salesians of Don Bosco are the third-largest order in the Catholic Church.

Finding God in Family

JESUS grew up in Nazareth. Like his foster father Joseph, Jesus was known as a carpenter. Raised a Jew, he learned Scripture, the commandments, hard work, respect, and obedience. It is in family life that we live out our full human experience just as Jesus did.

A Domestic Church

The family is the first place of education about faith and prayer. When a Christian family of faith worships and prays together, they become a **domestic church** where children learn to pray. But learning to pray is far more than memorizing words to particular prayers. When the words prompt a response to God, we recognize God's presence, follow Jesus' example, grow in faith, serve others, and receive God's grace.

Living the realities of Christian life daily means experiencing good times and challenging times. Faithful family life strengthens the Church and God's presence in the world. Consider what Pope John Paul II wrote about families in *On the Role of the Christian Family in the Modern World*: "Joys and sorrows, hopes and disappointments, births and birthday celebrations, wedding anniversaries of the parents, departures, separations and homecomings, important and far-reaching decisions, the death of those who are dear, etc.—all of these mark God's loving intervention in the family's history."

Who Is Family?

In Chapter 3 of Mark's Gospel, Jesus makes a radical attempt to change people's minds about how they define family. When the crowd tells Jesus that his family is outside asking for him, Jesus replies, "Who are my mother and [my] brothers?" (Mark 3:33) Referring to the faithful gathered around him, Jesus says, "Here are my mother and my brothers. [For] whoever does the will of God is my brother and sister and mother." (Mark 3:34–35)

Jesus tells us that gathering must come first. Jesus' presence depends on it. If we are to depend on Jesus to help us in a time of need, Jesus depends on us to realize that other people—whether we are related to them by blood or by law or by simple human biology—are our family. With one another, we abide in love.

Family's Role in Society

The family is the first place we learn tolerance, respect, patience, acceptance, forgiveness, and love. If we cannot live these virtues within our own family, how well can we live them for other people, those who are our brothers and sisters in Christ? Pope John Paul II pointed out that the family is an essential school for social life that teaches a true and mature way of expressing unity with others. The role of the family does not stop with educating children but extends to their service in society as they grow. In the 1987 encyclical *On Social Concern*, Pope John Paul II writes "Today perhaps more than in the past, people are realizing that they are linked together by a common destiny, which is to be constructed together, if catastrophe for all is to be avoided. . . ." We can grow and become a full person only through our relationships and participation in society.

Social Roles

Describe your roles in your family and in social service. Write your ideas below or on another sheet of paper.

_____

_____

_____

_____

Study Corner

Explore

DEFINE

domestic church

REMEMBER

Jesus promised that he would be present wherever two or more people were gathered in his name. Therefore, he is present in our families. We first learn values, virtues, and service to others in our families.

Meal, Marijan Detoni, 1935.

SACRED ART

Marijan Detoni, a Croatian artist, wants his art to reflect social reality. This oil painting of needy people sharing a meal reminds us that the family is a foundation for building broader community relationships. Family life can increase awareness of and responsibility to the needs of others. Pope John Paul II wrote "note must be taken of the ever greater importance in our society of hospitality in all its forms, from opening the doors of one's home and still more of one's heart to the pleas of one's brothers and sisters." (*On the Role of the Christian Family in the Modern World*)

Gifts Received, Gifts Given

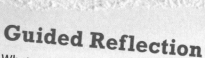

Guided Reflection

What are some things you have received freely from God? It might be a talent or an ability, or something you just enjoy doing. Maybe it's a supportive family or a friend who cares. Share your thoughts with Jesus.

Jesus reminds you that these gifts are meant to be shared. We are called to serve others by using our gifts, such as by spending time with an elderly relative or neighbor or befriending a new classmate. Talk over with Jesus some ways you might use your gifts to serve.

Jesus reminds you that serving others has hidden costs, like less free time or allowance, or maybe being teased. You will face challenges in living out your faith. But Jesus also reminds you that he is with you to help and encourage you in your service. Spend a moment just resting in Jesus' presence. Then thank him for your gifts and this time of sharing.

All: Lord Jesus, make us aware of the gifts we've received from your Father's hands. Encourage us to develop them. Inspire us to be open to the ways you call us to share our gifts. May we please you and help make the world a better place. We ask this with confidence in your name. Amen.

Ever since he called his first disciples, Jesus has been calling people to follow him. Followers of Jesus show their love for God by serving others.

Jesus instructed his first disciples:

> As you go, make this proclamation: ''The kingdom of heaven is at hand.'' Cure the sick, raise the dead, cleanse lepers, drive out demons. Without cost you have received; without cost you are to give.

Matthew 10:7–8

God gives us gifts and talents to accomplish his holy will. These gifts originate with God. We are not so independent that our gifts and talents come from ourselves. We foster and develop our gifts, but we realize that we are in a partnership with our Lord. We do our best to use our gifts, mindful that God the Father, God the Son, and God the Holy Spirit is the power in our lives that makes all things possible.

Saint Teresa of Calcutta echoes these ideas in her words about her service to those who are poor in India:

> "I do this because I believe I am doing it for Jesus. I am very sure that this is his work. I am very sure. I am very sure that it is he and not me."

WHERE Do I Fit In?

Even small experiences that seem insignificant at the time can shape the person you are becoming. Who or what helps you to discover the person God intends you to be?

by Claire Colombo

How Do I Discover My Real Identity?

Therefore, putting away falsehood,
speak the truth, each one to his neighbor,
for we are members one of another.

Ephesians 4:25

It happened when I was in the first grade. Winter was over, spring was on its way, and Sister Theresa Margaret wanted us to take down the snowflakes we'd taped to the windows back in December. She was very clear. "Children, when I say 'Go,' I want you to get up, find your snowflake, remove it, and return to your seat. No talking, no running, no grabbing."

Sister's orders threw me into a panic. December was ages ago! I had no idea where I'd taped my snowflake. The class sprang into action at Sister's "Go!" Everyone found their snowflakes easily because each one had its artist's name printed on the front. But mine was nowhere to be found. My heart thumped wildly. Where was my snowflake?

Then I remembered what happened on snowflake-hanging day. I had been unable to find a spot on the glass so Sister helped me. We taped my artwork to the window—with my name against the pane!

I looked around. Everyone was back in his or her seat—except me. I had not followed Sister's directions. I had not retrieved my snowflake. "Claire *Miller*!" she snapped. "Come *here*!" I was about to receive a consequence. I was paralyzed with fear.

Suddenly, though, I heard myself speaking—shy, awkward me, speaking with confidence, explaining the mix-up. "You helped me hang my snowflake," I was saying, "and my name ended up facing the pane." I tried to put it delicately, without blame. After several moments, Sister walked to the window and dislodged the single remaining paper snowflake. Sure enough, there was my name, facing the wrong way. Nevertheless, I did receive a consequence—a good one! Sister handed me the snowflake and gave my shoulders a little squeeze. "Thanks for telling the truth," she said.

To this day, I consider myself a truth-teller. I write for a living, which is all about telling the truth—even when it's hard to tell. At those moments, I feel Sister Theresa Margaret's arm around my shoulders. "Go on, Claire," she says. "It's who you are."

Who Are You Meant to Be?

Who are you becoming? Use your own photographs or pictures from magazines to make a collage on poster board that represents you. Cut out words or phrases that help explain your ideas and add them to your collage.

CLAIRE COLOMBO is a freelance writer and educator who lives in Austin, Texas, where snowflakes are never a problem.

Reflect

What's What?

Write answers using details from the text.

1 Where did Mary and Joseph find Jesus as a boy when he was lost? What was he doing there? (PAGE 72)

_____

_____

_____

2 How does Jesus surprise the Jewish elders? (PAGE 72)

_____

_____

_____

3 What are the four Cardinal Virtues? Why are they important to your faith? (PAGE 72)

_____

_____

_____

4 What does Jesus begin to understand when he is 12 years old? (PAGES 72–73)

_____

_____

_____

5 How does Jesus follow the Fourth Commandment? How do Mary and Joseph follow the Fourth Commandment? (PAGE 73)

_____

_____

_____

_____

6 Why is the family called a domestic church? (PAGE 74)

_____

_____

_____

7 What does Jesus teach about family in the Gospel of Mark? (PAGE 75)

_____

_____

_____

Say What?

Know the definitions of these terms.

Cardinal Virtues

domestic church

synagogue

Now What?

Describe one way your family demonstrates that it is a domestic church. Thank a family member for providing this way.

_____

_____

_____

_____

_____

_____

_____

_____

_____

Celebrating Advent and Christmas

WE prepare our hearts during the season of **Advent** to celebrate the birth of Jesus at **Christmas**. Advent begins four Sundays before Christmas and marks the start of the Church's liturgical year. When Advent ends, the season of Christmas begins. The Feast of the Baptism of the Lord, celebrated on the first Sunday after the Epiphany (January 6), closes the Christmas season.

Advent is a time for preparing ourselves to celebrate the coming of Jesus. It is a time for us to develop an attitude of hopefulness and joyful anticipation for the coming of Jesus. We can grow in this way as we celebrate liturgy and as we live our everyday lives. We remember the Jewish people who lived in hope awaiting the birth of the Messiah, and we joyfully anticipate the day when Christ will return in glory.

At Christmas we joyfully celebrate that Jesus' birth in Bethlehem brought God's promise of peace and salvation to the world. We respond to the miracle of the season by acknowledging that the one and only true gift we need to receive is Jesus. God's greatest gift to his people over 2,000 years ago is the greatest gift we receive today—his Son, our Savior Jesus Christ.

Explain what this sentence means to you: *God's gift of Jesus is the greatest gift we'll ever receive.* **What life experiences help you know this is true?**

PRAYER

Jesus, be with us as we prepare our hearts to celebrate your coming at Christmas. Help us experience and share the joy of your birth.

Living in the Light of Advent

ASSOCIATING ideas with darkness or light as a way to express a point that is important to our faith is found in both the Old and New Testaments.

Look at some common associations that follow:

- ➡ Darkness: evil, sin, living without following guidance from God, turning away from God

- ➡ Light: goodness, Jesus Christ, salvation, following God the Father and Jesus Christ, being in relationship with God

On various occasions, the prophet Isaiah used the contrast of darkness and light to speak to the Israelites about the promise of a Messiah, a Savior for humankind:

> I will lead the blind on a way they do not know;
>   by paths they do not know I will guide them.
> I will turn darkness into light before them,
>   and make crooked ways straight.
> These are my promises:
>   I made them, I will not forsake them.
>
> *Isaiah 42:16*

Jesus, who was promised to the Israelites and remains with us today, is the one true Light. The Israelites waited and prayed generation after generation for this light to come. Blessed with the gift of faith, they trusted that God would send them a Savior. Just as the Israelites believed and prepared, so do we. Advent is our time to ready our hearts and minds. Jesus, the Light of the World, has come to show us the way, and we look forward to the day he will return so that we can be with him forever.

Through Jesus Christ, our crooked ways are made straight. That's a comforting thought and a reason for great joy and hope. The promise of Christ's Light is why we celebrate Advent—why we get ready in our churches, in our homes, and in our hearts.

Our Catholic Character

During Advent we celebrate the Feast of the Immaculate Conception on December 8, which reminds us that Mary was born without Original Sin. Even before she was born, Mary was chosen by God to be the mother of Jesus. Several important celebrations occur during Advent. Many celebrations reflect ethnic and cultural traditions and recall saints or our Catholic Tradition. For example, the **Feast of Our Lady of Guadalupe** is an important Mexican celebration of Mary's appearance to Juan Diego. In the United States, it's celebrated on December 12. December 13 is the Feast of Saint Lucy, also known as Saint Lucia, whose name means "light." It is celebrated during the time of the longest nights of winter.

Awake from Sleep

The New Testament proclaims that the Messiah has come and that Jesus is in fact the Light of the World. This is good news—news to be happy about. And to prepare for Christ's coming again, Scripture tells us to examine our thoughts, words, and actions and check ourselves to be sure that we're ready. Consider this Scripture passage from Paul's Letter to the Romans:

> And do this because you know the time; it is the hour now for you to awake from sleep. For our salvation is nearer now than when we first believed; the night is advanced, the day is at hand. Let us then throw off the works of darkness [and] put on the armor of light; . . .
>
> *Romans 13:11–12*

"Awake from sleep" is our call to action—to be happy, present, and engaged in anticipating the coming of the Savior. Advent is our time of preparation, a time to awaken our faith. We don't want to go through the motions without consciously considering the coming of our Savior.

In History, Grace, and Glory

In History Jesus Christ came to us in history, born in a humble stable in the little town of Bethlehem. For centuries, God's Chosen People were promised a Messiah who would come to save the world. During Advent the Scripture readings at Mass remind us of how our ancestors in faith prepared for the Messiah. We can listen to the Word of God and take these messages to heart.

In Grace During Advent we reflect on the mystery of the Incarnation, our belief that the Son of God, Jesus Christ, became flesh in the womb of Mary and was born fully human, without loss of his divinity. Christ, the Light, comes to us today in grace through the people and events in our daily lives. He also comes to us through the sacraments, especially the Holy Eucharist, and in prayer.

In Glory Christ's final coming will be in glory to judge the living and the dead. He will come to take us to our eternal reward, revealed as "The city [that] had no need of sun or moon to shine on it, for the glory of God gave it light, and its lamp was the Lamb." (Revelation 21:23) To share his life in heaven, we prepare for his coming by loving and living as Jesus did.

Your Advent

You can celebrate Advent in your own unique way, in a way that gives you personal joy. If you like to spend time alone or reading, you might set aside five extra minutes before you go to bed to pray or read Scripture. You might also record reflections during Advent, perhaps thoughts from Scripture readings and the homilies from Mass or the Feast of the Immaculate Conception. How you prepare is up to you.

Explore

Awake or Asleep?

Think about where you are in life right now. Answer each question with an honest heart.

When it comes to faith, how do I show that I am awake rather than asleep?

_____

_____

What is one way that I show that I am living in the light?

_____

_____

When I celebrate Mass, what can I do to experience each moment fully?

_____

_____

_____

Study Corner

DEFINE

Feast of Our Lady of Guadalupe

REMEMBER

Advent is a time for us to prepare for the coming of Jesus and to develop an attitude of hopefulness and joyful anticipation.

Jesus is our Savior, the one true Light of the World.

The Gift of Christmas

MORE than 2,000 years ago, Jesus was born in the town of Bethlehem. Many of us can retell the story by heart. Only the Gospels of Matthew and Luke describe Jesus' birth.

Each writer of the **Nativity** story includes specific details. The Gospel of Luke begins with the announcement and birth of John the Baptist, tells about the Annunciation (the angel's announcement of Jesus' birth to Mary), and the Visitation (Mary's visit to her cousin Elizabeth). Luke explains Jesus' birth as an important world event by telling us that Caesar Augustus was the Roman emperor and that Mary and Joseph went to Bethlehem for the census. In Luke's story we read the Good News that Jesus' birth brings salvation to those who are poor and lowly. Born quietly in humble surroundings and first received by poor shepherds, Jesus comes into the world not as an earthly king but as a divine king. He has come as a light to shine on all people, especially those who are overlooked or forgotten: those who are poor, sinners, lepers, outcasts, and foreigners.

The Gospel of Luke highlights Mary's role and her response of yes to Jesus' birth. After the visit from the shepherds, Luke's Gospel tells us "And Mary kept all these things, reflecting on them in her heart." (Luke 2:19) In Luke's Nativity story, Jesus' birth is good news because Jesus brings salvation to the whole world.

Journey to Bethlehem,
Cathy Baxter,
20th century.

SACRED ART

This watercolor-and-pastel artwork shows Joseph leading a pregnant Mary out of Galilee. Joseph had to return to his hometown of Bethlehem for a census and to pay taxes being collected by the Roman government. Imagine taking a long journey on foot, with no paved roads, technology, or protection from the elements or other dangers. Now imagine taking this journey with a woman who is expecting a baby. Do you think that you would be motivated to reach your destination as soon as possible? Would your anticipation be one of joy, worry, or a mixture of both?

First Gifts

Only Matthew's Gospel records the visit from the Magi—astronomers from the East—who joyfully follow the star in the sky until they find Jesus. They are overcome at finding him, falling to their knees and offering him gifts. "Then they opened their treasures and offered him gifts of gold, frankincense, and myrrh." (Matthew 2:11) These gifts were signs that the Magi had come to serve a king. They recognized Jesus as their divine king and dedicated themselves to his will.

The Magi's gifts were symbolic of divine kingship. Gold is a precious metal, the currency of royalty and those who are wealthy. Frankincense was an incense that, when mixed with flour and oil, was offered on the outer altar of a **sanctuary.** A sanctuary is a holy place to worship God, such as a church or temple. The third gift, myrrh, was one of the most important perfumes in biblical times—it was used to perfume the oil with which kings were anointed and was also used in burials.

One True Gift

Today the season of Christmas has become a commercialized industry where shopping and gift exchanges overshadow the real reason we celebrate. Many people are tempted to focus on material gifts instead of the gift of Jesus, who is the only gift that we really need.

Think about a gift that you wanted for Christmas, but shortly after you got it, the excitement wore off, and you put it aside and forgot it. That's not what Christmas is about. Christmas is a lasting celebration of the Light of Christ entering the world, a precious gift for whom we await excitedly. Jesus is the gift we want and need—a gift to hold dear and never forget.

God blesses all of us with the gift of Jesus Christ. We are given a Savior who showed us how to live according to God's will. Through his Death and Resurrection, we are given the gift of forgiveness of sins so that we can walk with God now and be with him in heaven for all eternity. Jesus, the Light of the World, never disappoints us.

Past Meets Present

PAST: Why does the Church celebrate the Nativity on December 25? Many biblical scholars believe the choice of date is connected to the celebration of a pre-Christian feast. At the same time that Christianity was spreading, December 25 marked the Roman pagan custom of celebrating *Natalis Sol Invicti,* the rebirth of the sun at the winter solstice. Around A.D. 354 the Bishop of Rome called all Christians to celebrate the birth of Christ on that day. Early Christians would understand that Jesus is the Light of the World, brighter than the brightest light they knew, the sun.

PRESENT: Many Filipino Catholics participate in the Christmas novena known as *Simbang Gabi,* meaning "night worship." This predawn celebration of Mass lasts for nine days and is sometimes called *Misa de Gallo,* meaning "Mass of the Rooster." Beginning December 16 and leading up to Christmas Day, people awaken to the sound of church bells around 3:00 or 3:30 A.M., calling them to worship at Mass. Although the origin of this custom is obscure, most agree that the devotion requires a sacrifice of love to hear the Word of God so early in the morning before beginning daily duties. Ringing bells break the predawn silence with a message of hope and peace on earth.

Explore

Study Corner

DEFINE

Nativity
sanctuary

REMEMBER

Only the Gospels of Matthew and Luke describe Jesus' birth. Each includes unique details.

Jesus Christ is the one true gift of Christmas.

Welcome Jesus!

We welcome Jesus by celebrating feast days and holy days during Advent and Christmas.

A day when Catholics participate in the Eucharist to celebrate the great things that God has done through Jesus and the saints is called a **holy day of obligation**. In the United States, December 8 honors the Solemnity of the Immaculate Conception. We also celebrate Christmas on December 25 and Mary, Mother of God on January 1 during these two Church seasons.

In addition, Catholics celebrate these **feast days:** the Feast of the Holy Family on the Sunday after Christmas, the Epiphany on January 6, and the Baptism of the Lord on the first Sunday after the Epiphany.

Give Glory to the Lord

Leader: Let us begin our prayer with the Sign of the Cross.

Reader: A reading from the holy Gospel according to Luke. [Luke 2:1–7]
The Gospel of the Lord.

All: Praise to you, Lord Jesus Christ.

Leader: Let us offer our praise to God.

All: Glory to God in the highest.

Side 1: Sing to the LORD a new song;
sing to the LORD, all the earth.
Sing to the LORD, bless his name;
proclaim his salvation day after day.

Psalm 96:1–2

Side 2: Give to the LORD, you families of nations,
give to the LORD glory and might;
give to the LORD the glory due his name!
Bring gifts and enter his courts;
bow down to the LORD, splendid in holiness.

Psalm 96:7–8

Side 1: Let the heavens be glad and the earth rejoice;
let the sea and what fills it resound;
let the plains be joyful and all that is in them.

Psalm 96:11–12

Side 2: Then let all the trees of the forest rejoice
before the LORD who comes,
who comes to govern the earth,
To govern the world with justice
and the peoples with faithfulness.

Psalm 96:12–13

All: Glory to God in the highest.

Leader: Let us pray together the Glory Be to the Father.

WHERE Do I Fit In?

It's not always easy to find your way. You may struggle to do or say the right things. At times you may feel as if you don't know the way to go. Or you may take a wrong turn and lose your way. At these times, it is important to cultivate an attitude of hope and try to be a light to others, as Jesus is for us.

by Regina Kazanjian

Being a Light to Others

Many people I respect and love have a passion for apologetics, which is the art of forming solid arguments for faith. I am not scornful of this—it's a worthy pursuit. But one of my greatest personal pitfalls is striving to be good enough on my own. I'm ashamed to face God until I've pulled everything together, until I look worthy, until I've cleared this or that problem out of my life. It's a bottomless hole because I never can be perfect on my own. I begin to believe that if I know all the right facts, I can craft a flawless argument and convince everyone to join my side. Ironically, this makes me hesitate to even bring up subjects of faith with my friends because I tell myself that my arguments just aren't "right" yet.

I have an even greater problem in my discussions with those who don't share my faith. I concentrate on making myself a "perfect witness." If I've been talking about the joy of Christ, I mistakenly feel that now I have to be happy all the time. I think that my listeners may be watching me now, and I can't let myself slip up and undermine my own argument!

Thankfully, I've come to realize that the key to being a light to others is to humbly accept that the light is not mine—it is just a reflection of God's own light. A reflecting object must be oriented toward its light source. The goodness I know, the truth I see, or the love that's changed me is constantly streaming from God, the source of all goodness and beauty. It's impossible for me to figure out God and be perfect. However, he has called me to keep my eyes fixed on him, to never hide my love for him, and to be open about his work in my life.

Lighting a Way

A single flame casts a dim light. Dozens of flames may illuminate an entire space. God doesn't expect you to be a perfect person, but he invites you to share his light with others.

Show how you share your light with the world. Hold a flashlight and stand in a circle with your group in a darkened room. Think of one way in which you have been a reflection of God's love and care to others. After sharing your idea, turn on your flashlight. Notice the growing brightness in the room as each person speaks and then adds his or her light.

REGINA KAZANJIAN is an undergraduate student at the University of Cincinnati.

What's What?

After each topic sentence, write one supporting detail from the text.

After each topic sentence, write one supporting detail from the text.

1 Catholics celebrate Advent and Christmas during the Church's liturgical year for different reasons. (PAGE 79)

_____

_____

_____

_____

2 Themes of light and darkness appear in the Bible. (PAGES 80–81)

_____

_____

_____

_____

3 Advent is a good time for us to "awake from sleep." (PAGE 81)

_____

_____

_____

_____

4 Born quietly in humble surroundings and first received by poor shepherds, Jesus comes to us not as an earthly king but as a divine king. (PAGES 82–83)

_____

_____

_____

_____

5 The Light of Jesus is the one true gift of Christmas. (PAGE 83)

_____

_____

_____

_____

6 Catholics celebrate feast and holy days during Advent and Christmas. (PAGE 84)

_____

_____

_____

_____

Say What?

Know the definitions of these terms.

Advent

Christmas

feast days

Feast of Our Lady of Guadalupe

holy day of obligation

Nativity

sanctuary

Now What?

Jesus was born as one of us. His humble beginnings tell us that every person has dignity in the eyes of God. What is one thing you can do this week to promote the dignity of others?

_____

_____

_____

_____

_____

Respond

Faith in ACTION

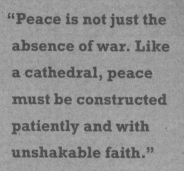

> "Peace is not just the absence of war. Like a cathedral, peace must be constructed patiently and with unshakable faith."
>
> —Saint John Paul II

Act

Part of the mission of the Catholic Church is to help shape the world. We are called to be part of the fabric of society, participating in social tasks and responsibilities. As members of society, Catholics take part in making the world a better place. Our families are the starting place for learning about justice.

In this unit we learned that Jesus, who is fully divine and fully man, expressed his humanity in profound ways, experiencing great joys as well as hardships and suffering. Jesus is "God with us," who is for all people. Our relationship with Jesus calls us to live in justice. One way that we can answer this call is to work for peace in the world. Here are some ideas to help you take a stand against violence and promote peace.

A Shelter from Violence

Purpose

Plan a project that raises awareness of the effects of domestic violence on families and society. Plan to provide assistance to people affected by domestic violence.

Background

Domestic violence is physical or mental abuse that is used to gain or maintain power and control over a partner or family member. Domestic violence can happen to anyone—children, teens, or adults. Although it is often inflicted by a family member, domestic violence can also occur in a dating situation.

Steps

1. Find organizations in your area that serve the needs of people who suffer from domestic violence.

2. Use these or other suggestions for ways to help:

   • Have the group write letters to government officials in support of legislation against domestic violence and to provide funding for agencies that deal with domestic violence.

(continued on page 88)

- Collect materials for arts-and-crafts projects that volunteers can use to teach children in shelters. Organize a time and date to visit a local shelter, and ask parents to chaperone.

- Educate your community by inviting experts to speak at a public forum, publish articles on domestic violence, and make available printed or online information that tells where to get help.

Toys Against Violence

Purpose

Become aware of the amount of violence people are exposed to on a daily basis; take a stand against violence by rediscovering peaceful activities.

Background

Our culture surrounds us with images of violence. Even simulated images, such as computer games, can desensitize us and make violence seem ordinary and more acceptable. What we see, what we read, and how we play really does shape us for better or worse.

Act

Steps

1. For one week, record every instance of your exposure to violence, either through your direct participation or witnessing someone else. For example, did you use toy weapons, view violence on TV, play violent video games, or engage in verbal violence, such as insults? At the end of the week, share your findings with the group. What insights did you gain from recording your observations?

2. Brainstorm ways that you can reduce the amount of violence around you.

3. Find ways to surround yourself with nonviolent, fun, and engaging things or activities.

4. Share your new insights with the group. For example, you could teach younger children a nonviolent game that encourages cooperation. Be creative and at the same time take a stand against violence.

"**Blessed are the peacemakers, for they will be called children of God.**"

—Matthew 5:9

PEACE

The Public Life of Jesus

Matthew, Mark, Luke, and **John** are the authors of the
Gospels, the first four books in the New Testament. The Gospels tell us
about the life of Jesus and his role as our Savior and Redeemer. If you look
closely, you'll discover that although the Gospels are all true and have
a great deal in common, they are not identical. Each one is written in a
different time for a different audience or community. None of the authors
of the four Gospels wrote a biography, telling absolutely everything they
knew about Jesus. Instead, inspired by the Holy Spirit, they recorded the
faith of the early Church, a faith that has been passed down to us.

**How the
Saints Relate** { Jesus performed signs and miracles, taught,
healed, loved, and forgave. The words of
Matthew, Mark, Luke, and John can help
answer the questions, "Who is Jesus?" and
"What does he teach?"

Four Gospels, One Lord

The Gospels are at the center of our faith because Jesus Christ is the center of the Gospels. The four Gospel writers, called the **Evangelists,** wanted to preserve the teachings of Jesus so that future generations would recognize his importance to our salvation. Each author tells us in a unique way what is important to know about Jesus and provides a point of view that is shaped by culture and historical time. The Gospels are the source of truth and understanding about how we are to live our lives.

Formation of the Gospels

The Gospels were not written simultaneously. They formed over a period of time. The first stage was the life and teachings of Jesus, including his birth and life in Nazareth, his public **ministry,** and finally his Death, Resurrection, and Ascension. When Jesus entered public life, he was accompanied by disciples, some of whom he chose to be Apostles. They saw the way Jesus lived and how he cared for others. They listened to his teachings. They spoke to Jesus after his Resurrection.

The second stage in the formation of the Gospels was the preaching of the Good News of the salvation of Jesus Christ by the Apostles. This passing on by word of mouth of what they received from Jesus' teaching and example and what they learned from the Holy Spirit is our Catholic Tradition. The Good News is passed on to us today by the Apostles' successors, the **bishops** and the **pope.**

The final stage was the actual writing of the Gospels. The writers recorded the words and stories about Jesus that they remembered or had been told. Each Gospel writer composed his own account to show what Jesus meant to him and to others living in his community.

Inspired by the Holy Spirit

Early leaders in the Church established some rules to help them choose which writings were inspired by the Holy Spirit and told the truth about Jesus Christ.

➡ Did the writing link to the teachings of one of the Apostles?

➡ Did the writing come from an authentic Christian community?

➡ Did the writing conform to the "rule of faith"; that is, did the writing reflect the authentic faith that had been learned from the Apostles?

The four Gospels we have today do all these things and are the only Gospels accepted by the Church as truly inspired by the Holy Spirit as teaching the truth about Jesus Christ.

Matthew

Mark

Luke

John

Jesus Prepares for His Ministry

Do messages that tell you how you should look, what you should wear, and what you should do always reflect Jesus' teaching? What values are at the heart of Jesus' messages? Which messengers do you trust the most? Why?

PRAYER

Beloved Jesus, help me learn what you value so that I may take up those values and make them my own.

Jesus, Son of God

JESUS' identity as the Son of God is revealed at his baptism by John the Baptist in the Jordan River. People were going to John for baptism as a public statement of their sinfulness and their repentance before the community.

Holy Spirit and Fire

When the crowds asked John what they must do to repent, he told them, "Whoever has two tunics should share with the person who has none. And whoever has food should do likewise." (Luke 3:11) To tax collectors, he said, "Stop collecting more than what is prescribed." (Luke 3:13) To soldiers, Luke instructed, "Do not practice extortion, do not falsely accuse anyone, and be satisfied with your wages." (Luke 3:14) Because John spoke this way, many in the crowd thought that he might be the long-awaited Messiah, an idea John dismissed. John told the people that he was baptizing with water, whereas the one to come after him would baptize "with the holy Spirit and fire." (Luke 3:16)

Our Catholic Character

The word *epiphany* takes its name from the Greek *epiphaneia*, meaning "manifestation, striking appearance." The Gospel writers used this term to describe events in the life of Christ when Jesus' divinity revealed itself. The Church recognizes four epiphanies of Christ when his divinity shines through his humanity: the Nativity, the adoration of the Magi, Jesus' baptism in the Jordan River, and Jesus' first sign at the wedding feast at Cana.

Anointed for the Mission

Jesus' coming to be baptized identified him as the Messiah that John had been talking about. By his baptism, Jesus submits entirely to the will of the Father. Jesus, who is without sin, takes the sins of the entire world upon himself so that we might have salvation. In his baptism, Jesus accepts his mission as Messiah. Jesus' immersion in the water symbolizes that he will redeem the world by being submerged in Death and then rise into new life. God the Father, delighting in his Son, voices his pleasure and reveals Jesus' identity. "[H]eaven was opened and the holy Spirit descended upon him in bodily form like a dove. And a voice came from heaven, 'You are my beloved Son; with you I am well pleased.'" (Luke 3:21–22)

Manifestation of God

Jesus' baptism is an **epiphany,** the revelation of Jesus as the Son of God. The Father's voice, the Holy Spirit like a dove descending upon Jesus, and Jesus the Son are the Revelation of the Trinity—Three Persons in one God. The Father strengthened Jesus for his mission, and the Spirit anointed him.

The Messiah's Test

Jesus, at around 30 years old, accepts his mission at his baptism by John. Immediately following his baptism, the Spirit leads Jesus into the desert for a time of solitude so that he can prepare for his mission.

For 40 days, Jesus remains in the harsh wilderness of the desert, living among wild animals. At the end of this time, when Jesus is tired and weak, **Satan** entices him with **temptation** three times, urging him to compromise his relationship with the Father or to live by values that would be completely different from those of the Father. (Luke 4:1–13)

Tempted in the Desert

Because Jesus has not eaten for 40 days, he is very hungry. Luke's Gospel tells us that the devil's first test of the Son of God takes advantage of Jesus' need for nourishment. "If you are the Son of God, command this stone to become bread." (Luke 4:3) Jesus rejects the suggestion because the Son of God is fed by God, not by bread alone. Satan persists and takes Jesus up to a very high mountain and shows him all the kingdoms of the world. He offers Jesus all the wealth and power of the world if only Jesus will worship him. Jesus replies that God alone is to be worshiped and served. (Luke 4:5–8) Then the devil takes Jesus to the top of the Temple and tells him to jump, for surely God will keep him safe from harm by sending angels to support him. Jesus replies that the Son of God does not put the Father to such foolish tests. Finally the devil leaves Jesus for a time. (Luke 4:9–13)

Jesus Is the Messiah

Satan tempts Jesus with power, honor, and wealth, which are all temporary and false sources of security. Satan tempts Jesus to be a different kind of Messiah, a Messiah with a material kingdom instead of a spiritual one. Because Jesus renounces the temptations, his true identity as the Messiah, the Son of God, is confirmed.

Jesus is the "new Adam" because he remains faithful, whereas Adam found temptation too hard to resist. Jesus' 40 days in the desert mirror the 40 years the Israelites spent wandering in the desert. While the Israelites lost faith in God over and over as they faced temptations, Jesus remains obedient and faithful to the will of God the Father. Jesus conquers Satan and his hollow promises, not for himself, but for love of humanity and the Father. "For we do not have a high priest who is unable to sympathize with our weaknesses, but one who has similarly been tested in every way, yet without sin." (Hebrews 4:15)

Recognizing Temptation

Write examples of temptations that people face today.

Temptations of pleasure:

_____

_____

_____

_____

Temptations of power:

_____

_____

_____

_____

Temptations of pride:

_____

_____

_____

_____

Study Corner

DEFINE

epiphany, Satan, temptation

REMEMBER

The baptism of Jesus was a sign that he accepted his mission as Messiah, taking on the sins of the world. Jesus' resistance to temptation reveals a Messiah who will make present the reign of God.

Facing Temptation

JESUS, like us except in sin, experienced real temptation in the desert. The temptations were ones all human beings face—things that look good on the surface but actually diminish our true calling.

The story of Jesus' temptation in the desert shows us how the Word of God is rooted in Jesus, how it helps him, and how it can help us. Temptation is an attraction that can lead us to disregard God's loving invitation. If the temptation starts with a person, he or she might try to convince you that you should have something or do something. The person might lie or make an attractive offer. Instead of giving you a lasting gift, the tempter really wants to take something away from you, such as your safety, your independence, your self-control, or your reliance on God and your obedience to him. Everyone is tempted, but the Holy Spirit helps us resist temptation and choose to do what God intends for us.

Christ in the Wilderness, Laura James, 20th century.

Jesus followed God perfectly and without sin, a grace shared with his mother, Mary. Even so, he still faced temptations. Because of this, Jesus understands how difficult it is for us when we face temptations. He did not leave us alone without guidance. Jesus gave the disciples the example of his own life and helped them understand his mission. When Jesus taught, he was also preparing his disciples to carry on his Word and lead his Church. Jesus often used a **parable** to give added explanations and to answer questions. At one point in the Gospel of Matthew, Jesus asked his disciples if they understood the meaning of his parables, and they answered yes. This is an important point because they would not have been able to pass along Jesus' teachings without this understanding. Jesus' teachings, safeguarded by the Apostles and by their successors, the pope and the bishops, are alive today in the Word of God.

Parable of the Sower

In Jesus' time, farmers understood the struggles of growing food on Israel's rocky land. Jesus used this knowledge to teach about hearing the Word of God, a tool for resisting temptation. In Jesus' telling of the parable of the sower, he uses familiar images. A sower drops seeds that fall in different places on the ground. Some seeds fall on the path, and birds eat it.

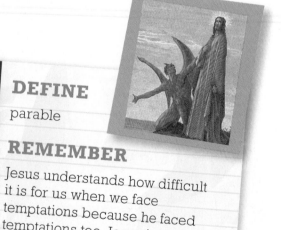

Study Corner

DEFINE
parable

REMEMBER
Jesus understands how difficult it is for us when we face temptations because he faced temptations too. Jesus is like us, but he alone follows God perfectly and without sin.

Some seeds fall on rocky ground. Because there is not enough soil to support them, they wither for lack of roots. Some seeds fall among thorns, and they are choked. But some seeds fall on rich soil, and much fruit is produced. (Matthew 13:3–9)

The seed, Jesus explained, is God's Word. Some of it falls in places where it can live and flourish, and some of it falls in places where it cannot sprout and grow. We are like the ground in the parable. The seed sown on the path is like the person who hears the Word without understanding it, allowing evil to come and steal it away. The seed sown on rocky ground is like a person who receives the Word joyously, but when faced with a test, falls away. The seed sown among thorns is the Word choked from someone's heart by worldly worries and desire for riches. Only the seed sown in rich soil flourishes and bears much fruit because God is at work in someone's life. (Matthew 13:18–23)

We Are Tested

As a young person, you face many temptations that get in the way of being faithful to the Word of God. Giving in to temptation makes you like stony ground where seeds can't take root and grow. Good intentions to avoid temptation can blow away like seeds in the wind if they are not rooted in prayer and perseverance. When you experience temptation, remember that Jesus faced temptation too. God wants you to live the best life you can. Moments of temptation can be overcome if you root yourself in determination to follow God.

Expect temptation so that you can prepare for it. Rely on the example of the saints who have gone before you. Put your energy into healthy activities, such as sports, the arts, music, and volunteer work. Remember Jesus' parable about the farmer. The Church is like the rich soil that will help the seed of faith grow in you. Turn to Jesus often in prayer. Receive the sacraments, listen to Scripture, and be determined to live a good life.

SACRED ART

Vincent Van Gogh's oil on canvas was inspired by an 1850 painting called *Sower* by Jean-François Millet. Van Gogh believed Millet's artwork brought the spirit of Christ to life on the canvas. Van Gogh, who had studied theology, regarded his art as a way to bring spiritual comfort and peace. Elements in this oil painting contain images from Jesus' parable of the sower, such as a path, the sun, and blackbirds eating some of the seed the sower is scattering. In the background, vertical stalks of grain show the seed that has taken root and grown.

Explore

Past Meets Present

PAST: Saint Thomas Becket (1118–1179) resisted temptation and held strong to faith and to the Church. Becket, a priest, had a friendship with King Henry II of England. Eventually, the king elevated Thomas to the highest position in the Catholic Church in England, the Archbishop of Canterbury. When the king wanted to use his power to control the Church, Thomas stood against him. As a result, the king had Thomas killed.

PRESENT: Although the Church recognizes the need for authority to govern people, Catholic social teaching insists that authority must be exercised for the common good of society, using morally acceptable means. "[T]here is no authority except from God, and those that exist have been instituted by God." (Romans 13:1)

Sower with the Setting Sun,
Vincent Van Gogh, 1888.

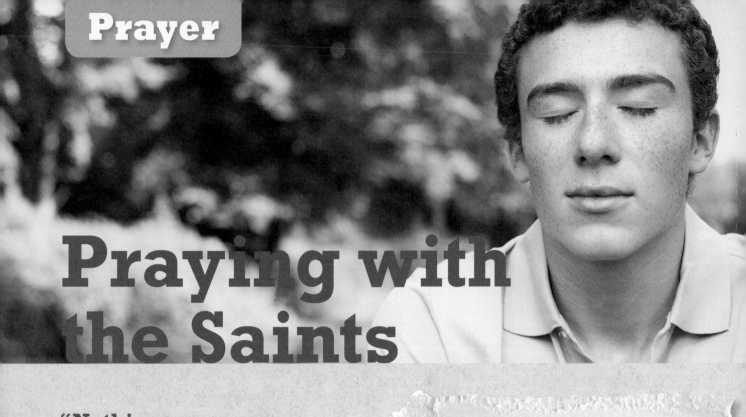

Praying with the Saints

"**Nothing** is more practical than finding God, that is, than falling in love in a quite absolute, final way. What you are in love with, what seizes your imagination will affect everything. It will decide what will get you out of bed in the mornings, what you will do with your evenings, how you spend your weekends, what you read, who you know, what breaks your heart, and what amazes you with joy and gratitude. Fall in love, stay in love, and it will decide everything."

Pedro Arrupe, S.J.

Pedro Arrupe is not a saint, yet similar to Saint Thomas Aquinas and other saints, he is a person who led a life of heroic virtue that set an example for all Christians.

Saints have witnessed to their faith in ordinary and extraordinary ways. The saints' love of God prompted them to know the heart of Jesus, taking what Jesus valued, and making it their own so that their hearts would be similar to Jesus'. This does not mean that the saints were perfect. Instead, it means that they trusted in God's love and mercy. God was able to work through them in powerful ways. Many saints wrote prayers that enrich the spiritual lives of all believers. Through their prayers we can see what they valued and try to follow their ways in our own lives.

Prayer of Saint Thomas Aquinas

Leader: In the name of the Father, and of the Son, and of the Holy Spirit. Amen.

Let us pray together a prayer by Saint Thomas Aquinas.

*Grant me, O Lord my God,
a mind to know you,
a heart to seek you,
wisdom to find you,
conduct pleasing to you,
faithful perseverance in waiting for you,
and a hope of finally embracing you.
Amen.*

All: Oh Lord, may we use our minds to comprehend the Catholic faith and to come to know what Jesus taught. May we come to know you through our love of others. May we treasure the grace of finding God in all things. May we act so that our behavior shows that we are disciples of your Son, Jesus. May we persevere in faith, overcoming all obstacles. May we keep in our imaginations the vision of ourselves embracing Jesus at the end of our lives. May we all live in eternal happiness in heaven with God. Amen.

WHERE Do I Fit In?

If you accept all messages blindly, you might fail to recognize God's invitation to live with integrity. Seeking deeper truths frees you to resist false trappings and allows you to live your life authentically as a follower of Christ.

by Jennon Bell

Seeking Real Truth

Once a week I meet a group of friends to play a trivia game. We win prizes or bragging rights, but primarily we get together for the good company and to flex our brain muscles. Usually, something interesting happens.

The announcer asks the question, and we stare blankly at one another, hoping the answer will magically come to us. Then as the clock clicks down and the tension rises, a nugget of information bursts into my brain. I blurt out the correct answer, right at the buzzer. My friends ask, "How did you know that?" I respond, "I'm not sure. I just *knew it*."

Some things I know because I've learned them, whether through study, experiments, or experience. But then there are things I just "know." I'm not sure how that information got there. I like to think that the mind is like a sponge, constantly absorbing data and tidbits that permeate our everyday lives. We're bombarded by information from the Internet, television, newspapers and magazines, lyrics, text messages, conversations, and advertisements. How can I know that the messages I'm hearing are trustworthy, worthwhile, and most importantly, a reflection of what I believe?

As Catholics, we have a multitude of resources to help us weigh the messages we receive. The Beatitudes, a Daily Examen, the Commandments,

a parish priest or church group, Scripture readings, family, or a quiet meditation can provide the support and guidance I need to focus my attention on what is influencing my daily choices. I like to think of these faith tools as a filter for my mind's inbox. And above all else, I trust the conscience I have cultivated as a Catholic so that when someone asks, "How do you know that?" I can say with confidence, "I just know it."

Unlocking the Message

What kind of media message is contrary to your Catholic values? What kind of media message supports your Catholic values? Write examples on the lines. If needed, continue on another sheet of paper.

False Message

_____
_____
_____

True Value

_____
_____
_____

JENNON BELL is a curriculum editor from Illinois who loves to read, bake, and perform improvisation.

What's What?

Finish each sentence to complete the crossword.

Across

2. Jesus accepts his mission as _____ . (PAGE 92)

3. The four writers of the Gospels are called the _____ . (PAGE 90)

6. Each Gospel was written for a different _____ . (PAGE 89)

9. An attraction that can lead to disobedience of God's commands is a _____ . (PAGE 93)

Down

1. God said, "You are my _____ Son." (PAGE 92)

4. The Gospels were inspired by the Holy _____ . (PAGE 90)

5. John the Baptist baptized in the _____ River. (PAGE 92)

7. In the Gospel of Luke, Satan tempts Jesus to perform a _____ by changing stone to bread. (PAGE 93)

8. In the early days of the Church, the Gospel was passed on by word of _____ . (PAGE 90)

Say What?

Know the definitions of these terms

bishops	parable
epiphany	pope
Evangelists	Satan
ministry	temptation

Now What?

Write some actions, attitudes, or practices that will help you stay away from temptation this week. Then choose one, write it on a slip of paper, and keep it with you as a reminder.

_____

_____

_____

_____

_____

_____

_____

_____

Respond

Jesus Performs Signs

To what are you committed? Even though you might be tempted to give up on commitments, relationships, or responsibilities when things get difficult, with courage and determination, you can see them through. When have you put in some extra effort to stick with a commitment?

PRAYER

Lord Jesus, bless my efforts to stay committed to you. Let me know the abundance of your love and grant me your salvation.

Miracle at Cana

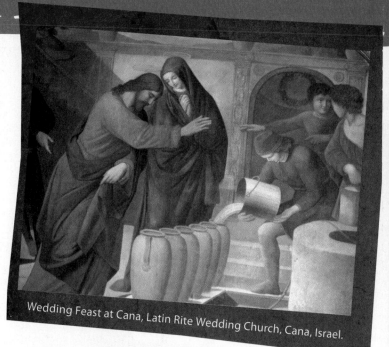

Wedding Feast at Cana, Latin Rite Wedding Church, Cana, Israel.

IN John 2:1–12, Jesus performs his first miracle, an act of power or wonder that is attributed to God. The first half of John's Gospel contains seven signs, each revealing the glory of God and giving us a glimpse of what the Kingdom of God is like. The wedding at Cana shows the significant role of Mary in Jesus' ministry.

Jesus, his mother, and the disciples are invited to a wedding in the town of Cana in Galilee. Although he has disciples, Jesus has not yet begun his public ministry. It was common for wedding feasts to last a long time, even days. At this wedding feast, the wine runs out, an embarrassment for the family, who will have to send everyone home.

In the midst of the celebration, Jesus' mother hears about the wine. When Mary tells Jesus the wine has run out, an interesting exchange between mother and Son takes place. Jesus says, "Woman, how does your concern affect me? My hour has not yet come." (John 2:4) Jesus is asking his mother how this fact involves him.

"Do Whatever He Tells You"

Mary directs the servers, "Do whatever he [Jesus] tells you." (John 2:5) John reveals Mary as an ever-faithful model of faith. She places her belief in Jesus. Interestingly, these are the last words we hear Mary speak in the Gospel of John.

Mary's words echo an occasion of famine when the Pharaoh of Egypt told the Israelites to go to Joseph, the son of Jacob, and do whatever he said to do. (Genesis 41:55) Pharaoh had entrusted Joseph with tremendous authority in Egypt, and Joseph fed the starving people to relieve the famine. In a similar way, the wine had run out at the wedding feast, and Jesus, to whom God had given authority, rewarded Mary's trust and faith by providing in abundance.

Jesus had not expected to perform any "sign" this day. Upon Jesus' direction the servers filled six water jars, each holding 20 to 30 gallons, and Jesus transformed the water into wine. The wine was very good; in fact, it was so good that the headwaiter was amazed it had been saved for last. (John 2:6–10)

Similarly, God provides for us in great abundance, and the world has been given all it needs through the coming of Jesus Christ. Mary's faith-filled words at the wedding feast set the stage for Jesus' glory to be revealed to his disciples. "Jesus did this as the beginning of his signs in Cana in Galilee and so revealed his glory, and his disciples began to believe in him." (John 2:11) The disciples' faith, then, followed from Mary's faith.

Our Catholic Character

The couple at the wedding feast at Cana made a promise, a personal covenant, with God and each other. In Jesus' time, religious authorities accepted divorce. Jesus refused to be drawn into the argument between sides that argued the grounds for divorce. Instead, he reminded them what God said at the beginning. "That is why a man leaves his father and mother and clings to his wife, and the two of them become one body." (Genesis 2:24) "Therefore, what God has joined together, no human being must separate." (Matthew 19:6)

Miracles of Abundance

The first 12 chapters of John's Gospel are referred to as the Book of Signs because Jesus performs many miracles that reveal God's glory. In different ways these signs, or miracles, show us God's abundant love for us. In John's Gospel, Jesus multiplies five barley loaves and two fish so that about 5,000 people can eat. Jesus takes the food, gives thanks, and distributes it, and the people eat as much as they want. When the disciples gather what is left, they are able to fill 12 wicker baskets. (John 6:9–13) Just as at Cana, Jesus performs a sign to reveal that God's promises are fulfilled with abundance.

The stories of signs in the Gospel of John reveal not only who Jesus is but also who the Father is. In Cana, Jesus shows that he is the one who fulfills the Father's promise to humankind with abundance. He says, "I came so that they might have life and have it more abundantly." (John 10:10) Jesus' love, mercy, and compassion are as abundant as food and drink multiplied for all people.

Jesus' greatest sign of his abundant love for us is his Crucifixion when he died for the sake of our salvation. Jesus calls us to follow his example and be a channel for God's abundant love and mercy—not distributing love or compassion with an eyedropper but acting in a way that reflects the divine love that has no limit.

Living Abundantly

God's abundant grace flows through us. We may not be able to turn water into wine, but God's grace enables us to do the good that we can do, such as

➡ **turning a negative outcome into a positive one by changing our outlook and our attitude.**

➡ **turning a stranger or an outcast into a friend.**

➡ **turning an enemy into someone we love and for whom we pray.**

While it is commendable to plan to do things of service for other people, Jesus' first miracle reminds us that opportunities to do good may come when we don't expect them. As Jesus did, we may initially ask, "What does this have to do with me?" Because we have Jesus' example, his words, his guidance, and the abiding Spirit of God within us, we *can* make a difference.

Explore

SACRED ART

Mosaic from the apse of Santi Maria e Donato, 12th century.

The Italian city of Murano is a miniature Venice, built on several islands and divided by canals. Famous for its glass-making, the city is home to the cathedral Santi Maria e Donato. Legend credits Emperor Otto I for the church's devotion to the Virgin Mary. When Otto's ship was caught in a terrible storm in the Adriatic, he promised to build and dedicate a church to Mary wherever she directed. When the storm ended, an apparition directed him to Murano. The cathedral includes a mosaic of the Virgin Mary set in an apse (a semicircular recess) of gold and overlooking a marble altar.

Sacraments as Signs

WE encounter Jesus at key times during our faith journey when we receive the **sacraments.** Sacraments are holy, visible signs that signify a divine reality. Through the sacraments, Christ acts in us to save us. The grace received through the Holy Spirit enables us to carry out our mission as disciples.

The seven sacraments are Baptism, Confirmation, Eucharist, Penance and Reconciliation, Anointing of the Sick, Matrimony, and Holy Orders. A sacrament is a sacred **rite,** a ceremonial religious act that is a sign of God's love and presence in our lives.

Instituted by Christ

Jesus gave us the sacraments so that we may encounter him on our journey of faith. Jesus' Great Commission to his disciples was to "Go, therefore, and make disciples of all nations, baptizing them in the name of the Father, and of the Son, and of the holy Spirit, . . ." (Matthew 28:19) At the Last Supper, Jesus offered his body and blood and then told his disciples, "[D]o this in memory of me." (Luke 22:19) Jesus told his disciples, "Whose sins you forgive are forgiven them, and whose sins you retain are retained." (John 20:23) Each sacrament was given to us by Jesus so that God's life and love could fill our lives.

The sacraments are Christ's actions in our lives. When you were baptized, Christ cleansed you of Original Sin and brought you into his Church. In Confirmation you are filled with the Holy Spirit. When you confess your sins to a priest, Christ acts through the priest to free you from the guilt and burden of your sinfulness. If you get married at some point in your life, it will be Christ who joins you and your spouse together, filling you with the love and grace you will need to live together to form a family. Sacraments help us remain healthy in body, mind, and soul. They strengthen the Church community and reinforce commitments among people and between people and the Church.

Signs and symbols taken from everyday life are present in the sacramental rites. For example, washing with water, breaking bread, or sharing a cup express the sanctifying presence of God in Baptism and the Holy Eucharist. Sacramentals, such as the oil used in Confirmation and the Anointing of the Sick, as well as the prayers and blessings, are important in the rites of the sacraments.

Sacraments of Initiation

Baptism In Baptism we are born into new life with Christ. Baptism takes away Original Sin and makes us members of the Church. Its sign is the pouring of water.

Confirmation Confirmation fills us with the Holy Spirit and seals our life of faith in Jesus. Its signs are the laying on of hands on a person's head, most often by a bishop, and the anointing with oil. Like Baptism this sacrament is received only once.

Eucharist The Eucharist nourishes our life of faith. We receive the Body and Blood of Christ. Its signs are bread and wine. Through the power of the Holy Spirit, the priest consecrates the bread and wine, which becomes the Body and Blood of Christ. This is a sign of Jesus' Death for our salvation.

Sacraments of Healing

Penance and Reconciliation In this sacrament we receive forgiveness and Jesus' healing grace. Forgiveness requires being sorry for our sins. The signs of this sacrament are our confession of sins to a priest, a **penance** to perform, our **repentance,** or sorrow for sins, and the words of absolution.

Anointing of the Sick This sacrament unites a sick person's sufferings with those of Jesus'. Oil, a symbol of strength, is the sign of this sacrament. A person is anointed with oil and receives the laying on of hands from a priest. This sacrament is a source of grace, helping people who are seriously ill or who are elderly to grow in faith and to trust in God that they are not alone. If God wills, the anointed person may experience physical healing. Jesus Christ is present, healing the person in a fundamental way and sharing his victory over sin and death.

Sacraments at the Service of Communion

Matrimony In Matrimony a baptized man and woman are united with each other as a sign of the unity between Jesus and his Church. Matrimony requires consent, as expressed in the marriage promises. The couple is the sign of this sacrament.

Holy Orders In Holy Orders, men are ordained priests to be leaders of the community or deacons to be reminders of our baptismal call to serve others. The signs of this sacrament are the laying on of hands and the prayer by the bishop asking God for the outpouring of the Holy Spirit.

Those who receive the Sacraments at the Service of Communion carry out the Church's mission by committing themselves to the salvation of others. Marriage partners help each other grow in holiness. Priests and deacons serve God's people. "[I]f they contribute as well to personal salvation, it is through service to others that they do so. . . . " (CCC 1534) Through their vocations, priests and married people give special witness to Christ's presence in the world.

In summary, God gave signs of his love by becoming one of us and giving us the Church as our home. All through our lives, he gives the special signs of his love that we call the seven sacraments.

Past Meets Present

PAST: Blessed Miguel Pro risked his life to bring people the sacraments. He was born in 1891 in Guadalupe, Mexico. From a young age, he was intensely spiritual and also intensely mischievous. He had a great sense of humor and loved to play practical jokes. He became a Jesuit priest and served the people of Mexico City during a terrible time of religious persecution. Churches were closed, and priests went into hiding. However, the brave Miguel Pro put on many disguises to carry out a secret ministry. He would dress as a beggar to baptize babies, bless marriages, and celebrate Mass in the middle of the night. When helping those who were poor, he would show up on the doorstep dressed as a wealthy businessman with a flower in his lapel. He died a martyr.

PRESENT: Today Catholic missionaries often put their lives at risk to bring the sacraments and God's Word to people around the world. In its year-end report for 2011, the Congregation for the Evangelization of Peoples listed 26 pastoral workers killed. Those who sacrificed their lives included priests, women religious, and lay missionaries in Latin America, Africa, Asia, and Europe. At one time Pope John Paul II called missionaries who lost their lives "unknown soldiers, as it were, of God's great cause."

Explore

Study Corner

DEFINE

sacraments, rite, penance, repentance

REMEMBER

Sacraments are sacred rites that are signs of God's love and presence in our lives.

The seven sacraments were given to us by Jesus so that God's life and love can fill our lives.

Filling Our Water Jars

If we want to grow closer to God, we have to spend time with him. Praying with Scripture is a way we get to know God and become aware of being filled with his love.

Think about Jesus' sign at the wedding feast at Cana. What images come to mind? Think about the water jars, which were filled to the brim, and meditate on the abundance that is God's love for us.

Using *lectio divina*, let's make the Scripture verses from the wedding feast at Cana our prayer. Remember that this kind of prayer is a way of spending time with the Word of God that is like a conversation with God.

Reading sacred text in the tradition of *lectio divina* invites us to listen for God's Word with trust and expectancy. The opening sentence of Saint Benedict's monastic *Rule* offers advice on a way to listen. "Listen, my son, to the master's instructions, and attend to them with the ear of your heart."

Lectio Divina

Read: John 2:1–12 (The Wedding at Cana)

Meditate: Imagine yourself at the wedding feast with Jesus, Mary, and the other guests.

Read a second time: John 2:1–12 (The Wedding at Cana)

Meditate: Use the space below to write the words or phrases that are most meaningful to you.

_____

_____

_____

_____

_____

_____

Pray: Share your meditations with God in your own words. Ask him if there is anything else in this Scripture story that he'd like you to notice. Thank him for this time of prayer and for his presence in your life.

Contemplate: Spend a few moments in prayerful silence with God.

All: Loving God, thank you for giving us an abundance of your life and love. Help us encounter your abundant love and grace in the sacraments. We ask this in Jesus' name. Amen.

WHERE Do I Fit In?

Life is full of small miracles—if only we take the time to pay attention to what is deep within our hearts or right in front of us.

by Vinita Hampton Wright

Miracles, Really

We don't know much about Jesus' life before the wedding feast at Cana. But it's interesting that his mother went right to him when a problem came up—as if she already knew he could perform a miracle. A person doesn't just suddenly develop a full-blown talent for miracles. You have to wonder: had Mary seen him develop as a miracle worker as he was growing up and discovering who he was? In the same way, we don't learn how to listen to the Holy Spirit in a few days or even a few years. The spiritual life is a daily thing, and as people who are part of God's miraculous family, we progress gradually, not all at once.

Since early childhood I was afraid of the dark—dark rooms, nighttime, any place where I couldn't see well. I was so embarrassed by my fear that I didn't talk about it to anyone until I was past 30 years old. One day I mentioned it to a friend, and we talked about patterns of fearful thinking that I had learned from people in my family. After that talk, I discovered that this fear had simply left me. It was a miracle! I wasn't paralyzed by fear of the dark anymore.

That "miracle" was part of a long process. I had spent a lot of time reflecting on my problem, praying for help, and developing a friendship with the person in whom I confided. Finally, I reached the point where I could admit to my friend, "I'm afraid of the dark." Then the miracle happened.

Jesus turned water into wine, performed healings, and multiplied food so that crowds could eat supper, be made whole, and be set free. Such miracles were

evidence of his divine nature. It seems for us, though, that the miracles that matter most are the interior changes that bring us freedom—from fear, anger, sorrow, and alienation. Those miracles take place in us day by day as we pay attention to what's really going on, within us and around us. Then we bring God, and people who love us, into the conversation.

Making Miracles Happen

Making a change for the better takes time, deeper spiritual awareness, and prayer. On the lines below, write the steps that the author took to overcome her fear of the dark. Then think of a "miracle" you'd like to happen in your own life. Write some steps you can take to make your miracle come true.

1. _____
2. _____
3. _____
4. _____

Making My Miracle Come True

1. _____
2. _____
3. _____
4. _____

VINITA HAMPTON WRIGHT is the author of *Days of Deepening Friendship* and *Simple Acts of Moving Forward*.

What's What?

Write a detail from the text that supports each main idea.

1 Jesus' first sign took place at a wedding feast at Cana. (PAGE 100)

_____

_____

_____

2 Mary, the mother of Jesus, plays a significant role in Jesus' ministry. (PAGES 100–101)

_____

_____

_____

3 In the Gospel of John, Jesus' signs reveal who Jesus is and who the Father is. (PAGES 100–101)

_____

_____

_____

4 Signs and symbols from everyday life are used during sacramental rites. (PAGE 102)

_____

_____

_____

5 The sacraments were instituted by Christ. (PAGE 102)

_____

_____

_____

6 Three sacraments are called the Sacraments of Initiation. (PAGE 103)

_____

_____

_____

7 Two sacraments are called the Sacraments of Healing. (PAGE 103)

_____

_____

_____

8 Two sacraments are called the Sacraments at the Service of Communion. (PAGE 103)

_____

_____

_____

Say What?

Know the definitions of these terms.

penance   sacraments

repentance   signs

rite

Now What?

Write key ideas about one particular sacrament. As you look forward to the days ahead, describe how the grace of this sacrament can help you follow Jesus more closely.

_____

_____

_____

_____

_____

_____

Write some rules for living a deeply satisfying life, the kind of life you and your parents, grandparents, and any future children you might have would be proud of. What do you think it takes to arrive at genuine happiness?

Jesus Is Our Teacher

PRAYER

Lord, teach me to be generous with my whole heart and soul. Teach me to give other people love, understanding, and kind words.

Sermon on the Mount

Sermon on the Mount, Laura James, 2010.

WHEN Moses encountered God on Mount Sinai, he received the Ten Commandments, a covenant of faith between God and the Israelites.

Matthew shows Jesus as the new Moses, the divine teacher of a new way to live. Similar to Moses, Jesus went up a mountain. We call Jesus' instructions the **Sermon on the Mount.** The centerpiece of Jesus' teaching in Matthew 5:3–10 has become known as the **Beatitudes,** eight guidelines for Christlike living that lead to happiness in this life and eternal joy in the next. The Beatitudes describe life the way it is lived in the **Kingdom of God,** on earth as it is in heaven.

Our Catholic Character

In the *Pastoral Constitution on the Church in the Modern World* in 1965, the bishops called the accumulation of nuclear weapons "one of the greatest curses on the human race." An arms race at the cost of helping the poor is an injustice that leads to excessive economic or social inequalities.

The just war doctrine outlines four conditions that must be met for a war to be considered just:

- The damage inflicted by the aggressor must be very serious.

- All ways to end the violence must have been shown not to work.

- A genuine chance of ending the violence through war must be indicated.

- The use of war must not produce evils and disorders worse than the evil that caused it.

The Church reminds us that even in a just war, combatants must follow the moral law. Acting in ways contrary to the law of nations is a crime.

The Beatitudes

"Blessed are the poor in spirit,
for theirs is the kingdom of heaven.
Blessed are they who mourn,
for they will be comforted.
Blessed are the meek,
for they will inherit the land.
Blessed are they who hunger and thirst
for righteousness,
for they will be satisfied.
Blessed are the merciful,
for they will be shown mercy.
Blessed are the clean of heart,
for they will see God.
Blessed are the peacemakers,
for they will be called children of God.
Blessed are they who are persecuted
for the sake of righteousness,
for theirs is the kingdom of heaven."

Matthew 5:3–10

The Kingdom of God

The eight Beatitudes describe the "blessed" as those who meet the challenge of living according to the values of Jesus. Living the Beatitudes helps us enter the **Kingdom of Heaven,** Matthew's term for the Kingdom of God. The Beatitudes are easily misunderstood. "Blessed are those who mourn" does not mean that Jesus wants you to suffer, but he does want you to comfort others during mournful times, just as he comforts you. The Beatitudes are not easy to accept. "Blessed are the poor in spirit" challenges you to detach yourself from craving wealth and comfort. Instead of watching out for your own good, the Beatitudes encourage you to be concerned for justice and to look out for the good of others. It takes courage to live the Beatitudes. It is not easy to be a peacemaker or to be merciful to those considered enemies. The Beatitudes challenge you to live in ways that society often discourages.

The Kingdom of God is the gathering by Jesus of those on earth who begin to live the divine life the Father calls us to live. The more you live the Beatitudes, the closer you come to the Kingdom of God. God intends us to be part of his Kingdom right now. The happiness promised to us in the Beatitudes asks us to make difficult moral choices, but the reward is eternal happiness with God.

The Commandments and the Beatitudes

Both the Ten Commandments, also called the Decalogue, and the Beatitudes are directives on how to live the life that God wants us to live. Like the Ten Commandments, the Beatitudes place great value on human life, the purity of spirit, and on respectful, loving relationships among people. Both offer the wisdom to live a good life in relationship with God and others.

But there are differences. Whereas Moses gave the instruction he received from God, Jesus spoke with his own authority as the Son of God. While Moses held up the two tablets of the Law as ideals of life, Jesus embodied the ideal. Jesus lived the ideal. "I am the way and the truth and the life. No one comes to the Father except through me." (John 14:6) While Moses was a messenger, Jesus was the message.

The Ten Commandments give God's law while the Beatitudes are reflections of attitudes and actions characteristic of Christian life. The Ten Commandments are concerned with what we shall and shall not do while the Beatitudes are concerned with what it takes to live a blessed life. The Beatitudes do not replace the Ten Commandments, nor are they "better." Both are necessary to understand the life to which God calls us.

The Ten Commandments and the Beatitudes each point the way to wisdom, peace, and eternal life. They represent two signposts, each beginning in God, and each leading to the same destination: sharing eternal life with God.

The Beatitudes

Choose a beatitude, and explain to a partner how you can live it in today's world. Draw a symbol to represent the beatitude, using the space below or another sheet of paper, and explain your idea.

Explore

Study Corner

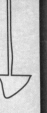

DEFINE
Sermon on the Mount
Beatitudes
Kingdom of God
Kingdom of Heaven

REMEMBER
The Beatitudes are the centerpiece of Jesus' Sermon on the Mount. The Beatitudes describe the Kingdom of God.

The Kingdom of God

COMMUNICATING an unfamiliar idea or experience can be difficult. Jesus brought important meaning to his lessons by helping his listeners understand big ideas.

Jesus knew the value of comparisons when describing the Kingdom of God, which is God's rule of love, justice, and peace in our hearts and in the world. Jesus spoke in parables—stories that compare an ordinary, everyday experience with a reality of God's truth. Jesus compared the Kingdom of God to ordinary objects such as a grain of wheat, a mustard seed, yeast, wheat and weeds, treasure, pearls, and a net cast into the sea.

The Mustard Seed

Jesus invited everyone into the Kingdom of God. The key to the Kingdom of God is acceptance of Jesus' Word. Jesus' audience had firsthand experience with farming, fishing, and making bread, so Jesus used language and analogies drawn from their daily lives. Jesus used ordinary objects and ideas to help people understand what it meant to belong to the Kingdom.

Mark 4:30–32 relates Jesus' parable of the mustard seed. "To what shall we compare the kingdom of God, or what parable can we use for it? It is like a mustard seed that, when it is sown in the ground, is the smallest of all the seeds on the earth. But once it is sown, it springs up and becomes the largest of plants and puts forth large branches, so that the birds of the sky can dwell in its shade." Through this parable, Jesus teaches that our faith takes root in small ways. God's grace grows and reaches far beyond what we are capable of doing on our own. It also teaches that our small, kind deeds in everyday life further the Kingdom of God. The kingdom shelters everyone and grows surprisingly beyond its small beginnings.

SACRED ART

Philippe de Champaigne, born in Brussels, painted in the Baroque style. Baroque art is a term that describes an artistic style that originated in Rome at the beginning of the 17th century. Baroque style reflects a preference for pictorial clarity and narrative relevance in religious art. Jesus is often shown as a shepherd because of his care for God's people. In Philippe de Champaigne's painting, Jesus is carrying the stray sheep he has found. Jesus, the Good Shepherd who proclaims the Kingdom of God, cares for every need.

The Good Shepherd, Philippe de Champaigne, ca. 1650–1660.

The Lost Sheep

Jesus made it clear that every person is important in the Kingdom of God. In Luke 15:3–7, Jesus tells the parable of a shepherd who had 100 sheep. When one strayed, the shepherd left behind 99 sheep to look for the one that was lost. When the lost sheep was found, the shepherd asked his friends to share with him in his joy. Jesus said, "I tell you, in just the same way there will be more joy in heaven over one sinner who repents than over ninety-nine righteous people who have no need of repentance." (Luke 15:7)

The Kingdom Is Now

So, what is the Kingdom of God? It's not a geographical place like the kingdoms of earthly kings. It is the reality that occurs when God's will is done on earth as it is in heaven. Taking Jesus' teachings to heart leads to action and change.

Jesus' parables teach that the Kingdom of God is among us. Parables challenge us to think in new ways. We wonder how the Kingdom of God really is like a wedding feast or a hidden treasure. We reflect on the nature of the tiny mustard seed and better understand what Jesus is saying about faith and small beginnings. While worldly kingdoms fade away, the values of the Kingdom of God are timeless.

Taking Jesus' words to heart, particularly the Beatitudes, can help you come to know more deeply the Kingdom of God. Living the words and putting their values into actions in daily life brings you closer to the kingdom. Jesus teaches that we do not have to wait until we die to enter the kingdom. He wants us to build the kingdom here and now.

If Only . . .

Our ability to imagine enables us to think about how things could be better for us, our community, or our world. You might think "If only there was no war . . ." "If only I hadn't lost my temper . . ." or "If only my teacher understood me better . . ." Paul tells us to put on "the mind of Christ." (1 Corinthians 2:16) Then our imagination can move us past how things are to how things could be. Our imagination is a gift from God and a tool for our enjoyment, but it is also for our growth in holiness. Our imagination, combined with Jesus' guidance and God's laws, can help us build the Kingdom of God as Jesus intended.

Past Meets Present

PAST: Jesus taught and prepared his disciples to lead his Church. He gave explanations and answered the Apostles' questions. "He answered, 'Knowledge of the mysteries of the kingdom of God has been granted to you; but to the rest, they are made known through parables so that they may look but not see, and hear but not understand.'" (Luke 8:10) With understanding, the Apostles were able to pass down Jesus' teachings to us.

PRESENT: The **Magisterium** is the office of the pope and bishops in communion with him, who are the authoritative teachers in the Church. The pope, who is the successor of Peter, joins with the assembly of bishops from all over the world, called the college of bishops, to govern the whole Church. Acting in the name of Christ, the Magisterium has full authority to preach the Catholic faith, which is to be believed and applied to moral life.

SOME YIELDED FRUIT

Study Corner

DEFINE

Magisterium

REMEMBER

Jesus invited everyone into the Kingdom of God.

The Kingdom of God begins here and now when we respond to God's love by loving him and others.

Jesus taught by using parables.

20/20 Vision

When Jesus gave us the Beatitudes, he showed us how to see with different eyes.

When we understand the values of the Beatitudes and translate them into action, the love of God illuminates the world. In this way we help build the Kingdom of God today on earth.

In the Beatitudes, Jesus teaches us to respect other people and to treat their lives as sacred. Jesus teaches us to love our enemies. Following the Beatitudes is a way to follow the will of God.

The Beatitudes teach us how to give. Instead of depleting us, we become richer. Matthew 6:32 assures us that the Father knows what we need before we ask him. God answers prayers, and if we ask, it will be given to us; if we seek, we will find; and if we knock, the door will be opened for us. As parents care and provide for their children's needs, so God the Father will provide for us and give good things to us if we ask.

Seeing as God Sees

Leader: God made us in his own image and likeness. It can be easy to think about ourselves or those we love as made in God's image. But what about other people? Sometimes we have to search for that likeness to God. We need a different kind of vision to help us see beyond the surface so that we can begin building the Kingdom of God right here, right now. Let us pray together.

All: God of All Creation, each of us is created in your image and likeness. We are a reflection of you that the world needs to see. We want to show others your face and to see you clearly in our brothers and sisters.

Side 1: Jesus, Light of the World, you are always with us to guide us. Sometimes our vision gets blurred by values that are different from the ones you teach us. We need courage to revere and respect your divine life in all creation. We want to let our light shine.

Side 2: Spirit of Life, you live in us and remind us that we are never alone. When we have difficult choices to make, send your light and truth to guide us. May your wisdom lead us to love others as the Father loves them. We want others to see your life in us. Help us see the divine life in others.

Leader: Let us pray the following blessing with and for one another and remember how important it is to support one another in living our life of faith.

All: May God bless you and be with you. May the holiness of God shine forth from you. May God grant you the vision to see his divine life in everyone you meet. Amen.

WHERE Do I Fit In?

The world is an imperfect place, but it is possible to transform it through acts of love, generosity, and selfless giving. Setting aside our own wants and needs in service of God and others really can happen.

by Fr. Paul Brian Campbell, S.J.

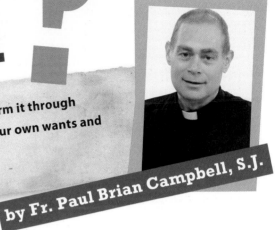

The Kingdom of God Is Like . . .

I was lucky enough to study in Paris for a couple of years. As my time there was ending, someone suggested that I should go and visit Lourdes in southwestern France. I knew that about 150 years ago, Our Lady appeared to Saint Bernadette at Lourdes and pointed her to a spring of healing water.

Over the years, many miracles are said to have occurred, but I was less than eager to visit. Friends had told me it was a total tourist trap, full of cheap souvenir stores and over-the-top pilgrims. It didn't sound like a good time could be had there. In the end, however, I decided to go and see it for myself.

The town was just as cheap and touristy as I had been told, with endless rows of stalls selling plastic statues, gaudy rosary beads, and all sorts of religious souvenirs. It made my flesh crawl, and I was reminded of Jesus throwing the money changers out of the Temple in Jerusalem.

What I was not prepared for, however, was the profound atmosphere of serenity and loveliness I witnessed the moment I entered the Shrine. It took me a little time to understand what was happening, but I slowly came to recognize that in this place the Reign of God was being made visible. Inside the Shrine, those who were sick, poor, and vulnerable took priority, and everyone cared for them. It was a place especially for them, and God was very present. Hundreds of volunteers, including lots of teenagers,

assisted those who were sick with a tenderness and joy that made them shine. It was such a holy place that everyone seemed to radiate peace and serenity. It is how every place on earth should be all the time.

It was a rare privilege to witness such goodness, and it is definitely the closest I've ever been to the Reign of God. I came away from Lourdes a better person or, at least, much less cynical than before.

Building the Kingdom

What can we do to build places of grace in our homes, communities, and world? Write your ideas on separate rectangles of construction paper. Cut out these "bricks." As a group, assemble and tape the bricks in the form of a structure on mural paper.

Donate my allowance to charity.

Volunteer time at the animal shelter.

Participate in park cleanup.

Help an elderly neighbor.

FR. PAUL BRIAN CAMPBELL, S.J., is a Jesuit priest and the Publisher at Loyola Press in Chicago, Illinois.

What's What?

Respond

Answer each question, using details from the text.

1 What is the centerpiece of Jesus' teaching on the Sermon on the Mount? (PAGE 108)

_____

2 What do the Beatitudes describe? (PAGE 108)

_____

_____

_____

3 What do the Beatitudes value? (PAGES 108–109)

_____

_____

_____

4 Why do we follow both the Beatitudes and the Ten Commandments? (PAGE 109)

_____

_____

_____

5 How did Jesus explain the Kingdom of God? (PAGE 110)

_____

_____

6 To what does Jesus compare the Kingdom of God? (PAGE 110)

_____

_____

_____

7 What is the meaning of the parable of the shepherd and the lost sheep? (PAGE 111)

_____

_____

_____

8 How do the Beatitudes ask you to live the Kingdom of God right now? (PAGE 111)

_____

_____

_____

Say What?

Know the definitions of these terms:

Beatitudes   Magisterium

Kingdom of God   Sermon on the Mount

Kingdom of Heaven

Now What?

What can you do to welcome the Kingdom of God in the coming week? Reread the Beatitudes and notice which one speaks to you most. Imagine Jesus speaking it directly to you. Think of one thing you can do in your life this week to live out the spirit of that beatitude.

_____

_____

_____

_____

_____

_____

_____

Jesus Heals and Forgives

Sometimes on the road of life we encounter difficulties—bumps in the road. Occasionally when life throws something unexpected at us, we might have to slow down or even change direction. What "bumps" have you encountered recently?

PRAYER

Dear Jesus, help me remember that no matter what I face, you are with me. Give me courage, hope, and strength when I encounter difficulty.

Jesus Heals

DURING his public ministry, Jesus healed many people. Perhaps the paralyzed man represents the most unusual way someone came to Jesus for healing.

The house where Jesus was preaching was jammed with people. Four men who were carrying a paralyzed man couldn't make their way through the crowd, but they had an idea. Like many of the small homes in Palestine, the house had a thatched roof. The men lifted the paralyzed man onto the roof, pulled apart the thatching, and lowered him down on a mat into the room.

Jesus was moved by the faith shown by the man and those who carried him. He saw not only the man's physical paralysis but also his need for spiritual healing. Jesus saw how the man's sins had been getting in the way of his well-being. Jesus' words surprised everyone. "Child, your sins are forgiven." (Mark 2:5) These words, considered **blasphemy** by the scribes, caused a stir. Didn't this man, Jesus, know that only God could forgive sins?

Jesus knew what they were thinking and said, "Why are you thinking such things in your hearts? Which is easier, to say to the paralytic, 'Your sins are forgiven,' or to say, 'Rise, pick up your mat and walk'? But that you may know that the Son of Man has authority to forgive sins on earth"—he said to the paralytic, "I say to you, rise, pick up your mat, and go home." (Mark 2:8–11) Jesus healed the man in body and soul with authority, telling him that he had been forgiven and healed. Jesus speaks, and it is so.

Jesus Cures the Man Born Blind

John 9:1–41 tells how Jesus cured a man born blind. Jesus put clay on the man's eyes and told him to wash in the pool of Siloam. When the man did so, he could see for the first time in his life. The religious authorities questioned him sharply, inquiring who had done this for him. The man claimed that Jesus, who must be a prophet and one sent from God, cured him. Unhappy with the explanation, the authorities questioned the man's parents and

The Palsied Man Let Down Through the Roof, James Jacques Joseph Tissot, ca. 1886–1894.

then returned again to challenge his faith. The man continued to proclaim Jesus' miraculous healing until he was thrown out of the Temple. Jesus sought out the man and asked him if he believed. Recognizing Jesus with eyes of faith, he worshiped him. The religious authorities, who could see with their own eyes, were spiritually blind while those who receive the gift of faith from God are the ones who see.

Jesus Empowers the Apostles to Forgive

Forgiveness is a central message throughout Jesus' ministry. When Peter asked Jesus how often he must forgive, Jesus responded, "I say to you, not seven times but seventy-seven times." (Matthew 18:22) Jesus prepared his Apostles for their ministry by giving them the authority to forgive sins. After his Resurrection, Jesus appeared to his disciples and said, "Receive the holy Spirit. Whose sins you forgive are forgiven them, and whose sins you retain are retained." (John 20:22–23)

Sacrament of Healing

Ordained priests have the same authority as the Apostles to forgive sins through the Sacrament of Penance and Reconciliation. This powerful sacrament invites us to draw closer to God. The Holy Spirit works through this sacrament to turn us away from sin and toward God the Father. When we say, do, or desire something that is contrary to God's will, we commit sin. Sin goes against reason and harms our relationship with God and others.

Even though Original Sin is washed away in the Sacrament of Baptism, human beings struggle against sin throughout their lifetimes. When sin becomes a habit, even **venial sins,** our less serious sins, can lead a person farther away from a close relationship with God and others. **Capital Sins** can lead someone to commit more serious sins. The Capital Sins are pride, covetousness, envy, anger, gluttony, lust, and sloth. **Mortal sins** are serious decisions to turn away from God by doing something known to be wrong. During confession, we receive God's merciful forgiveness for sin. After receiving the sacrament, we are reconciled with God, with others, and with all of creation.

Repentance

God does not give up on us when we sin. The Holy Spirit works within us and calls us to repentance to experience real sorrow for what we have done and to decide that we will stay away from sinning in the future. Repentance is also called **contrition.** When our sorrow is based on love of God above all else, we call it **perfect contrition.** When our sorrow is based more on the fear of punishment and other consequences we might receive for our sins, we call it **imperfect contrition.** The Sacrament of Reconciliation is a gift from Jesus to the Church that helps us recognize and remove the obstacles that sin puts in our way and gives us the grace we need to avoid sin in the future.

In the Sacrament of Reconciliation, we ask ourselves, "What direction am I heading? Am I moving toward God and my true self, or am I moving away from God and toward selfishness and sin?"

Seeking Forgiveness

Forgiveness of sins is important in order to have a healthy relationship with God, other people, and ourselves. After we take the first step of repentance, we go to a priest to confess our sins; express sorrow for them, usually by reciting the Act of Contrition; state our intention to avoid these sins in the future; and promise to repair any damage our sins may have

done to others. We confess all grave, or mortal, sins, as well as any venial sins that come to mind.

The ordained priest, who represents Jesus and the Church, gives an appropriate penance. Penance consists of prayers or actions that repair the damage caused by our sins and will help us turn away from sin and live closer to God. The priest then speaks the words of absolution through which we experience Jesus' forgiveness.

The Church encourages us to receive the sacrament regularly. In this way, we are reconciled with God and are filled with his life and love. We are reconciled with the Church and with the people we may have hurt. If we confessed a mortal sin, we are saved from eternal punishment. Our conscience is cleared, and we are at peace with God, others, and ourselves. We receive grace for future struggles with temptation and to avoid sin in the future.

Our Catholic Character

The practices of the modern Church for the Sacrament of Reconciliation focus on the need for reconciliation with God and with the community instead of an individual's private confession. People can now celebrate the sacrament in a confessional or talk with a priest face-to-face. In either practice the dignity of the person is most important. The priest is bound to absolute secrecy, called the **sacramental seal,** regarding the sins confessed to him.

Study Corner

DEFINE

blasphemy, venial sins, Capital Sins, mortal sins, contrition, perfect contrition, imperfect contrition, sacramental seal

REMEMBER

Jesus gave us the Sacrament of Penance and Reconciliation as a way to reconcile our sins.

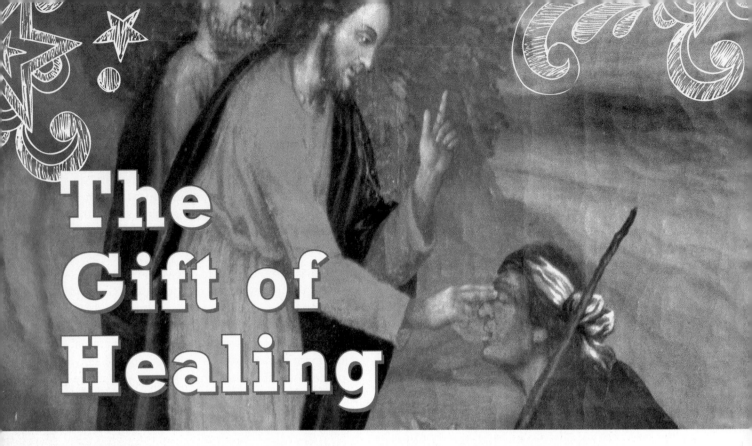

The Gift of Healing

JESUS came to heal spiritual and physical affliction. His words and touch freed and transformed hearts and bodies. With every healing, God's kingdom was manifested.

The Gospel of Mark reveals Jesus as a powerful healer. After Jesus healed the mother-in-law of Simon (later to be called Peter), the townspeople brought all who were sick to Jesus so that they might be healed. Among the people he cured were people thought to have unclean spirits within them and those with a terrible disease called leprosy. At that time people with such conditions were shunned by society. Lepers could not live with their families, and many wandered from town to town, begging in order to stay alive. They had to announce their condition as they walked to warn those who were near to stay away so as not to catch the contagious disease. But Jesus didn't stay away. He drew closer to those who needed healing, and they were healed.

When Jesus healed, he made it possible for people to return to a life with their families and society. In the Gospel accounts, much of Jesus' interaction with people involves healing them and welcoming them back to full acceptance in the community.

Apostolic Mission

Jesus sent his disciples on a mission to proclaim the Kingdom of God and to continue the care and concern he showed during his teaching. (Mark 6:6–13) Jesus told them to travel with few possessions, to trust in God to provide for them, and to preach repentance to the people. In Jesus' name, "[t]hey drove out many demons, and they anointed with oil many who were sick and cured them." (Mark 6:13)

The disciples were Jesus' ambassadors on a mission to tell the people that they were not alone, that the healing touch of God was in their midst. We know from the Letter of James that Jesus' appointed mission to his disciples—to anoint and heal those who were sick—continued in the early Church.

> "Is anyone among you sick? He should summon the presbyters of the church, and they should pray over him and anoint [him] with oil in the name of the Lord, and the prayer of faith will save the sick person, and the Lord will raise him up. If he has committed any sins, he will be forgiven."
>
> *James 5:14–15*

Sacrament of the Anointing of the Sick

The Church brings God's care and concern to those who are seriously ill by celebrating with them the **Anointing of the Sick.** This sacrament is meant for those who are suffering the difficulties of illness or old age. The sacrament brings healing on the spiritual level and, if it is God's will, on the physical level. The Anointing of the Sick is a source of grace, helping the person grow in faith and trust in God that he or she is not alone. The sacrament also provides forgiveness of sins, both venial and mortal, if the person is truly sorry but unable to make a confession. Jesus Christ is present, healing the person in a fundamental way and sharing his victory over sin and death.

Celebrating the Sacrament

When the priest approaches the person, who may be conscious or unconscious, he places his hands over the suffering person and prays. With the Sign of the Cross, he then anoints the forehead and hands of the person with oil that has been blessed by the bishop during Holy Week.

Before the **Second Vatican Council,** reception of the Anointing of the Sick took place only on a person's deathbed. Today the sacrament can be administered any time there is a danger of death, so it does not have to be a one-time occurrence. The Church wants to stay with the person throughout his or her journey of suffering and death. The anointing of a sick person is an action of the entire Church, and it must be administered by a priest or bishop.

Healing Has Many Faces

Write one way that you have experienced healing from others through these forms.

Presence _____

_____

Physical care _____

_____

Encouragement _____

_____

Prayers _____

_____

Explore

Study Corner

DEFINE

Anointing of the Sick
Second Vatican Council

REMEMBER

God's care for those who are elderly or seriously ill is shown through the Sacrament of the Anointing of the Sick.

Jesus heals not only physical sickness, but also the whole person.

SACRED ART

Little Girl Arise,
Laura James, 20th century.

Artist Laura James, born in Brooklyn, New York, is a self-taught painter. She made this painting, rendered in the Ethiopian art style, for one of the most sacred books in the Church, *The Book of the Gospels,* a lectionary published in 2000. The artist conveys the biblical theme of healing by blending colors, patterns, and imagery in an appealing, multicultural way. The painting reflects the Bible account of Jesus healing Jairus's daughter in the Gospel of Mark. (Mark 5:35–43)

Asking Forgiveness

In the Lord's Prayer,

Jesus teaches us to pray "forgive us our trespasses, as we forgive those who trespass against us."

The forgiveness that we ask of God is linked to the forgiveness that we grant to other people. In the Lord's Prayer, Jesus teaches us that the reconciliation we experience with God makes it possible for us to reconcile with others. We become peacemakers. The Holy Spirit can soften hard hearts, and we can experience forgiving and being forgiven in the compassionate love of God.

Jesus knows our need for forgiveness. When Jesus healed the paralyzed man, he saw beyond the man's physical illnesses. Jesus forgave the man's sins and healed his soul of its separation from God.

Lectio Divina

Read: Mark 2:1–12 (The Healing of the Paralyzed Man)

Meditate: In your imagination, place yourself in the crowded house. Look around you and notice the faces of those near you. Listen to Jesus teaching. What do you think when a hole appears in the roof and you see a man being lowered into the middle of the room? Listen to the passage a second time.

Read a second time: Mark 2:1–12 (The Healing of the Paralyzed Man)

Meditate: Now imagine that you are the person being lowered into the room. Hear Jesus speak these words to you, "Child, your sins are forgiven." Then notice what you feel inside.

Pray: Share your reflections with Jesus in your own words. In your prayer, ask him if there is anything else in this story he'd like you to notice or anything else he'd like you to understand. Then thank him for this time of prayer.

Contemplate: Spend a few moments in prayerful silence with God.

All: Jesus, you forgave the sins of the paralyzed man and healed his broken relationship with God. Help us know our need for forgiveness and come to you to be healed. May your healing grace direct our steps ever closer to God. Amen.

WHERE Do I Fit In ?

When drivers get behind the wheel, they adjust their rearview mirrors in an effort to eliminate any blind spots. Sometimes it is hard to see beyond our own human weaknesses. We suffer spiritual "blind spots" when we struggle to act or see with eyes of faith.

by Carl Reed

Two Wrongs Don't Make a Right

You never forget the day you get your face punched in by the school bully. I haven't. I remember the anger, the pain, and the humiliation as if it were only yesterday. I was walking home from school that mild spring day and carrying a couple of library books under my arm. I was daydreaming about the new *Star Trek* paperbacks and about the WWII *Spitfire* fighter plane I was assembling. Suddenly, someone jolted my arm, and the books catapulted out of my hand. I turned and there was Mike, the school bully, sneering at me. I yelled, and we went at each other. I got the worst of it—a black eye, bloodied nose, and torn lip. Mike was a year older, almost a hundred pounds heavier, and a foot taller.

I vowed revenge. I dreamed about it. I plotted it. Even though I prayed every night before getting into bed, this plot for revenge was one thing I didn't discuss with God. That was between Mike and me. A week later I got together with a couple of close friends who had also been bullied by Mike. We ambushed him in the alley behind his house and knocked him down. I had a baseball bat. I stood over him, ready to use it. My friends urged me on. But then I heard a voice in my head saying, "Whatsoever you do to the least of my brothers . . ."

Surely those words didn't apply to bullies! Besides, I'd already told God (by my silence) to stay out of this. I poked Mike in the chest with the bat, raised it, and had the thought, "Those who live by the sword, die by the sword." Part of me wanted to see Mike

hurt. But the other part of me knew that beating him up would be abject moral and spiritual failure. It would mean that I had become as monstrous, violent, and evil as the bully himself. I turned away. We left Mike there. He never bothered us again.

I learned something life-altering that day about the power of mercy. In the years that followed, I've prayed the Lord's Prayer many times: "[F]orgive us our trespasses, as we forgive those who trespass against us . . ." The words take on deeper, richer, truer shades of meaning with every passing decade of life. As a boy, I had told God to stay out of it. Thank God—O merciful God, O loving God—he didn't listen.

A Different Way to See

Stories of physical blindness in the Bible remind us that spiritual blindness afflicts all of us. Read Matthew 9:27–31. On the lines below, make a list of personal blind spots. Choose one, and on another sheet of paper, write ways to respond to it with eyes of faith.

_____

_____

_____

_____

_____

CARL REED has spent over thirty years in sales.

What's What?

Write the letter of the choice that best matches each clue.

1 _____ depicts Jesus as a powerful healer

2 _____ was lowered through a roof

3 _____ sacrament for someone who is seriously ill

4 _____ sacrament for forgiveness of sins

5 _____ has authority to forgive sins through the Sacrament of Reconciliation

6 _____ real sorrow and contrition for sin

7 _____ prayer said when we confess our sins

8 _____ sorrow that is based on the love of God

a. Act of Contrition (PAGE 117)

b. perfect contrition (PAGE 117)

c. ordained priest (PAGE 117)

d. repentance (PAGE 117)

e. Anointing of the Sick (PAGE 119)

f. Gospel of Mark (PAGE 118)

g. the paralyzed man (PAGE 116)

h. Sacrament of Penance and Reconciliation (PAGE 116–117)

Say What?

Know the definition of these terms.

Anointing of the Sick
blasphemy
Capital Sins
contrition
imperfect contrition
mortal sins
perfect contrition
sacramental seal
Second Vatican Council
venial sins

Now What?

Think of someone you care about who is sick, lonely, or elderly. How can you bring Christ's healing presence to that person this week?

_____

_____

_____

_____

_____

Respond

Celebrating Lent

CATHOLICS celebrate a time in the Church when they follow more closely the ways of Jesus. We take up spiritual practices and disciplines that help us identify with Jesus more closely as we prepare to celebrate Easter.

During **Lent** we come to a greater recognition of Jesus' dying and rising throughout our lives. To follow Jesus means that we must empty ourselves—our egos, fear, selfishness, and any attachments that threaten to become false gods so that we might rise to the new life of joy, courage, generosity, and freedom that Jesus won for us on the cross and in his Resurrection.

The liturgical season of Lent begins on **Ash Wednesday.** Marked by ashes traced in the Sign of the Cross on our foreheads as a sign of our dependence on God, the whole community is led by the Holy Spirit to prepare the way of the Lord and welcome him into our lives. Just as Jesus fasted in the desert for 40 days before beginning his ministry, we spend the 40 days of Lent with fasting, prayer, and charitable deeds done for others. Lent is a season of preparation for Jesus Christ's Resurrection at Easter and the promise of eternal life.

What is getting in my way of growing closer to God? What habits, beliefs, fears, or attachments stand between me and following Jesus? What would you like your Lenten journey to be?

PRAYER

Jesus, help me spend the season of Lent learning to live as you did so that I will be ready to celebrate your Death and Resurrection during Holy Week and Easter.

More Like Christ

Past Meets Present

PAST: All four Gospels include the story of the crowds who gathered to see Jesus. He recognized they would be hungry. Though the Apostles worried that there wasn't enough for everyone to eat, Jesus told them, "Give them some food yourselves." (Mark 6:37) That day everyone had enough to eat.

PRESENT: Catholic Relief Services (CRS) was founded by the Catholic bishops of the United States on the principle that each person possesses a basic dignity that comes directly from God. Its mission is to assist those who are poor and disadvantaged, alleviate the suffering of all people, promote the development of communities and individuals, and work for peace and justice throughout the world. CRS believes that we are all part of the global family; no matter where we come from, we are brothers and sisters to one another. CRS also provides ways that individuals and parishes can participate in this mission to help people in need.

BECAUSE Lent is a time for new beginnings, it is an appropriate time to consider the beginning of your own faith—your Baptism. Saint Paul says the best way to embrace your Baptism is to imitate Christ.

In the Letter to the Philippians, Paul pleads that we regard ourselves humbly. "Have among yourselves the same attitude that is also yours in Christ Jesus." (Philippians 2:5) Who is better for us to imitate than Christ? It is important for our spiritual life to think about who Jesus was and what he did so that we might recommit ourselves to following him.

A Man of Compassion

The writers of the Gospels tell many stories in which Jesus heals, forgives, or reconciles. "Moved with pity, Jesus touched their eyes. Immediately they received their sight, and followed him." (Matthew 20:34) They tell us that Jesus' motivation is always compassion for those who are suffering. Instead of seeing a crowd, he sees individuals who have their own stories, their own pain, and their own desire to be healed and reconciled. He sees a man who has leprosy, a woman beset by demons, and the father whose child is deathly ill. He not only sees their pain, but he also feels it and responds to it.

The word *compassion* means to "suffer with" another person, and that is the central message of the Gospel. Jesus became a man with a nature like ours who took on the pain of our sins so that we might have life.

A Man of Courage

Jesus showed courage in the way he lived and died. Even as a boy, Jesus entered into discussion with the elders in the Temple. Many times Jesus upset crowds because he spoke with the authority of God. When storms raged on the Sea of Galilee, Jesus courageously stood and calmed the waters. He confronted evil. When he saw money changers conducting business in the Temple where true sacrifice was supposed to take place, he cast them out of the Temple. Knowing that he was likely to be put to death when he reached Jerusalem, Jesus set out for Jerusalem. His complete trust in the Father and obedience to him led Jesus to pray, "[N]ot as I will, but as you will" during his agony in the garden. (Matthew 26:39) During Lent we pray for the courage to live our faith.

A Man of Service

"He said to them, 'The kings of the Gentiles lord it over them and those in authority over them are addressed as 'Benefactors'; but among you it shall not be so. Rather, let the greatest among you be as the youngest, and the leader as the servant." (Luke 22:25–26) During Jesus' temptation in the desert following his baptism, Satan offered Jesus power over all the kingdoms of the earth. Jesus, who knew his Father's heart, refused Satan because he understood that power was meant for service.

The night before he died, Jesus gave a great lesson in service. John's Gospel describes how Jesus washed the feet of his disciples. When Peter objected that the teacher should not put himself into a servant's role, Jesus told him that washing the feet of others was key to gaining a share in the kingdom. Jesus told his disciples, and he tells us, "[A]s I have done for you, you should also do." (John 13:15)

A Man of Promises

Jesus is the fulfillment of God's promise to send a Redeemer. He is our model of faithfulness to promises. Jesus told his disciples, "I will not leave you orphans." (John 14:18) He promised to send the Holy Spirit as an **Advocate** and guide; on **Pentecost** that promise was fulfilled. Jesus gave the disciples the Eucharist so that they might be strengthened and nourished every time they gathered to break bread. He taught them how to pray.

As we strive to imitate the life of Jesus during Lent and throughout the year, connecting with him is as easy as whispering the prayer, "Lord Jesus Christ, Son of God, have mercy on me, a sinner."

Study Corner

DEFINE

Advocate, Pentecost

REMEMBER

During Lent we follow more closely the way of Jesus by imitating the way he lived.

Explore

SACRED ART

Mosaics are pieces of marble, glass, or other material pressed into a design or picture. This mosaic of Jesus washing Peter's feet is in the Cathedral of Monreale, near Palermo, Sicily, which is home to a spectacular display of mosaics representative of Byzantine influence. A total of 130 mosaic scenes, all made on a background of yellow-gold tiles, show religious events that represent the Old and New Testaments. In this mosaic, Jesus leads as a humble servant to others.

Jesus and Saint Peter, detail from Jesus washing the feet of the Apostles, 12th century, mosaic.

Preparing the Way of the Lord

WHEN was the last time you were totally unplugged? In other words, you had no phone, no music, no TV or video, no email, texts, tweets, or distractions.

Did you get bored? Anxious? Confused? What did you think about? Did it become uncomfortable for you after 40 minutes? Or maybe 40 seconds?

Each year on the first Sunday of Lent, the Gospel reading at Mass tells how Jesus was led out to the desert for 40 days and 40 nights. Jesus removed himself from his daily activities and took the time to reflect and pray. He had plenty to contemplate. Just prior to his trip to the desert, during his baptism in the Jordan River, Jesus heard a voice from heaven, revealing that he was God's "beloved Son." Now, in the desert, he thought about what he had just experienced. He fasted and prayed in preparation for his public ministry of preaching, healing, and proclaiming the Good News of God's love and mercy.

Christ in the Desert, Maria Laughlin, 2006.

Get Unplugged

Lent is a time for us to follow Jesus' lead and get unplugged from distractions of all sorts. We might be distracted by unhealthy eating habits, ways we spend our free time, or ways we treat family and friends. The Church encourages us to use the time-honored spiritual practices of Lent, including fasting, prayer, and almsgiving, as ways to loosen the grip that habits and attachments have on us so that we can focus instead on being embraced by and embracing God. Lent calls us to repentance and recalling (or preparing for) our Baptism.

Repent, the Kingdom of God Is Near

The first recorded words of Jesus in his public ministry were "This is the time of fulfillment. The kingdom of God is at hand. Repent, and believe in the gospel." (Mark 1:15) Repentance, turning away from sin and changing your life to live as God wants you to live, is the doorway to the Kingdom of God. Taking the actions—both in your heart and in your behavior—to reconcile your life with God is at the heart of Lent.

Our Catholic Character

When we pray the *Kyrie, Eleison* at Mass, we echo the voices of millions of Catholics throughout the centuries. The *Kyrie,* one of the oldest prayers we pray at Mass, is Greek for "Lord, have mercy." Even when the Mass was spoken in Latin, the words were retained in Greek. Now this part of the Mass can be said in either English or the original Greek. Responding to the celebrant's lead, we say three times, *Kyrie, eleison. Christe, eleison. Kyrie, eleison.* (Lord, have mercy. Christ, have mercy. Lord, have mercy.) During Lent, these words take on special meaning as we repent and seek mercy from God.

The father's welcoming of his runaway son in the parable of the prodigal son conveys a truth that makes repentance not only possible but also appealing. We can rely on the promise of God's forgiveness and mercy.

Recall Your Baptism

Remember that in Baptism you were cleansed of Original Sin, joined to the Church, and received the Holy Spirit. With the help of these graces, you can live a new life, trusting in God and following the guidance of the Holy Spirit. By being plunged into the waters of Baptism, we connect to Jesus' dying as well as his rising.

Jesus calls us to **conversion,** which is the movement of a contrite heart away from sin and toward love of God and neighbor. Baptism celebrates our desire for conversion and our commitment to it. At Lent we renew our baptismal promises.

➡ Do you reject sin,
   so as to live in the freedom of God's children?

➡ Do you reject the glamour of evil,
   and refuse to be mastered by sin?

➡ Do you reject Satan,
   father of sin and prince of darkness?

➡ Do you believe in God, the Father almighty,
   creator of heaven and earth?

Practice of Prayer

During the season of Lent, you are asked to renew your commitment to prayer, the central action of your spiritual life. You might choose to read Scripture daily, pray the Rosary, or pray the Stations of the Cross. In addition to daily prayer, the Church encourages you to celebrate the Sacrament of Reconciliation.

Practice of Fasting

Another important spiritual practice to observe during Lent is fasting. **Fasting** is limiting the amount of food you eat for a period of time. When you fast, you do so to express sorrow for your sins and to become more aware of your dependence on God. Catholics between the ages of 18 and 59 are asked to fast on Ash Wednesday and Good Friday.

Another part of fasting is to choose to **abstain,** or not eat a particular food. Catholics 14 years and older are asked to abstain from meat on Ash Wednesday, Good Friday, and all the Fridays of Lent.

Some people choose to add their own personal fast or abstinence during Lent by choosing to give up a favorite food, such as pizza, as a reminder that God comes first in our lives and that we are dependent on God for everything.

Practice of Almsgiving

During Lent the Church asks you to practice **almsgiving.** To give alms is to offer money, possessions, time, or talent to those in need. Some people combine this practice with their fasting. For example, they might give up one meal each week and donate the money they would have spent on this food to those who are needy. By practicing prayer, fasting, and almsgiving, you can make Lent your own retreat to the desert, getting ready to rejoice in the Good News of Jesus' Resurrection on Easter.

Our Lenten Journey

During Lent we recognize our need to repent and recall our Baptism. We prepare ourselves through prayer, fasting, and almsgiving. When we receive ashes at the start of Lent, one of two prayers is prayed: "Turn away from sin and be faithful to the Gospel" or "Remember, man, you are dust and to dust you will return." Our Lenten journey, then, is a time to turn away from our sinfulness and recommit ourselves to following Jesus.

Explore

Study Corner

DEFINE
conversion, fasting, abstain, almsgiving

REMEMBER
During Lent we repent and recall our baptismal promises. We prepare by practicing prayer, fasting, and almsgiving.

Renew Our Hearts

Lent is a season of self-denial. This self-denial can be a time of self-discovery, where we realize our true identity and desires.

We say no to certain things to say a bigger yes to what matters more—our own relationship with God. We ask Jesus to be with us and renew our hearts as we undertake this journey of Lent.

Prayer of Renewal

Together pray the Lord's Prayer.

Leader: The grace of Lord Jesus be with us now and forever.

All: Amen.

Leader: During Lent we follow the model of Jesus in the desert. In our prayers and fasting, we remind ourselves of our need for God in our lives. In our almsgiving we show our commitment to those who are poor. As we begin Lent, let us ask God to renew our hearts and help us follow God's ways.

Reader: A reading from the Book of Joel. [Joel 2:12–17] The Word of the Lord.

All: Thanks be to God.

Leader: Let us pray silently as we consider how we will renew our lives this Lent through prayer, fasting, and almsgiving. Reflect silently on these questions.

- What can I do to renew my prayer life?
- How can fasting help me recognize what I really need from God?
- What can I do to help those in need this Lent?

Ask God what he wants you to do this Lent as you turn away from sin and grow more faithful to the Gospel.

Leader: We pray that God will accept our Lenten sacrifices and give us the strength to persevere in our promises. We ask this through Christ our Lord.

All: Amen.

WHERE Do I Fit In ?

Challenge yourself to avoid seeing Lent as a gloomy time filled with self-denial or a time to get on God's "good side." Instead, God invites you to see it as a time for self-discovery and personal growth.

by Sr. Jean Hopman, O.S.U.

Saying Yes to What Matters

When I was in junior high, I was a challenger. If I didn't see the meaning of a rule or tradition, I was the first to challenge it. If something didn't make sense to me, I wasn't going to do it. A rule in my house was to eat what was served. My mother fixed our plates, and we were expected to finish them or face the consequences, which in my home was to remain at the table until the plate was clean. To motivate us, my mother would say, "Think of the starving children in China." My flippant response would be to offer to send them the food.

One day at school I was talking with friends about what to give up for Lent—candy, soda, movies. I wondered, "How does giving up something for 40 days bring me closer to Jesus? Is that really what God wants?"

My questions challenged me to think of Lent in a new way. My religion class took on a Lenten project of making bag lunches once a week and distributing them with a local organization who fed the hungry. Seeing those who came for food—individuals, families, kids my own age—touched me. I decided to fast from lunch on our weekly food distribution day as a way to be in solidarity with other people's suffering—people I had actually met. These people didn't have hot food each evening or the ability to give up luxuries like candy.

Fasting from lunch one day a week in solidarity with the hungry of my town had more meaning to me than giving up candy. By fasting, I could offer a small sacrifice with great meaning. When I started to feel hungry on those days, I could thank God for what I had and pray for God's continued help for those in need. That Lent, my eyes were opened to the needs of people around me, and I learned the meaning of sacrifice.

Making Lent Meaningful

Solidarity is a theme of Catholic social teaching. See pages 298–300 in Prayers and Practices for information about the other themes. What is something you can do throughout Lent to follow a theme of Catholic social teaching?

Form an action plan of ways to return to God during Lent. Prepare a slide-show presentation of your ideas and share it with the group as a way to encourage one another on your Lenten journeys.

SR. JEAN HOPMAN, O.S.U., is vocation director for the Ursulines of the Roman Union, U.S.A.

What's What?

Unscramble each Lenten word. Then write the letters inside the circles to reveal a sentence that tells us how to live during Lent.

1. NERWE — K e N e r
2. TIEITMA *imitated* — e M M i t a t
3. AITEDTTU — a t t i t u d e
4. DELPSICI — D e c i p l e
5. RNPETCANEE — r e p a r t a n c e
6. LETN — L e n t
7. RAPYRE — P r a y e r s
8. ROJNEUY — J o r n e y
9. CEORUSTENRIR — r e s u r r e c t i o n
10. BIMTASP — B a p t i s m
11. SESJU — J e s u s
12. VIGNILGAMS — A l M s g i v i n g

Sentence: e M u L a t e J e s u s .

Say What?

Know the definitions of these terms.

abstain
Advocate
almsgiving
Ash Wednesday

conversion
fasting
Lent
Pentecost

Now What?

You can turn to Jesus and ask for strength to follow his example more closely. Write a short prayer asking for Jesus' help. Pray this prayer to yourself every day this week.

_____

_____

_____

_____

Faith in ACTION

As workers provide for the needs of their families at their jobs, they are also commissioned to promote workplace justice. Workplace justice includes the right to dignified work and acting in a way that supports the common good. We have the responsibility to contribute to a just environment by making moral decisions and living by the values that Jesus taught.

In this unit we explored the public life of Jesus. The signs Jesus performed were testaments of service to others. They showed us God's desire to care for and heal humanity. Jesus taught us that the true path to happiness is found in the Beatitudes and in the parables of the Kingdom of God. We are coworkers with God to build his kingdom on earth. Any good work that we do is valuable, no matter how small or seemingly insignificant. The following ideas show how you can value workers and promote workers' rights in today's world.

Act

"The human contribution is the essential ingredient. It is only in the giving of oneself to others that we truly live."

—Ethel Percy Andrus, founder of American Association of Retired Persons (AARP)

Behind the Scenes

Purpose

Recognize the people in your life whose helpful work often goes without recognition; show your appreciation for these people and how much you value their work.

Background

Many ordinary people work hard in support of others because it is the right thing to do. Selfless people who work behind the scenes may not get the appreciation they deserve. It is important to recognize and appreciate the contributions of workers who deserve part of the credit for success.

Steps

1. Look around your parish, school, or community. Who are the people who do behind-the-scenes work? Whose contributions make things work better and are vital to success? Who deserves a thank you?

2. Think of creative ways that you can show your appreciation for workers who are often taken for granted.

A Labor of Love

Purpose

Learn about the rights of workers and about child-labor abuse around the world; find out what you can do to raise awareness about child labor and poverty.

Background

The rights of workers are sometimes ignored and trampled on. Always a serious injustice, it is especially shocking when the workers are children. In 1995, 12-year-old Craig Kielburger decided to do something about the issue. Along with 11 school friends, Craig founded the group Free the Children to fight the abuse of child labor. The goal of the foundation is "to free children from abuse, exploitation, and the idea that they are not old enough or smart enough or capable enough to change the world."

Steps

1. Research child labor and learn its causes, effects, and what can be done to erase it.

2. Work with local or national organizations that seek solutions to this issue.

3. Take a stand and speak out. Raise awareness about child-labor abuse by writing to government officials. Protest child-labor abuse by refusing to buy goods that are made by child workers.

4. Consider ways that you can promote fair and just working conditions for young people in your community.

Act

"It does not require many words to speak the truth."

–Chief Joseph, leader of the Nez Percé tribe

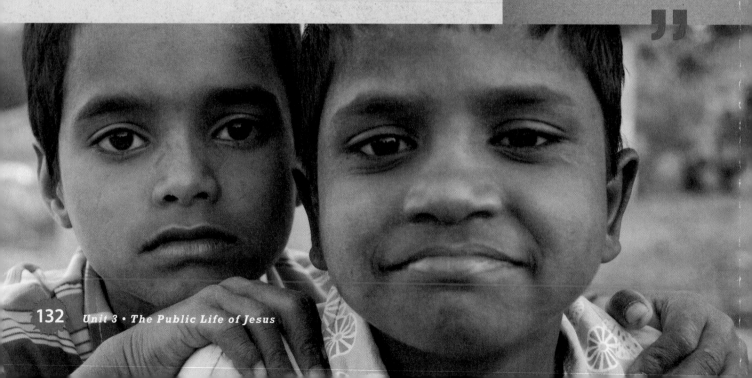

Jesus the Christ

Saint Teresa Benedicta of the Cross was born Edith Stein in Breslau, Poland, the youngest child in a large Jewish family. Her seemingly ordinary start in life would turn out to be anything but ordinary. Edith grew up to be a philosopher, teacher, writer, and social critic. She became interested in Catholicism and was baptized into the Church in 1922. Eventually she became a Carmelite nun, taking the name Sister Teresa Benedicta of the Cross. When the Nazis invaded the Netherlands, she was sent to a concentration camp, where her faith sustained her until her death.

How the Saint Relates { Saint Teresa Benedicta of the Cross accepted persecution and suffering with the strength that came from her faith and her belief in eternal life. She did not avoid the danger that living faithfully required and accepted death in her service of Jesus.

Strengthened by Faith

Edith Stein was an outstanding student in high school who enrolled at the University of Breslau in 1911 to study German and history. She had a special interest in philosophy and women's issues and transferred to Gottengen University in 1913 to study under the philosopher Edmund Husserl. This decision ended up affecting the path of her life. Edith wanted to be a professor, but because she was a woman and a Jew, she was refused. Years later she would teach at a school run by the Dominican Sisters. She would eventually earn the highest academic degree, a doctorate.

The Path to Baptism

As a young adult, Edith did not practice her Jewish faith. Looking back on her teen years, she said, "I consciously decided, of my own volition, to give up praying." Around 1917 she went to Frankfurt Cathedral and saw a woman stop in to pray. It made an impression on the future saint because this woman was clearly taking time out of her day to talk to God in an intimate way, instead of simply attending a scheduled service. That same year an associate and good friend died in World War I, and Edith went to console his widow. At first fearful of seeing how the widow would handle her loss, Edith was surprised by her faith. Later Edith said, "This was my first encounter with the Cross and the divine power it imparts to those who bear it. . . . It was the moment when my unbelief collapsed and Christ began to shine his light on me—Christ in the mystery of the Cross." In the summer of 1921, Edith read the autobiography of Saint Teresa of Ávila, a Carmelite nun. Edith later wrote, "When I had finished the book, I said to myself: 'This is the truth.'" She was baptized in 1922, and in 1934 she joined a Carmelite convent in Cologne, Germany, taking the name Sister Teresa Benedicta of the Cross. Sister Teresa, a convert, believed it was her vocation to intercede to God for everyone, in particular for Jewish people.

The Nazi Terror

By 1938 the German chancellor Adolf Hitler had begun persecuting the Jewish people. Although a devout member of the Carmelite Order, Sister Teresa's heritage as a Jew put her in danger. On New Year's Eve the prioress helped smuggle her to a convent in the Netherlands, where she submitted herself to God's will and began to prepare herself for death. Her sister Rosa, also a convert to Catholicism, was with her when the Gestapo arrested them in 1942. Her words to her sister were, "Come, we are going for our people." The two were among others who were transferred in August of that year to the infamous concentration camp Auschwitz. She and Rosa were killed by poison gas in a gas chamber probably two days later.

Sister Teresa Benedicta of the Cross was declared a saint on October 11, 1998. At her beatification ceremony in 1987, Pope John Paul II called her "an outstanding daughter of Israel and at the same time a daughter of the Carmelite Order. . . ." Her feast is celebrated on August 9.

Jesus Gives Us Himself

What kinds of events do you and your family enjoy remembering? Which memories are bittersweet—that is, they cause you to remember both sad and happy feelings? When has something really good come out of a difficult circumstance?

PRAYER

Lord, help me remember your great love for me. Show me how I can bring love to everything that I say and do.

A New Passover

THINK of a festive holiday meal you enjoy with your family. Gathering with family and friends in celebration is a way to lift our spirits, even when times are difficult.

The same was true when Jesus and his disciples gathered to celebrate the Passover in Jerusalem. Passover was a happy and celebratory occasion at which the Jewish people recalled the liberation of the Israelites from captivity in Egypt, as chronicled in the Book of Exodus. Passover was their story, and it was one of the holiest and most joyous celebrations of the year. Jesus and his disciples were celebrating just as their ancestors had celebrated for centuries before them. It was a time for the people to remember God's salvation—past, present, and future.

Past Meets Present

PAST: God made his presence known to the Chosen People in a burning bush, a column of smoke, a pillar of fire, the ark of the covenant, and in quail, manna, and water from a rock in the desert.

PRESENT: God's presence is most perfectly realized in the Eucharist at the **Institution Narrative**—when the priest recalls Jesus' words and actions at the Last Supper—and the bread and wine become the Body and Blood of Jesus Christ.

Jesus' Last Meal

What made this celebration of the Passover meal different was that Jesus knew something his friends did not. He knew that Judas Iscariot was plotting to betray him. He knew that Peter would deny him three times, and he knew that he was going to be arrested, tortured, and put to death on a cross. And so on this night, when Jesus gathered with his friends to eat the Passover meal, he wanted his disciples to remember this last meal with him. Luke 22:7–20 tells how Jesus gave his friends, the disciples, something of great importance.

The Passover meal follows a ritual that is outlined in Scripture. It includes a ceremony in which the family shares unleavened bread and a cup of wine. This sharing of bread and wine calls to mind the actual Passover event, when the people of Israel hurriedly ate unleavened bread before fleeing the slavery of Egypt. During the **Last Supper,** as Jesus and his disciples shared the bread and wine of Passover, Jesus gave these traditional items a completely different meaning.

Do This in Memory of Me

Luke tells us that as Jesus broke the bread and gave it to his disciples, he said a blessing. "This is my body, which will be given for you; do this in memory of me." (Luke 22:19) Jesus was giving himself to his disciples; he himself was the sacrifice. He gave the disciples the wine and said, "This cup is the new covenant in my blood, which will be shed for you." (Luke 22:20) Jesus was going to die on the Cross, and his sacrifice would establish a new covenant between the people and God. With these words, Jesus instituted the Sacrament of the Eucharist.

Food for the World

In the Eucharist we remember Jesus' gift of himself to the disciples and the entire Church at the Last Supper. As the celebration of Jesus' supreme sacrifice, the Eucharist is the heart and the high point of the life of the Church. We call the unique change of the bread and wine into the Body and Blood of the risen Jesus Christ **transubstantiation.** Jesus himself is food for the world.

The Eucharist is a celebration of Christ's Passover, his journey through life, Death, Resurrection, and Ascension that freed us from the slavery of sin and brought about our salvation. The Eucharist as a memorial means far more than a simple memory of past events.

The Eucharist makes Jesus' gift of himself real for us here and now. It is a proclamation of how God is working in our lives today. In celebrating his memorial, what Jesus did for us through his suffering and Death becomes present to us in our lives. The sacrifice of the Eucharist is offered by Christ himself, the high priest of the new covenant, acting through the priest presiding at every Mass in every Catholic community worldwide.

Sunday and Beyond

The principal day for celebrating the Eucharist is Sunday, which is the Lord's Day, the day of the Resurrection. This is the day of the Christian family, the day on which we rest from work and come together as God's people to worship God. Our coming together echoes what Jesus and the Apostles did long ago and shows that we are his followers. Just as Jesus gave himself as a sacrifice for others and continues to give himself to us in the Eucharist, we are to give ourselves to others. With the help of the grace of the Sacrament of the Eucharist, we serve others in Jesus' name.

Explore

Study Corner

DEFINE

Institution Narrative
Last Supper
transubstantiation

REMEMBER

The Eucharist is the heart of the life of the Church. With the grace we receive in the Eucharist, we serve others in Jesus' name.

SACRED ART

Judy McGrath, an artist living in Saint Louis, Missouri, is active in the community-arts movement. She is also an art therapist who has studied and taught in Central and South America. Her painting, *Last Supper,* is a reflection on the Eucharist as a meal with family and friends. At the table of the Lord, we seek spiritual nourishment given to us in the Eucharist. We long to be fed at the table of fellowship as we become what we receive, the Body of Christ. Jesus makes us one, just as he and the Father are one. We show reverence for the Body of Christ in the Eucharist and also in one another. Gathering at the table, we reveal our true nature as members of Christ's Body.

Last Supper, Judy McGrath, 2004.

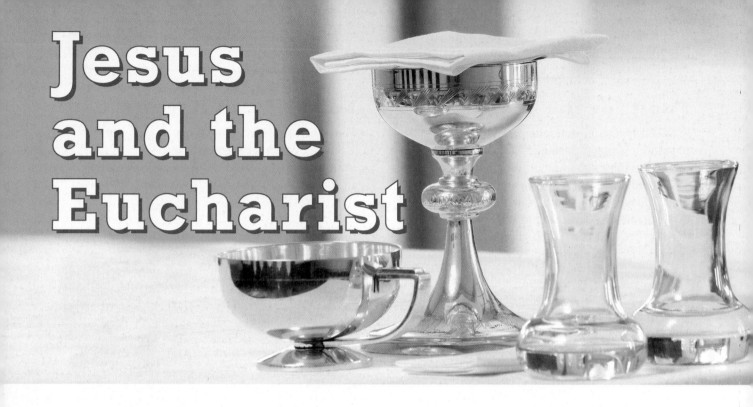

Jesus and the Eucharist

JESUS satisfied people's hungers. In Luke 9:11–17, Jesus was healing and preaching to a large crowd. Late in the day, his disciples encouraged him to send the crowd away so they could find food and lodging. Jesus blessed the small amount of food that was available, and his disciples distributed it. The crowd had plenty to eat, and the surplus filled several baskets.

Jesus came to satisfy more than physical hunger. He also satisfies our spiritual hunger. In the story of Jesus' birth in the Gospel of Luke, Mary laid the baby Jesus in a manger, a trough used to feed animals. Luke used this image to symbolize that Jesus had come to be food for the world. At the Last Supper, Jesus instituted the Sacrament of the Eucharist. The Eucharist is Jesus feeding his people with his Body and Blood. In receiving the Eucharist, our spiritual hungers are blessed and satisfied. We receive the love of God in Christ Jesus.

Food to Celebrate

Just as the disciples gathered with Jesus around a table where Jesus gave them his Body and Blood, the Last Supper continues today at the Eucharist with the altar as our gathering table. At the Eucharist our minds and hearts remember Jesus' life, Death, Resurrection, and Ascension. We experience anew the **real presence** of Jesus Christ because the glorified Christ who died for our sins and rose from the dead is truly present—body, blood, soul, and divinity—at the Consecration, when the bread and wine become the Body and Blood of Jesus Christ. The risen Christ's presence in the Eucharist is a mystery of God that we can never fully comprehend. In the Eucharist, Jesus' final gathering with his disciples continues around the world. The Eucharist is our celebration and reminder of Jesus' continued presence in our lives.

Food to Share

In every celebration of the Eucharist, Christ truly gives himself to us, and we are united with him. Catholic social teaching reminds us that we cannot gather at the Eucharist if Jesus' concern for those in need is not consistently reflected in our liturgical celebrations. Many people have no food to put on their table or even a table to gather around. Pope John Paul II wrote the following in preparation for the year of the Eucharist in 2004: "By our mutual love and, in particular, by our concern for those in need we will be recognized as true followers of Christ. This will be the criterion by which the authenticity of our Eucharistic celebrations is judged."

Together at the Table

In the Eucharist, Jesus Christ shows us how to be his followers. Just as he gave himself as a sacrifice for others and continues to give himself to us in the Eucharist, we are to give ourselves to others. When you receive Holy Communion with the words "The Body of Christ" or "The Blood of Christ," it is as if Jesus is saying, "Here I am," the same words God wants us to say to others. With the help of the grace of the Sacrament of the Eucharist, we serve others in Jesus' name.

Frequent reception of Holy Communion helps us better recognize the real presence of Jesus Christ in the Eucharist. We celebrate the Eucharist over and over because we constantly need spiritual nourishment as we go through life. However, we must be in a state of grace, free of mortal sin, to receive the Body and Blood of Christ in Holy Communion. Because sin damages our relationship with Christ, we need the Sacrament of Reconciliation to restore that relationship before we receive Holy Communion again.

Divorced Catholics may still receive Holy Communion. However, when divorced Catholics remarry without an annulment, they may not receive Holy Communion because the Church still considers them married to their original spouse. Catholics who seek an annulment, which is a finding by a Church tribunal that an essential element for a sacramental marriage was missing, are free to marry and receive Holy Communion. Either way, divorced Catholics still belong to the Church and can participate in the life of the Church.

Celebrating the Eucharist regularly is our way of renewing the commitments we made in Baptism and Confirmation to belong to God's people and to serve God's kingdom. In response to this gift of Christ's real presence, we are encouraged to engage ourselves fully at Mass, demonstrated by gathering with the community, listening with open hearts, singing, participating, and offering honest prayers to the God who welcomes us.

Reverencing the Body of Christ

The word *liturgy* means "the work of the people." We leave the church to go forth and put into practice our baptismal promises and to do the work of discipleship. When we receive the Body and Blood of Jesus Christ at the Eucharist, we become the Body of Christ. We show reverence for the risen Jesus who gives himself in the Blessed Sacrament. And we also show reverence toward the Church gathered in his name.

Saint John Chrysostom (A.D. 347–407) preached about our sending forth, our acceptance of mission, after we receive the risen Lord at the Eucharist. While preaching on the parable of the sheep and the goats (Matthew 25:31–46), he told his congregation, "Do you wish to honor the body of Christ? Do not ignore him when he is naked. Do not pay him homage in the temple [here at Mass] clad in silk, only then to neglect him outside where he is cold and ill-clad. He who said, 'This is my body,' is the same who said: 'You saw me hungry and you gave me no food,' and 'Whatever you did to the least of my brothers you did also to me. . . .'"

Jesus comes to us in Holy Eucharist and unites us with himself and to one another as members of the **Mystical Body of Christ.** Even those physically separated from the Liturgy of the Eucharist, such as those who are in a hospital or nursing home, remain united with the entire Catholic community when they receive the Eucharist from a priest, deacon, or extraordinary minister of Holy Communion.

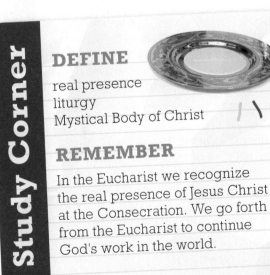

Study Corner

DEFINE

real presence
liturgy
Mystical Body of Christ

REMEMBER

In the Eucharist we recognize the real presence of Jesus Christ at the Consecration. We go forth from the Eucharist to continue God's work in the world.

Jesus Feeds Hungry Hearts

Jesus placed great emphasis on sharing meals with others. He ate with sinners and tax collectors, with crowds of people, and with the disciples.

Jesus also ate with **Pharisees,** a sect in Judaism that believed in strict observance of the Law and with whom he shared a mutually contentious relationship. Some of the parables of Jesus center on meals as a way to teach about the Kingdom of God. In one parable, Jesus instructs hosts to invite those who are poor and outcast to a fancy banquet instead of inviting the rich. (Luke 14:12–14)

Jesus' parables concerning meals give a deeper meaning to the Eucharist at the Last Supper, the most important meal Jesus shared with his disciples, and to the Emmaus story, when two disciples recognize the risen Christ in the breaking of the bread. In the Acts of the Apostles, Luke tells us that after Jesus' Death and Resurrection and following Pentecost, "They [the followers of Jesus] devoted themselves to the teaching of the Apostles and to the communal life, to the breaking of the bread and to the prayers." (Acts of the Apostles 2:42)

Petitions: Jesus Fills Us

PRAY the Sign of the Cross together.

Reader: A reading from the holy Gospel according to Luke. [Luke 22:14–20] The Gospel of the Lord.

All: Praise to you, Lord Jesus Christ.

Leader: Bring to mind all those who are hungry. *(Pause.)* For those who are hungry for food and drink, . . .
All: May we do all we can to provide for them. Let us do this in memory of you, Jesus.

Leader: For those who are hungry for friendship, . . .
All: May we reach out in kindness and generosity. Let us do this in memory of you, Jesus.

Leader: For those who are hungry for understanding, . . .
All: May we truly listen to their words. Let us do this in memory of you, Jesus.

Leader: For those who are hungry for forgiveness, . . .
All: May we forgive as God forgives us. Let us do this in memory of you, Jesus.

Leader: For all those who are hungry for joy, . . .
All: May we give them a smile and lift their spirits. Let us do this in memory of you, Jesus.

Leader: Lord, you sacrificed yourself for us. May we sacrifice for others. We believe in the Eucharist. Inspire us to celebrate the Eucharist and live the Eucharist. Amen.
Pray the Lord's Prayer together.

WHERE Do I Fit In?

Jesus has not left us alone. He nourishes us in the Eucharist and the other sacraments. He invites you to recognize his presence in others.

by Steve Connor

Lifting Burdens

> "Be still and know that I am God!"
> *Psalm 46:11*

She lived in the neighborhood. All day she walked around with her shopping cart full of bags. If it was a sunny and warm day, she might remove one of her four coats. If it was a cold and wet day, you could hardly see her beneath the hats and scarves. People brought her food. Most times she didn't speak. Sometimes you heard a muffled, "Thanks." When you gave her a cup of coffee, though, she would look out from her layers, look you straight in the eye, and say, "Thanks. I need that."

One drizzly, cool fall day I found out that my best friend had died. He had been sick with cancer, so the news was not totally unexpected, but it jolted me. I went for a walk. In a nearby park, I found a dry bench and sat down to pray. Closing my eyes, I asked God to help me and to be with me as I remembered my friend. As I prayed, I heard a noise. I opened my eyes, and there she was, wrapped in her layers, and pushing her cart. She came to the bench and sat down.

I wanted to be alone. As I stood to leave, she said, "How are you today?" I wasn't sure I heard her, but I responded, "OK." She looked up at me and said, "You seem a little sad." For someone who barely said anything, she had a lot to say! I sat back down and told her, "I am sad. My best friend just died." As I spoke the words, I started to cry. She moved closer to me, and from under her coats came a gloved hand.

She gently reached over and placed her hand on mine. The tears flowed. We sat like that for about ten minutes. No words were spoken, but my prayer had been answered. Just when I needed it, God sent me someone to help me grieve. I thanked her and got up to leave. Maybe remembering her own needs, she looked up and said, "I could really use a cup of coffee."

Mystical Body of Christ

How can you help someone in a time of trouble? Complete each phrase with your ideas.

When someone is bullied, I can . . .

_____

_____

When someone looks lonely, I can . . .

_____

_____

When someone suffers a disappointment, I can . . .

_____

_____

When someone is suffering physically, I can . . .

_____

_____

STEVE CONNOR has worked in pastoral ministry for over 25 years and is Director for Adult Spirituality Resources at Loyola Press.

What's What?

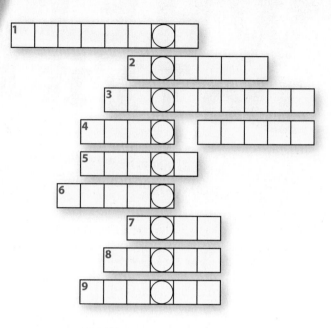

Complete each sentence using details from the text. Use the circled letters to discover the secret word.

1 The celebration that recalls the liberation of the Israelites from slavery in Egypt is _____ . (PAGE 136)

2 Jesus instituted the Eucharist at the Last _____ . (PAGE 136)

3 In the Eucharist we celebrate Jesus' supreme _____ . (PAGE 137)

4 Eucharist is the heart and the _____ of the life of the Church. (PAGE 137)

5 On the road to Emmaus, two disciples recognize the risen Christ in the breaking of the _____ . (PAGE 140)

6 Jesus knew that _____ would deny him three times. (PAGE 136)

7 Jesus Christ becomes truly present at the Consecration, when the bread and _____ become the Body and Blood of Jesus Christ. (PAGE 138)

8 _____ is spiritual nourishment for the world. (PAGE 137)

9 In every celebration of the Eucharist, Christ _____ us with himself and with one another. (PAGE 138)

Secret Word:

_ _ _ _ _ _ _ _ _ _

Say What?

Know the definitions of these terms.

Institution Narrative   Pharisees

Last Supper   real presence

liturgy   transubstantiation

Mystical Body of Christ

Now What?

When we celebrate the Eucharist, we recognize Jesus Christ as present in our lives. What can you do this week to receive Christ's presence and share it with others?

_____

_____

_____

_____

_____

_____

Respond

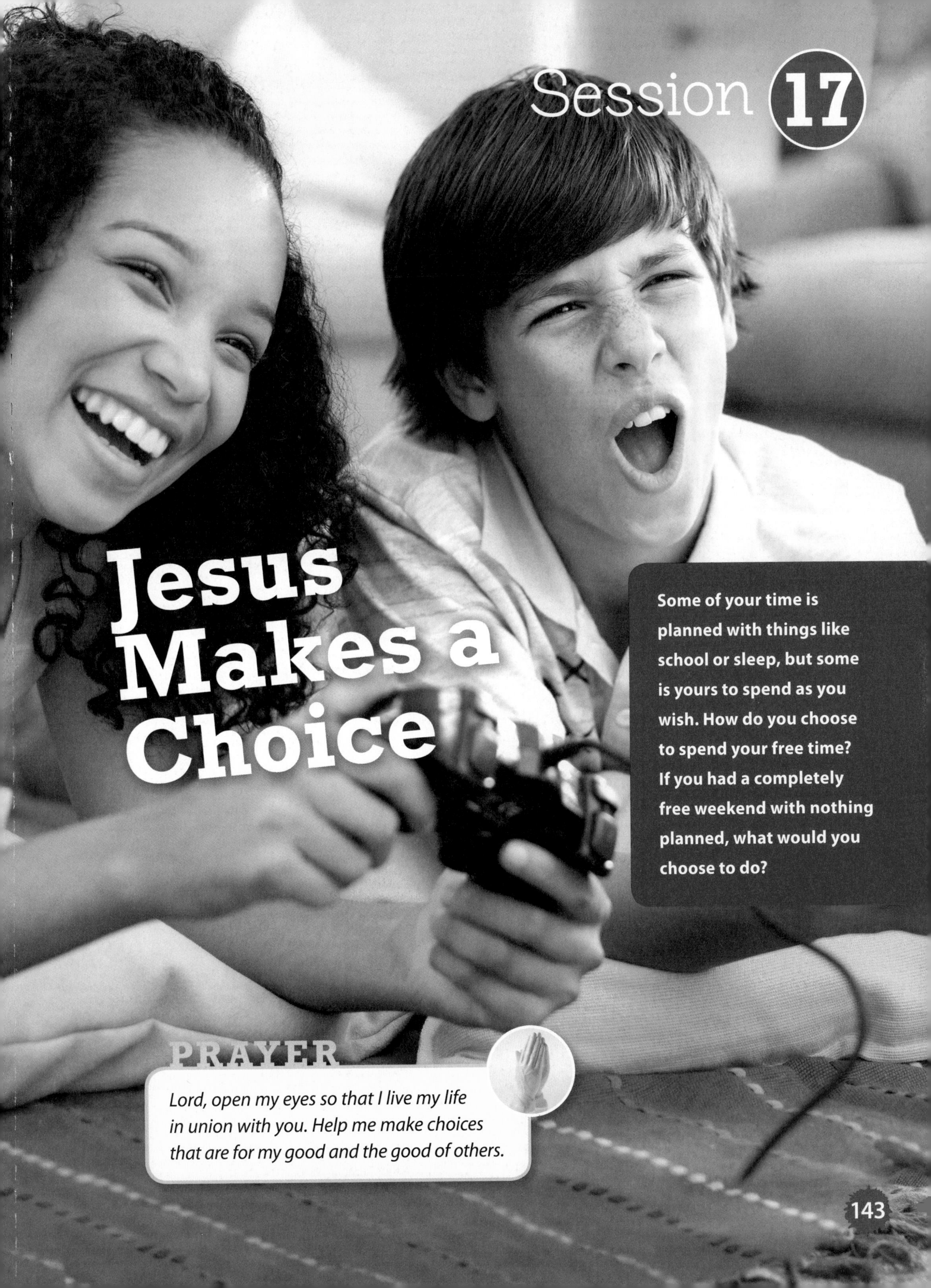

Jesus Makes a Choice

Some of your time is planned with things like school or sleep, but some is yours to spend as you wish. How do you choose to spend your free time? If you had a completely free weekend with nothing planned, what would you choose to do?

PRAYER

Lord, open my eyes so that I live my life in union with you. Help me make choices that are for my good and the good of others.

143

Jesus' Night of Sorrow

Golgotha Chapel ceiling detail of Gethsemane, Church of the Holy Sepulcher, Jerusalem.

AS a prelude to the creation of Eve, God said, "It is not good for the man to be alone." (Genesis 2:18) One of the hardest parts of life and the human condition is being alone—especially in times of trial and trouble.

In Chapter 14 of the Gospel of Mark, we learn about the night Jesus' disciples abandoned him. After the Passover meal, Jesus and the disciples went to a small garden called Gethsemane located outside the east wall of the city of Jerusalem, on the Mount of Olives. Knowing his arrest was imminent, Jesus was troubled and distressed. He was about to face the greatest test of love someone could face, a test that would ask him to live in accordance with the Father's divine plan. Jesus asked the disciples to keep watch while he prayed. "My soul is sorrowful even to death. Remain here and keep watch." (Mark 14:34)

Jesus prayed to his Father, "Abba, Father, all things are possible to you. Take this cup away from me, but not what I will but what you will." (Mark 14:36) The disciples, meanwhile, had fallen asleep. Three times Jesus left them to pray, and three times he returned to find the disciples asleep. The disciples could not stay awake with Jesus through his time of trial.

By the third incident, Jesus told them to get up because his betrayer (Judas Iscariot) had arrived, accompanied by a crowd with swords and clubs. After Judas betrayed him with a kiss, his accusers laid hands on Jesus and arrested him. Soon afterward the disciples left him and fled. Jesus, the Son of God, was abandoned by his friends, the same men he had loved and with whom he had walked, taught, shared meals, laughed, and prayed.

Stay Awake

The Gospel of Luke tells us that Jesus' prayers during his **Agony in the Garden** were so fervent that his "sweat became like drops of blood falling on the ground," and Jesus found the disciples "sleeping from grief." (Luke 22:44–45) Finally he said to his disciples, "Why are you sleeping? Get up and pray that you may not undergo the test." (Luke 22:46)

Jesus was fully awake in every sense of the word. God invites you to stay awake, too, to be vigilant against both personal sin and **social sin,** such as racism, sexism, denial of health care, and destruction of the environment. For what does God invite you to stay awake to see? To know? To feel? To do? To be?

As young people, it is good to pay attention to how you use video games, the Internet, or other distractions that can numb you to the present reality. If used as ways to avoid facing something painful, they can lull you into a state of indifference. Escaping through distractions might hinder your awareness of the needs of others. Instead of escaping life around you, Jesus invites you to turn yourself over to his care and pray for his mercy and help.

Thy Will Be Done

Jesus' words in the Gospel of Matthew reveal his troubled heart in words very similar to Mark's account. (Matthew 26:38) Jesus does not want to die. When he prays, he expresses his sorrow, fear, and a longing for companionship. He prays deeply and fervently. In verse 39 of Chapter 26, he asks his Father for this cup—this difficult moment—to pass him by. At this most difficult time, Jesus gives himself over to the Father's will.

It is okay to tell God and loved ones when you are afraid or confused. Living a Christian life requires staying fully awake and facing adversity. By turning to God in times of human weakness, you give yourself to God, relying on his grace to be your strength.

Jesus stayed close with the Father in the Garden of Gethsemane. He trusted the Father and acted on that trust. Jesus remained faithful in spite of the temptation to escape what was to come. Following God's will is not always easy, and it is hard to let go of the desire to control your own destiny. But God never abandons you. You are never truly alone.

God Is with Us

Jesus stayed true to his identity as the Son of God. The risen Christ would be with his friends again, sitting with them and even sharing a meal with them. Despite Peter's denials of him, Jesus would make him the rock of his Church. Despite Jesus' Crucifixion and Death, he would ascend to God his Father.

If Jesus suffered so that he may share in your suffering, the hope, life, and victory that Jesus experiences is something in which you also may share. Even when you feel alone or filled with deep sorrow, Jesus is with you—always near and waiting to be your source of strength.

SACRED ART

Georges Henri Rouault, a French artist who also worked in stained glass, was an Expressionist painter who tried to portray inner reality rather than focusing only on the exterior appearance of a subject. In this painting, he makes use of color, line, and form to represent Jesus' emotions as he faced his impending Death on the Cross.

Explore

Are You Awake?

Where in the world today do you find human suffering, and how can you respond to lessen it?

_____

_____

_____

_____

_____

_____

_____

Study Corner

DEFINE

Agony in the Garden

social sin

REMEMBER

In his Agony in the Garden, Jesus was tempted to avoid his suffering and Death, but he remained faithful to his Father. We are also called to remain true to our identity as sons and daughters of God, especially when we are tempted to run away from God.

Nocturne (Gethsemane), Georges Henri Rouault, oil on canvas, 1915.

Making Moral Choices

SOME choices require little thinking, such as what to eat for breakfast or what to wear. Other choices are more difficult, especially when they force you to choose between competing values.

Making a **moral choice** means choosing to do what is right or choosing not to do what is wrong. Saint Paul addressed moral issues with the early Christian community in Corinth, a port city in Greece between Asia and Western Europe. Similar to modern American port cities such as New York and Miami, Corinth was ethnically diverse and had lots of people with competing cultures and ideas. The Corinthian Christians, influenced by their Jewish roots, believed certain foods were acceptable to eat while others were not. This was an important issue for the time because following a proper diet was considered a way of honoring God's law.

Two Schools of Thought

Some Christians in Corinth chose to eat meat that had been sacrificed to pagan gods earlier in the day. They were not troubled by this because they believed that meat, after all, was only meat. They understood that there was one God and that Jesus was the Son of God. Other Christians, though, objected to the practice and were uncomfortable eating meat that had been used in Temple sacrifice. The Christians who chose to eat the meat thought that they had greater insight into the freedom won by Jesus Christ.

Letter to the Corinthians

Paul teaches about moral decisions in relation to eating the meat in 1 Corinthians 8. Moral choices are made by people who are free and take responsibility for their actions. The morality of any act has three dimensions: the act chosen, the intention behind the act, and the circumstances behind the act.

Our Catholic Character

In order to make good moral decisions, you have to have a fully formed **conscience,** which is the inner voice that helps you judge the morality of your actions. The Church understands that you must always obey the certain judgment of your own conscience. How do you form your conscience? You follow the guidance of parents and teachers. You learn from your mistakes and those of others. You also pray for guidance, read and listen to Scripture, and learn about the teachings of the Church. You learn to consider the effects of your actions on others. Without a fully formed conscience, you are left to make decisions without a guide. The consequence of a poorly formed conscience is that it may lead to a life of self-delusion and self-destruction.

The Act Chosen For the Corinthian Christians who decided to eat meat sacrificed to pagan gods, the act that was chosen was the good of feeding oneself and others. We need to eat to live, and offering hospitality to others is a Christian obligation. So those who served the meat or who were dining with friends in the Temple were acting in a morally good way because the meat helped fulfill their need for food.

The Intention Behind the Act If the intention was to serve themselves and their guests a good meal, this was a morally good thing to do. But suppose they knew that serving meat that had been part of a pagan sacrifice would make their guests uncomfortable, and they served it anyway to show off their superior understanding of Christian teaching? Then the act would be morally wrong because they did not have good intentions.

Circumstances Behind the Act Because food was scarce in Paul's time, people had to eat what was available. If meat from a pagan temple was all there was to eat, it would lessen the moral issue of whether the host was offending the conscience of his or her guest. Using similar reasoning, if a person is tricked or forced into committing an immoral act, his or her responsibility is lessened. It is never a good moral choice to do an immoral act for the sake of some imagined positive result.

Knowing How to Choose

Although Paul agreed in principle that meat was just meat, and the one group was correct in eating it, he believed their actions of superiority and their shaming of their fellow Christians were morally wrong. Paul wanted both groups of Christians in Corinth to support each other, not present situations in which one group built itself up at the expense of the other. "Thus through your knowledge, the weak person is brought to destruction, the brother for whom Christ died. When you sin in this way against your brothers and wound their consciences, weak as they are, you are sinning against Christ." (1 Corinthians 8:11–12)

How can you live a moral life? Gather for liturgical prayer with fellow Catholics on Sunday. The Lord's Day gives you the time for rest and leisure to help your family, cultural, social, and religious lives grow. Receive grace in the Eucharist and the other sacraments. Listen to your conscience. Follow the Ten Commandments, the Great Commandment, the new commandment, and the Beatitudes. Know the teachings of the Church, live the Golden Rule, and follow the example of the saints to help you make good moral choices.

Explore

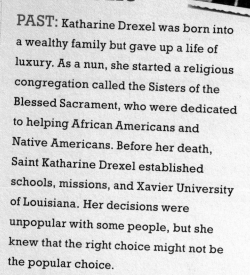

Past Meets Present

PAST: Katharine Drexel was born into a wealthy family but gave up a life of luxury. As a nun, she started a religious congregation called the Sisters of the Blessed Sacrament, who were dedicated to helping African Americans and Native Americans. Before her death, Saint Katharine Drexel established schools, missions, and Xavier University of Louisiana. Her decisions were unpopular with some people, but she knew that the right choice might not be the popular choice.

PRESENT: The Oblate Sisters of Providence, the first Catholic religious community for women of African descent, has been committed to the education of children and service to the poor for over 175 years. The order's ministry of providing a transitional place for neglected and abused girls continues at the Mary Elizabeth Lange Center in Baltimore, Maryland. The Sisters also provide eldercare, social services, and service to Hispanic ministry.

Study Corner

DEFINE
moral choice
conscience

REMEMBER
The morality of an act has three dimensions—the act chosen, the intention behind the act, and the circumstances behind the act. We develop a fully formed conscience through the guidance of parents and teachers, prayer, Scripture, Church teachings, and learning from our mistakes.

Acting in Good Conscience

Each one of us is called to take responsibility for living the Catholic faith and making good choices.

Prayer is an essential practice in developing a strong conscience. Praying helps us see the right path and gain the willingness to follow it. With the help of the Holy Spirit, we can consider how to make the correct choices in life.

Taking Responsibility

Leader: Let us begin this time of prayer together by praying the Sign of the Cross.

In the name of the Father, and of the Son, and of the Holy Spirit. Amen.

All: Loving God, we come before you with gratitude for all that you have given us. We ask for your help as we pause and take responsibility for our lives and the choices we make. We ask this through Christ, your Son and our Lord. Amen.

Reader: A reading from the Letter of Paul to the Romans.

Let love be sincere; hate what is evil, hold on to what is good; love one another with mutual affection; anticipate one another in showing honor. Do not grow slack in zeal, be fervent in spirit, serve the Lord. Rejoice in hope, endure in affliction, persevere in prayer.

Romans 12:9–12

The Word of the Lord.

All: Thanks be to God.

Leader: In light of the Word of God we've just heard, let's spend a few minutes in silence to reflect on how we take responsibility for living our faith. Think about these questions as I read them aloud.

- Do I make myself look good at the expense of others?
- Do I ever choose to do the right thing for the wrong reason?
- Do I learn from my mistakes as well as those of others?
- Do I consider what effect my actions may have on others?
- Do I show respect for my body and the bodies of others?

Pause and reflect.

Leader: The LORD bless you and keep you!
The LORD let his face shine upon you,
and be gracious to you!
The LORD look upon you kindly and
give you peace!

Numbers 6:24–26

All: Amen.

WHERE Do I Fit In?

When you are faced with a life-changing choice, a lot is at stake. Although some paths seem easier to take, they may lead you away from the person whom God intends you to be.

by Andy Laureano

What Does Courage Look Like?

"The pack" was a group of four eighth graders who walked around together, bullied kids, and vandalized the park. We called them "the pack" because they resembled a wolf pack. They sat by the soccer bench and laughed at the kids playing soccer. We always avoided them.

My friend Francisco and I always skateboarded by the basketball courts. One day "the pack" approached us and took our skateboards away. They made fun of us and said the only way we could get the boards back was to join them. The shortest kid handed Francisco a can of paint and ordered him to paint on the walls. Francisco shook his head in fear. Then the tallest kid snatched the paint from him and painted our skateboards red. They threw our boards across the basketball court and shoved us to the ground.

This continued to happen for a few days. Every day they used a different color of paint. Francisco decided that the best way to stop them was to join "the pack." I remember going home every day and putting my hands together to pray before I went to sleep. At first I thought praying was childish. I was 12 years old. I could have just stood up to them. Or I could have done what Francisco did and started to paint walls and school property. All I prayed for was to be safe and to get good grades.

"The pack" eventually stopped bothering me. But Francisco stopped skateboarding. I stopped talking to him. Eventually he got kicked out of school. My mother asked me where Francisco had gone, and I told her the story about "the pack." She told me that I had done the right thing. I think that I did the right thing too.

True to Yourself

The writer stuck to his convictions. Many martyrs, such as Blessed Miguel Pro, Saint Thomas Becket, and Saint Isaac Jogues sacrificed everything for their convictions.

When have you needed to stick to a conviction because you knew it was the right thing to do? In a brief essay, write about the experience on a separate sheet of paper.

ANDY LAUREANO is the Associate Director of Alumni Tracking and Support at the Cristo Rey Network. On a typical weekend, you may find him skateboarding in downtown Chicago.

Use details from the text to answer the questions.

1 Use your own words to describe what happened in the Garden of Gethsemane. (PAGE 144)

_____

_____

_____

_____

2 How did Jesus stay true to his identify as the Son of God? (PAGES 144–145)

_____

_____

_____

3 Why did Paul write to the Christians in Corinth? (PAGES 146–147)

_____

_____

_____

_____

4 How do we form our conscience? (PAGE 146)

_____

_____

_____

_____

5 What must be true of a person making a moral choice? (PAGE 147)

_____

_____

_____

_____

6 What are the three dimensions of a moral act? (PAGE 147)

_____

_____

_____

_____

Say What?

Know the definitions of these terms.

Agony in the Garden

conscience

moral choice

social sin

Now What?

If something was bothering your conscience, to whom or to what would you turn to for guidance? Why?

_____

_____

_____

_____

_____

_____

_____

Jesus Redeems Us

When you go through security at an airport or apply for a library card, you are asked to show identification. People want to make sure you are who you say you are. So who are you? What's the truest thing you can say about yourself?

PRAYER

I am your servant, Lord. Draw me close to your heart and never let me be parted from you.

The Suffering Servant

WHO do people say you are? Do people know you by a role—as a son or daughter, a cousin, a niece or nephew, an altar server, an artist, or a soccer player? But who are you, really? Are you all those things? Or are you some, none, or far more than those things?

Jesus knew what it was like to be known by many roles and titles. At various times in the Gospels, Jesus was called prophet, teacher, the Christ, Messiah, son of Mary and Joseph, Son of God, Lord, rabbi, Elijah, the Nazarene, healer, King of the Jews, Master, and the Savior. Jesus—who is he?

Prince of Peace icon, Father Gabriel Chavez de la Mora, O.S.B., Prince of Peace Abbey, Oceanside, California.

Past Meets Present

PAST: In 1 Corinthians 5:7, Christ is called "our paschal lamb." The word *paschal* is associated with the Hebrew word *pesach*, or Passover. Celebrated every year, Passover recalls when the Jewish people sacrificed a lamb and sprinkled its blood on their door posts so that the Angel of Death would pass over their homes and spare the lives of their firstborn children. The lamb became a symbol of redemption.

PRESENT: The **Paschal Mystery,** which is the work of salvation that Jesus Christ accomplished through his Passion, Death, Resurrection, and Ascension, is at the heart of our lives as Catholics. Jesus is the Lamb of God because by his Death he took away the sins of the world and redeemed us. We remember Jesus' saving Death when we celebrate the Eucharist in every Mass.

Who Is Jesus?

Although the very beginning of the Gospel of Mark proclaims that Jesus Christ is the Son of God, the revelation unfolds gradually throughout the entire Gospel. For example, when Jesus heals a number of people, he tells his disciples not to speak of it. Jesus is more than a miraculous healer.

When Jesus learned that people believed he was John the Baptist, Elijah, or one of the prophets, he asked his disciples, "Who do people say that I am?" (Mark 8:29) Peter answered for all of them, saying that Jesus was the Messiah. Jesus cautioned the disciples not to tell anyone. Why was Jesus reluctant to make himself known? Jesus knew that he was not the kind of Messiah the people expected. He was not an earthly king. He was the suffering servant who would endure physical and mental cruelty to redeem the world and make eternal life possible.

The Apostles Peter, James, and John witnessed the **Transfiguration,** when Jesus' appearance changed—his face shining like the sun and his clothes white as light—and he spoke with Elijah and Moses on the mountain. Afraid and hardly able to speak, the men witnessed a cloud overshadow them and heard a voice proclaim, "This is my beloved Son. Listen to him." (Mark 9:7) Even after witnessing this event and the disclosure of Jesus' divine glory, the Apostles still did not fully understand Jesus' mission as Messiah nor their role as his disciples. They wanted to pitch tents to honor Jesus, Moses, and Elijah, but Jesus knew the Apostles would be commissioned to go forth to spread the Word.

Who Is a Disciple?

The Gospel of Mark tells us how to be a disciple, a true follower of Jesus. The Apostles had a hard time understanding what it meant to follow Jesus. They thought that following Jesus would mean that they would have power and recognition in this world. But suffering was part of Jesus' life. Similarly, everyone has times of disappointment, sorrow, and suffering. In such times we recall the sufferings of Jesus and rely on our Christian faith to help us accept our hardships with trust in God.

The disciples had seen Jesus' miracles and heard his words when he taught to the crowds. It was hard for them to understand that Jesus would suffer on the cross. But Jesus knew that he would.

Words that describe the glory that will follow the Messiah's suffering are found in Isaiah 53:11.

> Because of his anguish he shall see the light;
> because of his knowledge he shall be content;
> My servant, the just one, shall justify the many,
> their iniquity he shall bear.

Jesus Predicts His Suffering

In the Gospels, Jesus tells the Apostles that the Son of Man will suffer greatly. He predicts his suffering and Death, or his **Passion,** and tells the Apostles about his rejection, Death, and rising after three days. Peter does not understand and is greatly disturbed by Jesus' words. Peter takes Jesus aside and rebukes him. In reply, Jesus scolds Peter. "Get behind me, Satan. You are thinking not as God does, but as human beings do." (Mark 8:33) Jesus refuses to avoid the suffering that lies ahead of him because that would be contrary to his obedience to his Father and to the fulfillment of God's plan for humankind.

Glory Through the Cross

Jesus' Crucifixion revealed the real meaning of who Jesus is. Looking at the bruised and battered Jesus on the Cross, the Roman centurion recognizes and exclaims, "Truly this man was the Son of God!" (Mark 15:39) It is at this point in Mark's Gospel that we too recognize that Jesus is the Messiah, the Anointed One, the Christ. Jesus' glory is revealed through his Death and Resurrection, and humankind is redeemed.

Jesus redeemed our sins on the Cross. His redemption helps us better understand our own times of suffering and how we are invited to respond as true disciples. Jesus told his disciples that along the way they would suffer. People would reject them and even be hostile toward them. In the midst of their journey, though, Jesus would be with them, helping them endure and follow him. (Mark 8:34–35)

God is with us in both happy and sorrowful times. He invites us to respond to our human suffering with a faith that makes us stronger, more resilient, and more able to follow the selfless example of Jesus.

Explore

Introducing Jesus

An introduction can be revealing. How would you introduce Jesus to someone who doesn't know him? Think about the session articles you have read and write a short introduction.

_____

_____

_____

_____

_____

_____

Study Corner

DEFINE

Paschal Mystery
Transfiguration
Passion

REMEMBER

We are called to reflect on, understand, and articulate who Jesus is and to live in a way that shows we know, understand, and follow him.

The Moment of Truth

WE only discover the depths of Jesus' love in his Death on the Cross. (Mark 15:33–39) In the Roman empire, crucifixion was not a punishment born of justice. It was a cruel and humiliating form of execution.

The Roman empire crafted crucifixion both to humiliate and degrade people perceived to be its "enemies." Most importantly, it was intended to put fear in the hearts of the people. Crucifixion was saved for rebels against Roman authority as a warning for anyone who would dare question their rule. After people saw or heard of Jesus' torture—his scourging, beating, mocking, and carrying of the instrument of his own death through the streets—no one would dare speak, act, or think in Jesus' name for fear of a similar punishment. Crucifixion was such a horrible death, in fact, that people believed it had to be a sign that the person had been abandoned by God.

Mark's Message

The Gospel of Mark tells us otherwise. This was the moment of truth. Jesus was alone on his Cross, despised by the Romans, ridiculed by his peers and countrymen, and abandoned by his disciples. Jesus was the suffering servant. If you want to know who Jesus really is, you have to look at the Cross. Once you understand its meaning, you can understand Jesus' miracles, parables, words, and deeds. Mark's Gospel tells us that Jesus' Death explains everything. He asks us to see the living God most clearly in Jesus' battered and bruised body.

Christian Suffering

Jesus was without sin and did not have to suffer. His love for humankind was so great and his obedience to the Father so strong that he freely chose to suffer.

SACRED ART

The *Pietà*, in Saint Peter's Basilica in Rome, is one of Michelangelo's most famous sculptures. The word *Pietà* means "pity" or "compassion." Carved from marble, the sculpture depicts the Blessed Mother holding the lifeless body of Jesus on her lap. This was a popular subject for northern European artists at the time, but Michelangelo's approach differs in his portrayal of Mary, which features a Catholic view of human suffering. Although Michelangelo shows a sorrowful Blessed Mother, she also has an attitude of serenity and faith.

The *Pietà*, Michelangelo, 1499.

Because of the Incarnation, Jesus' suffering was like ours. He understands our times of hopelessness, pain, and loneliness because he experienced them and shared our pain.

On the Cross, Jesus taught the most important lessons we have to learn in order to be his followers. Jesus' sacrifice shows us how much God loves us. Through his suffering, redeeming Death, Resurrection, and Ascension, Jesus saves all of God's creation. Jesus teaches us from the Cross to give our lives selflessly for others and to realize that doing God's work often involves sacrifice and suffering.

Mystery of Love

It may seem contradictory, but the instrument of execution used by the Romans, the cross, is a universal sign of hope for Christians. We pray the Sign of the Cross as a reminder that our whole life is lived under the sign that saved us, the Cross of Jesus. Jesus' Cross shows the depths of what it means to follow him. It reminds us of the conflict we often feel between our own will and submitting to the will of God the Father, and it proclaims that even senseless suffering can be redemptive if accepted with faith and love.

Forgiveness

Jesus taught us to love everyone, even our enemies, just as he offered his life for everyone, even those who hated him. As Jesus was crucified, he prayed, "Father, forgive them, they know not what they do." (Luke 23:34) Even in the worst of circumstances, Jesus chose to forgive.

He invites us to respond with a similar decision to forgive others as an act of faith and as a response to his own selfless love and forgiveness.

Jesus Saves, Even in Death

When we pray the **Apostles' Creed,** we acknowledge with the words "he descended into hell" that after Jesus died, and before he had risen, he went to the realm of the dead to gather all the just people who had died before him. What we believe is that Jesus met them as their Savior, proclaiming the Good News to them. He gathered them and brought them to heaven with him. This shows that Jesus' work of redemption is for the entire human family, of all times and in all places.

Our Response

When Jesus' followers saw him on the Cross, they must have thought, "This is the end." Everything changed for the disciples, including their notions of a Messiah, their hopes for the future with Jesus, and their role in Jesus' ministry. So often in our own lives, when things get difficult, we think, "This is the end." How does Jesus want us to respond to suffering in our own lives? Although we can never fully understand suffering, we can work to eliminate the evil that causes suffering. We can comfort others, and we can accept our suffering with strength and dignity to be a light to those around us. Through it all, Jesus is present, reassuring us that this is not the end as long as we place our faith in his Resurrection.

Explore

Our Catholic Character

When we see other people suffer, our response is to take action. In his encyclical letter *On the Christian Meaning of Human Suffering*, Pope John Paul II wrote, "Suffering is present in the world in order to release love, in order to give birth to works of love towards neighbor, in order to transform the whole of human civilization into a 'civilization of love.'" Jesus' words in the parable of the Last Judgment in Matthew 25:31–46 also help us understand how we find Jesus in acts of love and acts of assistance for those in need. Whenever we stop to feed the hungry, care for the sick, or visit the imprisoned, we do it to Jesus. He is present in everyone who suffers. All who suffer become sharers in Christ's suffering.

Study Corner

DEFINE

Apostles' Creed

REMEMBER

Jesus' Passion and Death help us understand the meaning of the Cross and our response as his disciples in the world.

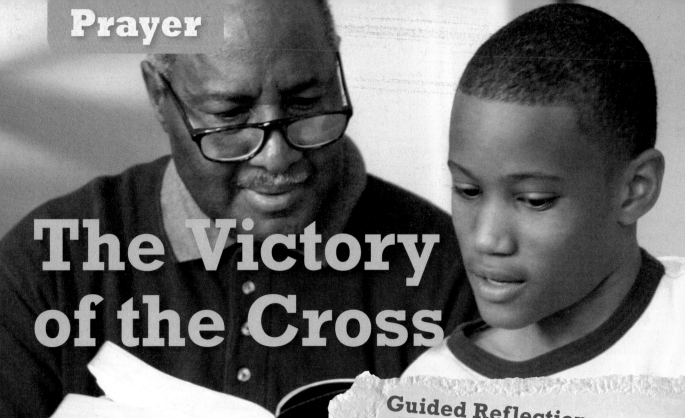

The Victory of the Cross

The Gospel of Mark

teaches us what it means to be one of Jesus' disciples.

It took a long time for the disciples to discover what Jesus meant about discipleship and how to carry on his teaching as true followers. Jesus invites us to reflect on the glory of redemption, won through his suffering, and what it means to us in our Christian lives.

Jesus summoned the crowd and said to them, "Whoever wishes to come after me must deny himself, take up his cross, and follow me. For whoever wishes to save his life will lose it, but whoever loses his life for my sake and that of the gospel will save it." (Mark 8:34–35)

Jesus does not promise that we will never suffer. His followers will experience the Cross. But we are hopeful because he never abandons us. By embracing our human suffering, we can become stronger in our faith and more united with Jesus' redemptive love.

Guided Reflection: Our Response to Suffering

Let's spend a few moments in silence and meditate on Jesus' message to his disciples in Mark 8:34–35.

In your imagination join the crowd that gathers around Jesus. What do you think of first when you hear him talk about denying yourself, taking up your Cross, and losing your life for his sake and the sake of the Gospel?

Take a moment and share your thoughts with Jesus.

As you look around the crowd, you notice that some people are leaving. Maybe Jesus' words sound too harsh to them. You stay. As Jesus speaks, you begin to understand a little better that a disciple is someone who follows Jesus, even when it gets difficult. How did Jesus respond to suffering? How do you respond to it?

When you are ready, share your thoughts with Jesus.

Now Jesus shares how much he loves you. He welcomes your courage to be his disciple. He wants you to know that he walks with you every step of the way through your hardships. Jesus reminds you that he will help you grow in wisdom and faith. Spend a moment resting quietly in Jesus' presence. Thank him for this time.

Knowing that following Jesus is about making God's kingdom visible on earth, let us close by praying together the Lord's Prayer.

Together, pray the Lord's Prayer.

WHERE Do I Fit In?

When you suffer, remember Jesus' Cross. He is with you, and he will keep carrying you with him. With faith in Jesus, you will make it to the other side.

by Amy Welborn

The Other Side of Suffering

In eighth grade, I was ruthlessly mocked by a bunch of truly mean girls.

I suffered.

During the years before and after eighth grade, things were weird and tense at home, and sometimes I was sure my world would fall apart completely.

I suffered.

Years later, I labored and gave birth.

Oh, I suffered.

And some years after that, one February morning, my husband had a heart attack and died.

My children and I suffered.

You've suffered, too, in all kinds of ways—some small, some great. Your times of suffering may be like mine, or they may be different. Your suffering may have been brought about by your own choices, the choices of others, or seemingly, no choices at all. The suffering just happened, and it *hurt*. Suffering, whether physical or emotional pain, means there's a huge distance between where we are and where we know we should be. God created us for love, truth, joy, wholeness, and life. When we suffer, we feel far away from all of these, and maybe even far away from God.

But here's the irony. When we live in Christ and let Christ live in us, that place of suffering is turned upside down. That place has a name—the Cross. For

Jesus was in that place—that place where he was mocked, where he hurt, where he was abandoned, where he seemed to have failed, where he asked God "Why?" and where his earthly life was stripped away.

Are you suffering? Jesus has been in the place where you are. He's there with you now, in whatever suffering you're enduring. He will always be with you. The Cross wasn't the end for Jesus, and if you live in faith, suffering won't be the end for you.

Reflect

The Victory of the Cross

Because Christ's Cross leads to Resurrection, we meet our human suffering with hope and encouragement. Read Luke 9:23.

Then explain how each example of renewed hope shown below is the other side of suffering. Write your ideas on another sheet of paper.

1. A woman loses her job and starts her own company.

2. You are cut from the team so you become the team manager.

3. The reflecting pools at Ground Zero in New York City become a national memorial.

4. A town rebuilds after a tornado.

5. After you lose your family pet, you help your elderly neighbor care for his dog.

AMY WELBORN is a mother of five and the author of *Wish You Were Here: Travels Through Loss and Hope.*

What's What?

Respond

Complete each sentence with details from the text.

1 The Gospel of Mark tells us _____ .
(PAGES 152–153)

_____

_____

_____

2 Jesus is the suffering servant because
_____ . (PAGES 152–153)

_____

_____

_____

3 After he predicts his own suffering, Jesus scolds Peter because Jesus _____ .
(PAGE 153)

_____

_____

_____

4 At his Crucifixion, Jesus is recognized as the Son of God by _____ . (PAGE 153)

_____

_____

5 Jesus' Crucifixion is the moment of truth for Christians because _____ .
(PAGES 154–155)

_____

_____

_____

6 For Christians the cross is a universal sign of hope because _____ . (PAGE 155)

_____

_____

_____

_____

_____

7 As Christians we can respond to our own suffering by _____ . (PAGE 155)

_____

_____

_____

_____

Say What?

Know the definitions of these terms.

Apostles' Creed

Paschal Mystery

Passion

Transfiguration

Now What?

How will you respond this week when faced with your own suffering or with someone else's suffering?

_____

_____

_____

_____

_____

_____

Jesus Brings Us New Life

What do you hope to find when you join a group? Are you looking for fun, a sense of belonging, or something else? How can your affiliation with a group challenge, support, or enliven your life?

PRAYER

Lord, I know that your life is within me. With all my brothers and sisters around the world, we are the family of God. Send your Holy Spirit to strengthen the Church.

An Empty Tomb

SOMETIMES we find what we're looking for when we join a group at school, in sports, or at church. Other times we might be surprised at what we find—or what we don't.

On the Sunday morning following Jesus' Death on the Cross, Mary Magdalene; Mary, the mother of James; and Salome were surprised when they went to the tomb to anoint Jesus' body. A young man clothed in a white robe said to them, "Do not be amazed! You seek Jesus of Nazareth, the crucified. He has been raised; he is not here." (Mark 16:6)

He told the women to bring a message to Peter and the disciples—that if they wanted to see Jesus, they would have to go to Galilee, as Jesus had told them. This was remarkable news, and the women fled the tomb, trembling and bewildered. They had received a message telling them where to find the risen Jesus.

Women at the tomb, Clayton and Bell, stained glass, St. Peter's Church, Albany, New York.

The Resurrection

For Christians, Jesus' Resurrection is the central mystery of our faith. Every Easter we celebrate Jesus' Resurrection and our hope for eternal life.

"Death is swallowed up in victory.
Where, O death, is your victory?
Where, O death, is your sting?"

1 Corinthians 15:54–55

After Jesus' Death on the Cross, his disciples probably felt confused, disappointed, and heartbroken. They probably felt alone and afraid. But on the third day, the women found an open and empty tomb. Jesus had triumphed over Death. Jesus' Resurrection is God's promise that if we live our lives well and follow his plan as his disciples, we will share eternal life with him.

Our Catholic Character

The Church's strong emphasis on **social justice,** the fair and equal treatment of every member of society, keeps us faithful to the Kingdom of God. The Kingdom of God is revealed when we work to assure justice for those who are poor, when we relieve the suffering of the oppressed, when we console the sorrowful, and when we actively seek a new social order in which the dignity of all human beings is recognized and respected. With the help of God's grace, we are able to continue the work of Jesus in building the Kingdom of God.

Where Will I Find Jesus?

Today we find the risen Christ in his Church—the worldwide community of baptized believers who work together to serve the coming Kingdom of God under the leadership of the bishops, with the Bishop of Rome—the pope—at the head. We also find Jesus in church every time the community gathers to celebrate the sacrifice of the Mass on Sundays and holy days of obligation.

We find Jesus in God's actions in the sacraments, especially in the Sacrament of the Eucharist, where we encounter the real presence of Jesus Christ in his Body and Blood, given to us as spiritual nourishment.

Today we do not see Jesus in his physical body, as he showed himself to his followers in Galilee. Instead, we have to look for Jesus in the types of places where he ministered. We find Jesus among the **marginalized,** those who are unimportant or powerless in society, such as victims of discrimination; those who are poor; or people who are mistreated in society because of their race, religion, or gender. We find Jesus among victims of war and among those who work for peace. We find him among those suffering from physical, mental, or emotional illness. When you help the elderly, make someone who is sick more comfortable, or assist those who are disabled, you are doing more than a nice act. As followers of Jesus Christ, you are blessed with opportunities to find Jesus in many people.

Jesus Is with Us

After Jesus was raised from the dead, he ascended to the Father in heaven. Jesus and the Father sent the Holy Spirit to teach and guide us and to aid us in understanding all that Jesus had done in saving us. It is the Holy Spirit who assists us to find the presence of God in all things. As we accept and welcome the grace of the Holy Spirit, every day becomes a discovery of the presence of God—sometimes in places where we least expect it.

The Gospel of Mark assures us that Christ is present with us in prayer and worship, in Christian community, in situations of love and respect, and in peacemaking and working for justice. What does Jesus call us to do as his followers?

Serving the Kingdom

As Christians, Jesus calls us to go forward and be among those who are poor and in need. In Mark 8:34, Jesus says that to be a true disciple means to deny yourself, take up your cross, and follow him. This means that we unite human suffering to the suffering of Jesus and join him in serving the needs of others in the Kingdom of God. "For the Son of Man did not come to be served but to serve and to give his life as a ransom for many." (Mark 10:45)

What will you do? Will you seek Jesus? Jesus said, "Then come, follow me." (Luke 18:22) We follow him away from the empty tomb and into life with its challenges and promises of redemption.

Explore

Study Corner

DEFINE

social justice
marginalized

REMEMBER

The Holy Spirit assists us to find the presence of God in all things.

We find the risen Christ among the suffering. Christ is present with us in prayer, in the Christian community, and in the sacraments.

Sacraments of Initiation

THE word *initiation* means "to make a beginning." Of the seven sacraments in the Catholic Church, three are designated as Sacraments of Initiation because they mark a new beginning in our journey of faith.

The first of these three is Baptism, in which Original Sin is washed away and we receive new life in the Holy Spirit. In the Sacrament of Confirmation, we are strengthened with the Holy Spirit and dedicate ourselves to serving the Kingdom of God on earth. In the Sacrament of the Eucharist, our bodies and souls are nourished with the Body and Blood of Jesus Christ.

The Sacraments of Baptism and Confirmation do not have to be repeated because they leave a permanent mark on our souls. We celebrate the Eucharist over and over again because we constantly need to remember who we are and what we are called to do as followers of Jesus Christ. Celebrating the Eucharist regularly is our way of renewing the commitments we made in Baptism and Confirmation.

Many Catholics are baptized as infants and later receive the Sacraments of the Eucharist and Confirmation. People of all ages can receive the Sacraments of Initiation, but Baptism is always the first sacrament received. Anyone who has reached the age of reason, which is seven years of age or older, and wishes to be baptized, can enter into a process called the Rite of Christian Initiation of Adults (RCIA), which prepares him or her to receive all three Sacraments of Initiation at the Easter Vigil on Holy Saturday.

Baptism

Our Baptism is not like the baptism of Jesus in the Jordan River by John the Baptist. Jesus' baptism was a way of showing his willingness to wade into the world of sin in order to save us and bring salvation. It was also the Father's way of showing that Jesus was indeed his only Son, filled with the Holy Spirit.

The Greek root of the word *baptism* means "to immerse." In Baptism we enter into the waters, where we symbolically die to sin and emerge to a new life of grace. In John 3:5, Jesus tells Nicodemus that "no one can enter the kingdom of God without being born of water and Spirit." Baptism gives us birth into a new life in Jesus Christ. We receive forgiveness of Original Sin and all personal sins, and we become members of the Body of Christ, the Church. The visible symbols of Baptism include water, a white garment, holy oils, and fire.

Confirmation

To *confirm* means "to strengthen." When we receive the Sacrament of Confirmation, we are strengthened in the Holy Spirit. In Acts of the Apostles 8:14–17, the Apostles Peter and John travelled to Samaria and "laid hands" on people who had been baptized so that they could receive the Holy Spirit. The tradition of prayer and laying on of hands continues to this day in the Catholic Church. In the Sacrament of Confirmation, the bishop anoints the forehead with Chrism and says, "Be sealed with the gift of the Holy Spirit."

Strengthened by the Holy Spirit, the confirmed person participates more fully in the mission of the Church and continues the spiritual journey with renewed inspiration. When Jesus appears to the Apostles in Jerusalem after his Resurrection, he says, "You are witnesses of these things. And [behold] I am sending the promise of my Father upon you; but stay in the city until you are clothed with power from on high." (Luke 24:48–49)

Eucharist

Receiving the Body and Blood of Christ for the first time is referred to as First Holy Communion. The Eucharist initiates us into the community of the faithful who regularly partake of the real presence of Jesus Christ.

Jesus told the Apostles at the Last Supper, "This is my body, which will be given for you; do this in memory of me." (Luke 22:19) Jesus himself is the sacrifice. When Jesus gave his disciples the wine, he said, "This cup is the new covenant in my blood, which will be shed for you." (Luke 22:20)

Jesus' sacrifice on the Cross establishes a new covenant between God and humankind, and so when we first receive the Eucharist, we enter into that covenant more fully. When we celebrate the Eucharist regularly, our salvation in Jesus Christ is made present to us in the most profound way.

Initiated Into the Body of Christ

Through the Sacraments of Initiation, we are incorporated into the Church. The word *incorporate* is based on the Latin word for *body* (corpus), and so we enter into the Body of Christ and the people of God.

The Church is the people of God throughout the whole world. The Church is also the Body of Christ. When Jesus died and rose, he established a community of believers as his own body so that we form one family and one people of God. Christ is the head of his people, and his law is love of God and neighbor. The Church's mission is to make the light of Christ evident to the world and to be a seed of unity, hope, salvation, and holiness for humankind.

When we receive the Sacraments of Initiation, we are not only initiated into the Church but are also called to initiate the Church's values and ideas into our own lives and the lives of people around us.

Explore

Study Corner

DEFINE

doxology

REMEMBER

The Sacraments of Initiation are Baptism, Confirmation, and Eucharist. They mark our entry into the community of the Church, which was born as a result of the Resurrection.

SACRED ART

Elizabeth Wang is a British artist who hopes her art will "encourage people to grow in holiness by believing and living the Catholic faith to its fullness." The title of this work of art reminds us of the words of the priest's prayer during the Concluding Doxology at the end of the Eucharistic Prayer. A **doxology** is a Christian prayer praising and giving glory to God, often referencing the three divine Persons of the Trinity. Through the Sacraments of Initiation, we enter into the life of the Church with Jesus Christ as its head. In Christ all people of the world are brought into unity.

Through Him, With Him,
Elizabeth Wang, 2006.

Reflecting God's Love

Witnesses for Christ

Reader 1: A reading from the holy Gospel according to John.
[John 15:12–13]
The Gospel of the Lord.

All: Praise to you, Lord Jesus Christ.

Reader 2: Think about what it means to lay down one's life for a friend. Have you ever gone out of your way to help someone? Or have you ever put your plans aside in order to be with your family? These are ways of laying down your life in order to serve others, and you become a living reflection of God's love.

Response: Lord, hear our prayer.

Reader 3: That through our prayer and reflection, we become true reflections of God's love in the world, let us pray to the Lord. ℟.

Reader 4: That we come to know Jesus more fully though his Passion, Death, Resurrection, and Ascension, let us pray to the Lord. ℟.

Reader 5: That we continue to grow in our ability to reach out to others, let us pray to the Lord. ℟.

Leader: Let us end our prayer with the words that Jesus taught us. Together let's pray the Lord's Prayer.

We belong to a Church that gives witness to Christ, worships God through the Holy Spirit, and serves Christ and his people.

Love is at the heart of what it means to follow Christ. Jesus tells us that of all the commandments, two are the greatest. First, you must love God with all your heart, with all your soul, and with all your mind. Second, you must love your neighbor as yourself. All the other laws are based on these two. (Matthew 22:36–40)

When Jesus died on the Cross, he taught us to give our lives for others. His willingness to suffer and die was the result of his deep love for the Father and us. The life, Death, Resurrection, and Ascension of Jesus reflect God's great love for us. As his followers, we look for ways to reflect God's love to those we meet each day.

WHERE Do I Fit In?

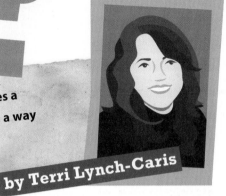

Seeing something with new eyes can change everything. Sometimes a place, event, or situation stays exactly the same, but you change in a way that allows you to live more abundantly.

by Terri Lynch-Caris

The Day Everything Changed

When I went away to college, I could make my own decisions. I decided what I was going to do each day. I decided when to go to bed and when to wake up. I could skip class if I wanted. I could decide who to see and where to go. On Sunday I could choose whether or not to go to church.

This new freedom was exciting, but it was also uncomfortable. Sometimes I felt lost and alone. It seemed that everyone knew where he or she was going on campus except me. Sometimes I felt like people were looking at me and laughing because they had friends and I didn't. I felt overwhelmed with coursework. Sometimes I slept in late or did schoolwork on Sunday mornings instead of going to church.

I am a Catholic, but I decided to try out different Christian churches on campus. They felt strange to me. The Bible message was the same, but the services were different, and they didn't offer Holy Communion. One day, almost by chance, I found the Catholic Church on campus. I went to Mass and immediately felt at home. I grew more excited as Mass went on, and when I received the Eucharist, it almost felt like my First Communion.

On that day, everything changed for me. The church became my anchor in new surroundings. Catholic life gave me a framework to make good choices. I realized that, just like God, I could depend on the Church. I had made the most important decision of my life—to rediscover and choose my Catholic faith.

TERRI LYNCH-CARIS is associate professor of industrial engineering at Kettering University in Flint, Michigan.

Reflect

Eyes of Faith

In what ways has a new perspective about your family, school, or community helped you live more fully? Write your ideas in each circle. Then continue writing on another sheet of paper.

Family

School

Community

What's What?

Fill in the letter blanks to complete each sentence. Use the circled letters to discover the secret word.

1 When the women arrived at the tomb of Jesus, they were told that he had __ _(○)_ __ __ __ and gone to Galilee. (PAGE 160)

2 We find Jesus in every celebration of the Mass, including Sundays and Holy Days of __ __ __ __ __ __ __ __ _(○)_. (PAGE 161)

3 We find Jesus in the types of places where he __ _(○)_ __ __ __ __ __ __ __ __ . (PAGE 161)

4 We find Jesus in God's action in the __ __ __ __ __ __ __ _(○)_ . (PAGE 161)

5 The __ __ __ __ __ __ __ __ __ _(○)_ __ helps us find the presence of God in all things. (PAGE 161)

6 _(○)_ __ __ __ __ __ is the first sacrament we receive. (PAGE 162)

7 We are nourished with the Body and Blood of Jesus Christ in the __ __ __ __ __ __ __ _(○)_. (PAGE 163)

8 The Church is the Body of __ __ __ _(○)_ __ __ . (PAGE 163)

9 In the Sacrament of _(○)_ __ __ __ __ __ __ __ __ __ __ __ , the bishop says, "Be sealed with the gift of the Holy Spirit." (PAGE 163)

10 Jesus Christ is the head of the people of God who love God and love their _(○)_ __ __ __ __ __ __ __ . (PAGE 163)

Secret Word:

__ __ __ __ __ __ __ __ __ __

Say What?

Know the definitions of these terms.

doxology
marginalized
social justice

Now What?

Write at least one thing you will do at school this week to reach out to someone in need of God's love.

_____

_____

_____

_____

_____

_____

_____

_____

_____

Celebrating Holy Week and Easter

OUR final preparations for Easter are made during Holy Week. We remember and commemorate the events that led to Jesus' acceptance of his Death on the Cross for our sins. We are hopeful because we know that Jesus will rise on Easter.

We often pray the **Stations of the Cross,** an important prayer through which we remember Jesus' Death for our salvation. When we pray the Stations of the Cross, we walk from station to station and remember events from Jesus' Passion and Death. We remember these events with great hope because we know that death and evil do not triumph. Jesus will rise on Easter!

Holy Week, the week that precedes Easter, begins with Palm Sunday. We remember Jesus' triumphant entry into Jerusalem on Palm Sunday. On Holy Thursday we celebrate the gift that Jesus gave us in the Eucharist as we remember Jesus' Last Supper. On Good Friday we venerate the Cross and remember Jesus' Passion and Death. During the **Easter Vigil,** we wait to celebrate Christ's Resurrection, and we welcome new members into the Church in the Sacrament of Baptism. The **Triduum** represents the three days—Holy Thursday, Good Friday, Holy Saturday—during which we enter into the suffering, Death, and Resurrection of Jesus, leading up to Easter. On Easter Sunday, we celebrate Christ's Resurrection and the promise of new life in this world and the next.

Where in your life do you experience sacredness and mystery? Name something in your life that you consider sacred. What do you do to honor and nurture your sense of God's sacred presence in your life?

PRAYER

Thank you, God, for raising Jesus from the dead so that we might know the promise of eternal life. Help us share the Good News of Jesus' Resurrection with others.

167

Journey Through Holy Week

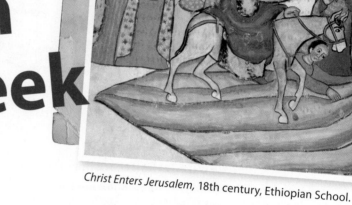

Christ Enters Jerusalem, 18th century, Ethiopian School.

DURING Holy Week we celebrate the most solemn liturgies of the Church year. The Church invites us to enter into the greatest mysteries at the heart of our faith—the suffering, Death, and Resurrection of Jesus.

Holy Week begins with Jesus' triumphant entry into Jerusalem on Palm Sunday and ends at the Easter Vigil on Holy Saturday. Through our participation in the sacred and ancient liturgies of Holy Week, we deepen our love for Jesus and come to better understand that he is the fulfillment of God's promise of salvation.

Entering Jerusalem

Palm Sunday commemorates Jesus' triumphant entry into Jerusalem. Jesus arrived before the celebration of Passover, one of the biggest feasts in the Jewish calendar. Jews from many countries were gathering in Jerusalem, and Jesus was met by people waving palm branches, crying out "Hosanna," and laying their cloaks on the road before him. These were actions fit for a king. But despite this royal reception, Jesus knew that he was proceeding toward his own Death.

On Palm Sunday we are invited to enter into the events surrounding Jesus' Passion, Death, and Resurrection. In the Palm Sunday liturgy, we enact the initial warm welcome of the crowds that changes to shouts of, "Crucify him! Crucify him!" In Holy Week, we enter into our faith's sacred mysteries.

Receiving Jesus

On Holy Thursday we celebrate the Evening Mass of the Lord's Supper. The Scripture readings recall how on the night before he died, Jesus instituted the Sacrament of the Eucharist. We focus on actions that ritually and symbolically express the meaning underlying Jesus' Paschal Mystery—new life comes when we lovingly sacrifice for others.

The Mass on Holy Thursday includes a ritual washing of the feet, recalling how Jesus washed the feet of his disciples. "I have given you a model to follow, so that as I have done for you, you should also do." (John 13:15) We receive the Body and Blood of Jesus Christ in the Eucharist, and we receive Jesus' example of how to lead through loving service.

At the Foot of the Cross

The solemn mood of Good Friday is established as the priests and deacons lay facing downward in a profound gesture of reverence before the altar. The silence of the church invites us to think and pray about Jesus' ultimate sacrifice of dying on the Cross so our sins would be forgiven. We bear witness to Jesus' Passion and Death, even as we anticipate the celebration of his Resurrection.

A focal point of the Good Friday liturgy is the veneration of the Cross when the congregation is invited to offer a gesture of respect and devotion by touching or kissing the Cross. The prayerful service ends, again with no music and no procession. We experience the emptiness of waiting—waiting on God's promise.

From Darkness to Light

A vigil is a watch kept the evening before a celebration. On the evening before Easter Sunday, the faithful gather in a darkened church in anticipation of the celebration of Christ's Resurrection. The Service of Light begins with the priest and deacon lighting and blessing a new fire. From those flames, they light the Easter candle. The deacon or priest, holding the Easter candle aloft, proclaims, "Light of Christ!" To which we respond, "Thanks be to God!" The Easter candle is processed to the sanctuary as the flame from this candle is spread to candles held by everyone in the assembly. As this is done, the **Exsultet,** a beautiful Easter hymn of praise, is sung. Soon the entire church is alive and lit with one light—the Light of Christ.

Liturgy of the Word

At the Easter Vigil, passages from the Old and New Testaments are read during the Liturgy of the Word. We hear the story of our salvation—beginning with creation and leading up to the discovery of Jesus' empty tomb. The readings help us understand God's tremendous love for us throughout thousands of years. We hear the struggles and challenges our ancestors faced waiting for the coming of a Savior. Jesus is the fulfillment of God's promises. Before the Gospel, we joyfully sing "Alleluia" for the first time since before Lent.

Liturgy of Baptism

After we listen to the readings, the Liturgy of Baptism is celebrated. This is the culmination of a journey that the participants in the Rite of Christian Initiation of Adults (RCIA) have made during the past year. The newly baptized are also confirmed and complete their initiation by receiving the Eucharist for the first time. As the congregation welcomes the new members of the Church, the members renew their baptismal promises.

Liturgy of the Eucharist

The Easter Vigil continues with the celebration of the Liturgy of the Eucharist. We hear the words "This is the Lamb of God" at every Mass. Hearing these words at the Easter Vigil reinforces the truth that Jesus, whose Good Friday sacrifice on the Cross gained our salvation, is present for us at every Eucharist we celebrate. Mass concludes with a blessing that sends us forth into the world, ready to proclaim the risen Christ to the world: "Christ is Risen! Indeed he is Risen! Alleluia!"

Explore

Our Catholic Character

The Church believes that God is the Father of everyone. It is important to recognize our common roots and respect the Jewish faith, which is already a response to God's Revelation in the old covenant. It is wrong for Catholics to blame members of the Jewish faith for crimes committed during Christ's Passion or to believe that Scripture desires them to do so. Over the years the Church has worked to improve Catholic-Jewish relations. One example is a request from Pope John Paul II at a special Mass at Saint Peter's in 2000, asking forgiveness for Christians' sins against the Jewish people.

Promise of the Resurrection

He Is Risen, He Qi, China.

CELEBRATING Holy Week and Jesus' Resurrection on Easter reveals God's response to some of the deepest issues that human beings ponder, such as how to make sense of suffering and what happens after death.

Jesus' Death teaches that suffering is a part of human life. Jesus modeled how to respond to suffering. Under the pressure of exhaustion, rejection, loneliness, and evil during his Passion and Death on the Cross, where did Jesus find the strength to endure violence and return only love? Jesus found strength in his union with his Father. Having experienced the depth of his Father's love, Jesus was filled with the love of the Holy Spirit. Through a life of prayer, he remained close to the Father through every trial.

Our Catholic Character

We continue to suffer the effects of our sins, even after we receive forgiveness; this is called temporal punishment. An **indulgence** is a lessening of temporal punishment gained through participation in prayer and works of charity. In addition to obtaining indulgences for ourselves, we can gain them for those in Purgatory, who benefit from the lessening of temporal punishment as they prepare to see the face of God.

To Love Like Jesus

Jesus found the strength to suffer on our behalf because he was grounded in the Father's love. The best response you can give is to love Jesus freely— not out of fear or because you are supposed to, but because he is good and worthy of your love. Pray for the grace to love Jesus because you *want* to love him.

In your daily life, you have many chances to love God and others. The choices you make in those situations make you who you are. If you offer actions of love toward others, you become more loving. If you do unkind and selfish things, you become less loving and may become insensitive to the needs of others. With each decision you make, you set a pattern for your life that shapes who you are becoming.

What Follows Death?

Jesus' Resurrection gives us a glimpse of what awaits us after our human lives are over. It is Jesus' promise of eternal life. Through Jesus' dying, rising, and ascending into heaven, we realize that we have a place in heaven with Jesus.

The Church invites us to reflect upon our beliefs in four last things: death, judgment, heaven, and hell. Everyone faces these four realities. Immediately following death is the judgment by Christ. The result of this judgment is heaven, hell, or Purgatory. The Church invites us to think about how we are living our lives. The choices we make each day matter. They have consequences now and into the future.

Death

At the moment of death, our hidden selves will be made plain to us, and we will realize whether the actions of our lives have brought us closer to or farther from Jesus. That moment is called the **particular judgment.** Have we followed Jesus or turned away? Our actions in life will determine whether we have a place with God in eternity.

Judgment

We all face God's judgment at the end of our mortal lives. God, in his tremendous compassion and love for us, will decide where we spend eternity based on how well we have loved others in this lifetime. Three possible outcomes accompany God's judgment.

➡ People who have followed Jesus perfectly in life can enter God's presence, which is the deepest goal of the human heart. They will see God face-to-face and experience complete and lasting joy. This is called heaven.

➡ People may need to be purified of any selfishness that remains because only those totally transformed by love can enter the Kingdom of God. This temporary state of purification is called **Purgatory**—when every trace of a soul's sin is cleared away so the person may enjoy God's presence in heaven.

➡ People who have freely refused in serious ways to follow God's command to love have put themselves in the state of mortal sin. Those who refuse to love cannot enter the Kingdom of God because God is love. They will be outside God's presence forever, and this eternal separation from God for whom we long is called hell. It is the result of the free choice of a person to reject God's love and forgiveness once and for all.

Mystery of Eternity

The mystery of eternity with God is beyond all understanding. The Scriptures describe heaven as life, light, peace, a wedding feast, wine of the kingdom, the Father's house, the heavenly Jerusalem, and paradise.

> "What eye has not seen, and ear has not heard, and what has not entered the human heart, what God has prepared for those who love him, . . ."
>
> *1 Corinthians 2:9*

We know that heaven responds to our deepest longings. These images give us clues to understanding what heaven will be like.

Study Corner

DEFINE

indulgence, particular judgment, Purgatory

REMEMBER

Jesus' Resurrection opens the promise of eternal life with him in heaven. After death we will be judged by a loving and merciful God who will determine how we will spend eternity.

Explore

SACRED ART

This Russian mosaic of the Resurrection depicts Jesus breaking the doors of death and freeing Adam and Eve along with other men and women of the Old Testament. Mosaic art is made with small pieces of glass, stone, or other material. The subject of this art reminds us that God desires for every person to be saved in order to enjoy eternal life in heaven with him. Jesus' Resurrection from the dead gives us hope of attaining that eternal life. Every Sunday when we celebrate the Eucharist, we celebrate Jesus' Resurrection from the dead and gain strength to follow him more faithfully.

Mosaic of the Resurrection, Moscow, Russia.

Enter the Kingdom

At Holy Saturday's

Easter Vigil liturgy, when the dark church is illuminated during the Service of Light, the people sing the _Exsultet_.

This beautiful Easter hymn of praise proclaims, "The power of this holy night dispels all evil, washes guilt away, restores lost innocence, brings mourners joy; it casts out hatred, brings us peace, and humbles earthly pride."

The hymn, a testimony to the light of Christ, gives us a vision of hope. It encourages us to walk in Christ's footsteps of forgiveness, reconciliation, and joy. Christ's light encourages us to become a guiding light for others as we do his work in the world.

People of Faith

Leader: In the name of the Father, and of the Son, and of the Holy Spirit. Amen.

Throughout his life, Jesus made it clear that in order to enter the kingdom, we have to recognize our need for God. We need God in a way that children need parents. Without God's help we could never enter the kingdom. If you want to enter the kingdom, you have to be a person of faith.

All: O God, we freely give ourselves to you. Help us nurture the gift of faith you have given us by following your Word, listening to what the Church teaches, and putting our faith into action.

Leader: If you want to enter the kingdom, you have to be a person of hope.

All: O God, without the gift of hope, our lives would have no meaning. Help us share our hope with others and look forward to the lasting joy and happiness of eternal life.

Leader: If you want to enter the kingdom, you have to be a person of love.

All: O God, when we look at your Son, Jesus, we learn what it means to love others. Help us love you above all things and show your love to all we meet.

Leader: Together let's pray.

All: Loving God, we want to enter eternal life with you. We know our need for you and count on your help. May we grow in our relationship with you during Holy Week and Easter as we prepare to accept the gift of your Son, Jesus Christ. We ask this in Jesus' name. Amen.

WHERE Do I Fit In?

Baptism is a gift from God and a lifetime process of initiation into the family of God. As Tertullian claimed, "Christians are not born. They are made."

by Joellyn Cicciarelli

Faith and Hope

I answered the telephone in my college dorm room. It was Aunt Nadine—my young, cool aunt whom I saw only a few times a year. "What's wrong?" I said instinctively, thinking that a family disaster would be the only reason she might call.

"Oh, nothing," she laughed. "I just have a question. Would you like to be John's godmother?" I quickly said yes, and after we chatted for a while, I scribbled the date in my Roman History notebook.

After I hung up, I wondered if I had done the right thing. Who was I to be someone's godmother? Does Aunt Nadine know that she asked a kid who is broke and always late for class? Why did she think I was worthy? I thought about calling her back—about declining and telling her that I wasn't ready.

But then I stopped myself. I thought that maybe my aunt might see something in me that she admired—something good. I remember thinking, "If I'm mature enough to take my little cousin's Baptism so seriously, then maybe I *am* ready."

And so I did call her back, but it wasn't to decline. It was to get a ride to the church. In retrospect, I know I actually had the makings of a good godmother. I had love to give, and I had commitment to my family, to baby John, and to God, who blessed us all with the gift of faith.

JOELLYN CICCIARELLI is the Director of Curricula Development at Loyola Press and the proud godmother of four fine young men.

What's What?

Complete the puzzle using details from the text.

Across

2 At the end of our lives, we all face God's _____ . (PAGE 171)

5 The _____ candidates are welcomed into the Church at the Easter Vigil. (PAGE 169)

7 We celebrate Jesus' Resurrection on _____ Sunday. (PAGE 168)

8 Participants touch or kiss the cross in a rite called the _____ of the Cross during the Good Friday liturgy. (PAGE 168)

9 The idea of eternity is a _____ of our faith. (PAGE 171)

Down

1 We catch a glimpse of our own afterlife through Jesus' _____ . (PAGE 170)

3 We remember Christ's sacrifice for our salvation every time we receive the _____ . (PAGE 169)

4 Holy Week begins on _____ . (PAGE 167)

6 One outcome of Christ's judgment, where one waits until the soul's sins can be cleansed, is _____ . (PAGE 171)

8 A _____ is a watch kept the evening before a celebration. (PAGE 169)

Say What?

Know the definitions of these terms.

Easter Vigil   Purgatory

Exsultet   Stations of the Cross

indulgence   Triduum

particular judgment

Now What?

In his suffering and Death, Jesus remained faithful to the Father and won our salvation. What is one thing that you can do this week to help ease the pain and suffering of others?

_____

_____

_____

_____

_____

_____

_____

Respond

Faith in ACTION

Acting as a disciple is to accept Jesus' message and to live as he did, sharing his mission, his suffering, and his joy. Jesus entrusted his disciples to continue his work in the world. As Catholics, working to build a just society that reflects the attitudes and values we believe as Jesus' followers is not optional.

In this unit we explored Jesus the Christ. Jesus sacrificed himself on the cross for our salvation. We receive the Body and Blood of Christ in the Eucharist. Instead of being defeated by temptation, betrayal, and Death, Jesus' Resurrection tells us that God invites us to eternal life. These ideas engage your faith in social and political issues with the self-giving and love that Jesus demonstrated.

Faithful Citizenship

Purpose

Explore what it means to be a faithful citizen by learning about significant witnesses of the Catholic social movement.

Background

In 2003 the United States bishops issued a statement on how our faith calls us to be active citizens in our nation and in our world. This statement served as a reminder that each person is responsible for witnessing to the Church's commitment to human life and dignity. Young people, too, are called to this mission. "We must ensure that our nation's young people—especially the poor, those with disabilities, and the most vulnerable—are properly prepared to be good citizens, to lead productive lives, and to be socially and morally responsible in the complicated and technologically challenging world of the twenty-first century." (USCCB, *Faithful Citizenship: A Catholic Call to Political Responsibility*, 2003)

Steps

1. Choose from among a list of significant witnesses of the Catholic social movement in the last century, such as Dorothy Day, César Chávez, Saint Oscar Romero, Saint Teresa of Calcutta, or Sister Helen Prejean. Research their lives and the stands they took in response to contemporary political thought in light of the call to social justice.

(continued on page 176)

> "There is plenty to do, for each one of us, working on our own hearts, changing our own attitudes, in our own neighborhoods."
>
> —Dorothy Day, social activist and founder of the Catholic Worker Movement

Act

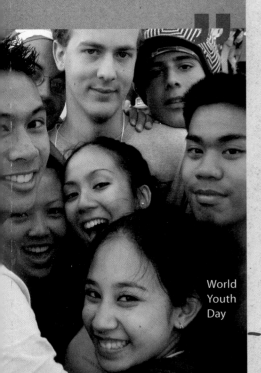

World Youth Day

2. Share your findings with one another and discuss ways that you can share the insights of people who have worked for justice in our world. Here are some ideas to jump-start your creativity.

- Make posters featuring the many people who have worked for justice. Include their pictures, vital statistics, contributions to justice, and compelling quotations. Display the posters in school, in the parish hall, or church.
- Invite a well-known local justice leader to talk with your parish, school, or community about what it means to be a faithful citizen.

Engaging in the Public Forum

Purpose

Design a project that allows you to express your faith publicly.

Background

Sometimes we might be reluctant to get involved in politics. However, we have a duty as citizens and as Catholics to engage with politics. "We are members of a community of faith with a long tradition of teaching and action on human life, and dignity, marriage and family, justice and peace, care for creation, and the common good. . . . Catholics have the same rights and duties as others to participate fully in public life. The Church through its institutions must be free to carry out its mission and contribute to the common good without being pressured to sacrifice fundamental teachings and moral principles." (USCCB, *Forming Consciences for Faithful Citizenship,* 2011)

Steps

1. Learn about the major public-policy issues in your community or state.
2. Choose one of the issues and research the topic. What are the different positions? What are the moral dimensions of the issue? How does Catholic social teaching address this issue?
3. Design a project that puts your faith into action. For example, your group can write letters to political leaders as a way to present your position. You might make a video or present a slideshow presentation to church or community leaders that raises awareness about the moral dimensions of the issue.

"We do not exist for ourselves."

—Thomas Merton, monk, social activist, poet, spiritual writer

Act

Jesus Lives On

Saint Maximilian Mary Kolbe grew up as a bright but mischievous boy. He was born Raymond Kolbe on January 8, 1894, in central Poland to a devout Polish Catholic family. When he was 10 years old, his mischievous ways tried his mother's patience. Exasperated, she asked him, "What is going to become of you?" Later, during prayer to the Virgin Mary, he asked himself this same question. Kolbe had a vision of Mary carrying two crowns: one white, for purity, and the other red, for martyrdom. When she asked him whether he would accept either of the crowns, he replied, "I choose both!" Kolbe, the mischievous boy, would live a life filled with passion for living out the example of Jesus Christ.

How the Saint Relates

Saint Maximilian Kolbe's life shows how one person who chooses to live for goodness and against evil can make a profound difference in the world. Kolbe spread Jesus' message of love and redemption wherever he was. His noble gift of his own life sends a message of love beyond his death.

Devoted to Mary

After his vision, Kolbe was especially devoted to Mary and pursued a life of prayer and service. In 1907 Kolbe and his brother Francis entered a Franciscan seminary in Lwów, the present-day city of Lviv, Ukraine. When he made his final vows in 1914, he chose the name Maximilian Mary in honor of the Blessed Virgin.

A gifted student, Kolbe earned doctorates in philosophy and theology. While he was a student in Rome, he witnessed demonstrations against the pope. In response, Kolbe organized a religious movement in 1917 called the Militia Immaculata to convert sinners and to win over enemies of the Catholic Church.

Missionary Travels

Kolbe wanted everyone to experience the happiness that comes from experiencing the presence of God. Between 1930 and 1936, he traveled to Japan, where he founded a monastery near Nagasaki. Kolbe chose to build the monastery on the side of the mountain, a site that many Japanese believed was not in harmony with nature. His decision later proved to be for the best. When the atomic bomb was dropped on Nagasaki in World War II, the monastery, shielded by the mountain, was unharmed.

A Soldier for Christ

In 1936, due to poor health, Kolbe returned to Poland. When the Nazis invaded Poland three years later, most people feared for their lives, but Kolbe spoke out against Nazi brutality. He hid 2,000 Jews from Nazi persecution, an undertaking that required great personal risks.

In 1941 Kolbe was arrested and sent to the concentration camp at Auschwitz. Later that year a man from his barracks escaped. In reprisal the camp commander chose 10 men to starve to death as a warning to the other prisoners. One of the men cried out, "My wife! My children!" Kolbe quietly stepped forward and asked to take the man's place. His request was granted, and the chosen 10 were placed together in a dark cell to die slowly from hunger and dehydration. During their time in the cell, Kolbe led the others in song and prayer to the Blessed Virgin. Finally, only Kolbe remained. The guards, impatient for the bunker to be emptied, executed him by lethal injection on August 14, the eve of the Feast of the Assumption. Saint Maximilian Mary Kolbe was a man who lived what he preached—total love for God and others. He was beatified in 1971 and canonized in 1982.

Jesus Opens Our Eyes

Think about your life's path so far. Which events have been most important? Where have you encountered God in work, play, joy, hardships, or ordinary life? Where have you recognized, or failed to recognize, Jesus along the way?

PRAYER

Loving God, help me remember you are always with me wherever the path in life takes me.

Recognizing Jesus in Our Lives

WHERE did Jesus go after his Resurrection? The angel at the tomb proclaimed that Jesus was going to Jerusalem.

Soon Jesus appeared on the road to Emmaus. Later Paul encountered him on the road to Damascus. In order to follow Jesus, you must recognize where to find him. Knowing this will help you clarify one of the key questions for your own life: "Where am I going?"

Do I Know You?

In the Gospel of Luke, two disciples are walking from Jerusalem to Emmaus on the morning of Jesus' Resurrection. Frightened and demoralized after witnessing the death of Jesus, they are no longer sure of their mission in life. Amazingly, the risen Christ appears and walks with them, but the two disciples don't recognize Jesus. (Luke 24:13–16)

The two disciples tell Jesus, "But we were hoping that he would be the one to redeem Israel." (Luke 24:21) Jesus challenges their interpretation of the role of the Messiah and speaks to them about seeing the Messiah in light of Moses and the prophets. (Luke 24:25–26)

When the risen Jesus breaks bread and prays with the disciples, they finally recognize him. With their hearts and minds burning, they recognize their mission, and they return to Jerusalem to announce their encounter with the risen Christ.

At God's Right Hand

After Jesus rose from the dead, he spent 40 days among his disciples before ascending to heaven, where he is now and will be eternally present at the Father's right hand. Jesus' Ascension celebrates the entrance of his humanity into divine glory. This astounding event, described in Acts of the Apostles 1:9–11, tells how Jesus was lifted up in a cloud while the Apostles looked on. From heaven,

SACRED ART

He Qi [Huh Chee], a Chinese artist, blends cultural traditions in this modernist work. Although the painting is rooted in Chinese culture, it is also universal because its subject is the Gospel, which rises above all cultures. In this painting, Christ is shown in the center, and the followers of Jesus are in the four corners. One interpretation suggests that Jesus' outstretched arms and body form a Eucharistic table for all his followers, who are the Body of Christ in the world.

The Risen Lord, He Qi, 1998.

Jesus and the Father sent the Holy Spirit. From heaven, Jesus will return again to gather all those who will join him and his mother, Mary, in the presence of God.

Jesus' life follows a pathway that leads through his life, Death, into Resurrection, and finally Ascension to heaven. As followers of Jesus, then, this means that this is our path, too, as we live with the hope and anticipation of being reunited with God.

Remember Me

At times we can be like the two disciples on the road to Emmaus, walking along the path of life, uncertain about our mission and unable to recognize that Jesus is walking with us. What is the key to recognizing Jesus and knowing your mission in life?

In the Gospel of Luke, the two disciples listen to Jesus explain Scriptures. They see the bread being blessed, broken, and shared, and they recognize the risen Christ. They recognize their role of discipleship. That is why the Eucharist is close to the hearts of Catholics, who know it is the real presence of the risen Christ in their midst. Christ sends them forth with the mission to continue his teachings in the world. At Mass we, too, listen to Scripture as it is read and explained. Likewise, just as the two disciples gathered around a table and received bread from Jesus, we come forward to receive the Body and Blood of Jesus Christ in the Eucharist. The Gospel of Luke tells us that this is what Christians have been doing since the time of Jesus—worshiping God by listening to the living Word of God and receiving the Eucharist.

People on a journey choose paths. The early Christian community identified itself as **the Way.** The two disciples on the road to Emmaus were on a journey, and Jesus came to them in the Eucharist and gave them strength to complete their journey. That is what the Eucharist is—strength to make our way through life. In the Eucharist we are nourished to complete our own journey on the Way.

Your Road to Emmaus

We don't always know what our mission in life is. Even when we follow Jesus, we don't know exactly where that path will take us. A path may take us to a new school, to a different state or country, or into a new group of people whom we serve or befriend.

If Jesus appeared to you as he appeared to the disciples on the road to Emmaus and said, "Come with me," would you follow him? Would you follow him even without knowing where he was leading you? Don't be afraid to answer yes. Wherever your path leads, Jesus is walking with you. His Word and his presence are with you, to guide you and give you hope. Recognizing Jesus' presence is a way to recognize your own mission in life and what God calls you to be and do in the world.

Explore

On the Road

Think about the Emmaus story and how the two disciples felt before they recognized the risen Jesus. What can you do when you are afraid and unsure about your path in life?

_____

_____

_____

_____

_____

Study Corner

DEFINE
the Way

REMEMBER
We can be uncertain about our mission in life when we fail to recognize Jesus' presence. We encounter and recognize Jesus in the Eucharist. Jesus' life follows a path through life, Death, into Resurrection, and finally Ascension to heaven. Following Jesus means that this is our path, too, as we live with the hope of being reunited with God.

Coworkers with God

THE Book of Genesis tells us that Adam, the first man, was created with a purpose—to tend and cultivate the Garden of Eden. (Genesis 2:15)

From the very beginning, human beings have had a job and a mission. God knows the importance and value of work to the body and soul. As with Adam, God creates each of us with a purpose. As time goes on, you will begin to see more clearly what your purpose, or mission, in life will be and how work will play an important part of that mission.

Jesus Understands Work

Jesus understood the **dignity of work,** the sense of purpose and achievement that comes from doing work well. In work, people fulfill part of their potential given to them by God.

Our Catholic Character

Monsignor George Higgins (1916–2002), the son of a Chicago postal clerk, grew up during the Great Depression. Moved by the struggles of workers, he soon became known as the "labor priest" because he worked tirelessly for the rights and dignity of the working person. He stood up for workers on strike, ministered to people in labor unions, and tried to convince politicians to support legislation that ensures fairness to working people. He was awarded the Presidential Medal of Freedom with these words: "For more than 60 years now, [Higgins] has organized, marched, prayed, and bled for the social and economic justice of working Americans."

Work gives people a sense of purpose, dignity, and accomplishment, and it makes it possible for them to provide a dignified life for themselves and for their families. But when people are paid unfair wages that keep them in poverty, or when they work in harmful or inhumane conditions, it is difficult for them to achieve dignity and independence. Dignity of work is a basic principle of Catholic social teaching. All workers have a right to productive work, decent and fair wages, and safe working conditions.

Jesus knew work. He worked alongside Joseph to learn carpentry as a trade. He knew what it was like to make something with his bare hands. Many images in Jesus' parables involve workers. For example, a farmer goes out to sow his fields, workers toil in the vineyard, and the good shepherd cares for his sheep.

Jesus worked to bring the Good News of salvation to all people. He didn't isolate himself, sit idly, or wait for the world to come to him. Instead, he traveled widely, preaching from place to place. The Gospels tell us that Jesus gathered disciples among fishermen. He ate with tax collectors. Jesus taught everyday people—working people leading ordinary lives. The Church looks to the example of Jesus as the model for issues related to work and workers.

Lure of Consumerism

One of the main reasons people work is to make money to meet their needs and the needs of those who depend on them. However, this reasonable goal can become blurred. At his opening address at World Youth Day in Australia in 2008,

Pope Benedict XVI warned young people against the lure of **consumerism** and "false idols." Consumerism is giving undue value to the acquisition of material goods. At its worst, consumerism puts things at the center of our lives, a place where only God should be. Speaking of the effects of consumerism, the pope said, "In our personal lives and in our communities, we encounter a hostility, something dangerous; a poison which threatens to corrode what is good, reshape who we are, and distort the purpose for which we have been created."

Material things are not sinful, but the misuse or hoarding of wealth and power is corrupt. We should not believe that life is all about the acquisition of material things and that the only point of work is to get a paycheck. Instead, we need to see that work is an important way to participate in God's creation. Jesus' example and teachings help give us perspective and direction when thinking about our own attitudes about work.

The Moral Use of Wealth

The Tenth Commandment teaches us not to desire more than we need or to desire what belongs to our neighbors. The *Pastoral Constitution on the Church in the Modern World,* a document from the Second Vatican Council, teaches that we should regard what we have as also meant for the benefit of others: ". . . people are bound to come to the aid of the poor and to do so not merely out of their superfluous goods."

Our Gifts, Our Calling

God has an active role in our lives, working in us to bring us to greater life and joy. When we take up his work, we are coworkers with God. God has given each of us gifts, talents, skills, and interests that are unique. Because these gifts come from God, they are spiritual gifts. Saint Paul speaks of these gifts in his first **Epistle,** or letter, to the Corinthians.

> There are different kinds of spiritual gifts but the same Spirit; there are different forms of service but the same Lord; there are different workings but the same God who produces all of them in everyone.
>
> *1 Corinthians 12:4–6*

When you think of your life's work, God encourages you to think about your mission or calling. Figuring out your calling often takes time and different experiences. Throughout this journey, Jesus is working with you, in you, and through you to guide the way.

Past Meets Present

PAST: The Wisdom of Ben Sira, also known by the title "Sirach," is a book of the Bible that was finished about A.D. 175. The writing covers topics such as law, poverty and wealth, and other matters, both religious and social. Recognized by the Catholic Church as canonical, the contents are divided into separate parts. Chapters 1–43 deal largely with moral instruction. Chapter 14 specifically instructs about the use of wealth.

PRESENT: All people have the right to the moral use of the earth's goods. Speaking to diplomats on June 16, 2005, Pope Benedict XVI reaffirmed that right. "The earth, in fact, can produce enough to nourish all its inhabitants, on the condition that the rich countries do not keep for themselves what belongs to all."

Explore

Study Corner

DEFINE

dignity of work
consumerism
Epistle

REMEMBER

Work gives people a sense of dignity and accomplishment. The work we do contributes to society and expresses our vocation to be cocreators with God. God creates us for a purpose. We discover our mission over time and with many experiences.

Refreshing Our Memory

In the story of the two disciples on their way to Emmaus, we learn that our memory is a valuable tool for our spiritual lives.

The two disciples had studied Scripture since their childhood. And they had eaten with Jesus before his Crucifixion. On this day their heavy hearts, cares, and burdens kept them from recognizing him. Jesus needed to refresh their memories. He reminded them of what they already knew but had temporarily forgotten.

Litany of Gratitude for the Gift of Memory

Leader: Have you ever forgotten something important because you were distracted by worry or fear, as the disciples were when they met Jesus on the road? Perhaps you forgot your manners and misbehaved. Or maybe you forgot a promise you'd made and disappointed someone you really cared about.

Think of a time you needed to be reminded of something you already knew. *(Pause.)*

How did you feel when your memory was refreshed and your thoughts or actions were resolved? *(Pause.)*

The two disciples described feeling as if their hearts were burning. What image would you use? *(Pause.)*

Let's gather our thoughts and pray together in gratitude for the gift of memory. *(Pause.)*

Response: We praise you, Lord, and give you thanks.

Reader 1: Jesus, thank you for the gift of memory and for all that we know of you from the Gospels, we pray to the Lord. ℟.

Reader 2: Jesus, thank you for the gift of yourself that we receive in the celebration of the Eucharist, we pray to the Lord. ℟.

Leader: Let's pause for a moment and pray aloud our own intentions. *(Pause.)* We pray to the Lord. ℟.

Together let's pray.

All: Lord Jesus, in the Eucharist we are refreshed with the Scriptures and with your own Body and Blood. Teach us to use the strength we receive to go out into the world and help others remember your message. Amen.

WHERE Do I Fit In?

When the women went to anoint Jesus' body, they found an empty tomb. Jesus Christ is as present today as he was more than 2,000 years ago. And if we take the time to notice, we can find him in the most unlikely people and in the most unexpected places.

by Keely Kriho

Meeting Jesus in a Surprising Way

I am a volunteer at a hospital during the school year (a volunteer called a "candy striper" because of my striped uniform). I help by wheeling patients around in gurneys and wheelchairs. I had a difficult time at first. I got very stressed out, especially when I had to wheel patients downstairs to be taken home after surgery. I wasn't sure what I was supposed to say to them, so most of the time, there was an uncomfortable silence between us. I felt very out of place, so much so that I was considering moving to a different department—until I was asked to bring down one very special patient.

Hesitantly, I approached this new patient, worried that she would either be too tired or too crabby to talk. As I neared her bed, I found a pleasant-looking, middle-aged woman who was chatting into a cell phone animatedly. She looked up at me, smiled, got off the phone, got out of bed, and placed herself in the wheelchair. "Hello!" she exclaimed merrily, getting settled in the chair. "Are you one of the candy stripers here?" "Yes," I replied. "I'm going to be taking you down to the parking garage today. Is that where you'll be picked up?" "Yes, honey," she replied kindly, smiling. I carefully wheeled her out, being careful not to disturb the bandages wrapped around her head and ears.

She chatted with me about school, jobs I wanted to look into, and why I had become a candy striper. She put me at ease, and we talked like old friends.

KEELY KRIHO is a sophomore at Lyons Township High School in LaGrange, Illinois.

Just before we got to the garage, we met the volunteer director, who recognized this lady. "How are you?" she asked. "Better," the patient replied. "They took out the brain tumor, but during the process my hearing was damaged. This surgery will hopefully help me hear better. In a while, they're going to try to fix my eye, but we don't know how that will go yet." She chatted calmly and matter-of-factly about the struggles she had gone through.

I thought to myself, "Who am I to complain when this seriously ill woman, perhaps dying, still manages to smile and meet life courageously?" I truly saw the risen Jesus in this woman. Out of the depths of sickness and despair, she met her unsure future with faith and showed that faith to me.

Build a Faith Community

We meet the risen Jesus in the Sacrament of the Eucharist, in Scripture, and in the faith community. Jesus opened his disciples' eyes to recognize him. Read John 20:16, Luke 24:30–35, John 20:26–28, and John 21:4–7. Discuss who recognized Jesus and tell how this happened.

Because the patient followed Jesus' example, the author recognized him. This patient encouraged the author in her own faith. On a separate sheet of paper, share a story about someone whose example deepened your love of Jesus.

What's What?

Circle the letter of the choice that best completes each sentence.

1 On the road to Emmaus, the disciples at first _____. (PAGE 180)

   a. feel happy and invigorated

   b. fail to recognize Jesus

   c. understand their mission

2 Jesus challenges the two disciples' _____. (PAGE 180)

   a. interpretation of the Messiah's role

   b. decision to go to Emmaus

   c. eyewitness account of the Crucifixion

3 The life of Jesus follows a pathway of life, Death, Resurrection, and _____. (PAGE 181)

   a. Assumption

   b. Ascension

   c. Scripture

4 We follow Jesus' pathway of life at Mass when we listen to Scripture and receive _____. (PAGE 181)

   a. the mission

   b. the Way

   c. the Eucharist

5 An important part of God's intended mission for us includes the role of _____ in our lives. (PAGE 182)

   a. work

   b. wages

   c. consumerism

6 The culture of consumerism places a high value on _____. (PAGE 183)

   a. conserving nature

   b. acquiring possessions

   c. sharing wealth

7 When we take up God's work in the world, we become his _____. (PAGE 183)

   a. coworkers

   b. parables

   c. consumers

8 The Church promotes the _____ of wealth. (PAGE 183)

   a. misuse

   b. hoarding

   c. moral use

Say What?

Know the definitions of these terms.

consumerism

dignity of work

Epistle

the Way

Now What?

How can you use your unique interests, gifts, and talents to nurture your calling, or mission, in life?

_____

_____

_____

_____

_____

_____

_____

_____

Jesus Sends Us Forth with His Spirit

Recall a time when someone sent you to do something. Was your mission simple, such as an errand, or was it more difficult, such as delivering bad news? What did you need to take with you—talents, special skills, money, patience, courage, or something else?

PRAYER

Here I am Lord. I want to do your will. Doing your work in the world, Lord, is my deepest desire.

The Gift of Pentecost

ARE you aware of how the Holy Spirit is at work in your life? Sometimes it's hard to notice. Prayer, a spirit of openness, and practice help us gain a steady awareness of the many ways the Holy Spirit is present every day.

The Third Person of the Trinity, the Holy Spirit, plays a prominent role in many parts of the Bible. The Gospel of Luke gives attention to the work of the Holy Spirit in the lives of Jesus, Mary, and the disciples.

➡ Luke tells how Mary is filled with the Spirit to conceive the Messiah.

➡ Inspired by the Holy Spirit, Elizabeth recognizes Mary as the mother of the Messiah.

➡ The Holy Spirit leads Jesus into the desert, and Jesus returns from the desert filled with the power of the Holy Spirit.

➡ Jesus proclaims in the synagogue that he is the one on whom the Spirit rests.

In Chapter 14 of the Gospel of John, Jesus tries to calm the Apostles' fears at the Last Supper. He promises not to leave them orphans, assuring them that the Father will send an Advocate, the Holy Spirit, in Jesus' name. The Holy Spirit will help and guide them. Through the Spirit, Jesus will remain with the whole Church. The gift of the Holy Spirit will be another sign of the Father's love for them, just as the gift of his Son had been a gift of love.

The Acts of the Apostles begins with Jesus ascending to heaven. Jesus' last words to his disciples are a promise and a commission.

> "But you will receive power when the holy Spirit comes upon you; and you will be my witnesses in Jerusalem, throughout Judea and Samaria, and to the ends of the earth."
>
> *Acts of the Apostles 1:8*

What the Apostles received from the risen Jesus was more than assurance. It was a continuing and abiding gift of God's presence and strength.

The Holy Spirit Descends

Fifty days after the Ascension, Jesus' disciples fearfully huddled together behind locked doors. They wondered how they were going to carry on without Jesus. The Acts of the Apostles tells how the Jewish holy day of Pentecost arrived and, as Jesus promised, the Holy Spirit descended on the disciples, with "tongues as of fire." (Acts of the Apostles 2:3) The Spirit filled them with courage and empowered them to preach in many languages about the risen Christ to the crowds that represented many nations. The Apostles' ability to speak in different languages showed that the **Good News** transcended boundaries of language and culture, country and race. We celebrate Pentecost as the birthday of the Catholic Church because that is the day when the disciples took up Jesus' ministry and brought it to the entire world.

The Good News Proclaimed

On that first Pentecost, Peter boldly proclaimed to the crowd that Jesus, who was crucified, was Messiah and Lord. The early disciples called people to repentance and to Baptism in Jesus Christ, and they healed in Jesus' name.

The Holy Spirit transformed the early Christian community and strengthened it for the task of witnessing to Jesus the Lord. This same Holy Spirit continues to strengthen the Church today. We are also called to faith by the Holy Spirit. We are initiated into the life of the Spirit in Baptism and Confirmation, and we are sustained in it through the Eucharist. Just as the Christians in Luke's time were called to live their values in the difficult Roman world, we recognize the Holy Spirit's guidance today. Each year on the Feast of Pentecost, we celebrate the Spirit's presence within us and within the Church.

Gifts of the Holy Spirit

We first receive the Holy Spirit in the Sacrament of Baptism. In the Sacrament of Confirmation, the grace of Baptism is strengthened, and we receive the **Gifts of the Holy Spirit.** Church Tradition has added the gift of piety to make a total of seven gifts.

> "The spirit of the LORD shall rest upon him:
>   a spirit of wisdom and of understanding,
> A spirit of counsel and of strength,
>   a spirit of knowledge and of fear of the LORD."
>
> *Isaiah 11:2*

Study Corner

DEFINE

Good News
Gifts of the Holy Spirit

REMEMBER

At Pentecost the Holy Spirit descended on the disciples, giving them the strength to embrace their mission to spread the Good News. The seven Gifts of the Holy Spirit are wisdom, understanding, counsel, fortitude, knowledge, piety, and fear of the Lord.

Explore

The Gifts of the Holy Spirit listed in Isaiah 11:2, along with piety, give Christians the strength to lead moral lives. These gifts are permanent dispositions within us that help us heed the promptings of the Holy Spirit. Where we are morally strong, they make us stronger. Where we are weak, they give us strength. Saint Paul says, "For those who are led by the Spirit of God are children of God." (Romans 8:14)

Our Catholic Character

The Holy Spirit leads us to better understand God's will for us. We cooperate with the Spirit by developing habits of prayer that deepen our love and understanding of Jesus. One spiritual practice of prayerful reflection is called the "virtuous circle." It begins with reflection, which leads to gratitude, which leads to service. Service leads you back to reflection. When we practice the virtuous circle, we open ourselves to God's grace in a profound way.

Father Paul Brian Campbell explains how this process helped him. When he was teaching at Le Moyne College in Syracuse, New York, he loved the enthusiasm of his students but reflected that something was missing. "I had little pastoral contact with the elderly. This reflection led me to volunteer at a local hospice." At the hospice, Campbell cleaned the house or chatted with the residents and their families. "I quickly learned that I was getting far more than I was giving," says Campbell. "The quiet and cheerful professionalism of the hospice staff, the dignity accorded to the dying residents and the care and compassion that was evident made a profound impression on me."

The Seal of Confirmation

PEOPLE often try to get confirmation for things such as facts, reservations, news, statistics, dates, and times of events.

We want to verify or prove what we seek to confirm. Once we confirm something, we don't need to confirm it again. It's done.

The word *confirmation*, whose Latin root means "to strengthen," is the name of a sacrament in the Catholic Church. The Sacrament of Confirmation places a spiritual mark on us that cannot be taken away, and so the sacrament is administered only once.

Sealed with the Spirit

The Sacraments of Baptism and Confirmation are closely tied together. Baptism welcomes us into the Church, and Confirmation strengthens us to live as full members of the Church. As with Baptism, there is no specified age when one can receive Confirmation, although many people are confirmed when they are young adults.

In order to receive the Sacrament of Confirmation, you must be in the state of grace. Additionally, you must want to receive the sacrament, profess your belief in the Catholic faith, and be ready to join with Jesus Christ in proclaiming the Kingdom of God.

As part of the Rite of Confirmation, the bishop places oil, called **Chrism,** on the forehead of the baptized person saying, "Be sealed with the Gift of the Holy Spirit." Confirmation ties us more closely to the Body of Christ. It helps us be witnesses to the Christian faith in the things we say and do. Confirmation involves us more closely in the Church's mission. In the Sacrament of Confirmation, the Holy Spirit fills us and charges us with helping the Church carry out its mission.

SACRED ART

Pablo Picasso, (1881–1973) a Spaniard, was one of the great artists of the 20th century. In 1952 while living in Vallauris, France, he painted the walls and ceiling of a 12th century chapel, which is now a museum. The full work is called *War and Peace*. The portion shown here is quite large and situated at the end of a room. For Picasso the dove was a symbol of peace. Notice the different colors of the figures and their positions in relation to the dove. At Pentecost the presence of the Holy Spirit is associated with fire and a dove. At Confirmation the Holy Spirit strengthens us to proclaim Christ to all the nations of the world.

The Four Corners of the World, Pablo Picasso, 1952–54.

Improved Vision

The Holy Spirit inspires us to see God's dream for us and for the world. We gain a vision of the kind of world God wants us to have. Jesus proclaimed the Kingdom of God in both word and deed.

➡ By curing the sick, he showed that the kingdom will be a place of health and wholeness.

➡ By raising the dead to life, he showed that it will be a place in which all life is respected.

➡ By caring for those in need and society's outcasts, he showed that in the kingdom, everyone will be respected and have what they need.

Guided by the Holy Spirit, we envision a better world and gain strength and inspiration to make the vision a reality.

Be Sent

When the disciples received the Holy Spirit, they embarked on a mission. Jesus sent them into the world to proclaim his message. We, too, are sent into the world at various times and in various ways. We are sent off to school or to camp. Later we may be sent off to college or into the world to find work. In addition to being sent in a literal sense, God invites us to grow spiritually, moving beyond our comfort zone into what we can become with God's help. The Holy Spirit inspires us to be the person God created us to be.

Be You

After you receive Confirmation, the Church's mission becomes your mission. As many people as there are in the Body of Christ reflects how many ways there are to fulfill that mission. God gives each of us unique spiritual gifts, and when we exercise those gifts—skills in helping people, talents for creativity, intelligence, or compassion—we honor God's gifts to us. Jesus tells us in the Sermon on the Mount, "Just so, your light must shine before others, that they may see your good deeds and glorify your heavenly Father." (Matthew 5:16)

Explore

Past Meets Present

PAST: Saint Julie Billiart (1751–1816) served the Church's mission by using her talent for teaching to spread the Catholic faith. Because the French government suppressed the Catholic Church at this time in history, she could have been arrested. However, she did not let fear stop her from telling others about Christ. Eventually she founded the Sisters of Notre Dame to care for orphans, to educate poor girls, and to train Christian teachers.

PRESENT: The Sisters of Notre Dame are an international congregation of Catholic women religious who are committed to acting as witnesses to God's loving care and goodness. They use gifts and talents received from the Holy Spirit in various ministries. Some ways they serve include educating children and adults, assisting the poor, ministering to refugees, or working as doctors, nurses, social workers, artists, or musicians. Their work continues to spread. Their first mission in Central America began in 2008, and in 2010 they welcomed their first novices to missions in Mozambique and the Philippines.

Study Corner

DEFINE

Chrism

REMEMBER

Confirmation ties us more closely to the Body of Christ. Confirmation helps us be witnesses to the Christian faith in the things we say and do.

Stretching Our Wings

Through prayer the Holy Spirit helps us stretch our wings, giving us the strength and grace to follow God's call.

At this time in your life, you take on greater responsibility. You embrace the positive values you've learned and begin to think for yourself. You begin to stretch your wings, try on new ways to think and act, and dream new dreams. During this time of great personal growth, ask the Holy Spirit to help you know God's will for you.

Prayer to the Holy Spirit

Leader: Let us pray to the Holy Spirit for help to know God's will for us. Let us pray that we follow God's will with a generous spirit.

All: Come, Holy Spirit, fill our hearts and kindle in us the fire of your love.

Side 1: Come, Holy Spirit, open our minds and hearts to hear God's voice and to know God's will for us.

Side 2: Come, Holy Spirit, help us know God's plan for the world and do our part to make it happen.

Side 1: Come, Holy Spirit, make us generous in using our gifts and talents to serve God's kingdom here on earth.

Side 2: Come, Holy Spirit, help us treat others with dignity and respect others as we begin to stretch our wings.

All: With faith and trust in the Holy Spirit, we ask God to hear and grant our prayers, which we make in Jesus' name. Amen.

WHERE Do I Fit In?

Confirmation is the sacrament that fulfills the grace we receive in Baptism. It seals, or confirms, this grace through the seven Gifts of the Holy Spirit. As confirmed members of the Catholic Church, we each accept our role as a disciple of Christ, fully participating in public worship, in the celebration of the sacraments, and in service to the Kingdom of God. In Confirmation we go forth to spread God's Word with others.

by Meredith Gould

My Way to Confirmation

I grew up in the Jewish faith before becoming a Roman Catholic. I waited nearly a decade between my Baptism and my Confirmation. I was already an adult, but only if you added up years logged on the planet. I was hardly a grown-up—at least, not in the spiritual sense. More growing would have to happen before I'd want to be confirmed. I had to figure out some stuff.

For one thing, I questioned why Confirmation was considered a Sacrament of Initiation. Initiation into what? After all, I thought, Baptism is what "makes" us Christian. When I was a teen, I celebrated my *bat mitzvah*, the occasion when a young Jewish woman becomes a "daughter of the commandment," at Temple Sinai. The preparation included learning more about Jewish beliefs, values, ethics, and history. It also included service and social justice projects, something that has become a key feature of Catholic Confirmation preparation.

Although the Holy Spirit is never mentioned explicitly, I noticed that *bar* and *bat mitzvah* ceremonies are scheduled to coincide with Shavuot. One of five "appointed feasts of the Lord," Shavuot commemorates God giving the Law (Torah) to the Israelites on Mount Sinai—something I consider a big-time Holy Spirit event. And what Greek word for Shavuot appears in Christian Scripture? *Pentecost*!

MEREDITH GOULD, PhD, is an author, blogger, and communications strategist for faith-based organizations.

These are some dots I connected over 10 years. I welcomed the Holy Spirit to show up in my life. I spent the years between Baptism and Confirmation seeking and finding comfort in the Eucharist, support in my parish, and finding God in community service.

Once, after Reconciliation, a priest told me, "For your penance, keep praying 'Come, Holy Spirit.'" I did, and I managed to get "un-confused" to the point of seeking out my parish's deacon. "I believe my Easter is coming up this year," I told him. At age 51, I understood finally what God was offering in calling me to complete the Sacraments of Initiation and celebrate Confirmation. I had returned to the sacraments, regularly celebrating the Sacrament of Reconciliation and the Eucharist, and in that state of grace, finally received the Sacrament of Confirmation.

A Big Impact

The author states that she was ready to declare publicly her commitment to being a Roman Catholic much later in life. Even though Jesus told his disciples, "Be not afraid," she had some self-doubts until she received the gift of faith. On a separate sheet of paper, tell how you might use each Gift of the Holy Spirit following your Confirmation.

wisdom   piety   understanding   counsel
knowledge   fear of the Lord   fortitude

What's What?

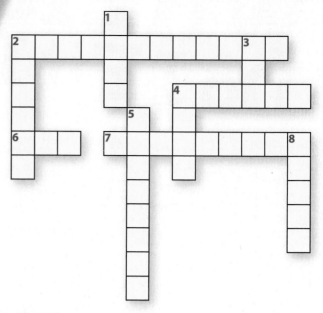

Finish each sentence to complete the crossword.

ACROSS

2 We receive the Holy Spirit at Baptism and _____ . (PAGE 190)

4 At Confirmation, the bishop says "Be _____ with the Gift of the Holy Spirit." (PAGE 190)

6 In his Sermon on the Mount, Jesus told the people, "Just so, your light must shine before others, that they may _____ your good deeds and glorify your heavenly Father." (PAGE 191)

7 Confirmation strengthens us so we can be _____ to the Christian faith in all we say and do. (PAGE 190)

DOWN

1 The Holy Spirit descended on the disciples with tongues as of _____ . (PAGE 189)

2 The Holy Spirit empowered the disciples to deliver the Good News of the risen _____ to the world. (PAGE 188)

3 At Confirmation the bishop anoints the forehead of the person receiving the sacrament with an _____ called Chrism. (PAGE 190)

4 In Confirmation, we too are _____ to be part of the Church's mission to continue the works of Jesus Christ. (PAGE 191)

5 We celebrate Pentecost as the _____ of the Church. (PAGE 188)

8 There are _____ Gifts of the Holy Spirit. (PAGE 189)

Say What?

Know the definition of these terms.

Chrism

Gifts of the Holy Spirit

Good News

Now What?

Reflect on God's dream for the world. What is one thing you can do this week to cooperate with his will and help build the Kingdom of God?

_____

_____

_____

_____

_____

_____

Respond

We Are Called and Sent

Think of a time when you were clearly on the wrong path morally or spiritually until you got turned back around. Did someone or something intervene to get you back on the right track? Who or what made the difference for you? Have you ever been that person for someone else?

PRAYER

Dear Lord, sometimes I need direction. Show me what I can do to spread your love to others and to make the world a better place.

Saint Paul Sees the Light

HAVE you ever had an experience that changed how you look at your own life? Maybe you met a new group of friends, were inspired by a book or movie, celebrated a victory, or suffered a loss.

Saul, a young Jewish man who lived during the time of Jesus, faced a situation that made him look at himself with new eyes. Saul was a brilliant student who wanted to be a Jewish teacher. He studied the first five books of the Bible, which are known as the Torah, or "the Law." These revered books in the Jewish faith tell the story of creation, of Abraham's faith, and of the liberation of the Hebrew people from slavery. They give the fundamental rules of how to follow God's will.

As a Jewish Pharisee, Saul believed in strict observance of the Law, both for himself and for all Jews. He was upset when a community of Jews believed that Jesus was the long-awaited Messiah. The Jewish leaders at the time denied that Jesus was the Messiah foretold by the prophets. To defend his religion, Saul led a persecution against those Jewish followers of Jesus in Jerusalem.

Our Catholic Character

As Catholics we are always being called to conversion. All baptized Christians, not only those who live in religious orders, are called to live holy lives by practicing the virtues of **poverty, chastity,** and **obedience.** Poverty requires living without an attachment to material goods. Chastity means respecting our bodies and the bodies of others. Obedience means respecting the authority of parents, teachers, and civil authorities.

Saul Encounters the Risen Jesus

As Saul continued his persecution of Jewish Christians throughout the land, he traveled to Damascus, where he encountered the risen Jesus Christ. "Saul, Saul, why are you persecuting me?" (Acts of the Apostles 9:4) Saul, shocked and blinded, had to be led by the hand to Damascus, where he fasted and prayed. This shattering experience led to Saul's conversion, his move from disbelief to belief. He began proclaiming that salvation had been won through the life, Death, Resurrection, and Ascension of Jesus Christ. Saul became Paul the Apostle, the greatest missionary of the early Church. Paul began to see the rules that he had learned as a youth in a new light. He recognized that the human race inherited the consequences of the sin of Adam and Eve that we call Original Sin. Because of Original Sin, we are stuck in a tar pit, and try as we might, we cannot free ourselves.

Helpless to Help Ourselves

If we get stuck in a real tar pit, we might panic and thrash around wildly until we give up, exhausted. Or our mind might consider dozens of survival rules, searching for one that will help. If we had a lever, we could attempt to pry ourselves out of the pit. Yet all our knowledge and wishful thinking are useless because being so deeply mired in the tar, we are helpless to free ourselves. Paul came to realize we have another choice.

Salvation Through Jesus Christ

Paul discovered that God longs for the human family to be freed. God has freely given us salvation through Jesus Christ by reaching out to us and reconciling us to himself. In Jesus, God provides us with the lever to pull ourselves out of the tar pit of sin. What we can't do for ourselves, God does for us. Through faith and Baptism, we receive the grace that we need to take away Original Sin and to live a new life in Jesus Christ. We also receive the daily graces we need to live as God wants.

God Makes Things Right

When we accept responsibility for hurting someone, we are willing to make the situation right. We may ask the person what we can do to heal the relationship—what we can do to make it right.

Paul says that the same thing happens in our relationship with God. Because of Original Sin, we can't make things right with God by ourselves. The good news is that God has provided a way to repair the relationship and reconcile us to himself. Paul calls this saving action of God **justification.** Justification is the action of the Holy Spirit in Baptism that cleanses us from sin and continually gives us the grace to walk in right relationship with God. Justification restores the right relationship between God and an individual. This right relationship between God and a person is called **righteousness.** Justification, then, is the act of God that gives us righteousness.

Called to Conversion

Like Saul, Jesus calls us to conversion because it is only through a change of heart that we can enter the Kingdom of God. It is by faith in the Gospel and through our Baptism that we gain salvation, the forgiveness of sins, and the gift of new life.

Conversion is a lifelong pursuit. We can practice conversion daily by turning away from sin and choosing God. We can choose God by turning away from selfishness and choosing generosity. We can turn away from lies and choose to be honest. We can turn away from temptation and turn to prayer.

Conversion is a central theme of the Lord's Prayer. We recognize God as our loving Father and ask his help to do his will. We ask to be forgiven by him and promise to forgive others. When we pray, the Holy Spirit opens our hearts to love God more deeply and serve him more fully. In true conversion we find the strength to extend the love of God to others.

Explore

SACRED ART

Masaccio included this image of Saint Paul as part of a large altarpiece for a church in Pisa, Italy. It depicts the saint in noble robes while holding a sword, an indication of his martyrdom since he was executed with a sword during the reign of Nero. Paul is carrying a book, which represents the Epistles he wrote. The 13 Epistles credited to Saint Paul make up one-fourth of the New Testament.

Saint Paul, detail from altarpiece, Masaccio, 1426.

Letters of Saint Paul

SAINT PAUL was not a professor who wrote essays on theological topics. He was an Apostle, one who preached the Gospel and taught the Christian community. Paul was a missionary and a pastor.

God called Paul to a life of faithfulness and commitment. Paul channeled his great yearning for God into a constructive, holy purpose. For the rest of his life, Saint Paul preached the living Word, guided growing Christian communities, and realized his life's true mission.

After Saint Paul had established a new church in a town or region, he would communicate with the new Christians with letters, the Epistles. He wrote Epistles in response to problems that had arisen mainly in the Christian communities that he himself had founded.

The New Testament contains many Epistles from Saint Paul. All together, 13 Epistles bear Paul's name, meaning that they were written personally by him or, in a few cases, by one of his followers. The Church accepts the Epistles as inspired by the Holy Spirit, and they are a wealth of counsel and wisdom that speak to us today.

Sincerely Yours

Paul, who experienced conversion and the Lord's forgiveness on the road to Damascus, never claimed to be perfect. He readily admitted his own faults to the people to whom he was writing, and he thanked friends and fellow believers who encouraged him. Paul possessed a humility and a humanity to which people could relate.

About the year A.D. 51, Paul wrote the first of two Epistles to the Christians in Thessalonica, which is currently the second largest city in Greece. Paul's letter to Thessalonica, the first Christian community he founded, was the first piece of New Testament literature written. Over the next 10 or more years, Paul traveled widely, preached, and wrote to other communities he had founded. During his many travels, Paul covered more than 14,000 miles.

A Lasting Message

Saint Paul's words are meant for us every bit as much as they were meant for the Christians of the first century. Why should we read letters that were written centuries ago? We face many of the same issues and struggles that Paul addressed almost 2,000 years ago. God's law and the principles of truth don't change.

While Paul wrote about doctrine and faith, he also wrote about fundamentals of Christian behavior, Christian virtue, and the best way to conduct oneself as a follower of Christ.

> "Put on then, as God's chosen ones, holy and beloved, heartfelt compassion, kindness, humility, gentleness, and patience, bearing with one another and forgiving one another, if one has a grievance against another; as the Lord has forgiven you, so must you also do."
>
> *Colossians 3:12–13*

Paul spoke with authority. His Epistles could be passionate and poetic, urgent, direct, and frank. The care and concern Paul had for his fellow Christians came through loud and clear in his letters.

It comes through to us today, too, as we read or listen to his letters in Scripture. We receive instruction, guidance, and support. Paul writes as one of us, in language that reflects the strength of his faith.

Called to Matrimony

Paul wrote that love was the preeminent gift from God. Many people who get married in the Church draw from Paul's first letter to the Corinthians as a reading in their wedding ceremony. "So faith, hope, love remain, these three; but the greatest of these is love." (1 Corinthians 13:13)

God created man and woman in his own image. As descendants of Adam and Eve, we are capable of entering into communion with other people through self-giving. This is most evident in the Sacrament of **Matrimony.** Love can call a man and a woman together for a shared mission in life. The selfless love and lifelong commitment between a man and a woman are signs of the enduring love that God has for us. The Sacrament of Matrimony, the lifelong union between husband and wife, is a sign of the union between Christ and the Church. This love is, in fact, the sign of the sacrament. The fidelity promised and kept between a wife and a husband reflects the faithfulness of God in his covenant with his people. This covenant was God's promise to always be with his people and care for them.

Called to Holy Orders

Men who receive **Holy Orders** continue the mission entrusted by Christ to his Apostles. Three degrees, or levels, of Holy Orders exist: **deacons,** priests, and bishops. Bishops, who enjoy the fullness of the priesthood, are the successors of the Apostles. As Christ's representatives, they are ordained to teach, sanctify, and govern. A bishop is the head of a diocese and can preside at all seven sacraments. Assisting the bishops are priests who, by virtue of their ordination, act in the person of Christ. They preach the Gospel, shepherd the faithful, and celebrate the sacraments—except for ordination, which is exclusively reserved for bishops to celebrate. Married deacons are ordained to a ministry of service and are authorized to baptize, preach, and preside at weddings and funerals when there is no Mass. There are also unmarried deacons who have taken a vow of chastity and serve in this capacity as a step toward ordination to the priesthood.

Both clergy and the laity have vocations in life— that is, ways in which God calls them to serve, each according to his or her particular gifts. All sacraments lead us to Jesus and the love that God pours out to us through him. We can never lead a life of holiness on our own. We need the saving power of Christ. The Sacraments of Matrimony and Holy Orders are called Sacraments at the Service of Communion. Through vocations as clergy or laity, these witnesses to Christ's presence in the world discover a call to serve others.

Study Corner

DEFINE

Matrimony
Holy Orders
deacons

REMEMBER

Paul's Epistles to early Christian communities provided guidance on topics of faith, virtue, daily conduct, and issues that still apply today. The Sacrament of Matrimony is a sign of the union between Christ and his Church. Men who receive Holy Orders continue the mission entrusted by Christ to his Apostles.

Accepting the Challenge

Jesus calls us to conversion. It is an essential part of the proclamation of the Kingdom of God.

Baptism is the event of our conversion. In the Gospel and through Baptism, we renounce evil and gain salvation. Jesus' call to ongoing conversion is addressed to us throughout our lives. We recognize it in the Lord's Prayer. The task of conversion is the movement of a contrite heart. The word *contrite* means "sorrow or remorse for sin." In prayer we are drawn and moved by grace to respond to the merciful love of God, who loved us first.

Called to Conversion

Leader: Christians who knew Paul before his conversion had to change their attitudes and learn to trust him. Those who heard Paul preach and were baptized experienced conversion to new life in Christ. God challenges each of us to ongoing conversion in our lives too.

Together pray the Lord's Prayer.

Side 1: You do amazing things, O God. Your ways and your thoughts are far beyond what we can imagine. You call people like Paul and like us to be followers of your Son, Jesus. Help us be true to our baptismal commitment to be the light of Christ in our world. Strengthen our desire to be open to your call and to be willing to accept your challenge to change our lives in order to stay close to you.

Side 2: We ask you also for the grace to allow other people to change and not to hold their pasts against them. Help us remember that as we grow closer to you, the change in our lives will have the same ripple effect in the lives of others that Paul's conversion did. May the grace we received at our Baptism be the strength we need to accept your challenge to conversion throughout our lives.

All: Amen.

WHERE Do I Fit In?

Our communication says a lot about who we are, but more importantly, it can let people know *whose* we are—God's! Let's strive to communicate the way of Jesus with peace, kindness, generosity, humility, and forgiveness in all that we say and do.

by Bret Nicholaus

Of Faith and Phones

I took a course in college called Basic Communication. I most clearly remember the words that the professor wrote on the board the very first day. *You cannot <u>not</u> communicate. Everything you say, everything you do, everything you wear—all of it communicates something about you.* Even silence can send a powerful message. It can tell people that you're upset, focused, bored, or a dozen other things.

In today's world, much of our communication is based on technology. Only sleep stops many of us from endless tweets, texts, calls, and e-mails. As followers of Jesus, what should our communication "look" like? Should our typed or spoken messages communicate something different *because* we are Christians? Saint Paul, in his letter to the Ephesians, provides instructions for Christian living that can be easily applied to our communication.

> All bitterness, fury, anger, shouting, and reviling must be removed from you, along with all malice, [And] be kind to one another, compassionate, forgiving one another as God has forgiven you in Christ.
>
> *Ephesians 4:31–32*

Here are things I consider in my own daily communication: Am I using technology to lift people up or to bring them down? Do my texts and tweets reflect the fact that Jesus is Lord of my life? Do my phone calls and e-mails shine Christ's love into the hearts and minds of others?

BRET NICHOLAUS is the author of more than 25 books, including the national best seller *The Conversation Piece*.

The Best Text

Text messages generally consist of few words. Write a reply that reflects a Christian mind-set for each situation.

 I can't believe Mike is wearing those ugly shoes!

_____

_____

_____

 I have no intention of speaking to Leticia ever again.

_____

_____

_____

 What can you do to help at the food pantry tonight?

_____

_____

_____

What's What?

Complete each sentence with details from the text.

1 Saul led a _____ against followers of Jesus in Jerusalem. (PAGE 196)

_____

2 As he was traveling to Damascus, Saul encountered the risen _____. (PAGE 196)

_____

3 The experience of meeting Jesus led to Saul's _____. (PAGE 196)

_____

4 Saul became Paul the Apostle, the greatest _____ in the early Church. (PAGE 196)

_____

5 Through faith and _____, we receive the grace that we need to take away Original Sin. (PAGE 197)

_____

6 The action of the Holy Spirit in Baptism that cleanses us from sin is called _____. (PAGE 197)

_____

7 We can read Paul's Epistles in the _____. (PAGE 198)

_____

8 The Sacrament of _____ is a sign of the union between Christ and the Church. (PAGE 199)

_____

9 The Sacrament of _____ continues the work begun by the Apostles. (PAGE 199)

_____

10 Three levels of Holy Orders are _____, _____, and _____. (PAGE 199)

_____

_____

_____

Say What?

Know the definitions of these terms.

chastity	Matrimony
deacons	obedience
Holy Orders	poverty
justification	righteousness

Now What?

What is one habit you could change that would make you a better disciple of Christ?

_____

_____

_____

_____

_____

_____

_____

_____

_____

_____

_____

_____

Respond

Jesus Calls Us to Eternal Life

Some things in life can be proven, and other things we take on the testimony of those we trust. Who is helping you make a plan for your future? Why do you trust what this person has to say?

PRAYER

You are my hope, Lord. Increase my trust in you.

The Struggle Between Good and Evil

WHEN you want to make a point, you might use descriptive language to describe what's going on. "I have *tons* of homework!" "Coach is *killing* us with those wind sprints!" You intend to paint an image in someone's head although you don't expect the person to interpret your words literally.

The Book of Revelation is one of the most misunderstood books in the Bible because it contains language and descriptions that are not supposed to be taken literally. The Book of Revelation was written during a time of crisis. Domitian, the Roman emperor from A.D. 81 to 96, was persecuting Christians. The Book of Revelation was intended as a message of support, encouraging Christians who had doubts about their future to remain faithful and strong in the midst of threat and oppression.

Good Versus Evil

The Book of Revelation is **apocalyptic literature,** a form of writing that uses symbolic language and imagery to describe the eternal struggle between good and evil. The author of Revelation, who refers to himself as John, uses extravagant language to describe a vision revealed to him.

Revelation, when interpreted in a literal and factual way, can be seen as a prediction of the end of the world—something it was never intended to be. In fact, despite disturbing language and imagery, the conclusion of the Book of Revelation is uplifting, a declaration of the everlasting reign of God and his defeat of evil. It says the forces of good always will prevail. The author of Revelation is not describing literal events. Rather, we read the author's vision while keeping symbolism in mind, recognizing that our future, though uncertain, holds the promise of everlasting salvation in Jesus.

As a message of encouragement and hope to Christians during a crisis, the Book of Revelation told them to endure suffering with the confidence that God would prevail. The central message of this book was that the victory had already been won in Jesus Christ. This message is meant for us today as well. We also experience times of conflict in our hearts between the forces of good and evil, and we sometimes have doubts about our future.

Jesus gave us a vision of eternity when he spoke about the Kingdom of God. Our faith in this kingdom gives us the confidence to pray the closing words of Revelation and of the Bible, "Come, Lord Jesus!" (Revelation 22:20)

The final chapter of Revelation points to a beautiful future to which we can pin our hopes.

> I heard a loud voice from the throne saying, "Behold, God's dwelling is with the human race. He will dwell with them and they will be his people and God himself will always be with them [as their God]. He will wipe every tear from their eyes, and there shall be no more death or mourning, wailing or pain, [for] the old order has passed away."
>
> *Revelation 21:3–4*

Understanding Symbolic Language

Catholics believe that in matters of religious truth, the Bible is free from error. Everything the Bible teaches about God and our relationship with God is true. At the same time, Catholics are not fundamentalists. We do not interpret every word or passage of the Bible literally. We recognize that the Bible contains many styles, or **literary forms,** of writing, such as history, proverbs, letters, parables, wisdom sayings, and poetry. At times stories and myth were seen as the vehicles through which the most essential and sacred truths of people were told and passed on. At other times apocalyptic literature, such as Revelation, was widely popular and seen as an appropriate way to reveal God's Word.

All forms of writing in the Bible have a sole purpose—to relay the truth found in God's Word.

Some forms work better than others to help listeners connect ordinary ideas or events in their lives in a way that reveals a deep spiritual truth or lesson in faith. For example, the story of Jonah and the whale is a divinely inspired parable that reveals what happens when a person tries to run away from God's call. When we run from God, as Jonah did, we encounter isolation. And even in our isolation, God can and will find us. The point of Jonah's story is not whether a man can factually survive in the belly of a large fish for three days. The greater truth is found in understanding our relationship with God.

Finding Truth

God speaks to us in sacred Scripture through the inspired writing of human authors. We need to study and seek what the authors intended to say and what God wants to show through their words. The writing of Scripture didn't happen by God dictating the message word by word as if to a scribe or secretary. The authors wrote while using their talents—and even their limitations—to convey God's message in the forms and language of their times, under the guidance and inspiration of the Holy Spirit.

We rely on the guidance of our pastors, teachers, catechists, and Scripture scholars to help us understand the meaning of Revelation and other books of the Bible. The pope and the bishops, known as the Magisterium, teach and guide the Church in matters of doctrine and morals, providing direction to the whole Church.

Explore

Study Corner

DEFINE

apocalyptic literature
literary forms

REMEMBER

To understand the Book of Revelation, we recognize that its literary form relies on symbols and images. It is not intended to be interpreted literally. In the Book of Revelation, God claims eternal victory over the forces of evil.

Revelation 14:14, *The Reaper, Vision of Armageddon*, German School, ca. 1530.

Assumption of the Blessed Mother

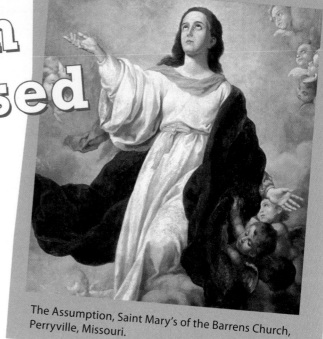

The Assumption, Saint Mary's of the Barrens Church, Perryville, Missouri.

WHAT happens to us after we die? The minds and imaginations of humankind have always pondered this question.

You have probably seen movies or TV shows that dramatize what the afterlife is like, and you may have read novels that deal with the subject. These are fictions, enjoyable in their own right as entertainment. To seriously consider and discuss what God has prepared for those who love him, we need to turn to the teachings of the Church, such as the Assumption of Mary, the mother of Jesus.

Our Catholic Character

In his encyclical *The Hope of Salvation (Spe Salvi)*, Pope Benedict XVI wrote that "The last Judgment is not primarily an image of terror, but an image of hope." Catholics believe that immediately after death, each person comes before God for an individual (particular) judgment and enters heaven, Purgatory, or hell. The **Last Judgment** refers to the end of time when Christ will return in glory and all will be raised from the dead to stand before God, at which time our relationship with him will be revealed to all. Jesus himself describes this last (general) judgment in Matthew 25:31–32, describing a shepherd separating the sheep from the goats. The message of the Last Judgment calls people to conversion so they are not separated from God forever.

Taken to Heaven

The root of the word *assume* means "to take," so when Mary was taken into heaven, both body and soul, we refer to it as her **Assumption.** We celebrate the Feast of the Assumption on August 15. In 1950 Pope Pius XII declared the beliefs of our Catholic faith. "By the authority of our Lord Jesus Christ, of the Blessed Apostles Peter and Paul, and by our own authority, we pronounce, declare, and define it to be a divinely revealed dogma: that the Immaculate Mother of God, the ever Virgin Mary, having completed the course of her earthly life, was assumed body and soul into heavenly glory." This is an **infallible** declaration, meaning that the Church accepts the decree as truth informed and inspired by the Holy Spirit of God.

Body and Soul

The Bible offers no information on how, when, or where Mary's life on earth ended. Pope Pius XII's decree states that Mary had "completed the course of her earthly life," meaning that her holy mission on earth was complete. The decree also clarifies that Mary did not ascend into heaven, as Jesus did; she was assumed, or taken, into heaven. (Luke 24:50–53) Mary's Assumption reflects her unique relationship to Jesus as the Mother of God. It also is an indication that believers in Jesus and in his Resurrection can anticipate eternal, never-ending life after death with God, granted to those who die as God's friends.

Communion of Saints

As the mother of Jesus, Mary holds an exalted place in the **Communion of Saints.** The Communion of Saints includes all who have been saved in Jesus Christ, whether living or dead. We are united in this union through our one faith and one Lord, whom we receive in the Eucharist.

A saint is not someone who is perfect. No one is perfect. Through God's grace, however, saints have received what we hope to receive one day after we complete the course of our earthly life—God's promised salvation. A canonized or declared saint is a person whom the Church believes now lives with God in heaven. By declaring a person a saint, the Church acknowledges God's grace at work in this person's life as an authentic witness to Christ. Because of the abundance of God's grace in their lives, the saints—just like Mary—can intercede before God on behalf of the living.

On November 1 we remember all these holy men and women recognized by the Church as saints. There are, however, many individuals who live now with God in heaven who haven't been officially declared saints by the Church. On All Saints Day, we also honor and remember these undeclared saints, for their prayers benefit us too. When Saint Paul wrote to the early Christian communities, he sometimes addressed the people as saints. Saint Paul was acknowledging their holy lives and their destiny—salvation through Christ.

What happens after we die? If we serve God as Mary did, faithfully and entirely, dedicating our lives to God, we anticipate salvation and a life of happiness in heaven. At death our life is changed, not ended. We know this by recalling Jesus' and Martha's conversation before the raising of Lazarus. Jesus assures Martha that her brother will rise again. Martha replies in faith, "I know he will rise, in the resurrection on the last day." Then Jesus identifies himself as the Resurrection and the Life. (John 11:17–27)

The soul is immortal, and we look forward to the final resurrection of the dead at the end of the world. In heaven we become part of the Communion of Saints.

Past Meets Present

PAST: In 1531, Juan Diego, a native Mexican, was walking to Mass when the Blessed Mother, dressed as an Aztec princess, appeared to him. She spoke to Juan Diego in his native language and sent him to the bishop of Mexico with a request to build a church on the site. When Juan Diego told the bishop, he demanded a sign before he would believe the story. The Blessed Mother told Juan Diego to pick roses on the site. Although it was December and freezing, roses were in full bloom. Juan Diego gathered the roses in his tilma, a cactus-cloth cape. When he shook them out in front of the bishop, an image of Our Lady of Guadalupe was imprinted on Juan Diego's tilma.

PRESENT: Saint Juan Diego's tilma with the image of Our Lady hangs in the Basilica of Our Lady of Guadalupe at Tepeyac. Millions from around the world visit the site every year. Scientific investigations cannot explain the way in which the image is imprinted on the cloth or why the tilma has not decayed more than 480 years later. The Feast of Our Lady of Guadalupe is celebrated on December 12.

Explore

Study Corner

DEFINE

Last Judgment
Assumption
infallible
Communion of Saints

REMEMBER

Through Mary we know that those who serve God can look forward to eternal life with him. Mary holds an exalted place in the Communion of Saints.

Enter the Kingdom

When we live in close relationship with God, we build the Kingdom of God right now as we wait for its fullness in the future.

When we practice virtues, we stay on the right path. Virtues are like good habits that become more familiar to us the more we use them. The **Theological Virtues**—faith, hope, and charity—are the most important virtues in our lives because they are gifts from God and lead to God. The virtue of faith helps us believe in him. We trust in God's promises and rely on the help of the grace of the Holy Spirit. In the virtue of hope, we desire the Kingdom of God and eternal life as our happiness. Charity is the virtue by which we love God above all things and love our neighbor as ourselves for the love of God.

We can cultivate other virtues by ourselves through education and positive actions. When we act with prudence, justice, fortitude, and temperance, we live the Cardinal Virtues. Although these virtues do not relate directly to the living God in the way that the Theological Virtues do, by incorporating them into our daily actions, they help us live Christian lives.

Prayer for Faith, Hope, and Charity

Leader: If you want to enter the Kingdom of God, you have to be a person of faith.

All: O God, we freely give ourselves to you. Help us nurture the gift of faith you have given us by trusting in your Word, by listening to what the Church teaches, and by putting our faith into action.

Leader: If you want to enter the Kingdom of God, you have to be a person of hope.

All: O God, without the gift of hope, our lives would have no meaning. Help us share our hope with others and always look forward to the lasting joy and happiness of living with you forever.

Leader: If you want to enter the Kingdom of God, you have to be a person of love.

All: O God, when we look at your Son, we learn what it means to love others. Help us love you above all things and show your love to all we meet.

Leader: Let us join together in prayer.

All: Loving God, we want to be eternally united with you. We know our need for you and count on your help. The virtues of faith, hope, and love are your gifts to us. May we grow in our relationship with you as we practice them in our daily lives. We ask this in Jesus' name. Amen.

WHERE Do I Fit In?

Jesus made powerful people nervous because he spoke truths that could be hard to hear. His teaching challenged people, institutions, and the status quo. When is it our Christian duty to take a stand against harmful policies?

by Anna Boekstegen

Witness for Peace in Haiti

When I was in Haiti in 1993, I experienced how subversive it can be to really live the Gospel message. At that time the Haitian people suffered not only from extreme poverty but also because their hope for democracy had been squashed by a military coup in 1991 against the popular elected president Jean-Bertrand Aristide, a champion of the poor. Aristide was sent into exile, and his followers were persecuted, severely beaten, or killed. Many were no longer able to stay in their own homes for fear of being killed by the Macoutes and Zenglendos in the service of the military. I had learned a lot about Haiti from a friend who had worked in a rural parish in northern Haiti for more than 20 years. She had to leave Haiti when the military took over because of threats to her life.

I wanted to help the Haitian people. When I heard about the Witness for Peace volunteer program through Pax Christi, the national Catholic peace organization, I decided to go. Witness for Peace organized teams of human rights observers to document the abuses and let the world know about them. I was part of a team of three, stationed in Cap Haitien, the second largest city in northern Haiti. We met people who had been severely beaten or were afraid of being killed or abused. The pastors of local parishes told us about their parishioners who were literally hiding in the mountains because they were not safe in their own homes.

ANNA BOEKSTEGEN is a retired French, Latin, and German high school teacher.

One of these pastors was Father Rex. He himself had been threatened and was living in hiding. He saw his ministry in the footsteps of Jesus' teaching. He took seriously his ministry among his poor illiterate parishioners. Father Rex's actions were considered subversive by the military because people started to think for themselves and to organize.

> "He has sent me to proclaim liberty to captives
>   and recovery of sight to the blind,
>   to let the oppressed go free,
>   and to proclaim a year acceptable to the Lord."
>
> *Luke 4:18–19*

As it turns out, in 1994 the United States intervened, and President Aristide was able to return. Did our work of documenting abuses contribute to this outcome? We don't know. Perhaps it did.

Response to Injustice

Look through newspapers or magazines to find articles about social injustice around the world. Work with a partner to choose one situation. Think of a Christian response or solution that imitates the teachings of Jesus, and report your ideas to the group.

What's What?

Write the letter of the choice that best matches each clue.

1 _____ August 15

2 _____ November 1

3 _____ December 12

4 _____ Revelation

5 _____ the Blessed Mother

6 _____ John

7 _____ Communion of Saints

8 _____ fundamentalists

a. book in the Bible that describes God's triumph over evil (PAGE 204)

b. the author, inspired by the Holy Spirit, of the Book of Revelation (PAGE 204)

c. people who interpret every word in the Bible literally (PAGE 205)

d. assumed into heaven body and soul (PAGE 206)

e. Feast of the Assumption (PAGE 206)

f. includes all who have been saved in Jesus Christ (PAGE 207)

g. Feast of all Saints (PAGE 207)

h. Feast of Our Lady of Guadalupe (PAGE 207)

Respond

Say What?

Know the definitions of these terms.

apocalyptic literature

Assumption

Communion of Saints

infallible

Last Judgment

literary forms

Theological Virtues

Now What?

How can you put a Theological Virtue into practice this week? List your ideas.

_____

_____

_____

_____

_____

_____

_____

_____

Celebrating Pentecost

THE feast of Pentecost is celebrated 50 days after Easter Sunday. It commemorates the day the Holy Spirit, sent by God, entered the Apostles' hearts and filled them with the strength and courage they needed to do God's work. We celebrate the gift of the Holy Spirit's presence among us on Pentecost.

In the Acts of the Apostles, we read that after Jesus ascended to heaven, the Apostles gathered together in a house. Suddenly, what appeared to be tongues of fire touched each of them. Filled with the Holy Spirit, they began to speak, and a crowd gathered outside the house. Members of the crowd, who represented many different nations, heard the Apostles speaking in their own language.

The Apostles, inspired by the Holy Spirit, began doing the work of the Church, calling the whole world to faith in Jesus. It took great courage and perseverance to act as witnesses to Jesus Christ, but the Good News eventually spread throughout the Roman Empire. With guidance from the Holy Spirit, the first Christian community grew.

Today, the Holy Spirit continues to inspire us to live our faith and carry out the mission of the Apostles—to spread Christianity throughout the world. The Holy Spirit makes us holy and helps us grow more like Christ as we act as his witnesses in the world.

> When have you faced a big challenge and felt hesitant or afraid to take action? Where did you find the strength and courage to do what you knew had to be done? How did you recognize the Holy Spirit's presence?

PRAYER

Thank you, Holy Spirit, for your gifts of courage and strength so I may live out my faith as a true witness of Christ.

The Holy Spirit Guides the Church

TIMES of change occur throughout your life, sometimes in rhythmic patterns just like the seasons. A school season begins, breaks, resumes, and ends. You may experience times of change in sports, entertainment, or family matters.

The Church celebrates seasons too. On the first Sunday of Advent, we celebrate the beginning of the Church year, remembering how God's people yearned for a Messiah. During the Christmas season, we celebrate the birth of Jesus, who is the fulfillment of God's promise to send a Savior. The Easter season is a 50-day celebration of the Resurrection of Jesus.

The Easter season comes to a close on the Feast of Pentecost, when we mark the beginning of the Church instituted by Jesus Christ. On this day we remember how a group of Jesus' followers, afraid and huddled together in a room, were filled with the Holy Spirit. The Spirit's coming fulfilled Jesus' promise that the Father would send them an Advocate, one who would be with them always.

On the night before he died, Jesus made a promise to the Apostles. Jesus knew they were worried about what would happen to them if he was arrested, or worse, put to death. The Apostles wondered what life would be like without Jesus there to lead them. Would he be completely gone from their lives after his Death and remain only as a mystery? They had followed Jesus and watched as he fed the hungry crowds, healed the sick, and walked on water. They listened as he spoke of his loving Father and described himself as the Good Shepherd. But now this life seemed to be coming to an end.

The Spirit

John's Gospel tells how Jesus spoke to the Apostles and calmed their worried hearts. He promised, "I will not leave you orphans; I will come to you. (John 14:18) Jesus explained, "The Advocate, the holy Spirit that the Father will send in my name—he will teach you everything and remind you of all that [I] told you." (John 14:26) This gift of the Holy Spirit would be another sign of the Father's love for them, just as the gift of the Son had been.

On the Jewish harvest feast of Pentecost, the Father sent the **Paraclete,** another name for the Holy Spirit. *Paraclete* is a Greek word that means "one who consoles or comforts, one who encourages or uplifts." Jesus kept his promise—the Spirit would remain with them and also with all of those who had come to believe, not just a chosen few.

The Holy Spirit would teach them everything, remind them of all that Jesus had said to them, and help them understand more fully Jesus Christ, the Messiah. With the inspiration of the Holy Spirit, the Apostles would continue Jesus' teaching through their preaching, writing, and actions. The successors of the Apostles, the bishops of the Church, continue this task for all generations until Jesus returns in glory. The mission of the bishops comes from the Holy Spirit in union with the Father and the Son.

Spirit Alive

The Holy Spirit is at the center of our lives, ready to motivate us at every moment to grow in holiness. When we allow ourselves to be led by the Holy Spirit, we are led by a God of strength and light. With this guidance, we will not go astray. The Holy Spirit helps us discern between good and evil and enlivens our lives of prayer. When we celebrate the sacraments, we are saved through the grace of the Holy Spirit.

In the Holy Spirit, we have a sure guide in our relationship with God and others. The Holy Spirit can help us live close to God and in loving relationship with those around us. We can pray the prayer of Saint John Vianney: "O God, send me thy Spirit to teach me what I am and what thou art."

Open Your Heart

To be open to the Holy Spirit means to allow him to enter into your life. Through prayer, the Holy Spirit teaches you to recognize and follow God's will. Whenever you pray the Lord's Prayer and say the words "thy will be done," you are practicing this openness. To be open to the Holy Spirit is to let go of your own willfulness. It means trusting in God's will, listening for what God wants you to do with your life, and learning how to make good choices.

What Is Truth?

Jesus promised to send the Spirit of truth. In Jesus' time there were two ways to talk about truth—the Hebrew way found in the Old Testament and the Greek way that would be reflected in the New Testament. The Hebrew view of truth was based on the reliability of the person speaking and that

Study Corner

DEFINE

Paraclete

REMEMBER

God fulfilled Jesus' promise to the Apostles by sending the Holy Spirit. They were filled with the faith and courage needed to spread his Word. Today we celebrate the strength given to us by the Holy Spirit when we live faithfully as Jesus' followers.

person's faithfulness to a relationship. This is what we mean when we say someone is true to his or her friends. The Greek view of truth was based on the reliability of the message. This is what we mean when we say that something is true or false.

The Holy Spirit is a spirit of truth in both senses. The Spirit represents God's faithfulness in love and what it means to live in a right relationship with God and others. Guided by the Holy Spirit, we are able to know the truth and be true to our calling.

Explore

SACRED ART

The Holy Spirit is commonly portrayed in four ways: as fire, wind, water, and a dove. Fire represents the transforming strength and force of the Holy Spirit. Wind symbolizes the breath of God breathing new life into the Church. Water represents the cleansing and life-giving gift of Baptism. In this oil-on-copper artwork, Hans Rottenhammer shows the Holy Spirit, portrayed as a dove, descending on the Apostles.

The Descent of the Holy Spirit, Hans Rottenhammer I, 1594–95.

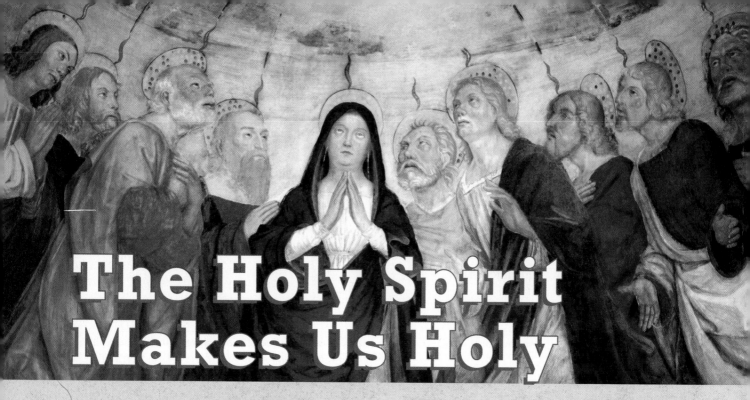

The Holy Spirit Makes Us Holy

THE Church began with the sending of the Holy Spirit on Pentecost. The Apostles were given the courage to proclaim the Good News of Jesus and the strength to face the challenge of carrying that message throughout the world.

One central part of Jesus' message that the Apostles proclaimed was that God wants to be close to us. By guiding us in prayer, the Holy Spirit helps us grow closer to God. When we are open to the Spirit's promptings, we grow in holiness and become more like Christ.

The Spirit: Our Teacher in Prayer

A key element of holiness is to develop lifelong habits of prayer, and the Holy Spirit leads the way.

God started it. The first thing to know about prayer is that, whether we recognize it or not, our prayer is always a response to God's initiative. In our relationship with God, it is always God who makes the first move. God created us, and the Holy Spirit is always inviting us to a deeper relationship with him.

You've already got God's attention. We don't pray to get God's attention. In fact, God is actively seeking to get *our* attention. Praying will help us notice the many ways God is reaching out to us, inviting us into a lifelong conversation.

Prayer doesn't change God; prayer changes us. When we are young, a lot of our prayer may be an attempt to persuade God to give us something we want or to influence the outcome of a situation. As we grow in the Spirit, we realize that prayer helps us know God's will and gives us the strength and wisdom to align our lives with that will.

It's about relationship. The best reason to pray is simply because we love God, and the optimal outcome of our praying is to grow in that love. When we pray, the Holy Spirit fills our hearts with divine life and love. We lift our minds and hearts to God.

You Are Not Alone

We can quickly become discouraged if we think that we alone are responsible for our prayer. Prayer comes from the Holy Spirit, not just from us. In the Gospel of John, we learn that the Advocate will teach us what we need to know. Every time we pray, it is the Holy Spirit who teaches us the way. The Holy Spirit is present in our prayer and makes it not just human prayer but divine prayer.

We have an emptiness inside us that only God can fill. What fills us is the Holy Spirit. The Holy Spirit is the living breath of our prayer. The Spirit is given to the Church so that through his power, the whole community of the People of God, even though living in diverse circumstances all over the world, might persevere in the hope in which we have been saved.

Gifts to Grow in Holiness

The Holy Spirit gives us seven gifts that prepare us to discover God's will for us and follow it throughout our lives. These Gifts of the Holy Spirit play an important role in all areas of our lives—at home, at school, in our worship, and even in our leisure activities. Think of how you experience these gifts in your own life. Ask the Holy Spirit to help you use the gifts to grow closer to God.

Wisdom

Wisdom helps us see as God sees. It helps us put God at the heart of our lives and love the things that God loves. Wisdom gives us the ability to know the real value of people and things.

Understanding

Understanding helps us open our eyes to the beauty, wisdom, and truth of our Catholic faith. Understanding helps us live our faith each day.

Counsel (Right Judgment)

Counsel helps us make good decisions in life. This gift helps us discern right from wrong and reminds us to seek good advice from others who are trustworthy guides. Counsel also helps us advise others.

Fortitude (Courage)

Fortitude is the courage to do what is right. Fortitude gives us the strength to follow God's will when we are tempted to take another path.

Knowledge

Knowledge is knowing the truth about God, about faith, and about the world.

Piety (Reverence)

Piety is also known as reverence. This gift of the Spirit helps us treat the people, places, and things in our life with reverence and respect because everything is a gift from God. Expressing our gratitude to God in prayer is a way of practicing piety.

Fear of the Lord
(Wonder and Awe in God's Presence)

This gift helps us appreciate the gift of life and God, the giver of life. It helps us remain aware that God is the Creator of everything that is.

Our Catholic Character

The Holy Spirit comes to us in Baptism and strengthens us in the Sacrament of Confirmation. Confirmation ties us more closely to the Body of Christ. It makes our link to the Church stronger and involves us more closely in the Church's mission. We become better witnesses to the Christian faith in the things we say and do.

In Confirmation we are charged with helping the Church carry out its mission. Jesus proclaimed the Kingdom of God and gave us a glimpse of that world by curing the sick, raising the dead to life, and caring for the poor. We gain the vision of the kind of world God wants us to have. The Holy Spirit inspires us to dream God's dream. Guided by the Holy Spirit, we work to bring about that dream by serving God's kingdom.

Explore

Study Corner

REMEMBER

The Holy Spirit is present in our prayers. We serve the Kingdom of God and grow in holiness when we use gifts received from the Holy Spirit.

Gifts of the Spirit

Saint John Vianney overcame many obstacles to become a priest. Guided by the Spirit, he had strength and vision to keep going.

Saint John Vianney encouraged liturgical prayer. He said, "Private prayer is like straw scattered here and there: If you set it on fire it makes a lot of little flames. But gather these straws into a bundle and light them, and you get a mighty fire, rising like a column into the sky; public prayer is like that."

Petitions to the Holy Spirit

Leader: Let us pray together the Lord's Prayer.

All: O God, send me your Spirit, to teach me what I am and who you are.

Leader: O God, send me your Spirit of Wisdom . . .

All: . . . to teach me to see the world as you see it and to know that you are the God who guides me.

Leader: O God, send me your Spirit of Understanding . . .

All: . . . to teach me to perceive your ways and to recognize that you are the God of Truth.

Leader: O God, send me your Spirit of Counsel . . .

All: . . . to teach me to seek advice and be open to our will and to believe that you are the God who calls me.

Leader: O God, send me your Spirit of Knowledge . . .

All: . . . to teach me to understand the truths of the universe and to know that you are the God who always stands ready to help me.

Leader: O God, send me your Spirit of Fortitude . . .

All: . . . to teach me what is right in the face of difficulties and to know that you are the God who strengthens me.

Leader: O God, send me your Spirit of Piety . . .

All: . . . to teach me to love and worship you and all that you created and to know that you are the God who is always present.

Leader: O God, send me your Spirit of Fear of the Lord . . .

All: . . . to teach me to recognize your glory and my dependence on you as the God of love.

Conclude with Saint Augustine's Prayer to the Holy Spirit.

Breathe in me, O Holy Spirit,
That my thoughts may all be holy.

Act in me, O Holy Spirit,
That my work, too, may all be holy.

Draw my heart, O Holy Spirit,
That I love but what is holy.

Strengthen me, O Holy Spirit,
To defend all that is holy.

Guard me, then, O Holy Spirit,
That I always may be holy.

WHERE Do I Fit In?

The idea of the Holy Spirit isn't so mysterious when we consider his work in our daily lives. Once we build this day-to-day awareness, we can begin to rely on the Holy Spirit to lead, guide, and provide.

by Fr. Richard J. Hauser, S.J.

Counting on the Holy Spirit

All my life I said the words in the Creed each Sunday: "I believe in the Holy Spirit, the Lord, the giver of life." It wasn't until I was in my 30s that I had any idea of any specific effects of the Holy Spirit in my life. I could recite the seven Gifts of the Spirit: wisdom, understanding, counsel, knowledge, fortitude, piety, and fear of the Lord. But these were just words for me with no reference to my life.

So what happened? Very simply, I began taking seriously what the New Testament says about the Holy Spirit. I was struck by Saint Paul's assertion in his Letter to the Galatians: "[T]he fruit of the Spirit is love, joy, peace, patience, kindness, generosity, faithfulness, gentleness, self-control." (Galatians 5:22–23)

I realized that I was experiencing the "fruit of the Spirit" when I was loving, joyful, and peaceful. The realization was incredible. All my life I had mistakenly assumed the Spirit was present only during times I was praying. I assumed God had nothing to do with my other activities since they were merely "secular" and not "holy."

I began to realize that all the treasured relationships of my life are the "fruit of the Spirit." To my surprise, the richest experiences of my life turned out to be God moments!

And the special guidance and strength that gets me through tough times also comes from the Gifts of the Spirit—wisdom, understanding, knowledge, and fortitude!

Even my ability to love my neighbor as I love myself—especially my most needy neighbors—is a Gift of the Spirit!

And on and on.

Being a Christian means to live in God. "For 'In him we live and move and have our being.'" (Acts of the Apostles 17:28)

In short, I count on the Spirit every day of my life. I can't imagine my life without God's presence.

With Us and For Us

On a separate sheet of paper, make a list of the Fruits of the Holy Spirit, leaving space between each word. Challenge yourself to identify a situation in which you received each fruit in the last 24 hours. Write a brief description of each situation. Pray a silent prayer thanking the Holy Spirit for his presence in your life.

FR. RICHARD J. HAUSER, S.J., is a professor of theology and the director of graduate programs in theology, ministry, and spirituality as well as the rector of the Jesuit Community at Creighton University. He is the author of *In His Spirit* and *Moving in the Spirit*.

What's What?

Respond

Complete each sentence using details from the text.

1. On the Feast of Pentecost, we mark the beginning of the _____ . (PAGE 212)

_____

2. Jesus promised that the Father would send an _____ , one who would be with them always. (PAGE 212)

_____

3. With the inspiration of the _____ , the Apostles would continue Jesus' teaching through their preaching, writing, and actions. (PAGE 212)

_____

4. Four common symbols for the Holy Spirit are fire, wind, water, and _____ . (PAGE 213)

_____

5. Our _____ is always a response to God's initiative. (PAGE 214)

_____

6. The Holy Spirit is the _____ of our prayer. (PAGE 214)

_____

7. The Holy Spirit gives us _____ gifts that prepare us to discover God's will for us and follow it throughout our lives. (PAGE 215)

_____

8. The gifts of the Holy Spirit are _____ . (PAGE 215)

_____
_____
_____
_____
_____
_____

Say What?

Know the definition of this term.

Paraclete

Now What?

On the lines below, write your own prayer to the Holy Spirit. Ask for help and guidance to be Christ's witness in the world.

_____
_____
_____
_____
_____
_____
_____
_____
_____
_____
_____
_____

Faith in ACTION

Many times the values of our Catholic faith clash with society's values. Discipleship requires that we apply Catholic social teaching to the issues of our time. These teachings guide our consciences and help us show our love for the world.

In this unit we explored how Jesus, who "came from the Father," returned to the Father in Ascension. After Jesus' Ascension, the Apostles, guided by the Holy Spirit, became witnesses of the Kingdom of God and spread Jesus' Word to the nations. We learned that the Apostle Paul was the greatest of the early Christian missionaries, and we explored our call to eternal life. In his life and teaching, Jesus showed his care for humankind and all creation. Here are some ideas to get involved in nature as a way of proclaiming Jesus to the world.

Plant Seeds

Purpose

Learn about the process of a seed taking root. Plant seeds of flowers or herbs that can be given to others as gifts.

Background

Paul teaches us that we must be generous in sowing the seeds of God's message in our world. (2 Corinthians 9:6) One way to sow the seed of God's message is to plant flowers, fruits, grains, vegetables, and trees to show our care for the earth. Their provision of beauty, shade, nourishment, habitat, or joy shows God's endless love for us to the world.

Steps

1. Read the parable of the mustard seed in the Gospel of Mark 4:30–32. Reflect on the power of one little seed to do so much good. Share your reflections with one another.

2. Research the nature of a seed. What is inside? What makes it start growing? What are the conditions that help it take root and grow strong?

3. Choose flowers or herbs that you can grow from seeds. Research how to plant these particular seeds.

4. Collect the supplies you'll need for those seeds. Yogurt cups and egg cartons make good pots for the initial planting of seeds.

5. Decide what you are going to do with the plants. How can you use them in ways that sow God's message for someone else?

"Judge each day not by the harvest you reap but by the seeds you plant."

—Robert Louis Stevenson, novelist, poet, and travel writer

Recycle-Bin Bonanza

Purpose

Establish or enhance recycling systems in your school or parish. Raise awareness about the importance of recycling.

Background

Almost everything that we use can be recycled and made into something new. When we throw things away, we add to landfills, and we unnecessarily take more of the earth's resources to make things that could have been made with recycled material.

Steps

1. Find out what recycling systems are already in place in your school or parish. If there are none, talk with school or parish leaders about how you can help.

2. Obtain recycling bins, or make them by reusing discarded containers and decorating them with fun colors, pictures, and words that remind people to recycle. Consult a local recycling facility to see how materials should be grouped. For example, you might have recycling bins for each of the following: mixed paper, glass, metal cans, batteries, printer cartridges, newspaper, and corrugated cardboard.

3. Place bins in high-trash zones.

4. Keep track of how much is recycled, and raise awareness by posting a chart online or in a printed publication that shows the impact of each month's recycling efforts.

Act

"Gather the fragments left over, so that nothing will be wasted."

—John 6:12

The Year in Our Church

The Liturgical Calendar

The liturgical calendar shows us the feasts and seasons of the Church year.

Ordinary Time

Christmas

Lent

Ash Wednesday

Holy Week

Palm Sunday
Holy Thursday
Good Friday
Holy Saturday

Easter

Easter Sunday

Epiphany

Christmas

Advent

First Sunday of Advent

All Souls Day
All Saints Day

Winter

Spring

Fall

Summer

Ascension
Pentecost

Ordinary Time

221

The Liturgical Year

The Year in Our Church

Advent marks the beginning of the Church year. It is a time of anticipation that begins four Sundays before Christmas.

The Christmas season includes **Christmas,** the celebration of Jesus' birth, and Epiphany, the day that Jesus was revealed as the Savior to the world.

Lent is a season of conversion that begins on Ash Wednesday. It is a time of turning toward God in preparation for Easter.

During **Holy Week** we recall the events leading to Jesus' suffering and Death. Holy Week begins with Palm Sunday and ends on Holy Saturday.

Easter is the celebration of the bodily raising of Jesus Christ from the dead. The Resurrection is the central mystery of the Christian faith. The Ascension celebrates Jesus' return to the Father in heaven.

The sending of the Holy Spirit from heaven is celebrated on **Pentecost.** With this feast, the Easter season ends.

All Saints Day celebrates the victory of all the holy people in heaven. On All Souls Day, we pray for those who have died but are still in Purgatory.

The time set aside for celebrating our call to follow Jesus as his disciples day by day is **Ordinary Time.**

Advent

> "May it be done to me according to your word."
>
> *Luke 1:38*

Advent begins on the fourth Sunday before Christmas and marks the beginning of the Church's liturgical year. During Advent, we remember how the people of Israel awaited the Messiah. We also prepare ourselves to celebrate the birth of Jesus. Advent is a time of joyful anticipation for the day when Christ will return in glory.

PRAYER

Thank you, God, for this new year and the anticipation it brings. Open our ears to your guiding words and give us the courage to follow them.

Mary Accepts God's Promise

Annunciation, from the *Hastings Hours,* ca. 1475–83, vellum, Flemish School.

WE celebrate Mary during Advent. **Luke 1:26–38 tells us how Mary was chosen by God to be the mother of Jesus and how she responded in faith. The angel's announcement of the birth of Jesus is called the Annunciation.**

Mary was from a small town in Galilee called Nazareth. She was engaged to marry a man named Joseph. An angel of God visited Mary and announced that she had been chosen by God to bear a son, who was to be named Jesus. The angel Gabriel told her that this child would be the Son of God.

Mary wondered aloud how this could be, since she was a virgin. The angel told her that she would conceive by the power of the Holy Spirit. He also told Mary that her relative, Elizabeth, long believed to be unable to have children, was pregnant. Mary accepted the message of the angel with the words, "Behold, I am the handmaid of the Lord. May it be done to me according to your word." (Luke 1:38) Then the angel left her.

After the visit from the angel, Mary traveled to see her relative Elizabeth and found her with child, just as the angel had said. We call this special event in Mary's life the Visitation. Elizabeth and Mary greeted each other joyfully because they recognized the wonderful things that God was doing for them. We're reminded to spend time during Advent remembering the great things God has done throughout history and in our own lives.

Mary is a model of discipleship for us. She responded to God's messenger with a resounding yes. Her words to the angel are sometimes called Mary's *fiat,* a Latin word that means "let it be done." During Advent, we reflect on Mary's acceptance of God's call to be the mother of Jesus. We pray that we'll be as open to God's call as Mary was and that we'll respond with our own *fiat.*

God had chosen Mary to be the mother of Jesus from the moment of her conception. We celebrate that Mary was born without Original Sin on December 8, the Feast of the Immaculate Conception, which is a holy day of obligation for Catholics.

Advent Prayer: The Advent Wreath

The Church provides us with special prayers and devotions during Advent. The Advent wreath decorates the church or home during Advent. Some people place an Advent wreath on their dinner table.

An Advent wreath consists of a circle of evergreens and four candles that represent each of the four Sundays of Advent. The greenery in the wreath reminds us of the new life that Jesus will bring to us. The circle of the wreath represents God's unending love. The candles on the wreath are usually purple, the liturgical color for Advent, or white. A pink candle ordinarily is used for the third Sunday of Advent. This color reminds us to rejoice because the Lord is near. The light from the candles represents the light that came into the world at Jesus' birth. A new candle is lit each week.

The Visitation, Bartholomaeus Bruyn, ca. 16th century.

Our Catholic Character

A number of Catholic prayers recognize Mary's special role in the mystery of Christ and the Incarnation of the Word. The words of the Hail Mary echo Luke's account of the Annunciation. (Luke 1:26–38) When Mary visits Elizabeth, her response to Elizabeth's greeting gives praise to God for the wonders he has done throughout the history of Israel. We find Mary's prayer, the *Magnificat*, in Luke 1:46–55. The *Magnificat* is prayed during Evening Prayer (Vespers), which is part of the Liturgy of the Hours.

God Is Great

Mary's prayer, the *Magnificat,* gives thanks to God and praises him for his wondrous deeds throughout the ages. Advent is a good time to offer our own prayers of thanksgiving as we get ready to welcome the light of Christ on Christmas.

Thanks and Praise to God

All: Praise be to God.

Leader: During this Advent season, we remember Mary's yes to God. Like Mary, we recognize that God has done marvelous deeds throughout history and in our own lives. Let us pray together Mary's *Magnificat* and praise God for all of his wondrous deeds.

All: "My soul proclaims the greatness of the Lord;
my spirit rejoices in God my savior.
For he has looked upon his handmaid's lowliness;
behold, from now on will all ages call me blessed.

Side 1: The Mighty One has done great things for me,
and holy is his name.
His mercy is from age to age
to those who fear him.

Side 2: He has shown might with his arm,
dispersed the arrogant of mind
and heart.

Side 1: He has thrown down the rulers
from their thrones
but lifted up the lowly.

Side 2: The hungry he has filled with good things;
the rich he has sent away empty.

All: He has helped Israel his servant,
remembering his mercy,
according to his promise to our fathers,
to Abraham and to his descendants forever."

Luke 1:46–55

Response: God has done great things for us!

Offer prayers of thanksgiving. ℟.

Leader: Lord our God, you fill us with good things. Continue to bless us as we prepare to celebrate the coming of your Son, Jesus Christ, who reigns with you and the Holy Spirit, now and forever.

All: Amen.

Christmas

"... I proclaim to you good news of great joy ..."

Luke 2:10

At Christmas, we celebrate the fulfillment of God's promise to send the world a Savior. We know this Savior to be Jesus, God's own Son. Jesus' birth in Bethlehem brings to the world God's promise of peace and salvation.

PRAYER

Thank you, God, for the amazing gift of your Son. Help us share this gift with everyone we meet by using words and actions that reflect Jesus' love.

The Birth of Jesus

The Nativity, Sir Edward Burne-Jones, ca. 19th century.

MOST of us can tell the story of Jesus' birth by heart, as the story has been told and retold every year. But there is more to understand about the story.

Only the Gospels of Matthew and Luke include the stories of Jesus' birth. While both Gospels have details in common, they also relate unique aspects surrounding Jesus' birth. You might be surprised to learn that only Matthew's Gospel records the visit of the Magi, who are sometimes called the Wise Men. Meanwhile, the account of the angels appearing to shepherds in the fields and announcing that the Messiah had been born is found only in Luke's Gospel. Because these two Gospels highlight different details from Jesus' birth, we will focus only on Luke's Gospel as we consider the mystery we celebrate at Christmas.

Luke's Infancy Narrative begins with the angel's announcement to Zechariah that his wife, Elizabeth, will bear a son (to be named John) in her old age. Luke's Gospel continues with the Annunciation, the angel's announcement of Jesus' birth to Mary, and the Visitation, Mary's visit to her now-pregnant relative, Elizabeth. In this way, Luke's Gospel connects the lives of John the Baptist and Jesus. Immediately after reporting the birth of John the Baptist, Luke tells the story of Jesus' birth.

Luke's Gospel provides historical perspective about the world into which Jesus was born. Caesar Augustus was the Roman emperor, a fact similar to identifying the president of the United States when you were born. Luke notes that a census had been announced, which explains why Mary and Joseph had traveled to Bethlehem, where Jesus was born. Luke's historical perspective reveals that Jesus' birth was an important event for the world, a theme that repeats throughout his Gospel.

The Gospel of Luke delivers the message that from his birth, Jesus was a different kind of king. He was not a king with material possessions; instead, he was a divine king. Jesus came to the world as someone who is poor and lowly. Because there was no room at the inn, Jesus was born in a stable and laid in a manger, which was a feeding trough for animals.

Jesus came for all people, not only the rich and powerful. Angels announced to shepherds in the fields the good news of Jesus' birth. Revealing this news to shepherds is an unexpected detail. Shepherds were simple workers, toiling in the fields and tending to animals. Yet these lowly ones were the first to receive and acknowledge the appearance of the Savior. The shepherds journeyed to Bethlehem and found Mary, Joseph, and Jesus just as the angels had said. They returned from Bethlehem singing praise and glory to God. By including these details, Luke delivers the message that those who responded most faithfully to Jesus' teaching were those least perceived to be chosen by God—those who were poor, sinners, lepers, outcasts, or foreigners.

In the Gospel of Luke, Mary plays a significant role. Mary is central to the mystery of the Incarnation. Because she responded yes to becoming the Mother of God, she is our first model of discipleship and our model of grace and trust in God. After the visit from the shepherds, Mary reflects on everything that has happened in her heart. She shows us a path to finding God in prayer, reflecting on his will, and following in faith.

We are called to respond in prayer to the miracle and mystery of Christmas. We are called to imitate Mary's faithfulness. The Christmas season includes the Solemnity of Mary, a holy day of obligation, on January 1, a feast day that is devoted to remembering Mary's role as Mother of God.

In the account of Jesus' birth in Luke's Infancy Narrative, we find plenty of good news to celebrate. Jesus' birth brings salvation to the whole world. In particular, Jesus' kingship is inclusive, bringing good news to those who are ignored or held in low esteem by society. During the Christmas season, we are called to pray and reflect on the events surrounding Jesus' birth and the story of salvation.

The First to be Told About Jesus, Clive Uptton, ca. 20th century.

Our Catholic Character

Angels, spiritual creatures in the Gospels who worship God in heaven and serve as God's messengers, reveal some of God's plans for salvation. In Luke's Gospel, angels bring news to Zechariah, Mary, and the shepherds. Eight days after his birth and at his circumcision, Mary gives Jesus his name—the name the angel Gabriel said when he announced that Mary had been chosen to be the mother of the Savior. By including these details, Luke makes clear Jesus' devout Jewish upbringing by Mary and Joseph. Angels in Luke's Gospel give more titles for Jesus when they announce his birth to the shepherds, calling Jesus "a savior," "Messiah," and "Lord."

Welcome Jesus!

We rejoice at Jesus' birth because he brought salvation to the whole world. Jesus, the Savior, came for everyone. The angels announced Jesus' birth to poor shepherds, who responded by journeying to Bethlehem to find Jesus. How will we respond to the good news?

He Is Born

Leader: Let us prayerfully reflect on the good news of Jesus' birth. Like Mary, let us ponder this mystery in the stillness of our hearts.

Reader: A reading from the holy Gospel according to Luke.
[Luke 2:1–14]
The Gospel of the Lord.

Leader: Glory to God in the highest.

All: Glory to God in the highest.

Side 1: Sing to the LORD a new song;
sing to the LORD, all the earth.
Sing to the LORD, bless his name;
proclaim his salvation day after day.
Psalm 96:1–2

Side 2: Give to the LORD, you families of nations,
give to the LORD glory and might;
give to the LORD the glory due his name!
Bring gifts and enter his courts;
bow down to the LORD, splendid
in holiness.
Tremble before him, all the earth; . . .
Psalm 96:7–9

Side 1: Let the heavens be glad and the
earth rejoice;
let the sea and what fills it resound;
let the plains be joyful and all that
is in them.

Side 2: Then let all the trees of the forest rejoice
before the LORD who comes,
who comes to govern the earth,
To govern the world with justice
and the peoples with faithfulness.
Psalm 96:11–13

All: Glory to God in the highest.

All: Praise to you, Lord Jesus Christ.

Allow time for silent meditation.

Leader: Let us pray. God sent to us a Savior, Jesus, our Messiah and Lord. He was born as one of us. May we, like the shepherds, give glory to God for the great gift of salvation. We pray this in Jesus' name.

All: Amen.

Lent

At once the Spirit drove him out into the desert, . . .

Mark 1:12

Lent is a season of repentance and renewal. The Holy Spirit guides us to turn away from our sinfulness and to recommit ourselves to following Jesus. Beginning with Ash Wednesday, we spend 40 days fasting and praying, just as Jesus fasted and prayed in the desert before his public ministry.

PRAYER

Thank you, God, for the gift of liturgical seasons and especially for the season of Lent. Help us make the most of this special time with you.

A Retreat in the Desert

SCRIPTURE tells us that after John the Baptist baptized Jesus in the Jordan River, the Holy Spirit led Jesus into the desert. Jesus prayed to God and fasted for 40 days. He prepared himself for his ministry. During this time, Jesus was tempted by Satan. In the desert's harsh and wild surroundings, angels tended to him. (Mark 1:12–13)

Christ in the Wilderness, Briton Riviere, 1898.

As we journey in faith and grow spiritually, we contemplate Jesus' baptism and retreat to the desert. Since the Second Vatican Council, Catholics recognize the celebration of Lent as a time to prepare for receiving the Sacrament of Baptism or a time to renew our baptismal promises. Jesus' acceptance of baptism from John the Baptist was acceptance of his Father's mission. At Jesus' baptism, a voice from heaven proclaimed to Jesus, "'You are my beloved Son; with you I am well pleased.'" (Mark 1:11)

Jesus needed to pray about his mission. We, too, need to pray about our actions and the events of our lives to learn what God intends for us. When something happens to us—good or bad—it's helpful to take time to pray and listen for what God is calling us to do.

When we receive ashes on Ash Wednesday, we signal that we accept our dependence on God. The priest, deacon, or lay minister traces the Sign of the Cross on our foreheads with the blessed ashes. As this is done, one of two prayers is prayed. One prayer reminds us that we are mortal beings who will stand before God one day for judgment: "Remember, man, you are dust and to dust you will return." The other prayer reminds us that we are baptized and called to conversion: "Turn away from sin and be faithful to the Gospel."

During Lent, members of the Church commit themselves to following their mission, imitating the footsteps of Jesus as he prepared for his mission in the wilderness of the desert. In order to follow our mission, we incorporate traditional Lenten practices into our lives.

Lenten Practices: Prayer, Fasting, and Almsgiving

Prayer Daily prayer is an important part of Christian life. During the season of Lent, we consider our life of prayer as a personal practice that prepares us for the celebration of Easter. The Church challenges us to renew our commitment to prayer, the central action of our spiritual life. We choose to deepen our commitment by praying for the grace to live out our baptismal promises. We pray for those who are preparing to receive the Sacrament of Baptism at Easter. During this season of conversion, as we change our hearts and turn away from sin, we receive the Sacrament of Penance and Reconciliation and pray for others who are reconciling themselves to God.

Fasting This spiritual practice increases awareness of our need for penance and conversion. Fasting, or limiting the intake of food and drink for a period of time, reminds us that Jesus fasted during his 40 days in the desert. Catholics between the ages of 18 and 59 are asked to fast on Ash Wednesday and Good Friday. Denying ourselves a full stomach helps make us more aware of our hunger for God and our dependence on him as his children. Fasting also works to remind us of our responsibility to ease the burdens of those who suffer physical, economic, or political hardships.

Catholics 14 years and older are also asked to abstain, or refrain, from eating meat on Ash Wednesday, Good Friday, and on the Fridays of Lent. Eating simple meals links us spiritually to the poor, who often have to do without proper food. Abstaining helps remind us of Lent's purpose.

Catholics both fast and abstain on Ash Wednesday and Good Friday. In addition to these spiritual practices, we might choose our own personal fast or abstinence during Lent. For example, you may choose not to eat candy, or you may give up television during Lent. Doing without some things we enjoy frees us to focus our lives on Jesus Christ alone. During Lent, we look at ways to simplify our lives by leaving behind things that don't really contribute to our fulfillment or to real happiness.

Almsgiving The Lenten practice of almsgiving is prompted by charity. To give alms is to assist those in need, such as an offering of money, possessions, time, or talent. Some people combine almsgiving with their practice of fasting. For example, you might give up buying lunch at the school cafeteria and donate the money that you would have spent on this food to those in need.

Through the spiritual practices of praying, fasting, and almsgiving, we make Lent our own retreat to the desert. Jesus speaks of praying, fasting, and almsgiving in Matthew 6:1–18, teaching us that we should not follow these practices as ways to be recognized, praised, or seen as holy. Instead, Jesus wants us to pray, fast, and give alms for love of God and neighbor. In this way, when it's time for Holy Week and Easter, we'll find ourselves ready to rejoice in the Good News of Jesus' Resurrection.

Past Meets Present

PAST: The Old Testament contains many references to wearing sackcloth and ashes as signs of repentance and as an acknowledgment of sinfulness, including Jeremiah 6:26, Isaiah 58:5, Daniel 9:3, and Jonah 3:6. In the early history of the Church, those seeking forgiveness wore sackcloth and ashes and begged members of the community to pray for them. The custom of distributing ashes arose from witnessing these public penitents. By the end of the 11th century, Pope Urban II called for the distribution of ashes on the Wednesday before Lent.

PRESENT: Receiving ashes, a sacramental, remains a popular devotion that begins the season of Lent. The ashes are made by burning palms that were blessed on the previous Palm Sunday. Some parishes invite parishioners to bring palms for burning to church before the season of Lent begins. Four ancient prayers are prayed in the blessing of the ashes, which are also sprinkled with holy water and perfumed with incense. The Ash Wednesday Scripture readings remind us of our call to conversion.

Renew Our Hearts

During Lent, we acknowledge our dependence on God. To prepare for Jesus' Resurrection, we turn back to God and turn away from sin. As we renew our hearts, we grow more faithful to God's Word. Lent is a good time to pray for the strength to be a better disciple.

Return to God

Leader: The grace of our Lord Jesus Christ be with us, now and forever.

All: Amen.

Leader: During Lent, we follow Jesus' footsteps into the desert. In our prayer and fasting, we remind ourselves of our need for God in our lives. In our almsgiving, we show our commitment to the poor. As we begin this season of Lent, let us ask God to renew our hearts and to help us return to him by following his ways more closely.

Reader: A reading from the Book of Joel.
[Joel 2:12–17]
The Word of the Lord.

All: Thanks be to God.

Leader: As we pray silently, let us consider how we will renew our lives this Lent through the spiritual practices of prayer, fasting, and almsgiving. Tell God what you will do this Lent as you turn away from sin and grow more faithful to the Gospel.

- What can I do to renew my prayer life? (*Pause.*)

- From what can I fast to help me hear what God is asking of me? (*Pause.*)

- What can I do to help those who are in need this Lent? (*Pause.*)

Reflect in the silence of your hearts.

Leader: We pray that God will accept our Lenten sacrifices and give us the strength to persevere in our promises. We ask this through Christ our Lord.

All: Amen.

Holy Week

> "Father, into your hands I commend my spirit."
> *Luke 23:46*

Holy Week commemorates Jesus' triumphant entry into Jerusalem; his gift of the Eucharist; and his suffering, Death, and Resurrection. The three solemn liturgies on Holy Thursday, Good Friday, and the Easter Vigil are called the Triduum.

PRAYER

Thank you, Father, for inviting us on the journey of Holy Week and for the precious gift of your Son, Jesus, whose steps we follow.

The Holiest Week of the Year

Jesus before Caiaphas, ceiling painting, Golgotha Chapel, Holy Sepulchre, Jerusalem.

AS we make our final preparations for Easter during Holy Week, we commemorate the events that led to Jesus' acceptance of his Death on the Cross for our sins. We remember these events with great hope because we know that death and evil do not triumph. Jesus will rise on Easter morning!

On Palm Sunday, the beginning of Holy Week, we remember that Jesus' journey to the Cross began with his glorious entry into Jerusalem. The crowds received him as their king. They laid out palm branches and shouted,

> "Blessed is the king who comes in the name of
> the Lord.
>   Peace in heaven and glory in the highest."
>
> *Luke 19:38*

Some Pharisees urged Jesus to rebuke the crowd for calling him a king, but Jesus would not. Jesus then went to the Temple, where he drove out the merchants and continued to teach. Shortly afterward, the religious leaders began to make plans to arrest Jesus. (Luke 19:28–48)

On Holy Thursday, we recall how Jesus celebrated his Last Supper with his disciples. This was a Passover meal, the Jewish feast that celebrated God's deliverance of Israel from slavery in Egypt. As Jesus celebrated Passover, he gave the feast a new meaning. Jesus said that his Death would begin the new covenant. He would give his life for the forgiveness of sins.

Following their Passover meal, Jesus and his disciples went to the Mount of Olives. Jesus, knowing his betrayal was imminent, wanted to pray. On Good Friday, we reflect on the events that begin with Jesus' arrest in the garden. Jesus was taken to the house of the high priest, Caiaphas, and tried by the Sanhedrin, which was the council of Jewish elders, chief priests, and scribes. Peter followed Jesus to the courtyard of Caiaphas's house, where he was recognized as one of Jesus' disciples. Just as Jesus had told him, Peter denied even knowing Jesus three times.

In the meantime, the Sanhedrin had determined that Jesus was guilty of inciting the people by claiming to be the Messiah and king. The Sanhedrin sent him to the Roman governor, Pontius Pilate. Because the Jews were under Roman rule, only Pilate had the authority to sentence Jesus to death.

At first, Pilate refused to find Jesus guilty of anything. To appease Jesus' accusers, he sent him to King Herod, the Jewish ruler of Galilee. Herod and his court questioned and mistreated Jesus and eventually sent him back to Pilate. Again, Pilate found Jesus free from guilt of the crimes for which he was accused, preferring to have Jesus flogged and released. But Jesus' accusers persisted and the crowd called for his crucifixion. In Jesus' place, they asked for the release of another prisoner, Barabbas. Pilate protested a third time, saying he found no guilt. But Pilate's resolve was not strong, and he gave in to the demands of the people. He released Barabbas and sentenced Jesus to death on the cross.

Jesus was led away and forced to carry a cross to the place of execution, as was the custom. Along the way, a bystander named Simon of Cyrene carried Jesus' Cross for a while. Jesus met some women followers and friends. He stopped to warn them of bad times to come. Finally, between two criminals, Jesus was nailed to the Cross.

As Jesus hung on the Cross, his garments were divided among the soldiers, and he was taunted by the crowd. A mocking inscription was placed above his head that read, "This is the King of the Jews." (Luke 23:38) One of the two criminals crucified with Jesus asked Jesus to remember him when he entered his kingdom. Jesus recognized the man's faith and promised that he would join Jesus in Paradise. Finally, Jesus cried out his last words, "Father, into your hands I commend my spirit," and died. (Luke 23:46)

In his Passion and Death for our sins, Jesus showed the full depth of his love for us. His sacrifice made our eternal life in heaven a possibility. We remember the events of Jesus' Passion and Death as we also strive to be with Jesus in Paradise at the end of our earthly lives.

Past Meets Present

PAST: The Stations of the Cross originated from the early Christian tradition of making a pilgrimage through Jerusalem to visit and pray along the path of Jesus' journey to the Cross. Along this pilgrimage were 14 stations—places to stop and recall important moments of Jesus' journey.

PRESENT: Praying the Stations of the Cross can take place any time of the year, but they are prayed more frequently during Lent and Holy Week. When we pray the Stations—most churches have depictions of them—we pray as we walk from station to station, recalling Jesus' way to his Crucifixion. Sometimes a 15th Station, the Resurrection of Jesus, is added to the prayer.

Jesus' Crucifixion, Tuscan School, ca. 12th century.

We Thank Jesus

We remember the events of Jesus' Passion and Death during Holy Week. We thank him for his abundant love and for his ultimate sacrifice for our salvation. We also recall Jesus' lesson of forgiveness. "Father, forgive them, they know not what they do." (Luke 23:34)

Our Petitions Before the Cross

Leader: Praise be to God, who fills our lives with love and joy.

All: Praise be to God.

Leader: Jesus died so that our sins might be forgiven. Let us pray that we will one day be received by Jesus in Paradise.

Reader: A reading from the holy Gospel according to Luke.
[Luke 23:33–46]
The Gospel of the Lord.

All: Praise to you, Lord Jesus Christ.

Reflect in the silence of your hearts.

Leader: Remembering all that Jesus has done for us, we offer our petitions to God:

That we follow the example of your only Son who, even as he died on the Cross, forgave those who crucified him, we pray to the Lord.

All: Lord, hear our prayer.

Leader: That we forgive those who do us harm so that we will not be filled with anger but with your love, we pray to the Lord.

All: Lord, hear our prayer.

Leader: Father, we pray to you with a spirit of forgiveness so that we can be free to accept the love you offer. Hear these prayers and the prayers of our heart. We pray through Jesus, your Son, and with the Holy Spirit.

All: Amen.

Easter

"He is not here, but he has been raised."

Luke 24:6

At Easter, we celebrate God's most amazing surprise. Each of the four Gospels tells how the disciples found an empty tomb. Jesus Christ had risen from the dead! He is still with us. We encounter his real presence in the Eucharist.

PRAYER

Thank you, God, for surprising us every day with your love. Keep us always open to your surprises and willing to share them with others.

Jesus Is Risen

Holy Women at Christ's Tomb, George Howard, 1869.

IMAGINE what it must have been like to be Jesus' friend, his disciple, on the day he was put to Death on the Cross. Jesus had been tried as a criminal, found guilty, tortured, and killed in a public and most horrible way.

After witnessing all that had happened, Jesus' friends might have shared intense feelings of sadness, fear, confusion, or anger. They probably tried to comfort one another as Jesus' body was taken from the Cross and placed in the tomb. Saturday, the day after Jesus' Death on Good Friday, was the Jewish Sabbath. The Sabbath laws restricted activities on this day, so no one could visit Jesus' tomb.

Amazing News: Jesus' Tomb Is Empty!

On the day after the Sabbath, some women disciples went to Jesus' tomb with spices to embalm his body. This practice was part of their Jewish custom. However, they returned from the tomb with an amazing report. The stone had been moved from the entrance to the tomb. Jesus' body was not there. And they had seen a vision of two men in white who told them that Jesus had been raised from the dead. (Luke 24:1–7)

The women reported this to other disciples. In first-century Jewish society, women couldn't serve as public witnesses. The men may have thought, "These women are crazy." Luke's Gospel tells us, "[T]heir story seemed like nonsense and they did not believe them." (Luke 24:11) Imagine what it must have been like to be one of those women. Only Peter got up and ran to Jesus' tomb, where he found the burial cloths but not Jesus' body. And Peter left amazed. (Luke 24:12)

But What Happened?

At first Jesus' disciples considered that Jesus' body had been stolen. That seemed possible, perhaps even logical. But why were the burial cloths found in the tomb? Even grave robbers would keep a dead body wrapped. It took time for the disciples to understand fully that Jesus had been raised from the dead.

What led the disciples to believe that Jesus had been raised from the dead? The angels at the tomb said to the women, "'Why do you seek the living one among the dead? He is not here, but he has been raised.'" (Luke 24:5–6) The angels reminded the women that Jesus had said that he would be put to death by sinners and would rise again on the third day.

The risen Jesus appeared to his disciples. The Gospel of Luke tells us about Jesus' appearance to two disciples on the road to Emmaus, a village about seven miles from Jerusalem. These two disciples engaged in conversation with a stranger. In the course of their conversation, the stranger, who was Jesus, explained and interpreted all that Scripture predicted about the Messiah. While breaking bread together at a meal, the disciples finally recognized that the stranger was Jesus.

Amazed and anxious to share their news, these two disciples returned to Jerusalem. As they gathered with the eleven Apostles and others, imagine their surprise at reports that others had also seen Jesus. "The Lord has truly been raised and has appeared to Simon!" (Luke 24:34) Then the two told those assembled what had happened and how they recognized Jesus in the breaking of the bread.

Our Encounter with Jesus

The amazing news of the risen Jesus didn't end there in Jerusalem. We share in this experience, too, when we encounter Jesus in the celebration of the Eucharist. In the Eucharist, we experience Jesus' real presence at the Consecration, when the bread and wine become the Body and Blood of Jesus Christ. Every Sunday we celebrate Jesus' Resurrection from the dead. Like the women who found the empty tomb and the disciples who encountered the risen Jesus, we can't help but share this amazing good news with others.

Our Catholic Character

Alleluia is a Hebrew word used to offer praise to God. During the season of Lent, the word *Alleluia* is not acclaimed during Mass. For instance, the *Alleluia* before the Gospel is replaced with an alternate acclamation. We pray and sing *Alleluia* with extra joy again during the Easter liturgies.

Alleluia! Jesus Is Risen

Jesus is God of the living. By his Resurrection, all of Jesus' works and teachings are confirmed. By his Death, he saves us from sin. Jesus' Resurrection opens a way for us to share eternal life with him in heaven. This is why we joyfully pray Alleluia.

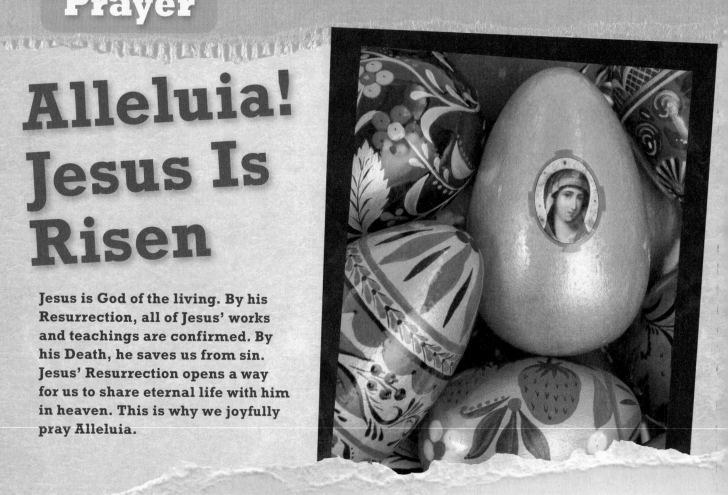

A Litany: The Victory of the Cross

Leader: The grace of the risen Jesus Christ be with us all, now and forever.

All: Amen.

Reader: A reading from the holy Gospel according to Luke.
[Luke 24:1–6]
The Gospel of the Lord.

All: Praise to you, Lord Jesus Christ.

Leader: Let us pray together in praise and thanksgiving. Jesus has been raised from the dead! Alleluia! Alleluia!

Response: Alleluia! Jesus is truly risen!

Leader: As the first disciples came to have faith in Jesus' Resurrection from the dead, so too may we have faith in the power of God, who has conquered death. ℟.

Leader: As the hearts of the disciples on the road to Emmaus were set on fire when Jesus talked with them about the Scriptures, so too may we be enlivened when we encounter Jesus through the words of Scripture. ℟.

Leader: As the disciples on the road to Emmaus recognized Jesus in the breaking of the bread, so too may we recognize Jesus' real presence in the Eucharist. ℟.

Leader: As the disciples proclaimed the Good News of Jesus Christ's Resurrection to others, so too may we be witnesses of his Resurrection to the world. ℟.

Leader: Lord, hear our prayers and continue to deepen our faith in the power of Christ's Resurrection. We ask this through your Son, who lives and reigns with you and the Holy Spirit for ever and ever.

All: Amen.

Pentecost

And they were all filled with the holy Spirit . . .

Acts of the Apostles 2:4

Before Jesus' Ascension into heaven, he had promised his disciples that he would not leave them alone. He had promised to send them a helper. So the disciples returned in faith to Jerusalem to wait for Jesus' promise to come true.

PRAYER

Thank you, Jesus, for keeping all your promises to us, especially your promise to send a helper. Make us always aware of your Spirit in our midst.

The Beginning of the Church

JESUS' Ascension into heaven appeared to signal the end of his encounters with his disciples. But they would soon find out that they were part of a new and wonderful beginning. The story of the beginning of the Church is found in the Acts of the Apostles.

The Acts of the Apostles was written by the same person who recorded the Gospel of Luke. The Gospel of Luke tells the story of Jesus' life, Death, Resurrection, and Ascension. The Acts of the Apostles continues the story by telling how the Holy Spirit led the Apostles to preach the message of Jesus throughout the Roman empire.

The Gift of the Holy Spirit

After Jesus was taken to heaven, the disciples returned to Jerusalem and gathered in the house where they had been staying. These disciples included the Twelve Apostles (Matthias had been chosen to replace Judas, Jesus' betrayer), as well as women disciples and Mary, the Mother of Jesus. As this group of Jesus' closest friends gathered on the Jewish feast of Pentecost, an extraordinary thing happened. The Acts of the Apostles tells us that a loud noise, like wind, filled the house. And then it looked as if tongues of fire touched each of them. The disciples felt themselves filled with the Holy Spirit, and they began to speak in different languages. (Acts of the Apostles 2:1–4)

As the disciples spoke, a crowd began to gather outside the house where they were gathered. The crowd took interest not only because the voices were so loud but because the disciples were speaking in a variety of languages. The crowd represented many different nations, yet each member heard the disciples speaking in his or her own language of "the mighty acts of God." (Acts of the Apostles 2:11)

People in the crowd offered differing opinions about this experience. Some were amazed but unsure about the meaning of the event. Others dismissed what they heard by scoffing, "They have had too much new wine." (Acts of the Apostles 2:13) Imagine yourself in the crowd. What would you have thought?

What Does This Mean?

At Pentecost, Jesus fulfilled his promise to send the Holy Spirit to the disciples. The disciples immediately began doing the work of the Church, proclaiming the life, Death, Resurrection, and Ascension of Jesus and calling the whole world to faith in him.

In the passage that follows the story of Pentecost, Peter boldly proclaims to the crowd that Jesus, who was crucified, is Messiah and Lord: "Therefore let the whole house of Israel know for certain that God has made him both Lord and Messiah, . . ." (Acts of the Apostles 2:36) The remainder of the Acts of the Apostles tells how the Holy Spirit led the first Christian community and how the Good News of Jesus spread throughout the Roman Empire.

The Holy Spirit transformed the early Christian community and strengthened it for the task of witnessing to Jesus the Lord. This same Holy Spirit continues to strengthen the Church today. This means that all of us who are baptized have been given the strength of the Holy Spirit, which empowers us to be Christ's witnesses in the world today. At Pentecost, we celebrate the Spirit's presence in us.

Our Catholic Character

We receive the Holy Spirit at our Baptism. In the Sacrament of Confirmation, the grace of Baptism is strengthened through the seven Gifts of the Holy Spirit. These seven gifts help us live as Christians. Six of the Gifts of the Holy Spirit are identified in the Book of Isaiah. Church Tradition has added the gift of piety to make a total of seven Gifts of the Holy Spirit.

> The spirit of the LORD shall rest upon him:
>   a spirit of wisdom and of understanding,
> A spirit of counsel and of strength,
>   a spirit of knowledge and of fear of the LORD.
>
> Isaiah 11:2

Lord, Send Down Your Spirit

Just as the Holy Spirit prepared the Apostles to preach God's Word, so does the Spirit encourage us to act as witnesses in the world. On the Feast of Pentecost, we pray that the Holy Spirit strengthens us as we continue the mission of the Church.

Pentecost, from the Hunterian Psalter, ca. 1170.

Welcome, Holy Spirit

Leader: Let us praise the God of wisdom and grace. Blessed be God forever.

All: Blessed be God forever.

Leader: Just as the Holy Spirit strengthened Jesus' first disciples and enabled them to witness to the Lord, so too may we be strengthened by the Gifts of the Holy Spirit.

Response: Lord, help us be open to your Spirit.

Reader 1: May we receive the gift of wisdom, that we may recognize God's action in our lives. We pray, . . . ℞.

Reader 2: May we receive the gift of fortitude, that we may persevere in our love of God. We pray, . . . ℞.

Reader 3: May we receive the gift of understanding, that our hearts may be open to the message of God's great love. We pray, . . . ℞.

Reader 4: May we receive the gift of knowledge, that we will always seek to know more about God. We pray, . . . ℞.

Reader 5: May we receive the gift of counsel, that we may always show right judgment in the decisions we make. We pray, . . . ℞.

Reader 6: May we receive the gift of piety, that others may see in us a life of faithfulness. We pray, . . . ℞.

Reader 7: May we receive the gift of fear of the Lord, that we may always be in wonder and awe of God's kindness to us. We pray, . . . ℞.

Leader: May the Gifts of the Holy Spirit make us faithful witnesses to Christ and strengthen the Church's mission today. We pray this in Jesus' name.

All: Amen.

All Saints Day

Beloved, we are God's children now; . . .
1 John 3:2

We celebrate the relationship we share with the holy women and men who have gone before us in the faith and who live now with God in heaven. We honor them on November 1, All Saints Day, and November 2, All Souls Day.

PRAYER

Thank you, God, for giving us the saints as guides in faith. Help us learn from them and follow in their ways.

Our Fan Club in Heaven

PRAYER for one another is an integral part of our Catholic Tradition. We believe prayer is central to our spiritual well-being and our relationship with God. Prayer also benefits the entire Christian community when we pray for one another's needs.

Prayer for one another doesn't end with death. We believe in the Communion of Saints, men and women who have been saved in Jesus Christ, who may be living or dead. Those who have died in friendship with God continue to pray for us and to intercede on our behalf before God. We, the living, pray for the dead in Purgatory who are being prepared to see the face of God. In this way, the living and the dead form one family before God.

Who Is a Saint?

The Church elevates certain individuals whose lives exemplify what it means to love God. The saints are not perfect people, but they are spiritual guides and companions. We believe that a saint has led a holy and virtuous life that models a path for us to follow. Through God's grace, the saints have received what we all hope to receive one day, which is God's promised salvation. A saint is a person whom the Church believes now lives with God in heaven. By declaring a person a saint, the Church acknowledges that evidence of God's grace was at work in this person's life as an authentic witness to Christ. Because of the abundance of God's grace in their lives, the saints can intercede before God on behalf of the living.

Litany of the Saints

A litany is a form of prayer in which a number of petitions are offered and the congregation responds. A special form of litany is the Litany of the Saints. In this prayer we ask the saints to pray for us by naming individual saints. This prayer is often prayed as part of the Easter Vigil and at ordinations. However, we might choose to pray this form of prayer anytime we wish to call upon the witness and prayers of those who have gone before us in the faith.

A Calendar Full of Saints

Our Church calendar is filled with the names of saints whom we believe live now with God in heaven. Many of us know the feast days for some popular saints. For example, March 17 is Saint Patrick's Day, March 19 is Saint Joseph's Day, and December 12 is the Feast of Our Lady of Guadalupe.

By popular devotion, some saints are considered patrons for particular needs or causes, which are usually related to an aspect of his or her life. We take our special needs to patron saints and ask them to intercede to God on our behalf. Saint Francis of Assisi is the patron saint of ecology because of his reverence for God's creation. Saint Frances Xavier Cabrini is the patron saint of immigrants because of all the work she did to help immigrants. Sometimes individuals, organizations, churches, and even countries are placed under the patronage of a particular saint. For example, Mary, the Mother of God, is the patroness of the United States.

We remember all these holy men and women whom the Church recognizes as saints on All Saints Day, November 1. In addition to the saints, there are many individuals who live now with God in heaven who haven't been officially declared saints by the Church. Many of us remember the life and witness of family members and friends whom we believe to be unofficial saints. On All Saints Day, we also celebrate these undeclared saints, who also pray for us before God.

All Saints Day Is Also Our Feast Day

In his letters to early Christian communities, Saint Paul often addressed the people as "the holy ones" or "the saints" to remind them of their call to holiness. We, too, are called to be saints. We dedicate our lives to God and pray that through his grace we may join the saints in heaven and live forever in his presence. Devotions to saints, such as pilgrimages to shrines or our use of sacramentals, are practices that deepen our spiritual values and help us learn the path to salvation.

Day of the Dead altar honoring family ancestors.

Our Catholic Character

Our Catholic Tradition distinguishes the prayer and worship we offer to God from the veneration and honor we give to Mary and the saints. Prayer is properly directed only toward God. Of all the saints, Mary is given a place of honor, and we offer special devotion to her. When we honor the saints, we ask for their intercession on our behalf with God. The effects of our devotion to the saints come from God's grace alone.

A Litany of the Saints

On November 1 we celebrate All Saints Day. These holy men and women, recognized by the Church for leading virtuous lives in the service of God, intercede before God on our behalf. The saints in heaven encourage and inspire us to act as witnesses for Christ.

Pray for Us

All: In the name of the Father and of the Son and of the Holy Spirit. Amen.

Leader: God, you have called us to be your children and have given us the grace to become holy. We thank you for uniting us with the holy men and women who have gone before us in the Communion of Saints. We long for the day when we will see you face to face.

Reader: A reading from the First Letter of John.
[1 John 3:1–3]
The Word of the Lord.

All: Thanks be to God.

Leader: Let us pray a Litany of the Saints, asking the holy men and women who are with God in heaven to pray for us.

Response: Pray for us.

Leader: Saint Mary Magdalene ℞.

Leader: Saint Basil ℞.

Leader: Saint Elizabeth ℞.

Leader: Saint Anthony ℞.

Leader: Saint Monica ℞.

Leader: Saint Thomas Aquinas ℞.

All are invited to invoke the names of their favorite saints. ℞.

Leader: May the example of the lives of the saints and their prayers for us lead us to join them one day in the presence of God. We ask this through Christ our Lord.

All: Amen.

Prayers and Practices of Our Faith

Luke

John

The Story of God's Promise

Christ on the Cross, Barthelemy d'Eyck, ca. 1445–50, Louvre, Paris, France.

GOD speaks to us in many different ways. One way that he has revealed himself to us is through Scripture. These collected writings make up the Bible. The Scriptures tell the story of God's promise to care for us, especially through his Son, Jesus. At Mass, readings from the Bible are proclaimed during the Liturgy of the Word. Christians all over the world pray with Scripture when they pray the Liturgy of the Hours or read the Bible on their own.

The Bible is not one book; it is a collection of books that is made up of two parts, the Old Testament and the New Testament. The events we read about in the Bible happened over a period of about 2,000 years. The Old Testament tells about events that unfolded over many centuries. The events in the New Testament happened, for the most part, in a single century. These events occurred during Jesus' lifetime and in the lifetime of his followers during the first century A.D.

Many of the stories that are included in the Bible were first developed in oral cultures. The stories were passed on by word of mouth from one generation to the next. Eventually the stories were written down, the earliest writings in the New Testament being Paul's first letter to the Thessalonians. The writings that make up the Bible were inspired by the Holy Spirit and were written by different authors who used various literary styles.

The Scriptures tell the story of God's promise to care for us.

Two Parts of the Bible

The Bible is made up of two parts: the Old Testament and the New Testament. The Old Testament contains 46 books that tell stories about the Jewish people and their faith in God before Jesus was born.

The New Testament contains 27 books that tell the story of Jesus' life, Death, Resurrection, and Ascension and the experiences of the early Christians. For Christians, the most important books of the New Testament are the four Gospels—Matthew, Mark, Luke, and John.

Finding a Passage

How can you find a passage in the Bible? Bible passages are identified by book, chapter, and verse, such as Genesis 1:28. The name of the book comes first. Sometimes the name is abbreviated. Your Bible's table of contents will help you determine what the abbreviation means. After the name of the book, there are two numbers. The first number identifies the chapter. So for Genesis 1:28, Chapter 1 is being referenced. The number or range of numbers following the colon identifies the verse or verses, which in the example below is verse 28.

Discovering the Truth in the Bible

When we read the Bible, we want to try our best to understand and interpret it accurately. We know that the Bible teaches truth because it is inspired by God. We use the word **inspiration** to explain that God is the author who, through the Holy Spirit, enlightened the minds of human authors while they were writing.

By acting through the authors, the Holy Spirit made sure that they would teach the truth about God with **inerrancy,** which means that the Bible is without error when it tells us a religious truth about God and about God's relationship with us. Religious truth is what we need to know for our salvation, but it is not necessarily a record of scientific and historic facts.

Even though the Bible is inspired by God and teaches religious truth without error, its message needs to be applied to people in every age and in every situation of life. So the Bible must be interpreted. **Interpretation** is a coming to an understanding of the words of Scripture, combining human knowledge with the wisdom and guidance of the teaching office of the Church.

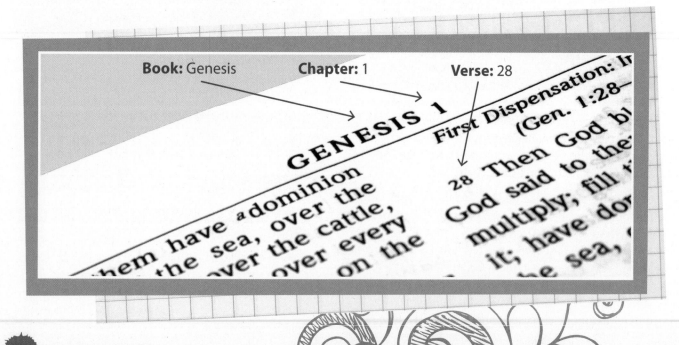

Book: Genesis   Chapter: 1   Verse: 28

GENESIS 1

First Dispensation: Ir
(Gen. 1:28—

...hem have a dominion the sea, over the ...over the cattle, ...over every ...on the

28 Then God bl God said to the ...multiply; fill ...it; have dor ...he sea,

Interpreting with Human Knowledge

Historical Perspective One way to use human knowledge to understand the Bible is to know how people lived, thought, and communicated during biblical times. When Jesus walked the earth, Palestine was occupied by Rome, which had conquered it in 63 B.C. In general, Rome respected Jewish religious practices, but the Jewish people resented the Roman taxes, laws, and troops. Jewish men who collected taxes for Rome were despised as traitors. Jews were not allowed to mix with Gentiles, or non-Jews.

The Jews were divided among various religious and political groups. The Pharisees, largely middle-class Jews, often interpreted the Torah strictly and added many regulations for living a life of holiness. The Sadducees were wealthy and politically powerful. Zealots were freedom fighters who sometimes used violence in attempts to overthrow Rome's control over Palestine. The Essenes were separatists who withdrew to the desert and lived simply as an expression of their desire to live the Jewish faith without contamination from other influences.

Literary Forms We recognize many styles of writing, or literary forms, in the Bible. Some of these literary forms are history, epic stories, gospels, proverbs, letters, wisdom sayings, parables, apocalyptic literature, and poetry. Each literary form serves a particular purpose in relaying God's Word. For example, the story of Jonah and the large fish in the Old Testament is not meant to relay historical facts. Instead, it is an inspired parable. The parable's purpose is to teach a lesson in faith that is divinely inspired. The essential religious truths revealed through the Jonah story are what matters, not the story's factual elements. Jesus used parables too. These stories helped listeners connect ordinary ideas or events in their lives in a way that revealed a deep spiritual truth or lesson about what it means to belong to the Kingdom of God.

The variety of literary forms in the Bible accomplishes what any one form cannot do by itself. Therefore, to discover the author's intention, "[T]he reader must take into account the conditions of their time and culture, the literary genres in use at the time, and the modes of feeling, speaking, and narrating then current." (*CCC* 710)

Interpreting with the Church's Magisterium

The key to understanding the Bible is to seek more than what the story says. The most important point is to unlock the story's meaning. In addition to human knowledge, the Church's Magisterium—the bishops in union with the pope and guided by the Holy Spirit—teach us how to interpret the Bible faithfully. As the official teachers of the Church, the Magisterium makes sure that we interpret the Bible faithfully by helping us understand what is essential for us to know for the sake of our salvation. ✝

Discovering Jesus in the Scriptures

THE Old Testament contains 46 books that tell stories about the Jewish people and their faith in God before Jesus was born. The sections of the Old Testament are the Pentateuch (called the Torah), the historical books, the wisdom books, and the prophetic books.

The Old Testament as we know it today did not begin to take shape until a period known as the Babylonian Exile (587–537 B.C.). It was in Babylon that members of the priestly class took many of the oral and written accounts of God's saving work and put them together in what we now call the Pentateuch.

The Old Testament

The Pentateuch The first five books of the Old Testament—Genesis, Exodus, Leviticus, Numbers, and Deuteronomy—are referred to as the Torah, meaning "instruction" or "law." The stories from the prehistory of Israel that are in the Book of Genesis were probably the first part of the Old Testament to be written. The author is probably King David's court historian, who wrote the stories around 1000 B.C. The author referred to God as Yahweh and spoke of God in human terms. It was this author who wrote the story of God walking in the Garden with Adam and Eve and the story of God's orderly creation of the world in six days and his rest on the seventh.

King David

Moses

Torah

Paul

The central story in the Torah is the Exodus. After the Hebrews had been enslaved by the Egyptians, God called Moses to lead them out of Egypt to the Promised Land. During the journey, God gave Moses and the people the Ten Commandments.

The Historical Books The historical books were put together from the court accounts of various kings of Israel and Judah, such as Saul, David, and Solomon. This section of the Old Testament records the story of the Israelites who fought to establish and maintain control of the Promised Land, to which God had delivered them during the Exodus.

The Wisdom Books These books are a collection of the wisdom teachings of the Israelites that surfaced over thousands of years. These writings include wisdom about the time when the people wandered the desert during the Exodus, their time living in the Promised Land, and their struggle during a period of exile known as the Babylonian Exile.

One of the best-known wisdom books is the Book of Psalms. A psalm is a prayer in the form of a poem. Each psalm expresses an aspect, or feature, of the depth of human emotion. Over several centuries, 150 psalms were gathered to form the Book of Psalms. They were once sung at the Temple, the house of worship first built by Solomon in Jerusalem. The psalms have been used in the public worship of the Church since its beginning. We often pray the psalms as part of our private prayer and reflection.

The Prophetic Books A large part of the Old Testament, 18 books, presents the messages and actions of the prophets. These were people called by God to speak for him to urge the Jewish people to be faithful to the covenant.

The New Testament

The second part of the Bible, the New Testament, contains 27 books. Even though the most important books of the New Testament are the four writings known as Gospels, in reality, one "gospel" of and about Jesus Christ, runs through the books. While the first three Gospels (Matthew, Mark, and Luke) reveal events of Jesus' life in different ways, the stories are similar enough to be read side by side. Because of this, we call them **synoptic.**

Many books of the New Testament are letters written by early Church leaders such as Paul. In reading about Jesus' public ministry, his Paschal Mystery, and the life of the early Church, we discover our own call to discipleship.

Mark

The Gospel of Mark reveals the nature of true discipleship.

The Gospel of Mark

The Gospel of Mark was most likely written between the years A.D. 65 and 70. These were troublesome years for both Jews and the first Christians in the Mediterranean world. The Church in Rome had just suffered the first large-scale persecution at the hands of the Roman government. The Church in Palestine, still close to its Jewish roots, watched as Roman armies invaded to crush a Jewish uprising. This invasion ended with the conquest of Jerusalem and the destruction of the Temple in the year A.D. 70. Early Christian converts who had embraced Jesus with a great spirit of hope and expectation discovered that they now lived in the midst of suffering and destruction.

In these times of trouble, what message of comfort and hope could be given to Christians? Mark responded by writing the first Gospel account. He proclaimed Jesus as the Son of God sent by the Father to save the human family through service and the sacrifice of his life for our salvation.

Writing the Gospel From his vantage point as Peter's companion in Rome, Mark collected Jesus' teachings and sayings, the stories and preaching about Jesus, and the stories of the events of the Last Supper and Jesus' Death on the Cross. He then shaped these stories into a larger story to help Christians recognize that Jesus was the Son of God. The Gospel of Mark was written in everyday Greek so it could be read by the mostly Greek-speaking audience. Mark presented Jesus as a dynamic figure who was always on the move, proclaiming the Kingdom of God to all who would listen. Mark's Gospel, being the first one written, strongly influenced the Gospels of Matthew and Luke, whose writings would follow.

Jesus as Healer and Teacher In the Gospel of Mark, Chapters 1—8, Jesus is a powerful healer and preacher. Even as he performs a number of miracles and explains the meaning of his parables, his disciples don't seem to understand the meaning of who he is. (Mark 4:13) After Jesus performs miracles, he orders his disciples not to talk about them, but

they continue to anyway. (Mark 7:36) The disciples don't understand that the real meaning of Jesus is not in his miracles and parables. The consistent theme in Mark is that it is not simply the miracles that reveal Jesus' true nature. It is Jesus' willingness to face the Cross that defines who he is for us. And if we are to be his disciples, we must face the same difficulties. "Whoever wishes to come after me must deny himself, take up his cross, and follow me." (Mark 8:34)

The Gospel of Mark reveals the nature of true discipleship. Jesus tells his followers that life in service to him is a life in service to others.

> "Rather, whoever wishes to be great among you will be your servant; whoever wishes to be first among you will be the slave of all. For the Son of Man did not come to be served but to serve and to give his life as a ransom for many."
>
> *Mark 10:43–45*

The Gospel of Mark describes the Crucifixion and Death of Jesus. When Mark writes that a Roman centurion who is witnessing Jesus' Death recognizes him as the Son of God, we hear Mark's message—we must look to the Cross to understand the depth of God's loving sacrifice for us.

The Gospel of Matthew

The Gospel of Matthew was written in a Jewish-Christian community in Syria about A.D. 70s–80s. One ancient tradition attributes the Gospel to the Apostle Matthew. It is more likely that the writer was a leader in the local church, possibly a converted rabbi, who was well-versed in the Scriptures. This Gospel writer faced the challenge of Jewish Christians interacting and worshiping with Gentiles, who were also members of the community. When it became clear that the majority of Jews would not become Christians, Matthew encouraged the Jewish-Christian community to recognize itself as the true heirs of God's promises to Israel.

The message and love of Jesus is not for Jews alone. To include the Gentile members of the community, Matthew showed that Jesus came to save everyone.

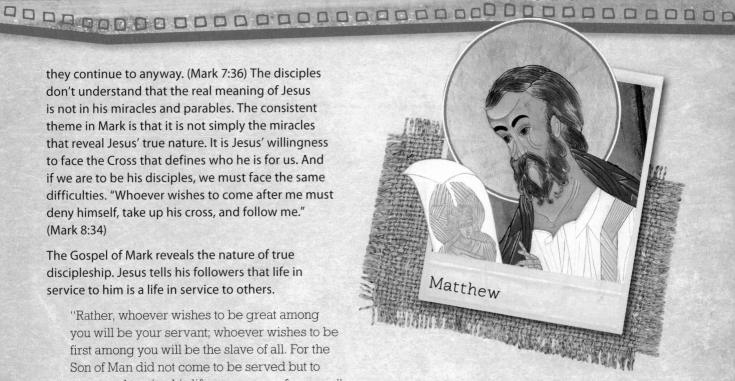

Matthew

Matthew incorporated Gentiles into the very beginning of Jesus' story. He told the story of the Wise Men from the East who were the first to pay homage to Jesus as the Messiah. (Matthew 2:10–11) The Wise Men were not Jews. They were Gentiles, an important segment of Matthew's audience. Matthew stressed that Jesus gave instructions to the disciples to proclaim the Gospel to the entire world, baptizing in the name of the Father, the Son, and the Holy Spirit. (Matthew 28:19–20)

Jesus as the New Moses Matthew presents Jesus as the new Moses. His Gospel describes how Jesus retraced the steps of Moses' journey. Mary and Joseph took the infant Jesus to Egypt to escape the murderous rage of King Herod. They stayed there until Herod's death. Like his Hebrew ancestors, Jesus was called out of Egypt, and he retraced their journey to the Holy Land. (Matthew 2:15)

Exodus chapters 19—20 tells us that Moses went up on Mount Sinai to receive the Law from God. Matthew chapters 5—7 recounts how Jesus went up a mountain not to receive the Law, but to deliver the New Law. Moses spoke with God's authority, but Jesus spoke with his own authority as the Son of God. As the Son of God, Jesus understands and proclaims the true meaning of the Law.

The New Law Matthew had great respect for the Law. He wished to emphasize its continuing validity for the both Jewish and Gentile Christians.

> "Do not think that I [Jesus] have come to abolish the law or the prophets. I have come not to abolish but to fulfill. Amen, I say to you, until heaven and earth pass away, not the smallest letter or the smallest part of a letter will pass from the law, until all things have taken place."
>
> *Matthew 5:17–18*

Jesus also understood and proclaimed the true meaning of the Law. Through their faith in Jesus, Christians followed the true intent of the Law.

Matthew and the Church Matthew viewed the Church as the way to pass on the real meaning of Jesus' identity. He stressed that Peter, as the head of the disciples, was the leader of the Church. (Matthew 10:2) Since Peter was the leader of the Church, he shared Christ's authority. (Matthew 9:8; 10:40) God is united with his people through the Church. (Matthew 28:18–20)

The Gospel of Luke and the Acts of the Apostles

By the year A.D. 85, Christianity was becoming well established in the cities of the Roman empire. Gentile citizens were becoming more interested in the Church, but they still had questions. Some Christians expected Christ to return soon, even within their lifetime. But it was becoming apparent that the Christian journey would continue through time. How could early Christians live by their values in a world dominated by Rome? The Gospel of Luke and the Acts of the Apostles, two different works by one author, are, in part, responses to this question.

The Writer of Luke Early Christian tradition attributes the Gospel of Luke and the Acts of the Apostles to Luke, a Syrian from Antioch. He is mentioned in the New Testament in Colossians 4:14, Philippians 1:24, and 2 Timothy 4:11. The writer of the Gospel of Luke identifies himself as a second-generation Christian who uses other sources to help

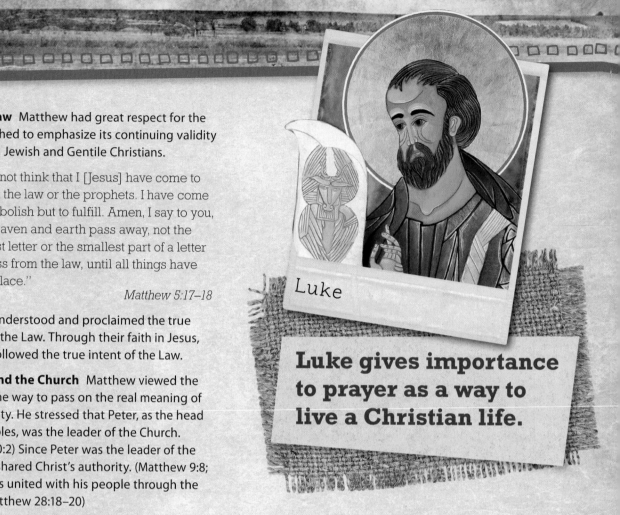

Luke

Luke gives importance to prayer as a way to live a Christian life.

him tell the story. Both the Gospel and the Acts of the Apostles were addressed to Theophilus, which means "friend of God" in Greek. The Gospel of Luke portrays the beginning of the Christian story from the announcement that the Messiah is coming to the Death and Resurrection of Jesus. The Acts of the Apostles starts with the Resurrection and Ascension of Jesus and then continues with events involving the spread of the Church.

Citizens of the Empire Luke sets his story in the Roman empire. Although Jesus was condemned by a Roman magistrate, Luke shows the Romans in a positive light. In Luke 7:9, Jesus says of the Roman centurion seeking a cure for his slave, "I tell you, not even in Israel have I found such faith." (Luke 7:9) Later, in Acts of the Apostles, Cornelius, a Roman centurion in Caesarea, is described as a prayerful, God-fearing man who gave generously to the Jewish people. (Acts of the Apostles 10:1–2) Luke wants his readers to understand that Christianity is compatible with the Roman world.

Guidance of the Holy Spirit The work of the Holy Spirit is highlighted in both the Gospel of Luke and the Acts of the Apostles. Through the power of the Holy Spirit, Mary conceives the Messiah. (Luke 1:35) Elizabeth, inspired by the Holy Spirit, recognizes Mary as the mother of the Messiah. (Luke 1:41)

The Holy Spirit is active in the life of Jesus. The Spirit leads Jesus into the desert. (Luke 4:1) Jesus returns from the desert in the power of the Spirit. (Luke 4:14) When Jesus returns and reads the Scriptures in the synagogue, he identifies himself as the one on whom the Spirit rests. (Luke 4:18)

The Holy Spirit is especially present in the Acts of the Apostles. The Holy Spirit empowers the disciples to preach the Gospel and sends them as missionaries (Acts of the Apostles 2:1–17; 16:6–7) Luke tells these stories to emphasize that the Holy Spirit is always a part of Christian life. The same Holy Spirit leads and guides the Church today.

Prayer Luke stresses the importance of prayer. salvation is first announced to Zechariah when he is serving in the Temple and the whole assembly is praying. (Luke 3:9–10) Simeon and Anna recognize the infant Jesus as the Messiah as a result of their years of prayer in the Temple. (Luke 2:25–38) Jesus prays before he chooses the Twelve Apostles. (Luke 6:12) He prays before the Transfiguration. (Luke 9:29) Active and enthusiastic prayer is also a characteristic of the early Christian community. (Acts of the Apostles 1:13–14; 2:42; 3:1) By telling these stories, Luke gives importance to prayer as a way to live a Christian life.

The Gospel of John

The Gospel of John was written around A.D. 90. This was 50 to 60 years after Jesus' life, Death, Resurrection, and Ascension. Although this Gospel has been attributed to the Apostle John, it is more likely to have been written by a few members of the early Christian community. It was common practice to write in the name of a person admired by the community so that people would pay attention to the writing. Since the Gospel was written nearly two

generations after Jesus walked the earth, the writer was able to reflect on what had already been written and taught about Jesus.

The Prologue in John 1:1–18 introduces the main theme of the Gospel—God's Revelation. It explains that the Word was with God from the beginning and that the Word of God became man in Jesus. Jesus, in turn, reveals the Father's great love for us. Jesus is fully God, fully man.

Reborn in Baptism through the power of the Holy Spirit, we participate in the divine nature of Jesus Christ. God dwells in us, and we become witnesses to his presence in the world. In Jesus, God's glory is revealed as a sign of his everlasting love.

The Book of Signs John's Gospel is divided into two major sections: the Book of Signs and the Book of Glory. The Book of Signs, John 1:19—12:50, recounts Jesus' wondrous deeds. Jesus transforms the water into wine at Cana not only to save his friends the embarrassment of running out of wine. The abundance of wine that Jesus provides is a sign that the kingdom has come in the person of Jesus.

John

St. Paul the Apostle, Claude Vignon, 17th century.

Chapter 3 of the Gospel of John tells about the Jewish leader Nicodemus, who comes in the night to speak with Jesus. He does not want to be recognized by his peers. Nicodemus is coming out of the darkness and into the light of Jesus. Jesus speaks to Nicodemus about faith and baptism. He tells Nicodemus that he has come because of the Father's great love for the world. Jesus has come to save the world.

The Book of Glory The second major section of John's Gospel, John 13:1 through 20:31, is known as the Book of Glory. These chapters recount the Last Supper and Jesus' Passion and Death. John shows how Jesus reverses the values of the world. Crucifixion was a Roman punishment, a horrible and slow death inflicted on those despised by the government. Instead of being a sign of shame, John reveals the glory of God through Jesus' victory of the Cross Through Jesus' ultimate sacrifice, we come to realize that we might be saved.

Before he returns to the Father, Jesus tells his disciples to be hopeful. Jesus promises that he will not leave them alone in the world. He will send an Advocate, the Holy Spirit, to be with them and to guide them. As time went on, the disciples experienced the glory of Jesus' presence, especially when they were persecuted for proclaiming the Good News. Jesus did not leave them orphans, and neither does he leave us.

The Letters of Paul

The Apostle Paul was the greatest of the early Christian missionaries. But before he did great work for God, he was a Pharisee and an early opponent of the Christian Church. Paul believed in the strict observance of God's Law, both for himself and for all Jews. While journeying to Damascus, Paul had an encounter with the risen Christ. (Acts of the Apostles 9:1–19) Paul became convinced that fellowship with the risen Jesus Christ, not the observance of the Law, was all that was needed to receive God's promise for salvation. (Galatians 1:11–12; 3:1–5)

Paul's Writings Thirteen Epistles bear Paul's name. However, scholars do not believe that he wrote them all. Paul was the author of 1 Thessalonians, 2 Thessalonians, Galatians, Philippians, 1 Corinthians, 2 Corinthians, Romans, and Philemon. The letters to the Ephesians, Colossians, Titus, 1 Timothy, and 2 Timothy bear Paul's name, but scholars believe that these were written after Paul's death. The writers of these letters were likely disciples of Paul who continued his teaching. Whoever the authors of these Epistles were, the writings have been accepted as inspired by the Holy Spirit and are part of the New Testament.

Centrality of Jesus Christ

Centrality of Jesus Christ The most profound day in Paul's life was when he met the risen Jesus Christ. Paul was well respected by the Jewish community and his peers. But he gave it all up for Christ. "More than that, I even consider everything as a loss because of the supreme good of knowing Christ Jesus my Lord." (Philippians 3:8)

Paul realized that Jesus had been sent by the Father to bring salvation for all. He taught that we are united with Christ in faith and Baptism. "We were indeed buried with him through baptism into death, so that, just as Christ was raised from the dead by the glory of the Father, we too might live in newness of life." (Romans 6:4)

Justification Paul believed that the justice of God was saving justice at its best. God is faithful, fulfilling the promises made in the covenant with his people. God has taken the initiative to call the human family back to him through Christ. This process of reuniting the human family with God is called justification. (Romans 3:21–31)

We cannot justify ourselves; we can only be justified by being united in faith with Jesus Christ and by accepting the grace won by Christ. (Romans 5:1–2) Christians can only be made right with God and set free from a life of immorality by accepting God's reconciling grace. Christians recognize that when they are united with and justified by Christ, they are given the grace needed to overcome sin and to live moral lives. (Galatians 5:16–26)

Life in the Spirit Paul teaches that it is through the Holy Spirit that the love of God has been poured out to us. (Romans 5:5) The Holy Spirit is the source of all love, and the Spirit creates a bond between ourselves and God like children bound to a father. (Romans 8:14–16) Even though we are weak, the Holy Spirit helps us live faithfully within that relationship. (Romans 8:26–27) It is through the Holy Spirit that we can live in love with all people. (1 Corinthians 13:3–7)

Other Epistles and the Book of Revelation

The remaining letters include the letters of Peter, which reflect the concerns of the Church in Rome; the letter to the Hebrews, a homily on early Christian themes; the letter of Jude; the letters of John; and the Book of Revelation. Revelation is an example of apocalyptic literature, a type of writing popular in Judaism at the time. Revelation presents a vision of the end of the world in which the good and just triumph. It was written to address a crisis—the persecution of Christians by the Roman emperor Domitian. Revelation offered encouragement to the people to endure during this difficult time and was not intended to be interpreted literally. ✝

Time Line of the New Testament

New Testament Books

A.D. 51	1 Thessalonians
51 or 90s	2 Thessalonians*
54–57	Galatians

56–57	Philippians
56–57 or 61–63	Philemon*
57	1 Corinthians, 2 Corinthians
58	Romans
60s or 70s–80s	Hebrews*

61–63 or 70–80	Colossians*
61–63 or 90–100	Ephesians*
62 or 70s–80s	James*
64 or 70s–80s	1 Peter*
65–70	Gospel of Mark
65 or 95–100	Titus*
65 or 95–100	1 Timothy*

66–67 or 95–100	2 Timothy*
70s–80s	Gospel of Matthew
70s–80s	Gospel of Luke, Acts of the Apostles
70s–90s	Jude*

| 90s | Gospel of John |
| 90s | 1 John, 2 John, 3 John, Revelation |

| 100–150 | 2 Peter |

Source: *The New Jerome Biblical Commentary*

History

A.D. 5

| 4 B.C. | Birth of Jesus in Bethlehem* |

15

| A.D. 14 | Death of Caesar Augustus; Tiberius becomes Roman emperor |

25

28	Death and Resurrection of Jesus—Pentecost; birth of the Church*
34	Martyrdom of Saint Stephen*
34–36	Conversion of Paul*

35

| 45 | Paul begins missionary travels |
| 49 | Council of Jerusalem |

45

55

62–63	Paul arrives in Rome*
64	Nero begins a persecution of Christians in Rome
67–68	Deaths of Peter and Paul in Rome
70	The Temple is destroyed by the Romans

65

75

85

95

| 96 | Death of Emperor Domitian, persecutor of Christians |
| Late 90s | Decision made on which books are part of the Old Testament |

105

| 122–135 | Final Jewish uprising under Bar Kochba; Jerusalem completely destroyed |

264

* Dates are approximate.

Saint Paul's Missionary Journeys

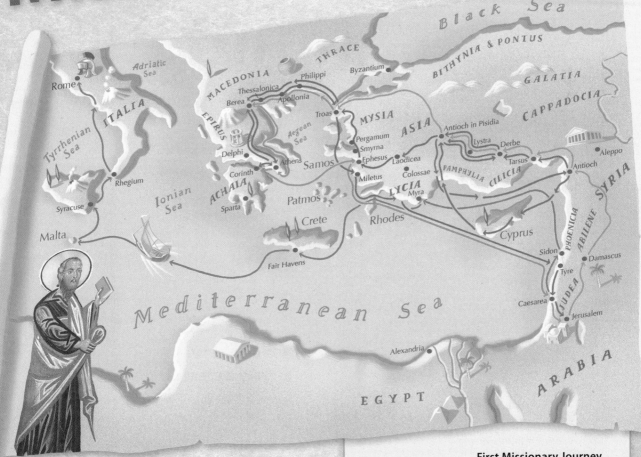

First Missionary Journey
(A.D. 47–49)

Second Missionary Journey
(A.D. 49–52)

Third Missionary Journey
(A.D. 53–58)

Journey to Rome
(A.D. 60–61)

0   100   200 MILES

0   100   200   300 KILOMETERS

Formulas of Catholic Doctrine

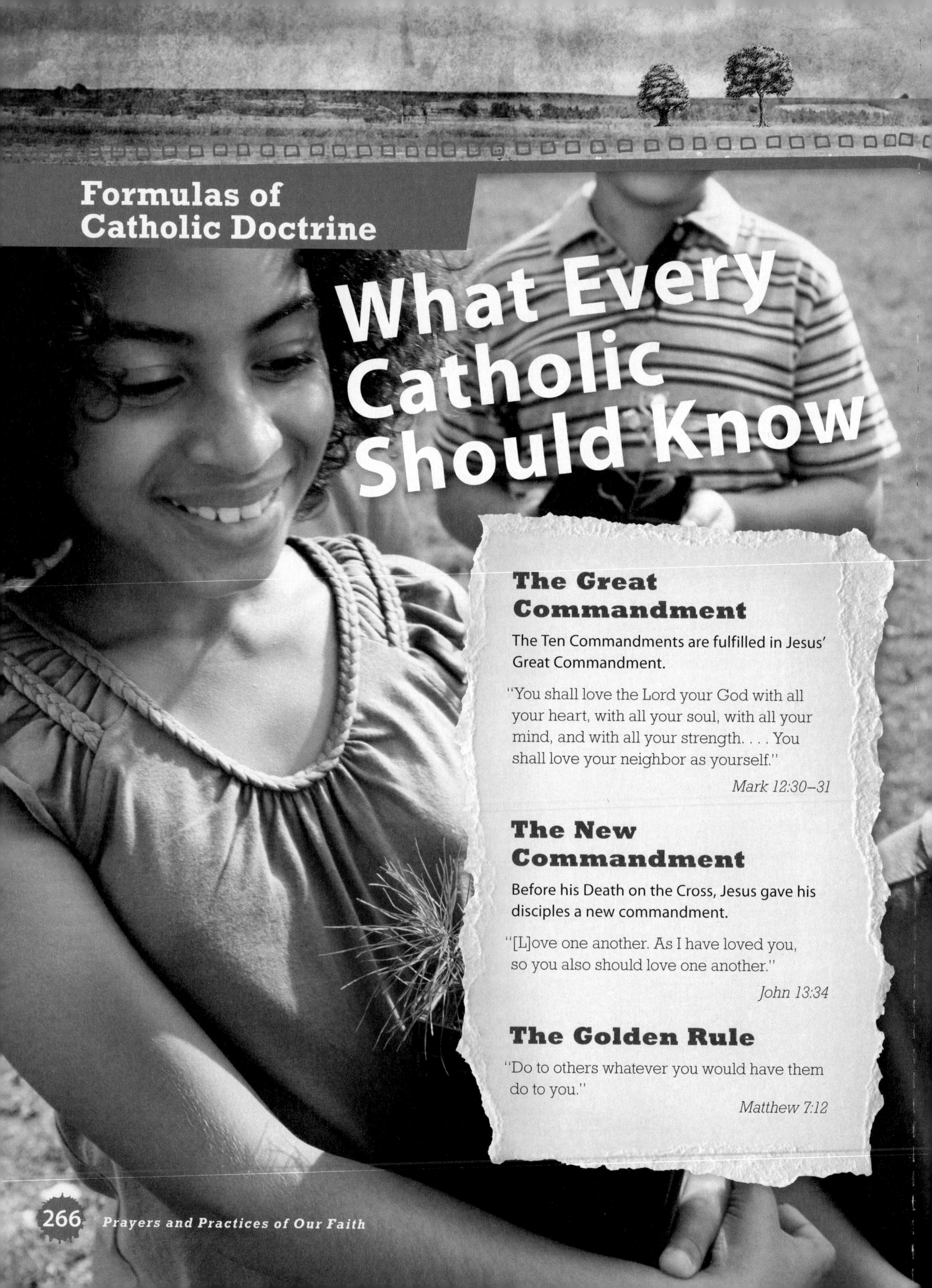

What Every Catholic Should Know

The Great Commandment

The Ten Commandments are fulfilled in Jesus' Great Commandment.

"You shall love the Lord your God with all your heart, with all your soul, with all your mind, and with all your strength. . . . You shall love your neighbor as yourself."

Mark 12:30–31

The New Commandment

Before his Death on the Cross, Jesus gave his disciples a new commandment.

"[L]ove one another. As I have loved you, so you also should love one another."

John 13:34

The Golden Rule

"Do to others whatever you would have them do to you."

Matthew 7:12

The Beatitudes

The Beatitudes are the teachings of Jesus in the Sermon on the Mount. Jesus teaches us that if we live according to the Beatitudes, we will live a happy Christian life. The Beatitudes fulfill God's promises made to Abraham and his descendants. Jesus' guidelines describe the rewards that will be ours in this life and eternal joy in the next as faithful followers of Christ.

''Blessed are the poor in spirit,
for theirs is the kingdom of heaven.
Blessed are they who mourn,
for they will be comforted.
Blessed are the meek,
for they will inherit the land.
Blessed are they who hunger and thirst
for righteousness,
for they will be satisfied.
Blessed are the merciful,
for they will be shown mercy.
Blessed are the clean of heart,
for they will see God.
Blessed are the peacemakers,
for they will be called children of God.
Blessed are they who are persecuted
for the sake of righteousness,
for theirs is the kingdom of heaven.''

Matthew 5:1–10

Sermon on the Mount,
Laura James.

The Ten Commandments

As believers in Jesus Christ, we are called to a new life and asked to make moral choices that keep us united with God. With the help and grace of the Holy Spirit, we can choose ways to act to keep us close to God, to help other people, and to be witnesses to Jesus.

The Ten Commandments guide us in making choices that help us live as God wants us to live. The first three commandments tell us how to love God. The other seven tell us how to love our neighbor.

1. I am the Lord your God: you shall not have strange gods before me.

2. You shall not take the name of the Lord your God in vain.

3. Remember to keep holy the Lord's Day.

4. Honor your father and your mother.

5. You shall not kill.

6. You shall not commit adultery.

7. You shall not steal.

8. You shall not bear false witness against your neighbor.

9. You shall not covet your neighbor's wife.

10. You shall not covet your neighbor's goods.

Precepts of the Church

The precepts of the Church provide the faithful with a foundation for living a Catholic life. These rules describe the minimum effort we must make in prayer and in living a moral life. All Catholics are called to move beyond the minimum by growing in love of God and love of neighbor. The precepts of the Church are as follows:

† attendance at Mass on Sundays and holy days of obligation

† confession of sins at least once a year

† reception of the Eucharist at least once a year during the Easter season

† observance of the days of fast and abstinence on prescribed days and times of the Church year as a way to grow in holiness through self-sacrifice

† providing for the needs of the Church. This includes supporting the Church with our talents, gifts, service, and financial assistance.

The Four Last Things

The end of human life is the beginning of eternal life. Immediately upon death, we are rewarded according to our deeds and faith. At death, Christ gives a judgment and destination for each soul.

The four last things describe the end of human life for all:

death   judgment   heaven   hell

Virtues

Virtues are gifts from God to do what is right and good. They lead us to live in a close relationship with God. Virtues are like good habits. They need to be practiced; they can be lost if they are neglected.

Theological Virtues

The three most important virtues are called Theological Virtues because they are gifts from God and lead to God. God gives us the Theological Virtues so we can live as his children and merit eternal life.

faith   hope   charity

Cardinal Virtues

The Cardinal Virtues are human virtues that can be acquired by education and good actions. *Cardinal* comes from *cardo*, the Latin word for "hinge," meaning "that on which other things depend."

prudence   justice   fortitude   temperance

Prudence This virtue helps us discern good from evil and abide by our conscience.

Justice Justice is the strong will to rightly give what is due to God and neighbor.

Fortitude Fortitude is the strength and courage to face difficulties and do what is right.

Temperance This is a virtue of moderation in pleasures, providing balance in the use of material goods.

Gifts of the Holy Spirit

The Holy Spirit makes it possible for us to do what God asks of us by giving us these many gifts.

wisdom   understanding   counsel   piety
fortitude   knowledge   fear of the Lord

Fruits of the Holy Spirit

The Fruits of the Holy Spirit are signs of the Holy Spirit's action in our lives.

love	kindness	faithfulness
joy	goodness	modesty
peace	generosity	self-control
patience	gentleness	chastity

Works of Mercy

Mercy is a virtue that influences a person's compassion for another. Mercy influences the will to ease another's misfortunes or suffering in either body or soul. The corporal and spiritual works of mercy are charitable actions that extend God's compassion and mercy to those in need.

However, the works of mercy are more than gestures or obligations. To gain merit in heaven, the actions must be performed as acts of love for our neighbor as a response to our deep love for God. The corporal and spiritual works of mercy work together as paths to salvation. They give Christians ways to live according to Jesus' Great Commandment.

Corporal Works of Mercy

The corporal works of mercy are kind acts by which we help our neighbors with their material and physical needs:

✝ feed the hungry

✝ give drink to the thirsty

✝ clothe the naked

✝ shelter the homeless

✝ visit the sick

✝ visit the imprisoned

✝ bury the dead

Spiritual Works of Mercy

The spiritual works of mercy are acts of compassion by which we help our neighbors with their emotional and spiritual needs:

✝ counsel the doubtful

✝ instruct the ignorant

✝ admonish sinners

✝ comfort the afflicted

✝ forgive offenses

✝ bear wrongs patiently

✝ pray for the living and the dead

" . . . 'Amen, I say
to you, what you
did not do for
one of these least
ones, you did not
do for me.'"

Matthew 25:45

Prayer and Forms of Prayer

GOD is always with us. He wants us to talk to him and to listen to him. In prayer we raise our hearts and minds to God. We are able to speak to and listen to God because through the Holy Spirit, God teaches us how to pray.

What Is Prayer?

Being a Christian requires that we believe all that God has revealed to us, that we celebrate it in the liturgy and the sacraments, and that we live what we believe. All of this depends on a vital and personal relationship with the living and true God. This relationship is found in prayer.

Prayer is, first of all, a gift from God. We can pray because God first seeks us out and calls us to meet him. We become aware of our thirst for God because God thirsts for us. Prayer arises from our heart, beyond the grasp of reason. Only the Spirit of God can understand the human heart and know it fully. Prayer is the habit of being with God—Father, Son, and Holy Spirit. This communion with God is always possible because through our Baptism we are united with Christ. Christian prayer is communion with Christ that branches out to all the members of his Body, the Church.

Meditate and Contemplate

To **meditate** is to think about God and to focus your attention on him alone. You may use Scripture, prayer books, or icons (religious images) to help you concentrate and to spark your imagination. Another way to pray is to **contemplate.** To contemplate is to rest quietly in God's presence.

Get Ready to Pray

You can get ready to pray by resting your body in a comfortable position. You might close your eyes and fold your hands comfortably in front of you. Concentrating on your breathing, slowly breathing in and out, helps quiet your thoughts.

Avoid Distractions

If distracting thoughts remove your focus from God, go back to thinking about your breathing. After some practice, you will be able to avoid distractions, pray with your imagination, and spend time with God in your heart and mind.

The Five Basic Forms of Christian Prayer

The Holy Spirit teaches us to pray. Our conversation with God can take different forms.

Blessing

To bless someone is to acknowledge his or her goodness. The prayer of blessing, or adoration, is our response to God's goodness because of all the gifts he has given us. In the prayer of blessing, God's gifts and our acceptance of them come together.

Petition

In prayers of petition, we do more than ask God for things we want or need. We express our relationship with God as our Creator and Father and we as his children, who depend on him for all good things. When we sin and turn away from God, we can turn back toward him and petition for forgiveness.

Intercession

In prayers of intercession, we ask God for something on behalf of another. Intercession is a prayer of petition that leads us to pray as Jesus did. Throughout his life on earth, Jesus interceded with the Father on behalf of all people. To pray in this way means that our hearts are turned outward, focused on the needs of others.

Thanksgiving

Thanksgiving as a form of prayer is especially realized in the Eucharist. *Eucharist* means "thanksgiving." Through his Death and Resurrection, Christ has reconciled us to God. His sacrifice is made present in the Eucharist. When we receive the Eucharist, we become a people of thanksgiving.

Praise

Praise is a form of prayer that recognizes God and gives him glory. Praise goes beyond thanking God for what he has done for us. A prayer of praise gives God glory simply because he is. Praise embraces the other forms of prayer and carries them to God, who is the source of all that is. †

Prayers to Take to Heart

WE can pray with any words that come to mind. Sometimes, when we find that choosing our own words is difficult, we can use traditional prayers. Likewise, when we pray aloud with others, we rely on traditional prayers to unite our minds, hearts, and voices. Memorizing traditional prayers such as the following can be very helpful. When we memorize prayers, we take them to heart, meaning that we not only learn the words but also try to understand and live them.

Pope Benedict XVI has identified four prayers that are shared by the universal Church. If they are learned in Latin, they can be prayed as a sign of the universal nature of the Church. Catholics throughout the world would be praying in the same language. The Latin versions of these four prayers are included across from each of them.

Lord's Prayer

Our Father, who art in heaven,
hallowed be thy name;
thy kingdom come,
thy will be done
on earth as it is in heaven.
Give us this day our daily bread,
and forgive us our trespasses,
as we forgive those who trespass against us;
and lead us not into temptation,
but deliver us from evil.
Amen.

Pater Noster

Pater noster, qui es in caelis,
sanctificetur nomen tuum.
Adveniat regnum tuum.
Fiat voluntas tua,
sicut in caelo et in terra.
Panem nostrum quotidianum da nobis hodie,
et dimitte nobis debita nostra
sicut et nos dimittimus debitoribus nostris.
Et ne nos inducas in tentationem,
sed libera nos a malo.
Amen.

Hail Mary

Hail Mary, full of grace,
the Lord is with you.
Blessed are you among women,
and blessed is the fruit of your womb, Jesus.
Holy Mary, Mother of God,
pray for us sinners,
now and at the hour of our death.
Amen.

Ave Maria

Ave Maria, gratia plena,
Dominus tecum.
Benedicta tu in mulieribus,
et benedictus fructus ventris tui, Iesus.
Sancta Maria, Mater Dei,
ora pro nobis peccatoribus,
nunc, et in hora mortis nostrae.
Amen.

The Sign of the Cross

In the name of the Father, and of the Son,
and of the Holy Spirit.
Amen.

Glory Be to the Father (Doxology)

Glory be to the Father, and to the Son, and to
the Holy Spirit. As it was in the beginning, is
now, and ever shall be, world without end.
Amen.

Morning Offering

My God, I offer you my prayers, works, joys
and sufferings of this day in union with the
holy sacrifice of the Mass throughout the world.
I offer them for all the intentions of your
Son's Sacred Heart, for the salvation of souls,
reparation for sin, and the reunion of Christians.
Amen.

Prayer Before Meals

Bless us, O Lord, and these your gifts
which we are about to receive from your goodness.
Through Christ our Lord.
Amen.

Prayer After Meals

We give you thanks
for all your gifts,
almighty God,
living and reigning
now and for ever.
Amen.

Signum Crucis

*In nomine Patris, et Filii,
et Spiritus Sancti.
Amen.*

Gloria Patri

*Gloria Patri, et Filio, et Spiritui Sancto.
Sicut erat in principio, et nunc, et semper,
et in saecula saeculorum.
Amen.*

Act of Contrition

My God,
I am sorry for my sins with all my heart.
In choosing to do wrong
and failing to do good,
I have sinned against you
whom I should love above all things.
I firmly intend, with your help,
to do penance,
to sin no more,
and to avoid whatever leads me to sin.
Our Savior Jesus Christ
suffered and died for us.
In his name, my God, have mercy.

Prayer to the Holy Spirit

Come, Holy Spirit, fill the hearts of your faithful.
And kindle in them the fire of your love.
Send forth your Spirit and they shall be created.
And you will renew the face of the earth.
Let us pray.

Lord,
by the light of the Holy Spirit
you have taught the hearts of your faithful.
In the same Spirit
help us to relish what is right
and always rejoice in your consolation.
We ask this through Christ our Lord.
Amen.

Nicene Creed

I believe in one God,
the Father almighty,
maker of heaven and earth,
of all things visible and invisible.

I believe in one Lord Jesus Christ,
the Only Begotten Son of God,
born of the Father before all ages.
God from God, Light from Light,
true God from true God,
begotten, not made, consubstantial
    with the Father;
through him all things were made.
For us men and for our salvation
he came down from heaven,
and by the Holy Spirit was incarnate of the
    Virgin Mary,
and became man.

For our sake he was crucified under
    Pontius Pilate,
he suffered death and was buried,
and rose again on the third day
in accordance with the Scriptures.
He ascended into heaven
and is seated at the right hand of the Father.
He will come again in glory
to judge the living and the dead
and his kingdom will have no end.

I believe in the Holy Spirit, the Lord,
    the giver of life,
who proceeds from the Father and the Son,
who with the Father and the Son is adored
    and glorified,
who has spoken through the prophets.

I believe in one, holy, catholic and
    apostolic Church.
I confess one Baptism for the forgiveness of sins
and I look forward to the resurrection of the dead
and the life of the world to come. Amen.

Apostles' Creed

I believe in God,
the Father almighty,
Creator of heaven and earth,
and in Jesus Christ, his only Son, our Lord,
who was conceived by the Holy Spirit,
born of the Virgin Mary,
suffered under Pontius Pilate,
was crucified, died and was buried;
he descended into hell;
on the third day he rose again from the dead;
he ascended into heaven,
and is seated at the right hand of God
    the Father almighty;
from there he will come to judge the living
    and the dead.

I believe in the Holy Spirit,
the holy catholic Church,
the communion of saints,
the forgiveness of sins,
the resurrection of the body,
and life everlasting. Amen.

Act of Faith

O my God, I firmly believe that you are one God in three divine Persons, Father, Son, and Holy Spirit. I believe that your divine Son became man and died for our sins, and that he will come to judge the living and the dead. I believe these and all the truths which the holy Catholic Church teaches, because you have revealed them, who can neither deceive nor be deceived.
Amen.

Act of Hope

O my God, relying on your infinite mercy and promises, I hope to obtain pardon of my sins, the help of your grace, and life everlasting, through the merits of Jesus Christ, my Lord and Redeemer.
Amen.

Act of Love

O my God, I love you above all things with my whole heart and soul, because you are all good and worthy of all my love. I love my neighbor as myself for the love of you. I forgive all who have injured me and I ask pardon of those whom I have injured.
Amen.

Prayer for Vocations

God, in Baptism you called me by name
and made me a member of your people, the Church.
Help all your people to know their vocation in life,
and to respond by living a life of holiness.
For your greater glory and for the service
   of your people,
raise up dedicated and generous leaders
who will serve as sisters, priests,
brothers, deacons, and lay ministers.

Send your Spirit to guide and strengthen me
that I may serve your people
following the example of your Son, Jesus Christ,
in whose name I offer this prayer.
Amen.

Jesus Prayer

Lord Jesus Christ, Son of God,
   have mercy on us sinners.

Prayer for Generosity

Eternal Word, only begotten Son of God,
Teach me true generosity.
Teach me to serve you as you deserve.
To give without counting the cost,
To fight heedless of wounds,
To labor without seeking rest,
To sacrifice myself without thought of any reward
Save the knowledge that I have done your will. Amen.

Suscipe

Take, Lord, and receive all my liberty,
my memory, my understanding,
and my entire will.
All I have and call my own.

You have given all to me.
To you, Lord, I return it.

Everything is yours; do with it what you will.
Give me only your love and your grace.
That is enough for me.

The Daily Examen

SAINT Ignatius of Loyola gave the Church a great gift—the Spiritual Exercises. Praying with the Spiritual Exercises helps us discover God's plan for us.

The Daily Examen is an important part of the Spiritual Exercises. When we pray the Daily Examen, we reflect on the events of the day so that we can discover God's presence and discern his will for us. The Daily Examen helps us recognize God's presence in our everyday lives.

The following steps are a version of the Daily Examen that we can use in our personal prayer.

Saint Ignatius of Loyola, 1882, engraving, London, England.

1. **Become aware of God's presence.** Take a moment to reflect on all the blessings you have received from God throughout the day. Ask yourself, "How did God reveal himself to me in the events I experienced and the people I met?"

2. **Review the day with gratitude.** Take a moment to thank God for the joys and delights you have experienced throughout the day. Ask yourself, "What joys have I experienced in my interactions with others? What sights, sounds, and smells have filled me with delight?"

3. **Pay attention to your emotions.** Reflect on the feelings you have experienced throughout the day. Ask yourself, "Have any of my emotions drawn me closer to God or led me away from him? What might God be telling me through my emotions?"

4. **Choose one feature of the day and pray with it.** Ask the Holy Spirit to help you identify something from your day that seems especially important. It may be a feeling, an encounter, or a recurring thought you've had. Spend a moment reflecting on the experience and pray a prayer from your heart.

5. **Look toward tomorrow.** Ask God for the grace to help you remain faithful to the call of discipleship. Then ask him to open your mind and heart so that you can continue to discover his presence in your everyday experience.

By praying this version of the Daily Examen, you can become more aware of God's action in your life so that you can find God in all things.

The Rosary

THE Rosary helps us pray to Jesus through the intercession of Mary. When we pray the Rosary, we think about the special events, or mysteries, in the lives of Jesus and Mary.

The Rosary is made up of a string of beads and a crucifix. We hold the crucifix in our hands as we pray the Sign of the Cross. Then we pray the Apostles' Creed.

Hail, Holy Queen (Salve Regina)

Hail, holy Queen, Mother of mercy,
hail, our life, our sweetness, and our hope.
To you we cry, the children of Eve;
to you we send up our sighs,
mourning and weeping in this land of exile.
Turn, then, most gracious advocate,
your eyes of mercy toward us;
lead us home at last
and show us the blessed fruit of your womb, Jesus:
O clement, O loving, O sweet Virgin Mary.

Next to the crucifix, there is a single bead, followed by a set of three beads and another single bead. We pray the Lord's Prayer as we hold the first single bead and a Hail Mary at each bead in the set of three that follows. Then we pray the Glory Be to the Father. On the next single bead, we think about the first mystery and pray the Lord's Prayer.

There are five sets of 10 beads; each set is called a decade. We pray a Hail Mary on each bead of a decade as we reflect on a particular mystery in the lives of Jesus and Mary. The Glory Be to the Father is prayed at the end of each set. Between sets is a single bead on which we think about one of the mysteries and pray the Lord's Prayer.

In his apostolic letter *Rosary of the Virgin Mary*, Pope John Paul II wrote that the Rosary could take on a variety of legitimate forms adapted to different spiritual traditions and different Christian communities. "What is really important," he said, "is that the Rosary should always be seen and experienced as a path of contemplation." With this in mind, it is traditional in some places to pray the Hail, Holy Queen after the last decade.

We end our prayer by holding the crucifix in our hands as we pray the Sign of the Cross.

Praying the Rosary

9. Pray 10 Hail Marys and one Glory Be to the Father.

10. Think about the fourth mystery. Pray the Lord's Prayer.

11. Pray 10 Hail Marys and one Glory Be to the Father.

8. Think about the third mystery. Pray the Lord's Prayer.

7. Pray 10 Hail Marys and one Glory Be to the Father.

12. Think about the fifth mystery. Pray the Lord's Prayer.

6. Think about the second mystery. Pray the Lord's Prayer.

5. Pray 10 Hail Marys and one Glory Be to the Father.

13. Pray 10 Hail Marys and one Glory Be to the Father.

4. Think about the first mystery. Pray the Lord's Prayer.

3. Pray three Hail Marys and one Glory Be to the Father.

Pray the Hail, Holy Queen. Many people pray the Hail, Holy Queen after the last decade.

2. Pray the Lord's Prayer.

14. Pray the Sign of the Cross.

1. Pray the Sign of the Cross and the Apostles' Creed.

Mysteries of the Rosary

THE Church has used three sets of mysteries for many centuries. In 2002, Pope John Paul II proposed a fourth set of mysteries—the Luminous Mysteries, which are also called the Mysteries of Light.

According to his suggestion, the four sets of mysteries might be prayed on the following days: the Joyful Mysteries on Monday and Saturday, the Sorrowful Mysteries on Tuesday and Friday, the Glorious Mysteries on Wednesday and Sunday, and the Luminous Mysteries on Thursday.

The Joyful Mysteries

1. **The Annunciation** Mary learns that she has been chosen to be the mother of Jesus.

2. **The Visitation** Mary visits Elizabeth, who tells her that she will always be remembered.

3. **The Nativity** Jesus is born in a stable in Bethlehem.

4. **The Presentation** Mary and Joseph take the infant Jesus to the Temple to present him to God.

5. **The Finding of Jesus in the Temple** Jesus is found in the Temple, discussing his faith with the teachers.

The Annunciation

The Luminous Mysteries

1. **The Baptism of Jesus in the River Jordan** God proclaims that Jesus is his beloved Son.

2. **The Wedding Feast at Cana** At Mary's request, Jesus performs his first miracle.

3. **The Proclamation of the Kingdom of God** Jesus calls all to conversion and service to the kingdom.

4. **The Transfiguration of Jesus** Jesus is revealed in glory to Peter, James, and John.

5. **The Institution of the Eucharist** Jesus offers his Body and Blood at the Last Supper.

Wedding Feast at Cana

The Sorrowful Mysteries

1. **The Agony in the Garden** Jesus prays in the Garden of Gethsemane on the night before he dies.

2. **The Scourging at the Pillar** Jesus is lashed with whips.

3. **The Crowning with Thorns** Jesus is mocked and crowned with thorns.

4. **The Carrying of the Cross** Jesus carries the cross that will be used to crucify him.

5. **The Crucifixion** Jesus is nailed to the cross and dies.

The Agony in the Garden

The Glorious Mysteries

1. **The Resurrection** God the Father raises Jesus from the dead.

2. **The Ascension** Jesus returns to his Father in heaven.

3. **The Coming of the Holy Spirit** The Holy Spirit comes to bring new life to the disciples.

4. **The Assumption of Mary** At the end of her life on earth, Mary is taken body and soul into heaven.

5. **The Coronation of Mary** Mary is crowned as Queen of heaven and Earth.

The Ascension

Stations of the Cross

THE 14 Stations of the Cross represent events from Jesus' Passion and Death. Even before the Gospels were in written form, the followers of Jesus told the story of his Passion, Death, Resurrection, and Ascension. When people went on pilgrimages to Jerusalem, they were anxious to see the sites where Jesus lived and died. Eventually, following in the footsteps of the Lord on the way to his Death on the Cross became an important part of the pilgrimage.

The stations that we pray today came about when it was no longer easy or even possible to visit the holy sites in Palestine. In the 1500s, villages all over Europe started making replicas of the Way of the Cross, setting up small shrines commemorating the places along the route in Jerusalem. Eventually, these shrines became the 14 stations we now reflect on.

The first thing to remember about the Stations of the Cross is that they are a prayer. They are not an exercise in remembering events from the past. They are an invitation to make present the final hours of Jesus' life and to experience who Jesus is. When we pray the Stations of the Cross and open our hearts to be touched by prayer, we can respond fully to Jesus' sacrifice on the Cross. Praying the stations moves our hearts and helps us know Jesus' love for us.

As we follow the Lord's footsteps on his way to the Cross, we use our senses and our imagination to reflect prayerfully on Jesus' suffering, Death, and Resurrection. The stations allow us to visualize the meaning of his sacrifice and lead us to gratitude. They can also lead us into a sense of solidarity with people around the world, especially those who suffer, who are unjustly accused or victimized, who sit on death row, who carry difficult burdens, or who face terminal illnesses.

1

Jesus Is Condemned to Death.
Pontius Pilate condemns Jesus to death.

2

Jesus Takes Up the Cross.
Jesus willingly accepts and patiently bears the cross.

3

Jesus Falls the First Time.
Weakened by torments and by loss of blood, Jesus falls beneath the cross.

4

Jesus Meets His Sorrowful Mother.
Jesus meets his mother, Mary, who is filled with grief.

5

Simon of Cyrene Helps Jesus Carry the Cross.
Soldiers force Simon of Cyrene to carry the cross.

6

Veronica Wipes the Face of Jesus.
Veronica steps through the crowd to wipe the face of Jesus.

7

Jesus Falls the Second Time.
Jesus falls beneath the weight of the cross a second time.

8

Jesus Meets the Women of Jerusalem.
Jesus tells the women not to weep for him but for themselves and for their children.

9

Jesus Falls the Third Time.
Weakened almost to the point of death, Jesus falls a third time.

10

Jesus Is Stripped of His Garments.
The soldiers strip Jesus of his garments, treating him as a common criminal.

11

Jesus Is Nailed to the Cross.
Jesus' hands and feet are nailed to the cross.

12

Jesus Dies on the Cross.
After suffering greatly on the cross, Jesus bows his head and dies.

13

Jesus Is Taken Down from the Cross.
The lifeless body of Jesus is tenderly placed in the arms of Mary, his mother.

14

Jesus Is Laid in the Tomb.
Jesus' disciples place his body in the tomb.

The closing prayer—sometimes included as the 15th station—reflects on the Resurrection of Jesus.

The Mystery of Faith Made Present

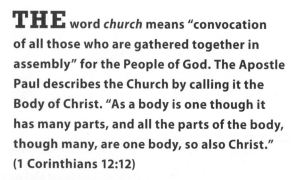

THE word *church* means "convocation of all those who are gathered together in assembly" for the People of God. The Apostle Paul describes the Church by calling it the Body of Christ. "As a body is one though it has many parts, and all the parts of the body, though many, are one body, so also Christ." (1 Corinthians 12:12)

The First Letter of Peter states that through faith and Baptism, Christians belong to the People of God. "But you are 'a chosen race, a royal priesthood, a holy nation, a people of his own, so that you may announce the praises' of him who you called out of darkness into his wonderful light." (1 Peter 2:9) Jesus Christ is the head of the Church.

> "He is before all things,
>   and in him all things hold together.
> He is the head of the body, the church."
>
> *Colossians 1:17–18*

In the Letter to the Ephesians, the Church is vividly described as the bride of Christ, who "loved the church and handed himself over for her to sanctify her, cleansing her by the bath of water with the word, that he might present himself to the church in splendor, without spot or wrinkle or any such thing, that she might be holy and without blemish." (Ephesians 5:25–28).

The Church was revealed to the world with the coming of the Spirit on Pentecost. This gift of the Spirit ushered in a new era in the history of salvation. This era is the age of the Church in which Christ makes present and communicates his work of salvation through the liturgy of his Church. The Church, as Christ's Body, is the first sacrament, the sign and instrument through which the Holy Spirit dispenses the mystery of salvation. In this age of the Church, Christ lives and acts through the sacraments.

The Seven Sacraments

Jesus touches our lives through the sacraments. In the sacraments physical objects or actions—water, bread and wine, oil, laying on of hands, and others— are signs of Jesus' presence.

Sacraments of Initiation

These sacraments lay the foundation for our Christian life.

Baptism In Baptism we are born into new life in Christ. Baptism takes away Original Sin and makes us members of the Church. Its sign is the pouring of water.

Confirmation Confirmation seals our life of faith in Jesus. Its signs are the laying on of hands on a person's head, most often by a bishop, and the anointing with oil. Like Baptism, it is received only once.

Eucharist The Eucharist nourishes our life of faith. We receive the Body and Blood of Christ often. Its signs are bread and wine.

Sacraments of Healing

These sacraments celebrate the healing power of Jesus.

Penance and Reconciliation Through Penance we receive God's forgiveness. Forgiveness requires being sorry for our sins. In Penance we receive Jesus' healing grace through absolution by the priest. The signs of this sacrament are our confession of sins, our repentance and satisfaction, and the words of absolution.

Anointing of the Sick This sacrament unites a sick person's suffering with Jesus'. Its signs are the laying on of hands by a priest and anointing with oil, which is a symbol of strength.

Importance of Baptism

The Church teaches us that, if God has called you to know the fullness of the truth about Jesus and his Church, you will not be saved if you refuse to believe. As Jesus said, "He who believes and is baptized will be saved; whoever does not believe will be condemned" (Mark 16:16). This does not mean that people who are not Christian will be condemned. People who search for the truth honestly and with a sincere heart, even if they are not called to God to the fullness of faith in Jesus, can be saved. But for us who are called, believing in Jesus Christ and in the one who sent him is necessary for salvation. In the unfortunate circumstance of children dying before they have been baptized, the Church entrusts them to the mercy of God and prays for their salvation.

From the earliest times the Church has practiced infant Baptism. The Church has celebrated this practice, recognizing Baptism is a gift of grace from God that is not connected to any human merit. By receiving this grace, children are more capable of fighting tendencies to be envious of others, and they can trust in God more completely.

Sacraments at the Service of the Community

These sacraments help members serve the community.

Matrimony In Matrimony, a baptized man and woman are united with each other as a sign of the unity between Jesus and his Church. Matrimony requires the consent of the couple, as expressed in the marriage promises. The couple are the sign of this sacrament.

Holy Orders In Holy Orders, men are ordained priests to be leaders of the community or deacons to be reminders of our baptismal call to serve others. The signs of this sacrament are the laying on of hands and the prayer by the bishop asking God for the outpouring of the Holy Spirit. ✝

Chastity and the Sacraments at the Service of the Community

Baptism challenges us to follow Christ, the model of chastity. Chastity is the essential virtue that helps us live out our sexuality in a proper manner. A chaste person is someone who is in control of his or her emotions and keeps them directed toward what is good for him or her.

Chastity is practiced differently by people according to their circumstances. Those who choose religious vocations take vows of chastity, which enable them to give themselves fully to God alone. For single people who are not in a religious order, chastity means learning to express sexuality in ways other than physical intimacy. For married couples, chastity means doing all those things that will help both the husband and the wife remain faithful to each other. It also means not practicing morally unacceptable means of birth control.

Celebrating the Lord's Day

THE Sabbath, the day on which God rested after creating the world, represents the completion of creation. Saturday has been replaced by Sunday for Christians because it recalls the beginning of the new creation through the Resurrection of Jesus Christ.

The Sunday celebration of the Lord's Day is at the heart of the Church's life. That is why on Sundays and holy days of obligation, we are required to participate in the Mass. We also rest from work, take time to enjoy our families, enrich our cultural and social lives, and perform works of mercy. On Sunday, people from all over the world gather at God's Eucharistic table.

The Order of Mass

The Mass is the high point of Catholic life, and it always follows a set order.

Introductory Rites—preparing to celebrate the Eucharist

Entrance Chant
We gather as a community and praise God in song.

Greeting
We pray the Sign of the Cross. The priest welcomes us.

Penitential Act
We remember our sins and ask God for mercy.

Gloria
We praise God in song.

Collect
We ask God to hear our prayers.

Liturgy of the Word—hearing God's plan of salvation

First Reading
We listen to God's Word, usually from the Old Testament.

Responsorial Psalm
We respond to God's Word in song.

Second Reading
We listen to God's Word from the New Testament.

Gospel Acclamation
We sing "Alleluia!" to praise God for the Good News. During Lent we use a different acclamation.

Gospel Reading
We stand and listen to the Gospel of the Lord.

Homily
The priest or the deacon explains God's Word.

Profession of Faith
We proclaim our faith through the Nicene Creed.

Prayer of the Faithful
We pray for our needs and the needs of others.

Liturgy of the Eucharist—celebrating Christ's presence in the Eucharist

Presentation and Preparation of the Gifts
We bring gifts of bread and wine to the altar.

Prayer over the Offerings
The priest prays that God will accept our sacrifice.

Eucharistic Prayer
This prayer of thanksgiving is the center and high point of the entire celebration.

† **Preface**—We give thanks and praise to God.

† **Holy, Holy, Holy**—We sing an acclamation of praise.

† **Institution Narrative**—The bread and wine become the Body and Blood of Jesus Christ.

† **The Mystery of Faith**—We proclaim the mystery of our faith.

† **Amen**—We affirm the words and actions of the Eucharistic Prayer.

Communion Rite—preparing to receive the Body and Blood of Jesus Christ

The Lord's Prayer
We pray the Lord's Prayer.

Sign of Peace
We offer one another Christ's peace.

Lamb of God
We pray for forgiveness, mercy, and peace.

Communion
We receive the Body and Blood of Jesus Christ.

Prayer after Communion
We pray that the Eucharist will strengthen us to live as Jesus did.

Concluding Rites—going forth to glorify the Lord by our lives

Final Blessing
We receive God's blessing.

Dismissal
We go in peace, glorifying the Lord by our lives.

Holy Days of Obligation

The holy days of obligation are the days other than Sundays on which we celebrate the great things God has done for us through Jesus and the saints. On holy days of obligation, Catholics attend Mass.

Six holy days of obligation are celebrated in the United States.

January 1—
Mary, Mother of God

40 days after Easter—
Ascension

August 15—Assumption of the Blessed Virgin Mary

November 1—All Saints Day

December 8—
Immaculate Conception

December 25—Nativity of Our Lord Jesus Christ

Making Good Choices

OUR conscience is the inner voice that helps us know the law God has placed in our hearts. Our conscience helps us judge the moral qualities of our own actions. It guides us to do good and avoid evil.

The Holy Spirit can help us form a good conscience. We form our conscience by studying the teachings of the Church and following the guidance of our parents and pastoral leaders.

God has given every human being freedom of choice. This does not mean that we have the right to do whatever we please. We can live in true freedom if we cooperate with the Holy Spirit, who gives us the virtue of prudence. Prudence helps us recognize what is good in every situation and make correct choices. The Holy Spirit gives us the gifts of wisdom and understanding to help us make the right choices in life in relationship to God and others. The gift of counsel helps us reflect on making correct choices in life.

The Ten Commandments help us make moral choices that are pleasing to God. We have the grace of the sacraments, the teachings of the Church, and the good example of saints and fellow Christians to help us make good choices.

Making moral choices involves the following steps:

1. Ask the Holy Spirit for help.

2. Think about God's law and the teachings of the Church.

3. Think about what will happen as a result of your choice. Ask yourself, "Will the consequences be pleasing to God? Will my choice hurt someone else?"

4. Seek advice from someone you respect and remember that Jesus is with you.

5. Ask yourself how your choice will affect your relationships with God and others.

Making moral choices takes into consideration the object of the choice, our intention in making the choice, and the circumstances in which the choice is made. It is never right to make an evil choice in the hope of gaining something good.

Human Sinfulness

When we sin, we offend God. We choose to turn away from him. Saint Augustine defines it as "an utterance, a deed, or a desire contrary to the eternal law."

Original Sin

Tempted by Satan in the Garden, Adam and Eve let their trust in their Creator die in their hearts and abused their freedom by choosing to disobey God. They chose themselves over God. They believed Satan and chose to "be like God." All subsequent sin would be disobedience toward God and lack of trust in his goodness. Adam and Eve committed a personal sin, but this sin affected the human nature that they would then transmit to humanity. Human nature would now be deprived of the original holiness and justice that God had intended. Original Sin is not a sin we commit but a state we are born into. Baptism, by giving us the life of Christ's grace, erases Original Sin and turns us back toward God. But the consequences of our nature, weakened and inclined to evil, remain in us.

Mortal Sin

Mortal sin destroys the love of God in our heart. A conversion of heart, through the Sacrament of Penance and Reconciliation, is necessary to experience God's mercy again. For a sin to be mortal, three conditions must be met: First, the matter of the sin must be serious. Second, mortal sin requires full knowledge of the seriousness of the act. Finally, there must be complete consent. In other words, the sin is really a personal choice.

Venial Sin

Venial sin allows the love of God to remain in our heart, but it offends and wounds that love. One commits a venial sin when the offense is of a less serious matter or, if the matter is serious, it is chosen without full knowledge or complete consent. Venial sin weakens love within us. It interferes with our practice of the virtues, makes it harder to do good, and can lead us to mortal sin. Venial sin is forgiven through the Sacrament of Penance and Reconciliation, the practice of good works, and reception of the Eucharist.

Capital Sins

Saint John Cassian and Saint Gregory the Great distinguished seven sins that they called Capital Sins because they produce other sins and other vices.

pride	covetousness	envy	anger
lust	gluttony	sloth	

Adam and Eve Driven Out of Paradise,
Siegfried Detler Bendixen, 20th Century.

The Morality of Human Acts

Human beings are able to act morally only because we are free to decide how we act. If we were not free to decide what to do, our acts could not be good or evil. Human acts that are freely chosen after a judgment of conscience can be morally evaluated. They are either good or evil.

The morality of human acts depends on

✝ the object chosen;

✝ the end in view or the intention; and

✝ the circumstances of the action.

For an act to be good, what you choose to do must be good in itself. If the choice is not good, the intention or the circumstances cannot make it good. You cannot steal a digital camera because it is your father's birthday and it would make him very happy to have one. But a good act done with a bad intention is not necessarily good as well. Participating in a hunger walk to impress a teacher from whom you want a good grade instead of out of genuine concern for those who are poor is not necessarily a good act. Circumstances can affect the morality of an act. They can increase or lessen the goodness of an act. Acting out of fear of harm lessens a person's responsibility for an act.

When Jesus gave us the Beatitudes in the Sermon on the Mount, he was teaching us to live in a healthy relationship with God and with others. Jesus wants us to respect other people and to treat their lives as sacred. It is good to think about our Christian values regarding people and their lives.

Life

Jesus and his Church teach us that every person is created in the image and likeness of God. The life of every single person, therefore, is holy because God created that life and wants it to exist.

Many plots in police dramas center on a murder taking place. Killing is depicted so often that it almost becomes an afterthought. Because murder is the deliberate taking of another person's life, it shows great disrespect for life and for the Lord of Life. God condemns murder because it goes against the dignity of the person and the holiness of God who made that person. Sometimes, however, someone will kill another person in self-defense. That is not murder, and it is not sinful if it is the only way to defend oneself.

Abortion

Protection of human life includes the life of the unborn. Every child has the right to life from the moment he or she is conceived. You might watch a movie or a TV show in which a woman who is expecting a baby has an **abortion.** Such an action is gravely wrong, and Catholic mothers who have abortions and those who aid them receive the severe penalty of excommunication. This means that the person is no longer part of the Church community and cannot receive the sacraments or participate in Church activities.

Euthanasia

As Catholics, we value the dignity of human life from conception until death. Often news reports and discussion programs raise issues about the quality of life that's possible if a person is severely disabled, terminally ill, or dying of old age. The question sometimes is whether it would be more merciful to kill that person. When a sick person is put to death so that he or she will not suffer any more, it is called **euthanasia.** Euthanasia is always wrong—it is a sin against hope. Instead, in situations of serious illness, the person should be treated with care and respect and helped to live as normal a life as possible.

Suicide

The act of a person taking his or her own life is suicide. Our life has been entrusted to us by God, and we do not have the authority to take it into our own hands. Neither do we have the authority to kill ourselves in such a way that our action takes the lives of others. Such actions are a denial of justice, hope, and love. These actions also break the bonds of human solidarity because we are called to love one another. When a person privately takes his or her own life, we should remember that it is not our place to pass judgment on this act. Only God knows what causes a person to commit suicide, and we should pray for the salvation of that person.

Human life is the most precious gift that God gives to us. God calls us to respect this gift in the way we value the lives of others and our own lives.

An Examination of Conscience

An examination of conscience is the act of looking prayerfully into our hearts and asking how we have hurt our relationships with God and other people through our thoughts, words, and actions. We reflect on the Ten Commandments and the teachings of the Church. The questions below help us in our examination of conscience.

My Relationship with God

☐ What steps am I taking to grow closer to God and to others? Do I turn to God often during the day, especially when I am tempted?

☐ Do I participate at Mass with attention and devotion on Sundays and holy days of obligation?

☐ Do I pray often and read the Bible?

☐ Do I use God's name and the names of Jesus, Mary, and the saints with love and reverence?

My Relationships with Family, Friends, and Neighbors

☐ Have I set a bad example through my words or actions? Do I treat others fairly? Do I spread stories that hurt other people?

☐ Am I loving toward those in my family? Am I respectful of my neighbors, my friends, and those in authority?

☐ Do I value human life? Do I do what I can to promote peace and end violence? Do I avoid talking about others in ways that could harm them?

☐ Do I show respect for my body and for the bodies of others? Do I keep away from forms of entertainment that do not respect God's gift of sexuality?

☐ Have I taken or damaged anything that did not belong to me? Have I cheated or copied homework?

☐ Have I told the truth even when it was difficult?

☐ Do I show concern for the poor and offer assistance to them in the ways I am able? Do I show concern for the environment and care for it as God has asked?

☐ Do I quarrel with others just so I can get my own way? Do I insult others to try to make them think they are less than I am? Do I hold grudges and try to hurt people who I think have hurt me?

How to Make a Good Confession

An examination of conscience is an important part of preparing for the Sacrament of Penance and Reconciliation. The Sacrament of Penance and Reconciliation includes the following steps:

1. The priest greets us, and we pray the Sign of the Cross. He invites us to trust in God. He may read God's Word with us.

2. We confess our sins. The priest may help and counsel us.

3. The priest gives us a penance to perform. Penance is an act of kindness or prayers to pray, or both.

4. The priest asks us to express our sorrow, usually by praying the Act of Contrition.

5. We receive absolution. The priest says, "I absolve you from your sins in the name of the Father, and of the Son, and of the Holy Spirit." We respond, "Amen."

6. The priest dismisses us by saying, "Go in peace." We go forth to perform the act of penance he has given us.

Catholic Social Teaching

HUNGRY PLEASE HELP GOD BLESS YOU

THE Catholic Church has developed a large body of teaching on social justice issues because action on behalf of justice to shape a more just world is an essential part of preaching the Gospel.

The major development of the social doctrine of the Church began in the 19th century when the Gospel encountered modern industrial society. There were new structures for the production of consumer goods, new concepts of society, new types of states and authorities, and new forms of labor and ownership.

Since that time the Church has been making judgments about economic and social matters that relate to the basic rights of individuals and communities.

The Common Good

A core principle of Catholic social teaching since the beginning has been that society as a whole is responsible for building up the common good. The common good is not the good for the greatest number of people. That would leave out some people. Rather every person must participate in the common good, not just the smartest, the most powerful, or the luckiest.

Following the principles of the common good means that people have the right to develop their talents and skills to become the best individuals they can be. The political, social, economic, and cultural environment must produce conditions that enable everyone to do this. The principles of the common good are best dealt with at the local level by the people most directly involved with the social issues.

The Church's social teaching is a rich treasure of wisdom about how to build a just society and live holy lives amid the challenges of the modern world.

Showing Our Love for the World

In the story of the Good Samaritan (Luke 10:29–37), Jesus makes clear our responsibility to care for those in need. The Catholic Church teaches this responsibility in the following themes of Catholic social teaching.

Life and Dignity of the Human Person

All human life is sacred, and all people must be respected and valued over material goods. We are called to ask whether our actions as a society respect or threaten the life and dignity of the human person.

Call to Family, Community, and Participation

Participation in family and community is central to our faith and to a healthy society. Families must be supported so that people can participate in society, build a community spirit, and promote the well-being of all, especially the poor and vulnerable.

Rights and Responsibilities

Every person has a right to life as well as a right to those things required for human decency. As Catholics, we have a responsibility to protect these basic human rights in order to achieve a healthy society.

Option for the Poor and Vulnerable

In our world, many people are very rich, while at the same time, many are extremely poor. As Catholics, we are called to pay special attention to the needs of the poor by defending and promoting their dignity and by meeting their immediate material needs.

The Dignity of Work and the Rights of Workers

The basic rights of workers must be respected: the right to productive work, fair wages, and private property; and the right to organize, join unions, and pursue economic opportunity. Catholics believe that the economy is meant to serve people and that work is not merely a way to make a living but an important way in which we participate in God's creation.

Solidarity

Because God is our Father, we are all brothers and sisters with the responsibility to care for one another. Solidarity is the attitude that leads Christians to share spiritual and material goods. Solidarity unites rich and poor, weak and strong, and helps build a society that recognizes that we all depend on one another.

Care for God's Creation

God is the Creator of all people and all things, and he wants us to enjoy his creation. The responsibility to care for all God has made is a requirement of our faith. ✝

Glossary

A

Abba the Aramaic word for "father" but more like the informal "papa" or "daddy." When Jesus spoke to God the Father, he called him "Abba." [Abba]

abortion the deliberate ending of a pregnancy that results in the death of the unborn child. The Church teaches that since life begins at conception, abortion is a serious crime against life and is gravely against the moral law. [aborto]

Abraham the model of faith and trust in God in the Old Testament. God made a covenant with Abraham, promising him land and many descendants. He became the father of the Chosen People. [Abrahán]

absolution the forgiveness we receive from God through the priest in the Sacrament of Penance and Reconciliation. Absolution places us in a state of grace and prepares us to receive other sacraments. [absolución]

abstain the choice to avoid certain foods or activities. Abstaining is a form of fasting that helps remind us that God comes first in our lives and that we are dependent on God for everything. [abstenerse]

Acts of the Apostles the second volume of Luke's two-volume work. Written for a Greek Christian audience, it continues the story of Jesus' Resurrection and Ascension and reports the beginnings of the Church at Pentecost. It then tells stories of the Apostles, including Paul, and how their evangelism spread the Church from Jerusalem to the ends of the earth. [Hechos de los Apóstoles]

actual grace the gift of God, freely given, that unites us with the life of the Trinity. Actual grace helps us make the choices that conform our lives to God's will. (See *grace, habitual grace,* and *sanctifying grace.*) [gracia actual]

adoration the act of giving reverence to God by recognizing and worshiping the real presence of Jesus Christ in the Blessed Sacrament, displayed in a monstrance. [adoración]

adultery a sin of unfaithfulness to one's marriage vows that injures the bond of the marriage covenant. It occurs when two people have sexual relations while at least one of them is married to another person. The Sixth Commandment forbids adultery because it undermines the institution of marriage and is harmful to children, who need the stability of their parents' marriage commitment. [adulterio]

Advent the four weeks before Christmas. It is a time of joyful preparation for the celebration of the Incarnation, Jesus' birth as our Savior, and a time for anticipating the coming of Jesus Christ at the end of time, which is known as the Second Coming. [Adviento]

Advocate Jesus' name for the Holy Spirit. The Holy Spirit comforts us and makes Jesus present to us. [Defensor]

Age of Enlightenment the shift in worldview that took place during the 1700s. The Age of Enlightenment included great advances in science and scientific understanding but also led to questions about religion, morality, and the existence of God. [Ilustración, la]

age of reason the age one must reach in order to receive Confirmation, usually around seven years old. The Church also requires that one reach the age of reason before celebrating the Sacraments of Reconciliation and the Eucharist. [edad de la razón]

Agony in the Garden the time Jesus spent in fervent prayer in the Garden of Gethsemane the night before his Crucifixion. Jesus' Agony in the Garden reminds us to remain true to our identity as sons and daughters of God, especially when we are tempted to run away from God. [Oración de Jesús en el Huerto, la]

All Saints Day November 1, the day on which the Church honors all who have died and now live with God as saints in heaven. This group includes those who are officially recognized as saints as well as people who have not been officially declared saints but now live in God's presence in heaven. The feast celebrates our union with those who have gone before us and points to our ultimate goal of union with God. [Día de Todos los Santos]

All Souls Day November 2, the day on which the Church prays that all who have died in friendship with God may rest in peace. Those who have died may need purification in Purgatory before living fully in God's presence. Our prayers and good works can help them in this process. Along with All Saints Day, this feast reminds us that all who love God, living and dead, are united with Jesus Christ and one another in the Communion of Saints. [Día de los Fieles Difuntos]

Alleluia a prayer of praise to God. It is usually sung as the Gospel Acclamation before the proclamation of the Gospel Reading at Mass except during Lent. [Aleluya]

almsgiving the offering of money, possessions, time, or talent to those in need. Along with fasting and prayer, almsgiving is an important spiritual practice during Lent. [limosna, dar]

altar the table in the church on which the priest celebrates Mass, where the sacrifice of Christ on the Cross is made present in the Sacrament of the Eucharist. The altar represents two aspects of the mystery of the Eucharist. It is the place where Jesus Christ offers himself for our sins and where he gives us himself in the Eucharist as food for eternal life. [altar]

ambo a raised stand from which a person proclaims the Word of God during Mass [ambón]

Amen the Hebrew word used to conclude Jewish and Christian prayers. It means "This is true," "So be it," or "Let it be so." We end prayers with *Amen* to show that we mean what we have just said. [amén]

angel a spiritual creature who worships God in heaven. Angels serve God as messengers. They tell us God's plans for our salvation. [ángel]

Angelus a Catholic devotion recited three times a day—morning, noon, and evening. The devotion reflects on the mystery of the Incarnation—the coming of the angel to Mary, her acceptance of the invitation to be the mother of Jesus, and the Word made flesh. [*Ángelus*]

anger an emotion that is not in itself wrong, but when not controlled can harden into resentment and hate, becoming one of the seven capital sins (See *Capital Sins*.) [ira]

annulment a finding by a Church tribunal that at least one essential element for a marriage was not present on the day of the wedding. The Church can declare that the Sacrament of Matrimony did not take place if one of the parties did not freely choose to marry, had been married before and that marriage was not annulled, or was not open to having children. An annulment cannot be considered until after a person is divorced. Catholics who receive an annulment are free to marry in the Church. [anulación]

Annunciation the announcement to Mary by the angel Gabriel that God had chosen her to be the mother of the Messiah. She would conceive a child through the Holy Spirit and name him Jesus. The Feast of the Annunciation is celebrated on March 25, nine months before Christmas. [Anunciación]

Anointing of the Sick one of the seven sacraments. In this sacrament a seriously ill person is anointed with holy oil and receives the strength, peace, and courage to overcome the difficulties associated with illness. Through this sacrament, Jesus brings the sick person spiritual healing and forgiveness of sins. If it is God's will, healing of the body is given as well. [Unción de los Enfermos]

antiphon one or more psalm verses sung in response during the liturgy. Although the Mass also uses antiphons, they are used in the Liturgy of the Hours to pray about the central events of the Christian faith. [antífona]

apocalyptic literature a form of writing that uses symbolic language and imagery to describe the eternal struggle between good and evil. The Book of Revelation is an example of apocalyptic literature. [literatura apocalíptica]

apologist a defender of the faith. Apologists defend Christianity against critics and proclaim the truths of the faith. [apologista]

Apostle one of the twelve chosen men who accompanied Jesus in his ministry and were witnesses to the Resurrection. *Apostle* means "one sent." These were the men sent to preach the Gospel to the whole world. [Apóstol]

Apostles' Creed a statement of Christian belief that developed out of a creed used in Baptism in Rome. The Apostles' Creed lists simple statements of belief in God the Father, Jesus Christ the Son, and the Holy Spirit. The profession of faith used in Baptism today is based on it. [Credo de los Apóstoles]

apostolic the Mark of the Church that indicates that Jesus continues to lead the Church through the pope and the bishops. The pope and the bishops are the successors of the Apostles. (See *Marks of the Church*.) [apostólico]

ark of the covenant the sacred box that God commanded Moses to build out of acacia wood to hold the restored tablets of the Law (Exodus 25:10–16) [Arca de la Alianza]

Ascension the entry of Jesus into God's presence in heaven. In the Acts of the Apostles, it is written that Jesus, after his Resurrection, spent 40 days on earth, instructing his followers. He then returned to his Father in heaven. [Ascensión]

asceticism the practice of self-denial and spiritual discipline as a way of training and forming oneself for the service of God and others. Asceticism can take many forms such as abstinence, fasting, celibacy, and prayer. [ascetismo]

Ash Wednesday the first day of Lent, on which we receive ashes on our foreheads. The ashes remind us to prepare for Easter by repenting and showing sorrow for offending God and hurting our relationships with others. [Miércoles de Ceniza]

assembly the People of God when they are gathered together to worship him [asamblea]

Assumption when Mary was taken into heaven, body and soul. Mary had a special relationship with her Son, Jesus, from the very beginning when she conceived him. Because of this relationship, she enjoys a special participation in Jesus' Resurrection and has been taken into heaven where she now lives with him. We celebrate this event in the Feast of the Assumption on August 15. [Asunción]

atone to make amends for sin. Jesus' obedience to God the Father by dying on the Cross atoned for the sins of the whole world. [expiar]

B

Baptism the first of the seven sacraments. Baptism frees us from Original Sin and is necessary for salvation. Baptism gives us new life in Jesus Christ through the Holy Spirit. The celebration of Baptism consists of immersing a person in water while declaring that the person is baptized in the name of the Father, the Son, and the Holy Spirit. [Bautismo]

baptismal font the water vessel where the Sacrament of Baptism is celebrated. The baptismal font may be located in a separate baptistry, near the entrance of the church, or in the midst of the community. [pila bautismal]

basic rights the human rights a government should protect, such as religious liberty, personal freedom, access to necessary information, right to life, and protection from terror and torture [derechos básicos]

basilica the term used to designate a certain church of historical significance in a local area. Major basilicas are in Rome and are designated churches of ancient origin that serve as places of pilgrimage. Minor basilicas are designated churches that have historical or devotional importance in local areas throughout the world. [basílica]

beatified recognized by the Church as having lived a life of great Christian virtue and declared to be in heaven. Beatified persons are referred to as *Blessed* and can be publicly venerated by the Church. [beatificado]

Beatitudes the teachings of Jesus in the Sermon on the Mount in Matthew's Gospel. The Beatitudes are eight guidelines for Christlike living that lead to happiness in this life and eternal joy in the next. They are the fulfillment of the Ten Commandments given to Moses. [Bienaventuranzas]

Bible the collection of books that contains the truths of God's Revelation. These writings, inspired by the Holy Spirit and written by different authors using different styles, are the Word of God. The Bible is made up of 46 books in the Old Testament and 27 books in the New Testament. [Biblia]

bishop a man who has received the fullness of Holy Orders. As a successor to the original Apostles, he cares for the Church and is a principal teacher in it. [obispo]

blasphemy any word, thought, or action done in hatred or defiance against God. It extends to using language that disrespects the Church, the saints, or holy things. It is also blasphemy to use God's name as an excuse to enslave people, to torture them, or to put them to death. Using God's name to do these things can cause others to reject religion. [blasfemia]

Blessed Sacrament the Eucharist that has been consecrated by the priest at Mass. It is kept in the tabernacle to adore and to be taken to those who are sick. [Santísimo Sacramento]

blessing a prayer that calls for God's power and care upon some person, place, thing, or special activity [bendición]

Body and Blood of Christ the Bread and Wine that has been consecrated by the priest at Mass. In the Sacrament of the Eucharist, all the risen Lord Jesus Christ—body, blood, soul, and divinity—is present in the consecrated Bread and Wine. [Cuerpo y Sangre de Cristo]

Bread of Life a title that Jesus gives himself in John 6:33–35. Jesus is food for the faithful. [Pan de Vida]

Buddhism a religion based on the teaching of Siddhartha Gautama, who was known as the Buddha, which means "Enlightened One." The Buddha was born to a royal family in northern India about five and a half centuries before Jesus. At age 29 he became disillusioned with life and left his comfortable home to find an answer to the question of why humans suffer. [Budismo]

Glossary

C

calumny (slander) a false statement about someone's reputation that makes others think bad of that person. Calumny is a sin against the Eighth Commandment. [calumnia]

Canaan the name of the land between Syria and Egypt in which the Israelites settled [Caná]

canon the official list of the 73 books that make up the Old and New Testaments of the Bible [canon]

canonization the process by which someone is declared a saint. The process ensures that the person who is a candidate for canonization lived an exemplary Christian life and can serve as a model for Christians around the world. [canonización]

canonize to declare that a Christian who has died is already a saint in heaven and may be looked to as a model of Christian life who may intercede for us [canonizar]

Capital Sins those sins that can lead to more serious sin. They are pride, covetousness, envy, anger, gluttony, lust, and sloth. [pecados capitales]

Cardinal Virtues the four virtues that lead a person to live in relationship with God and with others. Prudence, justice, fortitude, and temperance can be acquired by education and good actions. (See *fortitude, justice, prudence,* and *temperance.*) [virtudes cardinales]

cast lots to throw down small stones or pebbles called lots to help determine a decision needing divine guidance. Lots were cast to choose the disciple to replace Judas in the Acts of the Apostles 1:23–26. Roman soldiers also cast lots to divide Jesus' clothing among them as in John 19:24. [echar a suertes]

catechism a collection or summary of Church teachings for the education of the faithful. The current *Catechism of the Catholic Church* provides a contemporary summary and explanation of the Catholic faith. [catecismo]

catechumen a person being formed in the Christian life through instruction and by the example of the faith community. Through conversion and maturity of faith, a catechumen is preparing to be welcomed into the Church at Easter through the Sacraments of Baptism, Confirmation, and the Eucharist. [catecúmeno]

catechumenate the process of becoming a Christian. In the early Church, the process took several years. [catecumenado]

cathedral the main church in a diocese where a bishop presides and where the bishop's *cathedra,* or chair, is located. The *cathedra* represents the bishop's authority as the main teacher of the faith in the diocese. [catedral]

catholic one of the four Marks of the Church. The Church is catholic because Jesus is fully present in it, because it proclaims the fullness of faith, and because Jesus has given the Church to the whole world. The Church is universal. (See *Marks of the Church.*) [católica]

Catholic social teaching the body of teaching on social justice issues, action on behalf of justice, and work toward a more just world. The Church makes judgments about economic and social matters that relate to the basic rights of individuals and communities. The Church's social teaching is a rich treasure of wisdom about how to build a just society. [enseñanza social católica]

celebrant a bishop or priest who leads the people in praying the Mass. A deacon who baptizes or witnesses a marriage is also a celebrant. [celebrante]

celebrate to worship, praise, and thank God for what he has done for us with prayers and songs, especially in the celebration of the Eucharist [celebrar]

census a systematic counting of the citizens of a particular place. In addition to the census taking place when Jesus was born, the Bible records several censuses, including two in the Book of Numbers and one by King David. [censo]

character a permanent spiritual mark. Character shows that a person has a new relationship with Jesus and a special standing in the Church. Baptism, Confirmation, and Holy Orders each have a specific permanent character and therefore may be received only once. [carácter]

charism a special gift of the Holy Spirit given for the service of others, the good of the world, and particularly for the building up of the Church [carisma]

charity a virtue given to us by God that helps us love God above all things and our neighbor as ourselves. (See *Theological Virtues.*) [caridad]

chastity the integration of our physical sexuality with our spiritual nature. Chastity helps us be completely human, able to give to others our whole life and love. All people, married and single, are called to practice chastity. [castidad]

chasuble the visible liturgical vestment worn by the bishop or priest at Mass. A newly ordained priest receives a chasuble as part of the ordination ritual. [casulla]

Chosen People the people set apart by God to have a special relationship with him. God first formed a Chosen People when he made a covenant, or solemn agreement, with Abraham. He reaffirmed the covenant through Moses at Mount Sinai. The covenant is fulfilled in Jesus and his Church. [Pueblo Elegido]

Chrism a perfumed oil, consecrated by a bishop, that is used in the Sacraments of Baptism, Confirmation, and Holy Orders. Anointing with Chrism signifies the call of the baptized to the threefold ministry of priest, prophet, and king. [crisma]

Christ a Greek version of the Hebrew word *Messiah*, or "anointed one." It is another name for Jesus as priest, prophet, and king. [Cristo]

Christian the name given to all those who have been anointed through the gift of the Holy Spirit in Baptism and have become followers of Jesus Christ [cristiano]

Christmas the feast of the birth of Jesus (December 25) [Navidad]

Church the people of God throughout the whole world, or diocese (the local Church), or the assembly of those called together to worship God. The Church is one, holy, catholic, and apostolic. [Iglesia]

clergy those men who are set apart as sacred ministers to serve the Church through the Sacrament of Holy Orders [clero]

commandment a standard, or rule, for living as God wants us to live. Jesus summarized all the commandments into two: love God and love your neighbor. [mandamiento]

common good the sum total of the social conditions that allow people, individually and as a group, to reach their full potential. The common good requires peace, security, respecting everyone's rights, and meeting everyone's spiritual and worldly needs. People have a responsibility to contribute to the good of the entire society. It is one of the basic principles at the center of Catholic social teaching. [bien común]

communal prayer the worship of God together with others. The Liturgy of the Hours and the Mass are the main forms of communal prayer. [oración comunitaria]

Communion of Saints the unity of all, dead or living, who have been saved in Jesus Christ. The Communion of Saints is based on our one faith, and it is nourished by our participation in the Eucharist. [Comunión de los Santos]

community Christians who are gathered in the name of Jesus Christ to receive his grace and live according to his values [comunidad]

compassion God's fundamental attitude toward his people. This is best seen in Jesus' reaching out to heal those in need. Acting with compassion and mercy toward those in need identifies a person as belonging to God. [compasión]

confession the act of telling our sins to a priest in the Sacrament of Penance and Reconciliation. The sacrament itself is sometimes referred to as confession. [confesión]

Confirmation the sacrament that completes the grace we receive in Baptism. It seals, or confirms, this grace through the seven Gifts of the Holy Spirit that we receive as part of Confirmation. This sacrament also makes us better able to participate in worship and the apostolic life of the Church. [Confirmación]

conscience the inner voice that helps each of us judge the morality of our own actions. It guides us to follow God's Law by doing good and avoiding evil. [conciencia]

consecrate to make a thing or a person to be special to God through a prayer or blessing. At Mass the priest's words at the Consecration transform the bread and wine into the Body and Blood of Jesus Christ. People or objects set apart for God in a special way can also be consecrated. For example, men or women living in religious communities consecrate themselves to God through the evangelical counsels. [consagrar]

consubstantial the doctrine affirming that Jesus, the Son of God, assumed human nature while maintaining the same divine nature as God the Father. The Nicene Creed was written in part to make clear that Jesus is consubstantial with the Father. [consustancial]

consumerism giving undue value to the acquisition of material goods, acting in a way that puts things at the center of one's life where God alone should be [consumismo]

contemplate to focus on God while quieting and emptying our minds of all other distractions [contemplar]

contemplation the act of prayerfully and continuously focusing on God. Many religious communities and spiritualities in the Church are devoted to contemplation. [contemplación]

contemplative the character of an activity or a way of life that is prayerful and continuously focused on God. Many religious communities in the Church are devoted to contemplative life. [conemplativo]

Glossary

contrition the sorrow we feel when we know that we have sinned, followed by the decision not to sin again. Contrition is the most important act of the penitent preparing to celebrate the Sacrament of Penance and Reconciliation. (See *imperfect contrition* and *perfect contrition*.) [contrición]

conversion a radical or serious change of the whole life, a turning away from sin and toward God. The call to change of heart is a key part of the preaching of Jesus. Throughout our entire lives, Jesus calls us to change in this way. [conversión]

convert one who embraces a new faith or religion. At the beginning of the Church, whether Gentile converts needed to observe Jewish law was a major controversy resolved at the Council of Jerusalem. [converso]

convocation a gathering of people called together. We are called together in the Church as a convocation to work for the salvation of all people. [asamblea]

corporal works of mercy kind acts by which we help our neighbors with their everyday material needs. Corporal works of mercy include feeding the hungry, giving drink to the thirsty, clothing the naked, sheltering the homeless, visiting the sick and the imprisoned, and burying the dead.
[obras de misericordia corporales]

Council of Jerusalem the name of the meeting around A.D. 50 that is described in Acts of the Apostles. The meeting was the result of a disagreement between Paul and his followers and the Jewish Christian followers of James, the leader of the Jerusalem Church. James felt that those who became Christians should also observe Jewish customs. Paul said that there should be no such necessity. [Concilio de Jerusalén]

counsel one of the seven Gifts of the Holy Spirit. Counsel helps us make correct choices in life through reflection, discernment, consultation, and advisement. (See *Gifts of the Holy Spirit*.) [consejo]

covenant, the in the Old Testament, the solemn agreement between God and the Chosen People, Israel, that involved mutual commitments. God made covenants with Noah, Abraham, and Moses and prepared his people for salvation. In the New Testament, God's new and final covenant was established through Jesus' life, Death, Resurrection, and Ascension. *Testament* is another word for *covenant*. [Alianza]

covet to desire something belonging to someone else out of envy or jealousy. Coveting something is a desire that becomes an obsession. We are forbidden by the Ninth and Tenth Commandments from coveting others' spouses or possessions. [codiciar]

covetousness having a craving for wealth or for another's possessions (See *Capital Sins*.) [avaricia]

creation God's act of making everything that exists outside himself. Creation also refers to everything that exists. God said that all of creation is good. [creación]

Creator God, who made everything that is and whom we can come to know through everything he created [Creador]

crèche a Nativity scene depicting the birth of Christ. Crèches are popular ways to observe Advent and Christmas, and they can be found in homes, churches, and public places. [belén]

creed a brief statement of faith. The word *creed* comes from the Latin *credo*, meaning "I believe." The Nicene Creed and the Apostles' Creed are the most important summaries of Christian beliefs. [credo]

crosier the staff carried by a bishop that shows he cares for us in the same way that a shepherd cares for his sheep. It also reminds us that a bishop represents Jesus, the Good Shepherd. [báculo]

crucified the way in which Jesus was put to death, nailed to a cross. As the crucified one, Jesus died for the sake of the world. [crucificado]

Crucifixion refers to Jesus' Death on the Cross. In the ancient method of crucifixion used by the Romans, the victim was tied or nailed to a wooden cross and left to hang until dead, usually from suffocation. The cross with an image of the crucified Jesus on it is called a crucifix. [Crucifixión]

culture the activity of a group of people that includes their music, art, language, and celebrations. Culture is one of the ways people experience God in their lives. [cultura]

D

Daily Examen a prayer from the Spiritual Exercises that helps us become aware of God's presence, give thanks for the day we are given, pay attention to how we feel about our actions, and resolve to act more intentionally in the future. [examen diario de conciencia]

deacon a man ordained through the Sacrament of Holy Orders to the ministry of service in the Church. Deacons help the bishops and priests by serving the various charitable ministries of the Church. They help by proclaiming the Gospel, preaching, and assisting at the Liturgy of the Eucharist. Deacons can also celebrate Baptisms, witness marriages, and preside at funerals. [diácono]

detraction the act of talking about the faults and sins of another person to someone who has no reason to hear this and who cannot help the person. Detraction damages the reputation of another person without any intent to help that person. [detracción]

dignity of the human person a basic principle at the center of Catholic social teaching. It is the starting point of a moral vision for society because human life is sacred and should be treated with great respect. The human person is the clearest reflection of God among us. (See *Catholic social teaching*.) [dignidad de la persona humana]

dignity of work a basic principle at the center of Catholic social teaching. Since work is done by people created in the image of God, it is not only a way to make a living but also an important way we participate in God's creation. In work, people fulfill part of their potential given to them by God. All workers have a right to productive work, decent and fair wages, and safe working conditions. (See *Catholic social teaching*.) [dignidad del trabajo]

diocese the members of the Church in a particular area, united in faith and the sacraments, and gathered under the leadership of a bishop [diócesis]

disciple a person who has accepted Jesus' message and tries to live as he did, sharing his mission, suffering, and joys [discípulo]

discipleship for Christians, the willingness to answer the call to follow Jesus. The call is received in Baptism, nourished in the Eucharist, strengthened in Confirmation, and practiced in service to the world. [discipulado]

discrimination the act of mistreating other people because of how they look or act or because they are different [discriminación]

Dismissal the part of the Concluding Rites of the Mass in which the people are sent forth by the priest or deacon to do good works and praise and bless God (See *The Order of Mass*.) [despedida]

divine law the moral law as revealed by God in the Bible [ley divina]

Divine Praises a series of praises beginning with "Blessed be God," traditionally prayed at the end of the worship of the Blessed Sacrament in Benediction [alabanzas de desagravio]

Divine Providence the guidance of God over all he has created. Divine Providence exercises care for all creation and guides it toward its final perfection. [divina providencia]

Doctor of the Church a man or a woman recognized as a model teacher of the Christian faith [doctor(a) de la Iglesia]

doctrine the teachings that help us understand and accept the truths of our faith as revealed by Jesus and taught by the Church [doctrina]

dogma a teaching that the Church assures Catholics is true and that Catholics are obliged to believe. Papal infallibility, the Assumption, and the Immaculate Conception are all dogmas of the Church. [dogma]

domestic church the Christian home, which is a community of grace and prayer and a school of human virtues and Christian charity [iglesia doméstica]

doxology a Christian prayer praising and giving glory to God, often referencing the three divine Persons of the Trinity. The Glory Be to the Father and the *Gloria* at Mass are two common doxologies. [doxología]

E

Easter the celebration of the bodily raising of Jesus Christ from the dead. Easter is the festival of our redemption and the central Christian feast, the one from which other feasts arise. [Pascua]

Easter Vigil the celebration of the first and greatest Christian feast, the Resurrection of Jesus. It occurs on the first Saturday evening after the first full moon of spring. During this night watch before Easter morning, catechumens are baptized, confirmed, and receive the Eucharist for the first time. [Vigilia Pascual]

Eastern Catholic Churches a group of Churches that developed in the Near East in countries such as Lebanon and are in union with the Roman Catholic Church. These Churches have their own liturgical, theological, and administrative traditions. They show the truly catholic nature of the Church, which takes root in many cultures. [iglesias católicas orientales]

ecumenical council a gathering of Catholic bishops from the entire world, meeting under the leadership of the pope or his delegates. Ecumenical councils discuss pastoral, legal, and doctrinal issues. There have been 21 ecumenical councils recognized by the Catholic Church. The first was the First Council of Nicaea in 325. The most recent was the Second Vatican Council, which took place between 1962 and 1965. [concilio ecuménico]

Glossary

ecumenism the movement to bring unity among Christians. Christ gave the Church the gift of unity from the beginning, but over the centuries, that unity has been broken. All Christians are called by their common Baptism to pray and to work to maintain, reinforce, and perfect the unity Christ wants for the Church. [ecumenismo]

Emmanuel a Hebrew name from the Old Testament that means "God with us." In Matthew's Gospel, Jesus is called Emmanuel. [Emanuel]

encyclical a letter written by the pope and sent to the whole Church and sometimes to the whole world. It expresses Church teaching on some specific and important issue. [encíclica]

envy a feeling of resentment or sadness because someone has a quality, a talent, or a possession that we want. Envy is one of the seven capital sins, and it is contrary to the Eighth Commandment. (See *Capital Sins.*) [envidia]

epiphany an event in the life of Christ when Jesus' divinity revealed itself. The Church recognizes four epiphanies: the Nativity, the adoration of the Magi, Jesus' baptism, and Jesus' sign at the wedding feast at Cana. [epifanía]

Epistle a letter written by Saint Paul to a group of Christians in the early Church. Twenty-one books of the New Testament are letters written by Paul or other leaders. The second reading at Mass on Sundays and holy days is usually from one of these books. [epístola]

eternal life living happily with God in heaven when we die in grace and friendship with him. Jesus calls all people to eternal life. [vida eterna]

Eucharist, the the sacrament in which we give thanks to God for the Body and Blood of Christ. The Eucharist nourishes our life of faith. We receive the Body and Blood of Christ in the consecrated Bread and Wine. [Eucaristía, la]

Eucharistic liturgy the public worship, held by the Church, in which the bread and wine are consecrated and become the Body and Blood of Jesus Christ. The Sunday celebration of the Eucharistic liturgy is at the heart of Catholic life. [Liturgia Eucarística]

Eucharistic Prayer during the Mass the liturgical expression of praise and thanksgiving for all that God has done in creation and in the Paschal Mystery (Christ's dying and rising from the dead) and through the Holy Spirit (See *The Order of Mass.*) [Plegaria Eucarística]

euthanasia an act with the intent to cause the death of a person who is handicapped, sick, or dying. Euthanasia is considered murder and is gravely contrary to the dignity of the human person and to the respect due to the living God, our Creator. [eutanasia]

evangelical counsels the virtues of poverty, chastity, and obedience that help men and women live holy lives in accordance with the Gospel. All Christians are called to live the evangelical counsels, although members of religious communities consecrate themselves by making vows to live according to the evangelical counsels. [consejos evangélicos]

Evangelist one of the writers of the four Gospels: Matthew, Mark, Luke, and John. The term is also used to describe anyone engaged in spreading the Gospel. Letters in the New Testament and in the Acts of the Apostles list Evangelists, along with Apostles and prophets, as ministers of the Church. [evangelista]

evangelization the declaration by word and example of the Good News of salvation we have received in Jesus Christ. It is directed both to those who do not know Jesus and to those who have become indifferent about him. Those who have become indifferent are the focus of what is called the New Evangelization. [evangelización]

examination of conscience the act of prayerfully thinking about what we have said or done in light of what the Gospel asks of us. We also think about how our actions may have hurt our relationship with God and with others. An examination of conscience is an important part of our preparing to celebrate the Sacrament of Penance and Reconciliation. [examen de conciencia]

Exile the period in the history of Israel between the destruction of Jerusalem in 587 B.C. and the return to Jerusalem in 537 B.C. During this time many of the Jewish people were forced to live in Babylon, far from home. [Exilio]

Exodus God's liberation of the Hebrew people from slavery in Egypt and his leading them to the Promised Land. It is also one of the first five books in the Bible. [Éxodo]

Exsultet an Easter hymn of praise sung during the Service of Light that begins the Easter Vigil [Exsultet]

F

faith a gift of God that helps us believe in him. We profess our faith in the Creed, celebrate it in the sacraments, live by it through our good conduct of loving God and our neighbor, and express it in prayer. It is a personal adherence of the whole person to God, who has revealed himself to us through words and actions throughout history. (See *Theological Virtues*.) [fe]

fasting a spiritual practice of limiting the amount we eat for a period of time to express sorrow for sin and to make ourselves more aware of God's action in our lives. Adults ages 18–59 fast on Ash Wednesday and Good Friday. The practice is also encouraged as a private devotion at other times of penitence. [ayuno]

fear of the Lord one of the seven Gifts of the Holy Spirit. This gift leads us to a sense of wonder and awe in the presence of God because we recognize his greatness. (See *Gifts of the Holy Spirit*.) [temor de Dios]

feast day important liturgical celebrations in the life of the Church that mark an event in the life of Jesus or the life of a particular saint [día de fiesta]

Feast of Our Lady of Guadalupe feast day during the Advent season that celebrates Mary's appearance to Juan Diego. Widely celebrated on December 12, this feast is an important religious day for Catholics, especially those from Mexico and other parts of Latin America. [Solemnidad de Nuestra Señora de Guadalupe]

Feast of the Holy Family celebrated on the Sunday that falls within the octave of Christmas or, if no Sunday falls within the octave, on December 30. The feast celebrates the family of Jesus, Mary, and Joseph as a model for all Catholic families. [Fiesta de la Sagrada Familia]

forgiveness the willingness to pardon those who have hurt us but have then shown that they are sorry. In the Lord's Prayer, we pray that since God will forgive us our sins, we are able to forgive those who have hurt us. [perdón]

fortitude the strength to choose to do the right thing even when that is difficult. Fortitude is one of the seven Gifts of the Holy Spirit and one of the four central human virtues, called the Cardinal Virtues, by which we guide our conduct through faith and the use of reason. (See *Cardinal Virtues* and *Gifts of the Holy Spirit*.) [fortaleza]

four last things our belief in the four realities of death, judgment, heaven, and hell. The Church invites us to think about how the choices we make each day have consequences now and in the future. [los novísimos]

free will the ability to choose to do good because God has made us like him. Our free will is what makes us truly human. Our exercise of free will to do good increases our freedom. Freely choosing to sin makes us slaves to sin. [libre voluntad]

Fruits of the Holy Spirit the demonstration through our actions that God is alive in us. The Fruits of the Holy Spirit are love, joy, peace, patience, kindness, goodness, generosity, gentleness, faithfulness, modesty, self-control, and chastity. [frutos del Espíritu Santo]

fundamentalist a person who believes the Bible is literally true, word for word. Fundamentalists fail to recognize that the inspired Word of God has been expressed in human language, under divine inspiration, in different literary forms, by human authors possessed of limited capacities and resources. [fundamentalista]

G

Garden of Eden a garden created by God, filled with trees and lush vegetation, where God first placed Adam and Eve and from which they were later expelled [Jardín del Edén]

genealogy a listing of a person's ancestors through generations. Jesus' genealogy is listed in Matthew 1:1–17. [genealogía]

Gentile the name given by the Jews after the Exile to a foreign person. Gentiles were considered to be nonbelievers who worshiped false gods. They stand in contrast to the Jewish people who received God's Law. [gentil]

genuflect to show respect in church by touching a knee to the ground, especially before the Blessed Sacrament in the tabernacle [genuflexión]

gesture the movements we make, such as the Sign of the Cross or bowing, to show our reverence during prayer [gestos]

gift of peace the peace that Jesus gives to us that flows from his relationship with his Father. This is the peace that the world cannot give, for it is the gift of salvation that only Jesus can give. [don de la paz]

Gifts of the Holy Spirit the permanent willingness, given to us through the Holy Spirit, that makes it possible for us to do what God asks of us. The Gifts of the Holy Spirit are wisdom, understanding, counsel, fortitude, knowledge, piety, and fear of the Lord. [dones del Espíritu Santo]

gluttony excessive indulgence in food or drink (See *Capital Sins*.) [gula]

Glossary

God the Father, Son, and Holy Spirit, one God in three distinct Persons. God created all that exists. He is the source of salvation, and he is Truth and Love. [Dios]

godparent a witness to Baptism who assumes the responsibility for helping the baptized person along the road of Christian life [padrino/madrina]

Good News the meaning of the word *Gospel* in Greek. The spreading of the Good News began on Pentecost and continues today in the ministry of the Church. [Buena Nueva]

Gospel the Good News of God's mercy and love that we experience by hearing the story of Jesus' life, Death, Resurrection, and Ascension. The story is passed on in the teaching ministry of the Church as the source of all truth and right living. It is presented to us in four books in the New Testament: the Gospels according to Matthew, Mark, Luke, and John. [Evangelio]

grace the gift of God, given to us without our meriting it. Grace is the Holy Spirit alive in us, helping us live our Christian vocation. Grace helps us live as God wants us to live. (See *actual grace, habitual grace,* and *sanctifying grace.*) [gracia]

Great Commandment Jesus' commandment that we are to love both God and our neighbor as we love ourselves. Jesus tells us that this commandment sums up everything taught in the Old Testament. [mandamiento mayor]

Great Commission Jesus' command to the Apostles to spread the Good News to all people. Jesus commissioned the disciples before his Ascension. [misión de los discípulos]

Great Schism a split in the Church during the Middle Ages when two and then three men all claimed to be pope. The split began because the papal court had moved between Rome and Avignon, France. The schism was resolved at the Council of Constance (1414–1418) with the election of Martin V. [Gran Cisma]

Gregorian chant a form of liturgical music that began its development during the time of Pope Gregory the Great [canto gregoriano]

guardian angel the angel who has been appointed to protect, pray for, and help a person live a holy life [ángel de la guarda]

H

habit the distinctive clothing worn by members of religious orders. It is a sign of the religious life and a witness to poverty. [hábito]

habitual grace another name for sanctifying grace, as it refers to our God-given inclination and capacity for good. Habitual grace is a participation in God's own spirituality. (See *actual grace, grace, and sanctifying grace.*) [gracia habitual]

heaven union with God the Father, Son, and Holy Spirit in life and love that never ends. Heaven is a state of happiness and the goal of the deepest wishes of the human heart. [cielo]

Hebrew a descendant of Abraham, Isaac, and Jacob, who was enslaved in Egypt. God helped Moses lead the Hebrews out of slavery. [Hebreo]

hell a life of total separation from God forever. In his infinite love for us, God can only desire our salvation. Hell is the result of the free choice of a person to reject God's love and forgiveness once and for all. [infierno]

herald a messenger who announces important news. Angels served as the heralds of the birth of Christ. [heraldo]

heresy a false teaching that distorts a truth of the Catholic faith. Many of the Church councils have taught against heresies about the Trinity, Jesus, or the faith of the Church. [herejía]

holiness the fullness of Christian life and love. All people are called to holiness, which is made possible by cooperating with God's grace to do his will. As we do God's will, we are transformed more and more into the image of the Son, Jesus Christ. [santidad]

holy the Mark of the Church that indicates that the Church is one with Jesus Christ. Holiness is closeness to God, and therefore the Church is holy because God is present in it. (See *Marks of the Church.*) [santo]

Holy Communion the consecrated Bread and Wine that we receive at Mass, which is the Body and Blood of Jesus Christ. It brings us into union with Jesus and his saving Death and Resurrection. [Comunión]

holy day of obligation a principal feast day, other than Sundays, of the Church. On holy days of obligation, we celebrate the great things that God has done for us through Jesus and the saints. Catholics are obliged to participate in the Eucharist on these days, just as we are on Sundays. [día de precepto]

Holy Family the family of Jesus as he grew up in Nazareth. It included Jesus; his mother, Mary; and his foster father, Joseph. [Sagrada Familia]

Holy of Holies the holiest part of the Temple in Jerusalem. The High Priest entered this part of the Temple once a year to address God and ask his forgiveness for the sins of the people. [Sanctasanctórum]

Holy Orders the sacrament through which the mission given by Jesus to his Apostles continues in the Church. The sacrament has three degrees: deacon, priest, and bishop. Through the laying on of hands in the Sacrament of Holy Orders, men receive a permanent sacramental mark that calls them to minister to the Church. [sacramento del Orden]

Holy Spirit the third Person of the Trinity, who is sent to us as our helper and, through Baptism and Confirmation, fills us with God's life. Together with the Father and the Son, the Holy Spirit brings the divine plan of salvation to completion. [Espíritu Santo]

Holy Thursday the Thursday of Holy Week on which the Mass of the Lord's Supper is celebrated, commemorating the institution of the Eucharist. The season of Lent ends with the celebration of this Mass. [Jueves Santo]

holy water water that has been blessed and is used as a sacramental to remind us of our Baptism [agua bendita]

Holy Week the celebration of the events surrounding Jesus' establishment of the Eucharist and his suffering, Death, and Resurrection. Holy Week commemorates Jesus' triumphal entry into Jerusalem on Palm Sunday, the gift of himself in the Eucharist on Holy Thursday, his Death on Good Friday, and his Resurrection at the Easter Vigil on Holy Saturday. [Semana Santa]

Homily the explanation by a bishop, a priest, or a deacon of the Word of God in the liturgy. The Homily relates the Word of God to our lives as Christians today. (See *The Order of Mass*.) [homilía]

honor giving God or a person the respect that they are owed. God is given this respect as our Creator and Redeemer. All people are worthy of respect as children of God. [honrar]

hope the confidence that God will always be with us, make us happy now and forever, and help us live so that we will be with him forever (See *Theological Virtues*.) [esperanza]

human condition the general state of humankind. While the human family is created in the image and likeness of God, it is also wounded by sin and often rejects the grace won by Jesus Christ. So while called by God to the highest good, too often human behavior leads to personal and social destruction. [condición humana]

I

idolatry the act of worshiping something other than God. Originally idolatry meant the worship of statues or other images of gods, but the pursuit of money, fame, or possessions can become forms of idolatry. (See *consumerism*.) [idolatría]

Immaculate Conception the Church teaching that Mary was free from Original Sin from the first moment of her conception. She was preserved through the merits of her Son, Jesus, the Savior of the human race. Declared a dogma of the Catholic Church by Pope Pius IX in 1854, the Feast of the Immaculate Conception is celebrated on December 8. [Inmaculada Concepción]

imperfect contrition Sorrow for sin that is motivated by reasons other than loving God above all else. Imperfect contrition comes from fear of punishment or other consequences of our sin. Contrition is the most important act of the penitent preparing to celebrate the Sacrament of Penance and Reconciliation. (See *contrition* and *perfect contrition*.) [contrición imperfecta]

incarnate to take human form. The word *incarnate* comes from a Latin term meaning "to become flesh" and describes what happened in the mystery of the Incarnation when the Son of God, Jesus, became man, conceived and born of Mary. [encarnar]

Incarnation Jesus Christ, the Son of God, is God made flesh. The Son of God, the Second Person of the Trinity, is both true God and true man. [Encarnación]

indulgence a lessening of temporal punishment gained through participation in prayer and works of charity. Indulgences move us toward our final purification, after which we will live with God forever. [indulgencia]

Industrial Revolution the rapid economic change beginning at the end of the 18th century and continuing into the 19th century that resulted in a shift away from homemade and agricultural production and toward industry and manufacturing. [Revolución industrial]

inerrancy the absence of error in the Bible when it tells us a religious truth about God and his relationship with us. The Church teaches the inerrancy of Scripture on moral and faith matters. [inerrancia]

infallibility the inability to be in error or to teach something that is false. On matters of belief and morality, the Church is infallible because of the presence and guidance of the Holy Spirit. [infalibilidad]

infallible the quality of Church teachings in areas of faith and morals that have been proclaimed by the pope and the bishops, in their role as the Magisterium and guided by the Holy Spirit, to be without error [infalible]

Infancy Narrative an account of the infancy and childhood of Jesus that appears in the first two chapters of Matthew's and Luke's Gospels. Matthew's Infancy Narrative reveals Jesus as the fulfillment of prophecies. Luke's Infancy Narrative reveals Jesus as a Savior who came for everyone, not the privileged few. The intention of these stories is to proclaim Jesus as Messiah and Savior. [narración de la infancia]

inspiration the quality that explains God as the author who, through the Holy Spirit, enlightened the minds of human authors while they were writing the books of the Bible. God blessed the writers of Scripture with inspiration that enabled them to record religious truths for our salvation. [inspiración]

inspired influenced by the Holy Spirit. The human authors of Scripture were influenced by the Holy Spirit. The creative inspiration of the Holy Spirit made sure that the Scripture was written according to the truth God wants us to know for our salvation. [inspirado]

Institution Narrative the words prayed by the priest at the Eucharist that recall Jesus' words and actions at the Last Supper. During the Institution Narrative, the bread and wine become the Body and Blood of the risen Christ. [narración de la institución]

intercession a form of prayer on behalf of others. We ask for the intercession of those in heaven, such as Mary and the saints, or those still with us here on earth. [intercesión]

intercessor a person who prays for the needs of others. An intercessor can be someone still alive on earth or a saint in heaven. [intercesor]

interpretation coming to an understanding of the words of Scripture, combining human knowledge with the wisdom and guidance of the teaching office of the Church [interpretación]

interreligious dialogue the ongoing discussions between Christians and those of other faiths [diálogo interreligioso]

Islam the third great religion, along with Judaism and Christianity, that professes belief in one God. *Islam* means "submission" to that one God. [islamismo]

Israelite a descendant of Abraham, Isaac, and Jacob. God changed Jacob's name to "Israel," and Jacob's twelve sons and their children became the leaders of the twelve tribes of Israel. (See *Hebrew*.) [israelita]

J

Jerusalem the city conquered by David in 1000 B.C. to serve as his capital. David also made it the center of worship by bringing in the ark of the covenant, which held the tablets of the Law. [Jerusalén]

Jesse tree an Advent activity that helps us prepare to celebrate Jesus' birth. A small or an artificial tree is decorated with images of Jesus' ancestors. The image is based on Isaiah 11:1, "But a shoot shall sprout from the stump of Jesse, / and from his roots a bud shall blossom." [tronco de Jesé]

Jesus the Son of God, who was born of the Virgin Mary and who died and was raised from the dead for our salvation. He returned to God and will come again to judge the living and the dead. *Jesus* means "God saves." [Jesús]

Jews the name given to the Hebrew people, from the time of the Exile to the present. The name means "the people who live in the territory of Judah," the area of Palestine surrounding Jerusalem. [judíos]

Joseph the foster father of Jesus who was engaged to Mary when the angel announced that Mary would have a child through the power of the Holy Spirit. In the Old Testament, Joseph was the son of Jacob, who was sold into slavery in Egypt by his brothers and then saved them from starvation when famine came. [José]

Jubilee Year a holy year in which the pope calls people to witness to their faith in specific ways. Pope John Paul II announced that 1985 was a Jubilee Year. [Año jubilar]

Judaism the name of the religion of Jesus and all the people of Israel after they returned from exile in Babylon and built the second Temple [judaísmo]

justice the virtue that guides us to give to God and others what is due them. Justice is one of the four Cardinal Virtues by which we guide our Christian life. (See *Cardinal Virtues*.) [justicia]

justification the action of the Holy Spirit that cleanses us from sin in Baptism and that continually gives us the grace to walk in right relationship with God. Justification is the saving action of God that restores the right relationship between God and an individual. [justificación]

K

Kingdom of God God's rule over us, announced in the Gospel and present in the Eucharist. The beginning of the kingdom here on earth is mysteriously present in the Church, and it will come in completeness at the end of time. [Reino de Dios]

Kingdom of Heaven the term for the Kingdom of God in Matthew's Gospel. The Beatitudes help us enter into the Kingdom of Heaven by guiding us in ways to live according to the values of Jesus. [Reino de los cielos]

knowledge one of the seven Gifts of the Holy Spirit. This gift helps us perceive what God asks of us and how we should respond. (See *Gifts of the Holy Spirit*.) [ciencia]

L

laity those who have been made members of Christ in Baptism and who participate in the priestly, prophetic, and kingly functions of Christ in his mission to the whole world. The laity is distinct from the clergy, whose members are set apart as ordained ministers to serve the Church. [laicado]

Lamb of God the title for Jesus that emphasizes his willingness to give up his life for the salvation of the world. Jesus is the Lamb without blemish or sin who delivers us through his sacrificial Death. [Cordero de Dios]

Last Judgment the final judgment of all human beings that will occur when Christ returns in glory and all appear in their own bodies before him to give an account of all their deeds in life. In the presence of Christ, the truth of each person's relationship with God will be laid bare, as will the good each person has done or failed to do during his or her earthly life. At that time, God's kingdom will come into its fullness. [Juicio Final]

Last Supper the meal Jesus ate with his disciples on the night before he died. At the Last Supper, Jesus instituted the Sacrament of the Eucharist. [Última Cena]

lectio divina a reflective way of praying with Scripture. *Lectio divina* is Latin for "sacred reading" and is an ancient form of Christian prayer. It involves four steps: sacred reading of a Scripture passage, meditation on the passage, speaking to God, and contemplation or resting in God's presence. [*lectio divina*]

Lectionary for Mass the official book that contains all the Scripture readings used in the Liturgy of the Word [*Leccionario*]

Lent the 40 days before Easter (not counting Sundays) during which we prepare through prayer, fasting, and almsgiving to change our lives and live the Gospel more completely [Cuaresma]

Light of the World a name that helps us see that Jesus is the light that leads us to the Father. Jesus lights up our minds and hearts, replacing sin and darkness with the knowledge of God. [luz del mundo]

litany a prayer that consists of a series of petitions, often including requests for the intercession of particular saints [letanía]

literary forms the different styles of writing found in the Bible. Some forms are history, proverbs, letters, parables, Wisdom sayings, and poetry. They all have as their purpose the communication of the truth found in God's Word. [géneros literarios]

liturgical year the celebration throughout the year of the mysteries of the Lord's birth, life, Death, Resurrection, and Ascension. The cycle of the liturgical year constitutes the basic rhythm of the Christian's life of prayer. [año litúrgico]

liturgy the public prayer of the Church that celebrates the wonderful things God has done for us in Jesus Christ, our High Priest, and the way in which he continues the work of our salvation. The original meaning of *liturgy* was "a public work or service done for the people." [liturgia]

Liturgy of the Eucharist the part of the Mass in which the bread and wine are consecrated and become the Body and Blood of Jesus Christ. We then receive Christ in Holy Communion. [Liturgia de la Eucaristía]

Liturgy of the Hours the public prayer of the Church to praise God and sanctify the day. It includes an office of readings before sunrise, morning prayer at dawn, evening prayer at sunset, and prayer before going to bed. The chanting of psalms makes up a major portion of this prayer. [Liturgia de las Horas]

Liturgy of the Word the part of the Mass in which we listen to God's Word from the Bible and consider what it means for us today. The Liturgy of the Word can also be a public prayer that is not followed by the Liturgy of the Eucharist. [Liturgia de la Palabra]

Glossary

living wage the amount of income that is enough to support a person and a family in reasonable comfort. Pope Leo XIII defined what a living wage was in his encyclical *On the Condition of Labor.* [salario digno]

Lord a title that indicates the divinity of God. *Lord* replaced *Yahweh*, the name God revealed to Moses and was considered too sacred to pronounce. The New Testament uses the title *Lord* for both the Father and for Jesus, recognizing him as God himself. (See *Yahweh*.) [Señor]

lust the excessive craving for or indulgence of bodily pleasure that makes the other a victim of our desires (See *Capital Sins*.) [lujuria]

M

Magi, the the men who came from the East to Bethlehem by following a star. They were the first Gentiles to believe that Jesus was the Messiah. [Reyes Magos]

Magisterium the living, teaching office of the Church. This office, through the bishops and with the pope, provides an authentic interpretation of God's Revelation. It ensures faithfulness to the teaching of the Apostles in matters of faith and morals. [Magisterio de la Iglesia]

Magnificat Mary's song of praise recorded in the Gospel of Luke. Sung before Jesus' birth, the *Magnificat* shows Mary's understanding of Jesus' mission and her role as a disciple. [*magníficat*]

manna the food provided by God when the Israelites were in the desert [maná]

marginalized those who are viewed as unimportant or powerless in society. We find Jesus among the marginalized, such as people who are poor, mistreated, discriminated against, and the victims of war. [marginados]

Marks of the Church the four most important aspects of the Church found in the Nicene Creed. According to the Nicene Creed, the Church is one, holy, catholic, and apostolic. (See *apostolic, catholic, holy,* and *one*.) [atributos de la Iglesia]

martyr one who has given his or her life for the faith. *Martyr* comes from the Greek word for "witness." A martyr is the supreme witness to the truth of the faith and to Christ to whom he or she is united. In chapter 7 of Acts of the Apostles, the death of the first martyr, the deacon Stephen, is recounted. [mártir]

Mary the mother of Jesus. She is called blessed and "full of grace" because God chose her to be the mother of the Son of God, the Second Person of the Trinity. [Virgen María]

Mass the most important sacramental celebration of the Church, established by Jesus at the Last Supper as a remembrance of his Death and Resurrection. At Mass we listen to God's Word from the Bible and receive Jesus Christ in the consecrated Bread and Wine that are his Body and Blood. [Misa]

Matrimony a solemn agreement between a woman and a man to be partners for life, for their own good and for bringing up children. Marriage is a sacrament when the agreement is properly made between baptized Christians. [Matrimonio]

meditate to focus the mind prayerfully on an image or a word in order to experience God and understand God's will [meditar]

meditation a form of prayer using silence and listening. Through imagination, emotion, and desire, it is a way to understand how to adhere and respond to what God is asking. By concentrating on a word or an image, we move beyond thoughts, empty the mind of contents that get in the way of our experience of God, and rest in simple awareness of God. [meditación]

memorial a remembrance of events that have taken place in the past. We recall these events because they continue to affect us since they are part of God's saving plan for us. Every time we remember these events, we make God's saving action present. [memoria]

Mendicant Order a unique variety of religious order that developed in the 13th century. Unlike monks who remain inside a monastery, members of Mendicant Orders have ministries of preaching, teaching, and witnessing among people. They are called mendicant from the Latin word for "begging," which is their major means of supporting themselves. The two main Mendicant Orders are the Dominicans, founded by Saint Dominic de Guzman, and the Franciscans, founded by Saint Francis of Assisi. [orden mendicante]

mercy the gift to be able to respond with care and compassion to those in need. The gift of mercy is a grace given to us by Jesus Christ. [misericordia]

Messiah a title that means "anointed one." It is from a Hebrew word that means the same thing as the Hebrew word *Christ*. Messiah is the title given to Jesus as priest, prophet, and king. [Mesías]

ministry service or work done for others. All those baptized are called to a variety of ministries in the liturgy and in service to the needs of others. [ministerio]

miracle a sign or an act of wonder that cannot be explained by natural causes and that is the work of God. In the Gospels, Jesus works miracles as a sign that the Kingdom of God is present in his ministry. [milagro]

mission the work of Jesus Christ that is continued in the Church through the Holy Spirit. The mission of the Church is to proclaim salvation through Jesus' life, Death, Resurrection, and Ascension. [misión]

missionary a person sent by Church authority to spread the Gospel through evangelization and catechesis. Missionaries may serve in areas where few people have heard about Jesus or in small, underserved communities of isolated believers. [misionero]

monastery a place where men or women live out their solemn vows of poverty, chastity, and obedience in a stable community. People who live in monasteries spend their days in public prayer, work, and meditation. [monasterio]

monasticism a form of religious life in which men and women live out their vows of poverty, chastity, and obedience in a stable community. The goal of monasticism is to pursue a life of public prayer, work, and meditation under the guidance of a rule for the glory of God. Saint Benedict of Nursia, who died about 550, is considered the father of Western monasticism. [monacato]

monstrance a vessel that holds the Blessed Sacrament for adoration and Benediction [custodia]

moral choice a choice to do what is right or not to do what is wrong. We make moral choices because they help us grow closer to God and because we have the freedom to choose what is right and avoid what is wrong. [decisión moral]

moral law a rule for living that has been established by God and people in authority who are concerned about the good of all. Moral laws are based on God's direction to us to do what is right and avoid what is wrong. Some moral laws are "written" in the human heart and can be known through our own reasoning. Other moral laws have been revealed to us by God in the Old Testament and in the new law given by Jesus. [ley moral]

mortal sin a serious decision to turn away from God by doing something that we know is wrong. For a sin to be mortal, it must be a very serious offense, the person must know how serious it is, and the person must freely choose to do it anyway. [pecado mortal]

Mother of God the title for Mary proclaimed at the Council of Ephesus in 431. The council declared that Mary was not just the mother of Jesus, the man. She became the Mother of God by the conception of the Son of God in her womb. Because Jesus' humanity is one with his divinity, Mary is the mother of the eternal Son of God made man, who is God himself. [Madre de Dios]

Muslim a follower of the religion of Islam. *Muslim* means "one who submits to God." [musulmán]

mystery a religious truth that we can know only through God's Revelation and that we cannot fully understand. Our faith is a mystery that we profess in the Creed and celebrate in the liturgy and the sacraments. [misterio]

mystic a person who has a special understanding of God from intense, private experiences [místico]

Mystical Body of Christ the members of the Church formed into a spiritual body and bound together by the life communicated by Jesus Christ through the sacraments. Christ is the center and source of the life of this body. In it, we are all united. Each member of the body receives from Christ gifts fitting for him or her. [Cuerpo Místico de Cristo]

N

Nativity the mystery of Jesus' birth as told in the Gospels of Matthew and Luke. Although the two Nativity stories focus on different details, they relate the same truth that Jesus is the promised Savior. [Natividad]

natural law the moral law that is "written" in the human heart. We can know natural law through our own reason because the Creator has placed the knowledge of it in our hearts. It can provide the solid foundation on which we can make rules to guide our choices in life. Natural law forms the basis of our fundamental rights and duties and is the foundation for the work of the Holy Spirit in guiding our moral choices. [ley natural]

neighbor according to Jesus, this includes everyone, as each person is made in God's image. We are all meant to develop mutually supportive relationships. [prójimo]

neophyte a person who has recently been initiated into the Church through the Sacraments of Initiation [neófito]

New Evangelization the work of missionaries in traditionally Christian areas with people who may already know about Jesus and the Gospel [nueva evangelización]

New Testament the 27 books of the Bible that tell of the teaching, ministry, and saving events of the life of Jesus. The four Gospels present Jesus' life, Death, and Resurrection. Acts of the Apostles tells the story of Jesus' Ascension into heaven. It also shows how Jesus' message of salvation spread through the growth of the Church. Various letters instruct us in how to live as followers of Jesus Christ. The Book of Revelation offers encouragement to Christians living through persecution. [Nuevo Testamento]

Nicene Creed the summary of Christian beliefs developed by the bishops at the first two councils of the Church held in A.D. 325 and 381. It is the Creed shared by most Christians in the East and the West. [Credo Niceno]

novena a Catholic tradition repeated over a set number of days, usually nine, in devotion to a particular mystery or saint [novena]

novice a monk or nun who has not yet taken vows. Novices deepen their faith and learn about the customs, practices, and obligations of the religious life. [novicio]

O

obedience the act of willingly following what God asks us to do for our salvation. The Fourth Commandment requires children to obey their parents, and all people are required to obey civil authority when it acts for the good of all. To imitate the obedience of Jesus, members of religious communities make a special vow of obedience. [obediencia]

obey to follow the teachings or directions given by God or by someone who has authority over us [obedecer]

oil of catechumens the oil blessed by the bishop during Holy Week and used to anoint catechumens. This anointing strengthens them on their path to initiation into the Church. Infants are anointed with this oil right before they are baptized. [óleo de los catecúmenos]

oil of the sick the oil blessed by the bishop during Holy Week and used in the Sacrament of the Anointing of the Sick, which brings spiritual and, if it is God's will, physical healing [óleo de los enfermos]

Old Testament the first 46 books of the Bible, which tell of God's covenant with the people of Israel and his plan for the salvation of all people. The first five books are known as the Torah or Pentateuch. The Old Testament is fulfilled in the New Testament, but God's covenant presented in the Old Testament has permanent value and has never been revoked. [Antiguo Testamento]

one the Mark of the Church that indicates the unity of the Church as a community of Christian believers as well as the unity of all the members with Christ (See *Marks of the Church.*) [una]

option for the poor the principle of Catholic social teaching that holds that Christians must promote social justice and serve those who are poor (See *Catholic social teaching.*) [opción por los pobres]

ordained men who have received the Sacrament of Holy Orders so that they may preside at the celebration of the Eucharist and serve as leaders and teachers of the Church [ordenado]

Order of Mass, The the sequence of the prayers, gestures, readings and Eucharistic rites of the Mass [Ordinario de la Misa, el]

Order of Penitents a group of people within the Church, practicing intense repentance. The Order of Penitents first began in the early centuries of the Church, and many of the practices of Lent, including the use of ashes, come from the Penitents. [orden de penitentes]

Ordinary Time the longest liturgical season of the Church. It is divided into two periods—the first after the Christmas season and the second after Pentecost. The first period focuses on Jesus' childhood and public ministry. The second period focuses on Christ's reign as King of Kings. [Tiempo Ordinario]

ordination the rite of the Sacrament of Holy Orders by which a bishop gives to men, through the laying on of hands, the ability to minister to the Church as bishops, priests, and deacons [ordenación]

Original Sin the consequence of the disobedience of the first human beings. Adam and Eve disobeyed God and chose to follow their own will rather than God's will. As a result, human beings lost the original blessing God had intended and became subject to sin and death. In Baptism we are restored to life with God through Jesus Christ, although we still experience the effects of Original Sin. [pecado original]

Orthodox Church the Eastern Churches that split with the Roman Catholic Church in 1054. These Churches are distinct from the Roman Catholic Church in their liturgy and some of their traditions. [Iglesia Ortodoxa]

P

Palm Sunday the celebration of Jesus' triumphant entry into Jerusalem on the Sunday before Easter. Today it begins a week-long commemoration of the saving events of Holy Week. [Domingo de Ramos]

pantheism the belief that rejects a personal God and instead considers that God and the universe are identical. Pantheism was condemned in the *Syllabus of Errors*. [panteísmo]

parable one of the stories that Jesus told to show us what the Kingdom of God is like. Parables present images drawn from everyday life. These images show us the radical choice we make when we respond to the invitation to enter the Kingdom of God. [parábola]

Paraclete another name for the Holy Spirit. Jesus promised to send a Consoler and Advocate who would help the Apostles continue his mission. [Paráclito]

parish a stable community of believers in Jesus Christ who meet regularly in a specific area to worship God under the leadership of a pastor [parroquia]

participation one of the seven principles of Catholic social teaching. All people have a right to participate in the economic, political, and cultural life of society. It is a requirement for human dignity and a demand of justice that all people have a minimum level of participation in the community. (See *Catholic social teaching*.) [participación]

particular judgment Christ's judgment made of every person at the moment of death that offers either entrance into heaven (after a period of purification in Purgatory if needed) or immediate and eternal separation from God in hell. At the moment of death, each person is rewarded by Christ in accordance with his or her works and faith. [juicio individual]

Paschal Mystery the work of salvation accomplished by Jesus Christ through his Passion, Death, Resurrection, and Ascension. The Paschal Mystery is celebrated in the liturgy of the Church, and we experience its saving effects in the sacraments. In every liturgy of the Church, God the Father is blessed and adored as the source of all blessings we have received through his Son in order to make us his children through the Holy Spirit. [Misterio Pascual]

Passion the suffering and Death of Jesus. The Passion is part of the Paschal Mystery that accomplished Jesus Christ's saving work and that we celebrate and remember in the Eucharist. [Pasión]

Passover the Jewish festival that commemorates the delivery of the Hebrew people from slavery in Egypt. In the Eucharist, we celebrate our passover from death to life through Jesus' Death and Resurrection. [pascua]

pastor a priest who is responsible for the spiritual care of the members of the parish community. It is the job of the pastor to see that the Word of God is preached, the faith is taught, and the sacraments are celebrated. [párroco]

patriarch, Catholic the title used by leaders of certain Eastern Catholic Churches [patriarca, católico]

patriarch, Old Testament a leader of a family or clan within ancient Israel. More specifically, in biblical studies, the patriarchs are the founders of the Hebrew people described in Genesis chapters 12–50. Prominent among the patriarchs are Abraham, Isaac, Jacob, and Jacob's twelve sons. [patriarca, Antiguo Testamento]

patriarch, Orthodox the title used by leaders of Orthodox Churches. The bishop of Constantinople is known as the Ecumenical Patriarch. [patriarca, ortodoxo]

peacemaker a person who teaches us to be respectful in our words and actions toward one another [paz, los que trabajan por la]

penance the turning away from sin with a desire to change our life and live more closely the way God wants us to live. We express our penance externally by praying, fasting, and helping those who are poor. Penance is also the name of the action that the priest asks us to take or the prayers that he asks us to pray after he absolves us in the Sacrament of Penance and Reconciliation. (See *Sacrament of Penance and Reconciliation*.) [penitencia]

Penance and Reconciliation, Sacrament of the sacrament in which we celebrate God's forgiveness of sin and our reconciliation with God and the Church. This sacrament includes sorrow for the sins we have committed, confession of sins, absolution by the priest, and doing the penance that shows our willingness to amend our ways. [sacramento de la Penitencia y de la Reconciliación]

Penitential Act a formula of general confession asking for God's mercy at Mass. The priest may lead the assembly in praying the *Confiteor* ("I confess to almighty God . . .") or a threefold invocation echoed by "Lord have mercy . . . Christ have mercy . . . Lord have mercy" in English or in Greek. (See *The Order of Mass*.) [acto penitencial]

Pentecost the 50th day after Jesus was raised from the dead. On this day the Holy Spirit was sent from heaven, and the Church was born. It is also the Jewish feast, called *Shavuot* in Hebrew, that celebrated the giving of the Ten Commandments on Mount Sinai 50 days after the Exodus. [Pentecostés]

People of God another name for the Church. In the same way that the people of Israel were God's people through the covenant he made with them, the Church is a priestly, prophetic, and royal people through the new and eternal covenant with Jesus Christ. [Pueblo de Dios]

Glossary

perfect contrition the sorrow for sin that arises from a love of God above all else. Perfect contrition is the ideal act of the penitent preparing to celebrate the Sacrament of Penance and Reconciliation. (See *contrition* and *imperfect contrition*.) [contrición perfecta]

personal prayer the kind of prayer that rises up in us in everyday life. We pray with others in the liturgy, but also we can listen and respond to God through personal prayer every moment of our lives. [oración personal]

personal sin a sin we choose to commit, whether serious (mortal) or less serious (venial). Although the consequences of Original Sin leave us with a tendency to sin, God's grace, especially through the sacraments, helps us choose good over sin. [pecado personal]

petition a request to God, asking him to fulfill a need. When we share in God's saving love, we understand that every need is one that we can ask God to help us with through petition. [petición]

Pharaoh the Egyptian word for "Great House," referring to the royal palace of the king of Egypt. The reference to Pharaoh became known for the king himself, just as "White House" might refer to the president. Pharaoh was both the political and religious leader of Egypt. [faraón]

Pharisee a member of a party or sect in Judaism that began more than 100 years before Jesus. Pharisees saw Judaism as a religion centered on the observance of the Law. The Gospels depict tension between Jesus and the Pharisees. Pharisees were later found in the Christian community in Jerusalem. (Acts of the Apostles 15:5) Before his conversion, Paul was proud to call himself a Pharisee. [fariseo]

piety one of the seven Gifts of the Holy Spirit. It calls us to be faithful in our relationships both with God and with others. Piety helps us to love God and to behave responsibly and with generosity and affection toward others. (See *Gifts of the Holy Spirit*.) [piedad]

plague a natural calamity or disease that is seen as being inflicted by God as a remedial event to make people more conscious of their duties toward God and one another. In the Book of Exodus, the plagues inflicted on the Egyptians are seen as the means by which God convinced the Egyptians to free the Hebrew people from slavery. [plaga]

pope the Bishop of Rome, successor of Saint Peter, and leader of the Roman Catholic Church. Because he has the authority to act in the name of Christ, the pope is called the Vicar of Christ. The pope and all the bishops together make up the living, teaching office of the Church, the Magisterium. [papa]

poverty the quality of living without attachment to material goods. All baptized persons, not only those called to religious life, are called to live a holy life by practicing the virtues of chastity, obedience, and poverty. [pobreza]

praise the expression of our response to God, not only for what he does, but also simply because he is. In the Eucharist, the whole Church joins with Jesus Christ in expressing praise and thanksgiving to the Father. [alabanza]

prayer the raising of our hearts and minds to God. We are able to speak to and listen to God in prayer because he teaches us how to pray. [oración]

prayer of intercession a prayer of petition in which we pray as Jesus did to the Father on behalf of people. Asking on behalf of others is a characteristic of a heart attuned to God's mercy. Christian intercession recognizes no boundaries. Following Jesus' example, we pray for all people—for those who are rich, for political leaders, for those in need, and even for persecutors. [oracione de intercesión]

precepts of the Church those positive requirements that the pastoral authority of the Church has determined are necessary to a moral life. The precepts of the Church ensure that all Catholics move beyond the minimum by growing in the love of God and neighbor. [mandamientos de la Iglesia]

precursor a title for John the Baptist as the immediate forerunner of Jesus, the Messiah. John the Baptist is considered the last of the prophets. [precursor]

presbyter a word that originally meant "an elder or a trusted advisor to the bishop." From this word comes the English word *priest*, one of the three degrees of the Sacrament of Holy Orders. All the priests of a diocese under the bishop form the presbyterate. [presbítero]

pride a false image of ourselves that goes beyond what we deserve as God's creation. Pride puts us in competition with God. It is one of the seven Capital Sins. (See *Capital Sins*.) [soberbia]

priest a man who has accepted God's call to serve the Church by guiding it and building it up through the ministry of the Word and the celebration of the sacraments [sacerdote]

priesthood all the people of God who have been given a share of the one mission of Christ through the Sacraments of Baptism and Confirmation. The ministerial priesthood, which is made up of those men who have been ordained bishops and priests in Holy Orders, is essentially different from the priesthood of all the faithful because its work is to build up and guide the Church in the name of Christ. [sacerdocio]

Promised Land the land first promised by God to Abraham. It was to this land that God told Moses to lead the Chosen People after they were freed from slavery in Egypt and received the Ten Commandments at Mount Sinai. [Tierra Prometida]

prophecy a divine communication that comes through a human person. Prophecy in the Old Testament often tells of the coming of Jesus or conveys an important message to God's people. [profecía]

prophet one called to speak for God and to call the people to be faithful to the covenant. Eighteen books of the Old Testament present the messages and actions of the prophets. [profeta]

prudence the virtue that directs us toward the good and helps us choose the correct means to achieve that good. When we act with prudence, we carefully and thoughtfully consider our actions. Prudence is one of the Cardinal Virtues that guide our conscience and influence us to live according to the Law of Christ. (See *Cardinal Virtues*.) [prudencia]

psalm a prayer in the form of a poem, written to be sung in public worship. Each psalm expresses an aspect of the depth of human prayer. Over several centuries, 150 psalms were assembled into the Book of Psalms in the Old Testament. Psalms were used in worship in the Temple in Jerusalem, and they have been used in the public worship of the Church since its beginning. [salmo]

Purgatory a possible outcome of particular judgment following death. Purgatory is a state of final cleansing after death of all our human imperfections to prepare us to enter into the joy of God's presence in heaven. [purgatorio]

R

racism the opinion that race determines human traits and capacities and that a particular race has an inherent, or inborn, superiority. Discrimination based on a person's race is a violation of human dignity and a sin against justice. [racismo]

rationalist a person who regards human reason as the principal source of all knowledge. Rationalism was developed by René Descartes and dominated European thought in the 17th and 18th centuries. Rationalists recognize as true only those religious beliefs that can be explained rationally and stress confidence in the orderly character of the world and in the mind's ability to make sense of this order. [racionalista]

real presence the way in which the risen Jesus Christ is present in the Eucharist in the consecrated Bread and Wine. Jesus Christ's presence is called real because in the Eucharist his Body and Blood, soul and divinity, are wholly and entirely present. [Presencia Real de Cristo]

reconciliation the renewal of friendship after that friendship has been broken by some action or lack of action. In the Sacrament of Penance and Reconciliation, through God's mercy and forgiveness, we are reconciled with God, the Church, and others. [reconciliación]

Redeemer Jesus Christ, whose life, sacrificial Death on the cross, and Resurrection from the dead set us free from the slavery of sin and bring us redemption [Redentor]

redemption our being set free from the slavery of sin through the life, sacrificial Death on the cross, and Resurrection of Jesus Christ. [redención]

reform to put an end to a wrong by introducing a better or changed course of action. The prophets called people to reform their lives and return to being faithful to their covenant with God. [reforma]

refugee a person who flees his or her home country because of a natural or a manmade disaster. Jesus was a refugee when Joseph and Mary escaped to Egypt to keep Jesus safe from King Herod. [refugiado]

relic a piece of the body of a saint, something that belonged to a saint. The first relics were from the bodies of martyrs and were enshrined in Christian basilicas and churches. [reliquia]

religious life a state of life recognized by the Church. In religious life, men and women freely respond to a call to follow Jesus by living the vows of poverty, chastity, and obedience in community with others. [vida religiosa]

repentance our turning away from sin, with a desire to change our lives and live more closely as God wants us to live. We express our penance by prayer, fasting, and helping those who are poor. [arrepentimiento]

Resurrection the bodily raising of Jesus Christ from the dead on the third day after his Death on the cross. The Resurrection is the crowning truth of our faith. [Resurrección de Cristo]

Glossary

Revelation God's communication of himself to us through the words and deeds he has used throughout history to show us the mystery of his plan for our salvation. This Revelation reaches its completion in his sending of his Son, Jesus Christ. [Revelación]

righteousness an attribute of God used to describe his justice, his faithfulness to the covenant, and his holiness in the Old Testament. As an attribute of humans, righteousness means being in a right relationship with God through moral conduct and observance of the Law. We have merit in God's sight and are able to do this because of the work of God's grace in us. Paul speaks of righteousness in a new way that is no longer dependent on observance of the Law. It comes through the faith in Jesus and his saving Death and Resurrection. To be made righteous in Jesus is to be saved, vindicated, and put right with God through his grace. [rectitud]

rights and responsibilities an important idea within Catholic social teaching. All people have the right to the necessities for a full and decent life, such as dignified work, health care, and education. All people also have responsibilities to promote the common good and to help others. (See *Catholic social teaching*.) [derechos y responsabilidades]

rite one of the many forms followed in celebrating liturgy in the Church. A rite may differ according to the culture or country where it is celebrated. A rite is also the special form for celebrating each sacrament. [rito]

Rite of Christian Initiation of Adults (RCIA) the process through which unbaptized adults join the Church. Catechumens receive instruction in preparation for their initiation into the Church. Lent marks the beginning of the catechumens' final period of preparation. During Lent they participate in the Rite of Election, during which their sponsors stand as witnesses to their faith, moral character, and desire to join the Church. During the Easter Vigil on Holy Saturday, the Elect profess their faith in Christ and the Church, and they promise to live as Jesus' disciples in the world. They are welcomed into the Church through the Sacraments of Initiation. [Ritual de la Iniciación Cristiana de Adultos]

Rosary a prayer in honor of the Blessed Virgin Mary. When we pray the Rosary, we meditate on the mysteries of Jesus Christ's life while praying the Hail Mary on five sets of ten beads and the Lord's Prayer on the beads in between. In the Latin Church, praying the Rosary became a way for ordinary people to reflect on the mysteries of Christ's life. [Rosario]

S

Sabbath the seventh day, when God rested after finishing the work of creation. The Third Commandment requires us to keep the Sabbath holy. For Christians the Sabbath became Sunday, the Lord's Day, because it was the day that Jesus rose from the dead and the new creation in Jesus Christ began. [sabbat]

sacrament holy, visible signs that signify a divine reality. Through the sacraments, Christ acts in us to save us. Grace received through the Holy Spirit enables us to carry out our mission as disciples. [sacramento]

sacramental an object, a prayer, or a blessing given by the Church to help us grow in our spiritual life [sacramental]

sacramental seal the obligation of priests to keep absolutely secret the sins confessed during the Sacrament of Penance and Reconciliation [sello sacramental]

Sacraments at the Service of Communion the Sacraments of Holy Orders and Matrimony. These two sacraments contribute to the personal salvation of individuals by giving them a special way to serve others. [sacramentos al Servicio de la Comunidad]

Sacraments of Healing the Sacraments of Penance and Reconciliation and Anointing of the Sick, by which the Church continues Jesus' healing ministry of body and soul [sacramentos de la Curación]

Sacraments of Initiation the sacraments that are the foundation of our Christian life. We are born anew in Baptism, strengthened by Confirmation, and receive in the Eucharist the food of eternal life. By means of these sacraments, we receive an increasing measure of the divine life and advance toward the perfection of charity. [sacramentos de la Iniciación]

sacrifice a ritual offering of animals or produce made to God by the priest in the Temple in Jerusalem. Sacrifice was a sign of the people's adoration of God, giving thanks to God, or asking for forgiveness. Sacrifice also showed union with God. The great High Priest, Christ, accomplished our redemption through the perfect sacrifice of his Death on the Cross. [sacrificio]

Sacrifice of the Mass the sacrifice of Jesus on the Cross, which is remembered and made present in the Eucharist. It is offered in reparation for the sins of the living and the dead and to obtain spiritual or temporal blessings from God. [sacrificio de la Misa]

saint a holy person who has died united with God. The Church has said that this person is now with God forever in heaven. [santo]

salvation the gift, which God alone can give, of forgiveness of sin and the restoration of friendship with him [Salvación]

sanctify to make holy. Sacramentals and other Church practices make holy the everyday events and objects in our lives. [santificar]

sanctifying grace the gift from God, given to us without our earning it, that introduces us to the intimacy of the Trinity, unites us with its life, and heals our human nature, wounded by sin. Sanctifying grace helps us respond to our vocation as God's adopted children, and it continues the work of making us holy that began at our Baptism. (See *actual grace, grace,* and *habitual grace.*) [gracia santificante]

sanctuary a holy place to worship God. A sanctuary in church is the place where a religious rite is celebrated. [santuario]

Sanhedrin the Jewish court that ruled on matters of faith and practice among Jews. The Sanhedrin was the only Jewish court allowed to inflict the death penalty. [Sanedrín]

Satan a fallen angel and the enemy of anyone attempting to follow God's will. Satan tempts Jesus in the Gospels and opposes his ministry. In Jewish, Christian, and Muslim thought, Satan is associated with those angels who refused to bow down before human beings and serve them as God commanded. They refused to serve God and were thrown out of heaven as a punishment. Satan and the other demons tempt human beings to join them in their revolt against God. [Satanás]

Savior Jesus, the Son of God, who became man to forgive our sins and restore our friendship with God. *Jesus* means "God saves." [Salvador]

scriptorium the room in a monastery in which books were copied by hand. Often beautiful art was added to the page to illustrate a story. [scriptorium]

Scriptures the holy writings of Jews and Christians, collected in the Old and New Testaments of the Bible [Sagradas Escrituras]

seal of confession also called the sacramental seal. It declares that the priest is absolutely forbidden to reveal under any circumstances any sin confessed to him in the Sacrament of Penance and Reconciliation. (See *sacramental seal.*) [sigilo sacramental]

Second Coming the return in glory of Jesus Christ to the world. The Church looks forward to the Second Coming with joy. [Segunda Venida]

Second Vatican Council the 21st and most recent ecumenical council of the Catholic Church. It met from October 11, 1962, to December 8, 1965. Its purpose, according to Pope John XXIII, was to renew the Church and to help it promote peace and unity among Christians and all humanity. [Concilio Vaticano Segundo]

seminary a school for the training and spiritual formation of priests. Seminaries first became widespread in the Church during the renewals of the 1500s. [seminario]

seraphim the heavenly beings who worship before the throne of God. One of them purified the lips of Isaiah with a burning coal so that he could speak for God. (Isaiah 6:6–7) [serafín]

Sermon on the Mount the words of Jesus, written in Chapters 5–7 of the Gospel of Matthew, in which Jesus reveals how he has fulfilled God's law given to Moses. The Sermon on the Mount begins with the eight Beatitudes and includes the Lord's Prayer. [Sermón de la Montaña]

sexism a prejudice or discrimination based on sex, especially discrimination against women. Sexism leads to behaviors and attitudes that foster a view of social roles based only on sex. [sexismo]

Sign of Peace the part of the Mass in which we offer a gesture of peace to one another as we prepare to receive Holy Communion. This signifies our willingness to be united in peace before we receive the Lord. (See *The Order of Mass.*) [Rito de la Paz]

Sign of the Cross the gesture we make that signifies our belief in God the Father, the Son, and the Holy Spirit. It is a sign of blessing, a confession of faith, and a way that identifies us as followers of Jesus Christ. [Señal de la Cruz]

signs events in the world that point to a deeper reality. The first half of the Gospel of John presents seven signs that reveal the glory of God and give us a glimpse of what the Kingdom of God is like. [signos]

sin a deliberate thought, word, deed, or failure to act that offends God and hurts our relationships with other people. Some sin is mortal and needs to be confessed in the Sacrament of Penance and Reconciliation. Other sin is venial, or less serious. [pecado]

Glossary

sloth a carelessness of heart that leads a person to ignore his or her development as a person, especially spiritual development and a relationship with God. Sloth is one of the seven capital sins, and it is contrary to the First Commandment. (See *Capital Sins*.) [pereza]

social justice the fair and equal treatment of every member of society. It is required by the dignity and freedom of every person. The Catholic Church has developed a body of social principles and moral teachings described in papal and other official documents issued since the late 19th century. This teaching deals with the economic, political, and social order of the world. It is rooted in the Bible as well as in the traditional theological teachings of the Church. [justicia social]

social sin social situations and institutions that are against the will of God. Because of the personal sins of individuals, entire societies can develop structures that are sinful in and of themselves. Social sins include racism, sexism, structures that deny people access to adequate health care, and the destruction of the environment for the benefit of a few. [pecado social]

solidarity the attitude of strength and unity that leads to the sharing of spiritual and material goods. Solidarity unites rich and poor, weak and strong, to foster a society in which all give what they can and receive what they need. The idea of solidarity is based on the common origin of all humanity. (See *Catholic social teaching*.) [solidaridad]

Son of God the title revealed by Jesus that indicates his unique relationship to God the Father. The revelation of Jesus' divine sonship is the main dramatic development of the story of Jesus of Nazareth as it unfolds in the Gospels. [Hijo de Dios]

soul the part of us that makes us human and an image of God. Body and soul together form one unique human nature. The soul is responsible for our consciousness and our freedom. The soul does not die and will be reunited with the body in the final resurrection. [alma]

Spiritual Exercises a spiritual retreat written by Ignatius of Loyola, designed to help people become aware of the presence of God in all things. The Spiritual Exercises are a major part of Ignatian spirituality. [Ejercicios Espirituales]

spirituality our growing, loving relationship with God. Spirituality is our way of expressing our experience of God in both the way we pray and the way we love our neighbor. There are many different schools of spirituality. Examples of these schools are Franciscan and Jesuit.

These are guides for the spiritual life and have enriched the traditions of prayer, worship, and living in Christianity. [espiritualidad]

spiritual works of mercy the kind acts through which we help our neighbors meet the needs that are more than material. The spiritual works of mercy include counseling the doubtful, instructing the ignorant, admonishing sinners, comforting the afflicted, forgiving offenses, bearing wrongs patiently, and praying for the living and the dead. [obras de misericordia espirituales]

Stations of the Cross a prayer for meditating on the final hours of Jesus' life, from his condemnation by Pontius Pilate to his Death and burial. We pray the Stations by moving to each representation of 14 incidents, based on events from Jesus' Passion and Death. [Vía Crucis]

stewardship the careful and responsible management of something entrusted to one's care, especially the goods of creation, which are intended for the whole human race. The sixth Precept of the Church makes clear our part in stewardship by requiring us to provide for the material needs of the Church, according to our abilities. [corresponsabilidad]

subsidiarity the principle that the best institutions for responding to a particular social task are those closest to it. The responsibility of the closest political or private institution is to assist those in need. Only when issues cannot be resolved at the local level should they be resolved at a higher level. [subsidiaridad]

Summa Theologiae a work of Christian theology in five volumes written by Saint Thomas Aquinas. In the *Summa Theologiae*, Aquinas asks questions about thousands of theological topics that continue to influence Christian theology today. [*Summa Theologiae*]

superior the leader of a community of consecrated religious men or women [superior]

swaddling wrapping an infant in strips of cloth for warmth and comfort. Jesus' swaddling clothes symbolized the humility and poverty of his birth and foreshadowed the shroud he would be wrapped in after his Crucifixion. [envolver en pañales]

Syllabus of Errors a document issued by Pope Pius IX condemning false claims and ideas about the nature of God and the world. The condemned views included claims related to pantheism, socialism, communism, the rights of the Church, and many other topics. [Syllabus Errorum]

synagogue the Jewish place of assembly for prayer, instruction, and study of the Torah. After the destruction of the Temple in 587 B.C., synagogues were organized as places to maintain Jewish faith and worship. Jesus attended the synagogue regularly for prayer and to teach. When visiting a city, Paul would first visit the synagogue. The synagogue played an important role in the development of Christian worship and in the structure of Christian communities. [sinagoga]

synod a meeting of bishops from all over the world to discuss doctrinal or pastoral matters. Synods offer suggestions to the pope, which may or may not become official teachings at a later time. [sínodo]

synoptic the way in which three of the four Gospels—Matthew, Mark, and Luke—tell similar stories in similar ways about the life and Death of Jesus. The Gospel of John's structure and stories are often different from the other three. Although none of the Gospels agree on every detail, each one conveys unique truths from their own perspectives about Jesus' life and mission. [sinóptico]

T

tabernacle the container in which the Blessed Sacrament is kept so that Holy Communion can be taken to those who are sick and dying. It is also the name of the tent sanctuary in which the Israelites kept the ark of the covenant from the time of the Exodus to the construction of Solomon's Temple. [sagrario]

temperance the Cardinal Virtue that helps us control our attraction to pleasure so that our natural desires are kept within proper limits. This moral virtue helps us choose to use goods in moderation. (See *Cardinal Virtues*.) [templanza]

Temple the house of worship of God, first built by Solomon. The Temple provided a place for the priests to offer sacrifice, to adore and give thanks to God, and to ask for forgiveness. It was destroyed and rebuilt. The second Temple was also destroyed and was never rebuilt. Part of the outer wall of the Temple mount remains to this day in Jerusalem. [Templo]

temptation an attraction, from outside us or inside us, that can lead us to disobey God's commands. Everyone is tempted, but the Holy Spirit helps us resist temptation and choose to do good. [tentación]

Ten Commandments the 10 rules given by God to Moses on Mount Sinai that sum up God's law and show us what is required to love God and our neighbor. By following the Ten Commandments, the Hebrews accepted their covenant with God. [Diez Mandamientos]

theologian an expert in the study of God and his Revelation to the world [teólogo]

Theological Virtues the three virtues of faith, hope, and charity that are gifts from God and not acquired by human effort. The virtue of faith helps us believe in God, the virtue of hope helps us desire eternal life and the Kingdom of God, and the virtue of charity helps us love God and our neighbor as we should. [virtudes teologales]

Torah the Hebrew word for "instruction" or "law." It is also the name of the first five books of the Old Testament: Genesis, Exodus, Leviticus, Numbers, and Deuteronomy. [Torá]

Tradition the beliefs and practices of the Church that are passed down from one generation to the next under the guidance of the Holy Spirit. What Christ entrusted to the Apostles was handed on to others both orally and in writing. Tradition and Scripture together make up the single deposit of faith, which remains present and active in the Church. [Tradición católica]

Transfiguration an event witnessed by the Apostles Peter, James, and John that revealed Jesus' divine glory. Jesus' face shone like the sun, his clothes became dazzlingly white, and he spoke with Elijah and Moses on the mountain. [Transfiguración]

transubstantiation the unique change of the bread and wine in the Eucharist into the Body and Blood of the risen Jesus Christ, while retaining their physical appearance as bread and wine [transubstanciación]

trespasses unlawful acts committed against the property or rights of another person or acts that physically harm a person [ofensas]

Triduum a Latin word meaning "three days" that refers to Holy Thursday, Good Friday, and Holy Saturday. The liturgies of the Triduum are among the most solemn celebrations of the Catholic faith. [Triduo Pascual]

Trinity the mystery of the existence of God in three Persons—the Father, the Son, and the Holy Spirit. Each Person of the Trinity is God, whole and entire. Each Person is distinct only in the relationship of each to the others. [Trinidad, Santísima]

Truce of God an act of the Church in the 11th century that banned fighting on Sundays and that was eventually extended to more than half the year [tregua de Dios]

Glossary

U

understanding one of the seven Gifts of the Holy Spirit. This gift helps us make the right choices in life and in our relationships with God and with others. (See *Gifts of the Holy Spirit.*) [consejo]

universal Church the entire Church as it exists throughout the world. The people of every diocese, along with their bishops and the pope, make up the universal Church. (See *catholic.*) [Iglesia universal]

V

venerate to show respect for someone or something. Although only God should be worshiped, Christians venerate the saints and objects associated with them to show respect for God's work in their lives. [venerar]

venial sin a choice we make that weakens our relationship with God or with other people. Venial sin wounds and lessens the divine life in us. If we make no effort to do better, venial sin can lead to more serious sin. Through our participation in the Eucharist, venial sin is forgiven when we are repentant, strengthening our relationship with God and with others. [pecado venial]

viaticum the Eucharist that a dying person receives. It is spiritual food for the last journey we make as Christians, the journey through death to eternal life. [viático]

Vicar of Christ the title given to the pope who, as the successor of Saint Peter, has the authority to act in Christ's place. A vicar is someone who stands in for and acts for another. (See *pope.*) [Vicario de Cristo]

virtue an attitude or a way of acting that enables us to do good [virtud]

Visitation one of the Joyful Mysteries of the Rosary, a reference to Mary's visit to Elizabeth to share the good news that Mary is to be the mother of Jesus. Elizabeth's greeting of Mary forms part of the Hail Mary. During this visit, Mary sings the *Magnificat,* her praise of God. [Visitación]

vocation the call each of us has in life to be the person God wants us to be and the way we each serve the Church and the Kingdom of God. Each of us can live out his or her vocation as a layperson, as a member of a religious community, or as a member of the clergy. [vocación]

vow a deliberate and free promise made to God by people who want especially to dedicate their lives to God. Their vows give witness now to the kingdom that is to come. [voto]

Vulgate the Latin translation of the Bible by Saint Jerome from the Hebrew and Greek in which it was originally written. Most Christians of Saint Jerome's day no longer spoke Hebrew or Greek. The common language, or vulgate, was Latin. [Vulgata]

W

Way, the what Saint Paul called the early faith and those who follow Jesus. Like the disciples on the road to Emmaus, our life is a journey of faith on "the Way" for which Jesus gives strength in the Eucharist. [Camino, el]

wisdom one of the seven Gifts of the Holy Spirit. Wisdom helps us understand the purpose and plan of God and live in a way that helps bring about this plan. It begins in wonder and awe at God's greatness. (See *Gifts of the Holy Spirit.*) [sabiduría]

Wisdom Literature the Old Testament books of Job, Proverbs, Ecclesiastes, Song of Songs, Wisdom, and Ben Sira. The purpose of these books is to give instruction on ways to live and how to understand and cope with the problems of life. [literatura sapiencial]

witness the passing on to others, by our words and our actions, the faith that we have been given. Every Christian has the duty to give witness to the good news about Jesus Christ that he or she has come to know. [testimonio]

worship the adoration and honor given to God in public prayer [culto]

Y

Yahweh the name of God in Hebrew, which God told Moses from the burning bush. *Yahweh* means "I am who am" or "I cause to be all that is." [Yavé]

Index

Index

Acknowledgments

Excerpts from the *New American Bible, revised edition* © 2010, 1991, 1986, 1970 Confraternity of Christian Doctrine, Washington, D.C., and are used by permission of the copyright owner. All rights reserved. No part of the *New American Bible* may be reproduced in any form without permission in writing from the copyright owner.

The English translation of the Act of Contrition from *Rite of Penance* © 1974 International Commission on English in the Liturgy Corporation (ICEL); the English translation of Prayer to the Holy Spirit and Hail, Holy Queen *(Salve Regina)* from *A Book of Prayers* © 1982, ICEL; the English translation of Prayer Before Meals and Prayer After Meals from *Book of Blessings* © 1988, ICEL; the English translation of Nicene Creed and Apostles' Creed from *The Roman Missal* © 2010, ICEL. All rights reserved.

Excerpts from the English translation of the *Catechism of the Catholic Church, Second Edition* for the United States of America © 2000 United States Catholic Conference, Inc.—Libreria Editrice Vaticana.

Excerpt from *Economic Justice for All: Pastoral Letter on Catholic social teaching and the U.S. Economy* © 1986 United States Conference of Catholic Bishops, Washington, D.C. All rights reserved. Used by permission.

Excerpt from *Faithful Citizenship: A Catholic Call to Political Responsibility* © 2003 United States Conference of Catholic Bishops, Washington, D.C. All rights reserved. Used by permission.

Excerpt from *Forming Consciences for Faithful Citizenship* © 2007, 2011 United States Conference of Catholic Bishops, Washington, D.C. All rights reserved. Used by permission.

Excerpts from papal encyclicals and other Vatican documents are © Libreria Editrice Vaticana. All rights reserved.

The Prayer for Generosity and the *Suscipe* are from *Hearts on Fire: Praying with Jesuits* by Michael Harter, S.J. © 2005 Loyola Press.

Loyola Press has made every effort to locate the copyright holders for the cited works used in this publication and to make full acknowledgment for their use. In the case of any omissions, the publisher will be pleased to make suitable acknowledgments in future editions.

Art and Photography

When there is more than one picture on a page, positions are abbreviated as follows: **(t)** top, **(c)** center, **(b)** bottom, **(l)** left, **(r)** right, **(bg)** background, **(bd)** border.

Photos and illustrations not acknowledged are either owned by Loyola Press or from royalty-free sources including but not limited to Art Resource, Alamy, Bridgeman, Corbis/Veer, Getty Images, iStockphoto, Jupiterimages, Media Bakery, PunchStock, Shutterstock, Thinkstock, and Wikipedia Commons. Loyola Press has made every effort to locate the copyright holders for the cited works used in this publication and to make full acknowledgment for their use. In the case of any omissions, the publisher will be pleased to make suitable acknowledgments in future editions.

Frontmatter: i Rafael Lopez. **ii–iii** iStockphoto/Thinkstock. **iii** (t) © iStockphoto.com/keeweeboy. **iii** (c) The Crosiers/Gene Plaisted, OSC. **iii** (b) Jupiterimages/Creatas/Thinkstock. **iv** (t) Zvonimir Atletic/Shutterstock.com. **iv** (bl) © iStockphoto.com/hadynyah. **iv** (br) © iStockphoto.com/botsman141.

© iStockphoto.com: 4 (t) Jbryson. **6** (t) -Mosquito-. **6–7, 21, 31** (t, b) blue67. **8** (t) Maica. **12** (t) TonyBaggett. **15** (t) blue67; (br) Luseen. **21** (cl) lawcai; (cr) Allkindza; (cl, bc) deeAuvil; (bc) Crisma. **22** (bl) iStockphoto. **30** (tl) blue67; (b) Auki. **32** (t) eyecrave. **37** (bc) alexsl. **38** (bl) Liliboas. **44** (tr) evilclown.

46 (t) mixformdesign. **48** (b) ranplett. **58** (t) Chelnok; (bl) kryczka. **64–67** (tl, b) blue67. **64** Hogie. **65** (c) Hogie. **72** (bl) ranplett. **76** (t) arieliona. **82–83** (bd) blue67. **87** (t) ChrisSteer; (b) jabejon. **88** (t) peepo. **100** (bd) trigga; (b) Fos4o. **102** (bd) ChuckStryker. **108–109** (b) artplay711. **110** (bd) ChuckStryker. **118** (tl, tr, b) blue67. **123** (cb) iStockphoto.com. **126–127** (b) Beastfromeast. **128** (b) blue67. **132** (t) hadynyah; (b) Vardhan. **134** (t) keeweeboy; (b) javarman3. **138–139** (b, t) Beastfromeast. **139** (cr) kryczka. **145** (cr) LokFung. **146** (br) diane555. **147** (br) bubaone. **148** (t) Beastfromeast. **154–155** (b) LokFung. **161** (cr) blue67; (b) Beastfromeast. **163** (t) stdemi. **167** (cr) aldegonde. **167–169** (b) Beastfromeast. **168** (t) duncan1890. **168–169** (b) Beastfromeast. **170** (t) abzee; (c) aleksandarvelasevic. **171** (br) elsen029. **176** (t) JennaWagner; (bl) lisafx; (br) kali9. **178** (c) cstar55. **181** (br) princessdlaf. **183** (b) blue67. **184** (t) Slonov; (c) blue67. **196** (bd) abzee. **204** (t) Beastfromeast; (b) svetikd. **205–206** (b, tl) Beastfromeast. **219** (t) HeikeKampe; (b) OllieMac. **221** (tr) 7io; (bg) Jasmina007. **222** (bl) beastfromeast. **224** (bd) kamisoka. **225** (b) huronphoto. **229** (b) chankimlungistock. **230** (c) blue67. **233** bopshops. **234** (c) blue67. **242** botsman141. **244** (t) javarman3. **246** (bd) kentarcajuan. **248** (b) kulicki. **251** (t, bd) Jasmina007; (tr) WPChambers. **252** (ct) ankh-fire; (cr) beastfromeast. **253** (bd) makkayak. **254** blue67. **257** (t) duncan1890; (bl) jgroup; (br) ZU_09. **270** (cb) kevinruss. **272–273** (bg) Trifonov_Evgeniy. **273** grandriver. **274** livjam. **275** blue67. **277** (b) beastfromeast. **283** (t) ajt. **287** teekid. **290** duckycards. **296** AndrisTkachenko. **298** LeggNet; eyedear. **300** (c) MariaAngelaCiucci.

Thinkstock: 4 (t) iStockphoto. **43** (tl) Jupiterimages/Creatas. **52** (b) iStockphoto. **56–57** (b) iStockphoto. **72** (c) PhotoObjects.net/Hemera Technologies. **112** (t) Jupiterimages/Creatas. **138** (t) Jupiterimages/Photos.com. **144** (b) Hemera. **184** (b) Brand X Pictures. **198** (c) iStockphoto. **199** (bd) Brand X Pictures. **212** (bd) iStockphoto. **212–213** (r, t) iStockphoto. **215** (bd) Brand X Pictures. **216** (t) iStockphoto. **221** (t) iStockphoto. **236** (b) iStockphoto.

Unit 1: 1 (t) Andrew R. Wright. **2** (br) Andrew R. Wright. **3** (t) Ocean Photography/Veer. **5** (tr) Susan Tolonen; (br) Scala/Art Resource, NY. **7** (cr) AgnusImages.com. **9** (t) Loyola Press Photography; (b) James Woodson/Digital Vision/Getty Images. **11** (t) OJO Images Photography/Veer. **13** (tr) The Crosiers/Gene Plaisted, OSC; (br) AgnusImages.com. **14** (t) Don Hammond/Design Pics/Corbis. **15** (bc) Fotosearch. **16** (t) Fancy Photography/Veer. **19** (t) Blend Images Photography/Veer. **20** (t) Detail: Murillo, Bartolome Esteban (1618–1682) The Nativity. Pen and brown ink, brush and brown wash, over traces of leadpoint or soft black chalk. 10-3/4 x 9 in. (27.3 x 22.9 cm). Purchase, Clifford A. Furst Bequest, by exchange, and Harry G. Sperling Fund, 1995 (1995.375). The Metropolitan Museum of Art, New York, NY, U.S.A. Photo Credit: Image copyright © The Metropolitan Museum of Art/Art Resource, NY; (b) SuperStock/Getty Images. **22** (t) Rui Vale de Sousa/Shutterstock.com; (br) Alinari/The Bridgeman Art Library International. **23** (t) Olga Kushcheva/Jupiterimages; (b) The Crosiers/Gene Plaisted, OSC; (br) The Crosiers/Gene Plaisted, OSC. **24** (t) Alloy Photography/Veer. **27** (t) Corbis Photography/Veer. **28** (t) Scala/Art Resource, NY; (b) Daily Mail/Rex/Alamy. **29** (cr) The Crosiers/Gene Plaisted, OSC; (br) Giraudon/The Bridgeman Art Library International. © 2013 Artists Rights Society (ARS), New York/ADAGP, Paris. **30** (t) Blend Images Photography/Veer. **31** (t) Jupiterimages. **35** (cr) Image Source Photography/Veer. **36** (t) Fancy Photography/Veer; (b) Royalty-free image. **38** (t) The Crosiers/Gene Plaisted, OSC; (cl) Jupiterimages; (cr) The Crosiers/Gene Plaisted, OSC. **39** (b) Fine Art Photographic Library/Corbis. **40** (b) Ocean Photography/Veer. **41** Mark Poulalion. **43** (bl) Wikimedia public domain. **44** (b) Warling Studios.

Unit 2: 45 (t) Andrew R. Wright. **46** (c) Museu Nacional d'Art de Catalunya, Barcelona, Spain/The Bridgeman Art Library International; (br) Andrew R. Wright. **47** (t) Blend Images Photography/Veer. **48** (t) The Crosiers/Gene Plaisted, OSC. **49** (tr) Zvonimir Atletic/Shutterstock.com; (br) The Crosiers/Gene Plaisted, OSC. **50** (t) Corbis Photography/Veer. **51** (tr) Warling Studios; (br) Michael O'Brien. **52** (t) Ocean Photography/Veer. **55** (t) Fancy Photography/Veer. **56** (t) The Crosiers/Gene Plaisted, OSC. **57** (tr) The Crosiers/Gene Plaisted, OSC; (bc) Private Collection/The Bridgeman Art Library International. **59** (t) W.P. Wittman Limited; (br) Phil Martin Photography. **60** (t) Monkey Business Images/Veer. **63** (t) Blend Images Photography; (t) Laurence Mouton/PhotoAlto/Corbis. **64** (tr) The Crosiers/Gene Plaisted, OSC. **64, 68, 80** (tr) Jupiterimages. **65** (t) The Crosiers/Gene Plaisted, OSC. **66** (tl) Jupiterimages; (t) The Crosiers/Gene Plaisted, OSC; (t) SeDmi/Veer. **67** (tr) Jesus Mafa; (br) © Look and Learn/The Bridgeman Art Library International. **68** (t) Alloy Photography/Veer. **71** (t) moodboard Photography/Veer. **72** (t) Ocean Photography/Veer; (bl) AgnusImages.com. **73** (cr) The Crosiers/Gene Plaisted, OSC. **74** (t) Corbis Photography/Veer. **75** (cr) W.P. Wittman Limited; (br) Alinari/The Bridgeman Art Library International. **79** (c) The Crosiers/Gene Plaisted, OSC. **80** (t) Warling Studios; (br) W.P. Wittman Limited. **81** (br) The Crosiers/Gene Plaisted, OSC. **82** (t) The Crosiers/Gene Plaisted, OSC; (br) Private

Collection/The Bridgeman Art Library International. **83** (br) Private Collection/The Bridgeman Art Library International. **84** (t) Alloy Photography/Veer; (b) Photodisc Object Series. **88** (b) Echo/Cultura/Getty Images.

Unit 3: 89 (t) Andrew R. Wright. **90** Jupiterimages; (t) Andrew R. Wright. **91** (t) is/Veer. **92** (t) The Crosiers/Gene Plaisted, OSC; (b) National Gallery, London, UK/The Bridgeman Art Library International. **93** (br) The Crosiers/Gene Plaisted, OSC. **94** (tr) Private Collection/The Bridgeman Art Library International; (c) Bettmann/Corbis. **95** (br) Erich Lessing/Art Resource, NY. **96** (t) Oliver Rossi/Corbis. **99** (t) Barbara Reddoch/Veer. **100** (t) The Crosiers/ Gene Plaisted, OSC. **101** (tr) The Crosiers/Gene Plaisted, OSC; (bl) Cameraphoto Arte Venezia/The Bridgeman Art Library International. **102** (tr) W.P. Wittman Limited. **103** (br) Alessandra Cimatoribus. **104** (t) Alloy Photography/Veer. **105** Jim Wright. **107** (t) Corbis Photography/Veer. **108** (t) Private Collection/ The Bridgeman Art Library International; (bd) SeDmi/Veer. **109** (br) Media Bakery. **110–111** (t) Rafael Lopez. **110** (br) Giraudon/The Bridgeman Art Library International. **111** (br) The Crosiers/Gene Plaisted, OSC. **113** Loyola Press Photography. **115** (t) Blend Images Photography/Veer. **116** The Palsied Man Let Down Through the Roof, illustration for 'The Life of Christ', c.1886–94 (gouache on paper), Tissot, James Jacques Joseph (1836–1902)/Brooklyn Museum of Art, New York, USA/The Bridgeman Art Library International. **117** (br) Warling Studios. **118** (t) The Crosiers/Gene Plaisted, OSC. **119** (cr) Greg Kuepfer; (bl) Private Collection/The Bridgeman Art Library International. **120** (t) Sean Justice/Corbis. **123** (ct) Jupiterimages. **124** The Crosiers/Gene Plaisted, OSC. **125** (tr) W.P. Wittman Limited; (br) Giraudon/The Bridgeman Art Library International. **126** (tl) Jupiterimages; (tr) Maria Laughlin; (c) Jupiterimages. **127** (t) Warling Studios. **128** (t) Warling Studios. **129** Loyola Press Photography. **131** (t) Warling Studios; (b) Blend Images Photography/Veer.

Unit 4: 133 Andrew R. Wright. **134** (br) Andrew R. Wright. **135** Lisafx/Veer. **136** (t) Jupiterimages; (t) Regional Art Museum, Zaporizhia, Ukraine/The Bridgeman Art Library International; (br) Rafael Lopez. **137** (t) AgnusImages. com; (br) Judy McGrath. **140** (t) SW Productions/Media Bakery. **141** (t) Loyola Press Photography. **143** (t) OJO Images Photography/Veer. **144** (t) The Crosiers/Gene Plaisted, OSC. **145** (br) Nocturne (Gethsemane) 1915 (oil on canvas), Rouault, Georges (1871–1958)/Allen Memorial Art Museum, Oberlin College, Ohio, USA/© DACS/R.T. Miller, Jr. Fund/The Bridgeman Art Library International. © 2013 Artists Rights Society (ARS), New York/ADAGP, Paris. **146** (t) Floresco Productions/Media Bakery. **147** (t) Courtesy of the Archives of the Sisters of the Blessed Sacrament, Bensalem, PA. **148** (t) Auslöser/Media Bakery. **151** (t) Walter Lockwood/Media Bakery. **152** (t) The Crosiers/Gene Plaisted, OSC; (b) Bill Perry/Shutterstock.com. **153** (br) Galleria degli Uffizi, Florence, Italy/The Bridgeman Art Library International. **154** (t) The Crosiers/ Gene Plaisted, OSC; (br) St. Peter's, Vatican, Rome, Italy/The Bridgeman Art Library International. **156** (t) Media Bakery. **159** (t) Ocean Photography/Veer. **160** (t) The Crosiers/Gene Plaisted, OSC; (t) Jupiterimages; (br) Nic Neufeld/ Shutterstock.com. **161** (t) Image Source Photography/Veer. **162** (t) Alessandra Cimatoribus; (t) Jupiterimages. **163** (cr) W.P. Wittman Limited; (br) Image by Elizabeth Wang, Code: T-00535-OL-V2, Copyright © Radiant Light 2000, Title: "At the Mass, if we unite ourselves with Christ's self-offering, we are like jewels on His robe." **164** (t) Don Hammond/Media Bakery. **165** Carrie Gowran. **168** (t) © The Trustees of the Chester Beatty Library, Dublin/The Bridgeman Art Library International. **169** (t) Photodisc/Getty Images. **170** (tr) He Qi, www.heqigallery.com. **172** (tr) Tim Pannell/Media Bakery. **175** (t) W.P. Wittman Limited; (b) W.P. Wittman Limited.

Unit 5: 177 Andrew R. Wright. **178** (l) Jupiterimages; (r) Andrew R. Wright. **179** moodboard Photography/Veer. **180** (t) Warling Studios; (br) He Qi, www. heqigallery.com. **182** (t) Image Source Photography/Veer; (bd) Jupiterimages; (br) Wikipedia. **187** cultura Photography/Veer **188** (t) The Crosiers/Gene Plaisted, OSC. **190** (t) W.P. Wittman Limited; (br) Musee Nat. Picasso La Guerre et la Paix, Vallauris, France/The Bridgeman Art Library International. © 2014 Estate of Pablo Picasso/Artists Rights Society (ARS), New York. **191** (b) The Crosiers/Gene Plaisted, OSC. **192** (t) Image Source Photography/Veer **195** Blend Images Photography/Veer. **196** (t) The Crosiers/Gene Plaisted, OSC. **197** (t) The Crosiers, OSC; (b) Scala/Art Resource, NY. **198** (t) Klaus Mellenthin/Getty Images; (b) The Crosiers/Gene Plaisted, OSC. **199** (tr) The Crosiers/Gene Plaisted, OSC. **200** (t) PT Images/Veer. **203** (t) Ian Lishman/ Juice Images/Corbis **205** (cr) Bible Society, London, UK/The Bridgeman Art Library International. **206** (tr) The Crosiers/Gene Plaisted, OSC; (b) bokononist/ Shutterstock.com. **207** (t) The Crosiers/Gene Plaisted, OSC. **208** (t) Warling Studios. **211** (r) Ben Blankenburg/Corbis. **212** (l) © Radiant Light/The Bridgeman Art Library International. **213** (br) © Museumslandschaft Hessen Kassel Ute Brunzel/The Bridgeman Art Library International. **214** Ivan Vdovin/

Alamy. **215** (t) Tim Pannell/Corbis; (b) The Crosiers/Gene Plaisted, OSC. **220** (t) Corbis Photography/Veer; (b) cultura Photography/Veer.

The Year in Our Church: 221 (cl) Jupiterimages; (cl) Plush Studios/Digital Vision/Getty Images; (cr, clockwise) Andrew R. Wright; (br) SeDmi/Veer. **222** (t) The Crosiers/Gene Plaisted, OSC; (ct) The Crosiers/Gene Plaisted, OSC; (cb) The Crosiers/Gene Plaisted, OSC; (br) The Crosiers/Gene Plaisted, OSC. **223** Warling Studios. **224** (t) © British Library Board. All Rights Reserved/The Bridgeman Art Library. **225** (t) Rafael Valls Gallery, London, UK/The Bridgeman Art Library. **226** The Crosiers/Gene Plaisted, OSC. **227** Private Collection/The Bridgeman Art Library. **228** (t) Birmingham Museums and Art Gallery/The Bridgeman Art Library; (bd) Phecsone/Shutterstock.com. **229** (t) © Look and Learn/The Bridgeman Art Library. **230** (tr) The Crosiers/Gene Plaisted, OSC. **231** Warling Studios. **232** (tr) © Guildhall Art Gallery, City of London/The Bridgeman Art Library; (bd) Jupiterimages. **233** (tr) Warling Studios; Stockdisc Classic/Alamy. **234** (tr) Warling Studios. **235** Copyright 2001 TheoLogic Systems, Inc. All rights reserved. Usage subject to license agreement. **236** (tr) The Crosiers/ Gene Plaisted, OSC. **237** Galleria degli Uffizi, Florence, Italy/The Bridgeman Art Library. **238** (tr) ReligiousStock/Alamy. **239** The Crosiers/Gene Plaisted, OSC. **240** (tr) Private Collection/The Bridgeman Art Library. **241** (c) Warling Studios. **243** The Crosiers/Gene Plaisted, OSC. **244** (tr) The Crosiers/Gene Plaisted, OSC; (bc) ColonialArts.com **245** Warling Studios. **246** (tr) © Glasgow University Library, Scotland/The Bridgeman Art Library. **247** John Nava/Los Angeles Cathedral of Our Lady of the Angels. **248** (tr) Werner Forman/Art Resource, NY. **249** (cl) Charles O. Cecil/Alamy; (cr) Siede Preis/Photodisc; (b) Siede Preis/ Photodisc. **250** (tr) National Gallery, London, UK/The Bridgeman Art Library; (bd) Thunderstorm.

Prayers and Practices of Our Faith: 251–300 (bd) Greg Becker. **251** (cl) © Hermitage Art, Inc./Reproductions at www.Bridgebuilding.com; (cr) © Hermitage Art, Inc./Reproductions at www.Bridgebuilding.com. **251** (b) Steph Fowler/Media Bakery. **252** (cb) The Crosiers/Gene Plaisted, OSC; (b) Warling Studios. **253** (c) Giraudon/The Bridgeman Art Library. **255** (c) Michael Runkel Ethiopia/Alamy. **256** Lebrecht Music and Arts Photo Library/ Alamy. **258** (c) © Hermitage Art, Inc./Reproductions at www.Bridgebuilding. com; (b) SeDmi/Veer. **259** (c) © Hermitage Art, Inc./Reproductions at www. Bridgebuilding.com. **260** (c) © Hermitage Art, Inc./Reproductions at www. Bridgebuilding.com. **261** (c) © Hermitage Art, Inc./Reproductions at www. Bridgebuilding.com. **262** (c) Alinari/The Bridgeman Art Library; (b) **263** (b) The Crosiers/Gene Plaisted, OSC. **264** (tl, b) Bill Wood; (tr) Bettmann/Corbis; (br) Bill Wood. **265** (c) Bill Wood. **266** Corbis Photography/Veer **267** (b) Private Collection/The Bridgeman Art Library. **268** (b) Christina Balit. **269** ImageZoo/ Corbis. **270** (c) Warling Studios. **271** (b) KidStock/Media Bakery. **272** (c) Rick Becker-Leckrone/Shutterstock.com; (bd) Jupiterimages. **276** The Crosiers/ Gene Plaisted, OSC. **277** (br) Warling Studios. **278** (b) Fancy Photography/Veer; (br) Warling Studios. **279** (c) Engraving from; Jesuits; Loyola; Saint Ignatius; The Illustrated Globe Encyclopaedia of Universal Knowledge; Vol. V (London 1882). **279** (b) Jupiterimages. **280** (cr) The Crosiers/Gene Plaisted, OSC. **281** Greg Kuepfer. **282** (c) The Crosiers/Gene Plaisted, OSC; (b) The Crosiers/ Gene Plaisted, OSC. **283** (cr) The Crosiers/Gene Plaisted, OSC; (br) The Crosiers/ Gene Plaisted, OSC. **284** (l) James, Laura/Private Collection/The Bridgeman Art Library; (cl) James, Laura/Private Collection/The Bridgeman Art Library; (cr) James, Laura/Private Collection/The Bridgeman Art Library; (r) James, Laura/ Private Collection/The Bridgeman Art Library. **285** Top left to right (a) James, Laura/Private Collection/The Bridgeman Art Library. (b) James, Laura/Private Collection/The Bridgeman Art Library; (c) James, Laura/Private Collection/The Bridgeman Art Library; (d) James, Laura/Private Collection/The Bridgeman Art Library; (e) James, Laura/Private Collection/The Bridgeman Art Library; (f) James, Laura/Private Collection/The Bridgeman Art Library; (g) James, Laura/Private Collection/The Bridgeman Art Library; (h) James, Laura/Private Collection/The Bridgeman Art Library; (i) James, Laura/Private Collection/ The Bridgeman Art Library; (j) James, Laura/Private Collection/The Bridgeman Art Library. **286** (cr) The Crosiers/Gene Plaisted, OSC. **287–288** Alessandra Cimatoribus. **289** (t) AgnusImages.com; (b) W.P. Wittman Limited. **291** (tl) The Crosiers/Gene Plaisted, OSC; (tc) Private Collection/The Bridgeman Art Library; (tr) Louvre, Paris, France/Giraudon/The Bridgeman Art Library; (bl) © Radiant Light/The Bridgeman Art Library; (bc) The Crosiers/Gene Plaisted, OSC; (br) Photo © Boltin Picture Library/The Bridgeman Art Library. **292** (cr) Granger Wootz/Media Bakery. **293** (br) © Look and Learn/The Bridgeman Art Library. **294–295** chbaum/Shutterstock.com. **295** (cr) The Crosiers/Gene Plaisted, OSC. **297** (cr) Warling Studios; (cr) Warling Studios; (cr) Warling Studios; (b) Warling Studios. **299** (cr) Alex Mares-Manton/Asia Images/Getty Images. **300** (br) Safia Fatimi/Taxi/Getty Images.